FROM
MATCH
FIXING
TO
MURDER

101 Sporting Encounters with the Law

REVIEWS OF THE FIRST EDITION (previously entitled *Sporting Justice*)

'I have a fine book on my desk … a treasure trove of human folly.'
(Simon Barnes, *The Times*)

'An excellent idea of bringing together the most important, interesting or just fun-to-read cases … tells the stories clearly and entertainingly.'
(Marcel Berlins, *The Guardian*)

'A well-judged blend of cases running the gamut from the famous to the obscure.'
(Simon Redfern, *Independent on Sunday*)

'Refreshing … this is a book worthy of any sports fan's bookshelf … an easy read and free of legal jargon.'
(*The Press*)

'An illuminating book, meticulously researched and entertainingly written.'
(Anton Rippon, *Sports Journalists' Association News*)

'The book is a delight … well-written … very easy to read.'
(*Iusport*)

'I can heartily endorse … complete with glittering legal analysis and stories from golf to motor and horse racing this is a thoroughly entertaining legal book to fall asleep over after dinner.'
(Edward Fennell, *The Times*)

'A marvellous pot pouri of cases … If you like sport and generally care about it, this is a must-read book. If you happen to be a lawyer as well, so much the better but it is not a pre-requisite.'
(Mel Goldberg, *Sport & the Law Journal*)

FROM MATCH FIXING TO MURDER

101 Sporting Encounters with the Law

IAN HEWITT

VSP

This edition published by Vision Sports Publishing in 2015
First edition (entitled *Sporting Justice*) published by SportsBooks Limited in 2008

Vision Sports Publishing
19–23 High Street
Kingston upon Thames
Surrey
KT1 1LL

www.visionsp.co.uk

ISBN: 978 1 9095 3454 4

Edited by: Jim Drewett
Copy editing: Paul Baillie-Lane
Design: Neal Cobourne
Images: Getty Images

A CIP Catalogue record for this book is available from the British Library

Printed and bound in the UK by TJ International, Padstow, Cornwall

CONTENTS

INTRODUCTION

Swiss plain-clothes police, working in co-ordination with America's FBI, arrived around 6am on a Wednesday morning in May 2015 at a luxury hotel in Zurich. Seven officials of football's world governing body, FIFA, were arrested on charges of corruption and led away, shielded from public sight by crisp linen bedsheets. Six days later, Sepp Blatter, FIFA's president, announced that he was resigning. His 17-year, seemingly permanent, reign was ending. The law had again impacted significantly the landscape of the sporting world.

This book is a collection of such sporting encounters with the law - 101 stories of cases involving sport or sporting personalities which have ended up before courts or tribunals. Many are of serious import, others more light-hearted. The range is wide: from the 'body in the trunk' murder by a former Wimbledon finalist to an ugly football challenge resulting in a charge of manslaughter; from the fixing of baseball's 1919 World Series to a transsexual tennis player seeking to play in the women's singles at the US Open; from litigation to prevent the formation of football's Premier League to a wife's claim in the divorce courts that 'golf was his mistress'; and more.

'Lawyers have no place in sport.' A familiar cry. Yes, but … sport does not and cannot exist without a framework of rules: rules of the game itself, disciplinary rules and procedural rules for enforcement. Sport is also subject to the laws of the land: the rules of criminal law, laws imposing liability for negligence, employment law and laws relating to libel, misrepresentation and unfair trading.

Most sporting disputes are resolved quickly – by a referee on the field, by an appeal body within the particular sport or by commercial negotiation. But not all. Some have important consequences – for an individual, a team, a competition, a sporting event, sponsors, broadcasters or the spectating public. Some involve prosecution under the criminal law. A court or appeal tribunal may be called upon to make a judgment, impose a penalty or provide a remedy. This is where sport encounters the law. This is the arena for the stories in this book.

Sporting disputes do, of course, reflect sport itself. They can be unpredictable and colourful. They can involve lively personalities, great sporting venues and extraordinary events. Stories in this book involve many well-known sporting figures. Among them: Bobby Moore, Eric Cantona, John Terry and Harry Redknapp from the world of football; Tony Greig, Hansie Cronje and Ian Botham from cricket; Ben Johnson,

Christine Ohuruogu and Dwain Chambers from athletics; golfers Tiger Woods and Rory McIlroy; Ayrton Senna and Lewis Hamilton from motor racing; Lester Piggott and Kieren Fallon from horse racing; rugby's JPR Williams; snooker player Stephen Hendry; and cyclists Floyd Landis and Lance Armstrong. All make an appearance, together with many others. All have contributed, some reluctantly, to the history of sporting encounters with the law.

So, how were the cases included in this book selected? I have focused on four ingredients. Did the encounter involve a leading sporting personality, venue or event? Did it illustrate or establish an important legal principle affecting sport? Were there significant consequences for the particular sport? Was it an entertaining story? Each encounter satisfies at least one of these criteria. In a large number of cases, I believe all four are satisfied. It is, however, a personal choice and I know that many strong candidates for inclusion have been omitted.

There has been no shortage of material. The flow of sporting disputes before courts or tribunals in recent years has been continuous. More than two-thirds of the stories in this book arise from events or incidents that have occurred in the last 25 years. (This second edition has itself enabled the inclusion of a dozen or so fresh stories since the book's first publication seven years ago.) 'We'll meet at the bar' has taken on a new meaning in sport.

In several cases, I want to exclaim the sports fan's cry: 'I was there!' I remember as a child the 1960s 'football bribery sensation' headlined in *The People* (a popular sports paper at the time); I was at the Belfry watching the Ryder Cup in 1989 and at Augusta in awe of Tiger Woods in 1997; I saw Bruce Grobbelaar play at Southampton (we thought he was a pretty good goalkeeper); I worked, as a lawyer, on the formation of the Premier League; I have stayed, by chance, at the Amsterdam hotel used by talkSPORT for their Euro 2000 broadcasting; and the incident at Buckpool golf course vividly reminds me of my own tendency to slice at golf. So, there were many personal memories as I compiled this book.

I hope you, the sports fan, enjoy this journey along the many diverse paths where sport and sporting personalities have encountered the law.

Ian Hewitt
1 August 2015

Chapter One

SPORT, CRIME AND THE PLAYING FIELD

We start with a fundamental question. Does the criminal law, the law of the land, apply to activities on the sporting field of play?

All major sports have disciplinary rules and procedures which enable sanctions to be imposed 'within the sport' on participants who are guilty of serious misconduct. Should the criminal law simply stay outside the touchline? How does the criminal law permit direct combat sports such as boxing? Should different rules or standards apply to sport and exempt acts of violence on the field of play which would be criminal if they took place off the field? Does it make a difference if violence occurs in a major, televised match?

Many of the encounters in this chapter are striking because of the sporting personalities involved. Others because of the important legal principles established. Our journey to explore sport's relationship with the criminal law takes us to a wide range of sporting venues, including a makeshift fighting ring near Ascot, the famous football stadiums of Ibrox, St James' Park and Selhurst Park, an ice-skating rink in Detroit, the Imola racing circuit in Italy and a village tennis club in France.

1. A PRIZE FIGHT NEAR ASCOT

When is boxing unlawful?

Were fighters in a bare-knuckle prize fight guilty of criminal assault? Was a spectator at the fight guilty of aiding and abetting?

Our story starts near Ascot, after the races in 1881, off the country road to Maidenhead. A surprising venue, perhaps, for a case which would settle whether bare-knuckle prize fighting was unlawful or not.

Prize fighting was still common in the early 1880s. Just over 20 years earlier, a bare-knuckle fight between England's champion Tom Sayers and America's leading fighter John Heenan had captured national attention when they fought, in Farnborough in Hampshire, for nearly two and a half hours to the point of exhaustion and broken limbs in a 'world championship'. Stories vary as to whether the police tried to stop the fight but could not get through the crowd to the ring, or whether they waited until the ring rope broke at the end and a near riot ensued. The fight was declared a draw.

Even under the London Prize Ring Rules introduced in 1838, it was a rough and violent 'sport' with very few accepted rules and restrictions. To many this form of combat had become increasingly distasteful. The Queensberry Rules, introduced in 1865, were leading to a more humane and orderly form of boxing more acceptable to Victorian society, with the use of padded gloves, no wrestling or throwing of an opponent, three minute rounds and the introduction of weight divisions. Amateur boxing clubs were growing in popularity.

Raw bare-knuckle prize fighting nevertheless continued – albeit under an increasing cloud of illegality. Fuelled by gambling, many fights were mismatches or fixed; others endured to the bitter end of exhaustion. Fights tended to be arranged secretly. Local police sometimes took action – but generally on the grounds that such fights incited unlawful assembly and riot rather than the essential nature of the 'sport', the infliction by one person of physical injury on another. Did bare-knuckle prize fighting involve unlawful assault or not? The issue was finally put to the Court of Criminal Appeals in 1882. And there was a surprise twist to the prosecution.

Back to Ascot. After leaving the races one afternoon in June 1881, an unnamed witness spotted a number of people coming out of a gap in the woods by the side of the road between Ascot and Maidenhead. Curious, he took a closer look. On private land, a ring of rope supported by four blue stakes had been set up. Two men, Jack Burke and Charley Mitchell, were ready to fight. Bets were exchanged between some of the

Did bare-knuckle prize fighting involve unlawful assault or not?

150-strong crowd. A man called Coney was one of the spectators among the throng. Burke and Mitchell, supported by their 'seconds', took off their coats and waistcoats, went into the ring and fought for just under an hour.

The local police were alerted and decided to take action. Burke and Mitchell were arrested and charged on the basis of criminal assault. And the surprise twist to the prosecution? Coney, as a member of the crowd watching the fight, was also charged with assault. A supporting spectator, the police alleged, was aiding and abetting and that was equivalent to assault.

Legal Question: Should Burke and Mitchell be guilty of criminal assault even if, as consenting adults, each agreed to the risk of injury from the other's blows? If so, should Coney be treated as aiding and abetting the crime and therefore himself guilty of unlawful assault?

For: A blow struck in anger, and likely to cause physical injury, was an assault. The consent of the person struck should be immaterial. Consent should not render innocent acts which were deliberately aimed at another person and were knowingly dangerous (for example, a duel). Burke and Mitchell were guilty. Prize fighting was contrary to the public interest. The presence of spectators watching the fighters, and knowing that bets were being made, encouraged these assaults. They were therefore aiding and abetting the crime and, in the eyes of the law, Coney should also be found guilty of assault.

Against: Burke and Mitchell had agreed to fight. They were consenting adults. There should be no conviction of criminal assault where there was clear consent. Parliament, as legislature, had not made prize fighting illegal. Burke and Mitchell should therefore not be found guilty. Even if they were found guilty, Coney himself was only a spectator. His mere presence was not sufficient to constitute active aiding and abetting.

Decision: They were all convicted at the Berkshire Quarter Sessions. Given the importance of the case, however, the chairman referred the case to the Court of Criminal Appeals to review whether his direction to the jury had been correct. It was a landmark case. An extraordinarily large 11-strong court − yes, 11 judges in their full regalia – sat in judgment. The guilty verdict on Burke and Mitchell was unanimously confirmed. Each was guilty of criminal assault on the other. Their sentences were confirmed – six weeks imprisonment with hard labour.

The court determined that the deliberate infliction of physical injury by one person on another was an assault. Consent could not render it lawful. Bare-knuckle prize fighting was clearly now a criminal activity in England. Summing up, Justice Hawkins declared: '… *a prize fight … is illegal and the parties to it may be prosecuted for assaults upon each other*'. He distinguished, rather quaintly, prize fighting from '*friendly encounters not calculated to produce real injury or to rouse angry passions*' such as sparring with gloves without any intention of the parties to beat each other until exhaustion or one of them was subdued by force. Such '*friendly encounters*', he said, were on the right side of the law.

As for Coney, he was more fortunate. His conviction was overturned. By an eight to three majority, the Court of Criminal Appeals decided that Coney was not guilty of aiding and abetting an assault merely by being a spectator.

Where does that leave the modern professional boxing contest?

Simply, there is no decision of the courts – or specific law of Parliament – which positively renders a boxing contest legal. It remains an anomaly. The courts have said that sparring with gloves, where boxers do not aim to injure or fight to exhaustion, is acceptable. Consent does not justify dangerous or masochistic acts beyond that level. But professional boxing is a 'sport' where blows, such as an uppercut to the jaw, are deliberately aimed at the head with the objective of causing damage. The British Medical Association, among others, continues to call for a total ban on boxing due to brain damage sustained cumulatively by boxers from blows to the head.

The modern professional bout is, apart from the wearing of gloves, the direct descendant of the prize fight. The fighters do box for money and often do so to the point of near exhaustion. They are not 'friendly encounters'. And that is without any additional violence such as when Mike Tyson bit off part of Evander Holyfield's ear – an assault by any measure.

Today, the careful regulation of boxing as a sport under the rules of the various boxing authorities would, however, undoubtedly influence any modern-day court. It is highly unlikely that any court would now find a professional boxer guilty of assault in the ring. The enjoyment and social role of regulated boxing would almost certainly be judged, as a matter of policy, to outweigh the risk of injury. An anomaly, though, it remains.

Their sentences were confirmed – six weeks imprisonment with hard labour.

2. A TRAGIC FOOTBALL CHALLENGE

Was it manslaughter?

Henry Moore committed a foul in an ugly clash which resulted in the death of an opposition player. Should he be convicted of manslaughter?

Can a footballer be liable for manslaughter as a result of a reckless tackle? The issue was, tragically, put to the test in 1898.

The case arose in Aylestone, a village south-west of Leicester. It was in the early days of association football and the game was growing rapidly in popularity. The amateur village team in Aylestone were playing local rivals Enderby in a Saturday scene repeated up and down the land. It was the background, though, to an incident which would give rise to the basic question: does the criminal law apply to tackles on the football field in the course of play?

A lively match was in progress. Aylestone were on the attack. John Briggs, a young forward, received a pass and pressed forward. He dribbled past Henry Moore, an Enderby central defender, and kicked the ball firmly towards the Enderby goal. Moore ran after Briggs. The chase was on. The Enderby goalkeeper ran forward to kick the ball clear and save his goal. Just as he kicked the ball clear, the defender Moore jumped with his knees up against Briggs' back, forcing him violently forward against the knee of the advancing goalkeeper. Briggs fell to the ground, with serious internal injuries. Sadly, he died a few days afterwards.

Moore was charged with manslaughter. The case came before a jury trial at the Leicester Assizes.

Legal Question: The issue was stark. Although the injury was not intentional, was Moore so reckless in using force likely to cause injury that a verdict of manslaughter was appropriate?

For: Sport, including football, was not above the criminal law of the land. The fact that the game was governed by its own rules was irrelevant. Football was a rough game and people who play it must be careful not to inflict bodily harm on another person. No one had a right to use force which was likely to injure another. If he did use such force, and death resulted, the crime of manslaughter was committed. Moore should be found guilty.

Against: Football was a physical game. The players knew this. Serious injuries did occur. There was no intention to kill. Allowance must be made for the rough-and-tumble of a contact sport even if the contact went beyond the technical level permitted by the rules. The use of the criminal law was inappropriate to apply to such an incident. Moore should be found not guilty.

Decision: Moore was found guilty of manslaughter. The following extract from the contemporary law report summarised the direction of the judge to the jury:

'Football was a lawful game, but it was a rough one ... No one had a right to use force which was likely to injure another, and if he did use such force and death resulted the crime of manslaughter had been committed. If a blow were struck recklessly which caused a man to fall, and if in falling he ... was injured and died, the person who struck the blow was guilty of manslaughter.'

This case is a vivid illustration that the criminal law does not stop at the touchline. An earlier football case, extraordinarily also at Leicester Assizes, had resulted in a 'not guilty' verdict on a manslaughter charge – but the court had affirmed that sport was not above the law: *'No rules or practice of any game whatever can make that lawful which is unlawful by the law of the land.'*

Football was clearly a particularly dangerous game in those early days. One extraordinary feature of this case against Henry Moore was that a young player in this same match named Veasey, who had given evidence against Moore, was himself killed a few weeks later in another football match.

All that is known is that the vicar of Enderby gave him an excellent character reference.

The conviction of Henry Moore is the only reported case of a successful manslaughter charge arising from an on-the-ball incident during a football match. Criminal prosecution for on-the-ball incidents has become rare. Off-the-ball incidents are different. Indeed, as recently as 2006 an amateur footballer, Julian Clarke, received an 18-month jail sentence for manslaughter after an opponent died as a result of a head injury following a punch at the end of a Birmingham Sunday League game.

What was the sentence given to Henry Moore? All that is known is that the vicar of Enderby gave him an excellent character reference. Sentence was postponed and no record appears of the final outcome.

3. TONYA HARDING

An assault that gripped the sporting world

Preparing for the 1994 Winter Olympics, leading US skater Nancy Kerrigan was struck down by a heavy blow. Was a rival competitor involved?

Next, a sporting soap opera. A bizarre story started in downtown Detroit in January 1994 and went on to become a saga which would remain etched in the minds of all with memories of sport in the 1990s. In the words of US talk-show host Oprah Winfrey: 'The story had it all… drama, scandal, heartbreak, controversy and competition.'

The Cobo Arena in Detroit was the scene for the final build-up to the Winter Olympics which began the following month in Lillehammer, Norway. Skaters were practising for the US National Women's Figure Skating Championships after which the two skaters to represent the USA in the individual event at the Olympics would be selected. The story centred on two characters, leading US skaters Tonya Harding and Nancy Kerrigan.

Tonya Harding was a feisty, fair-haired 23 year-old raised from a tough background in Portland, Oregon. She had already won the US Championships twice: 1991 was her great year; achieving second place in the World Championships and becoming the first American woman to complete a triple Axel jump in competition. Now, in 1994, her form had slipped a little, although she had still come fourth in the previous year's US Championships and was seeking a shot at glory in the Olympics.

Nancy Kerrigan, her great US rival, was a polar opposite in temperament and background. She was an elegant, dark-haired 24 year-old from a well-educated middle-class background in east coast Boston. She was the current US champion and the leading US medal hope.

Kerrigan had just finished her practice session at the Cobo Arena on 6th January. As she left the rink, an unidentified man suddenly ran towards her and, wielding a metal bar or club, struck her on the outside of the right knee. An eye-witness said: 'Before she could say anything, a guy ran by, crouched down, whacked her on the knee and kept running.' The man escaped as Kerrigan fell to the ground, screaming and clutching her knee. Officials rushed to the scene.

As she left the rink, an unidentified man suddenly ran towards her and, wielding a metal bar or club, struck her on the outside of the right knee.

Fortunately, a doctor was on hand to treat her. Kerrigan was forced to withdraw from the US Championships in Detroit. Harding went on to win the title. Fears grew that Kerrigan would miss the Olympics.

A few days later, extraordinary rumours began to spread that the attack – which occurred just eight months after an on-court knife attack by a 'fan' of Steffi Graf on the leading tennis player, Monica Seles – might have involved associates of Tonya Harding.

Events moved quickly. On 19th January, less than two weeks after the assault, Harding's ex-husband, Jeff Gillooly, and her bodyguard, Shawn Eckhardt, were arrested along with the alleged hired attacker, Shane Stant, for an alleged plot to injure Kerrigan. Harding denied any prior knowledge of the attack.

Harding had a tempestuous relationship with Gillooly. They had married in 1990 when she was a 19 year-old. The marriage lasted for only three years and they were divorced in 1993. They were reconciled for a short period afterwards, but apparently not for long. On 1st February, less than one month after the attack, in a dramatic turn of events, Gillooly agreed to a plea bargain. He pleaded guilty to his role in the attack in exchange for giving testimony against Harding who, he claimed, was deeply involved in the conspiracy to injure Kerrigan. Harding continued to deny any involvement. Gillooly was later sentenced to two years in prison, of which he served six months, and fined $100,000.

Where did this leave Harding's imminent participation in the Olympics? Could the USA still select her if she was under suspicion for a criminal attack on a rival? The US Olympic Committee (USOC) sought to suspend Harding from competing in the Olympics. Harding continued to protest her innocence and threatened legal action for $20 million damages against USOC if they did suspend her. USOC were in a dilemma.

A day or so after the opening ceremony for the Olympics had taken place in February at Lillehammer, USOC did a deal with Harding. Fearing protracted legal battles and distractions that could disrupt the Winter Olympics, USOC agreed to allow Harding to skate in the Olympics. In return, Harding withdrew her lawsuit against them. A USOC statement continued: 'We are appalled still by the attack on Nancy Kerrigan, which was not only an attack on the athlete, but an assault on the basic ideals of the Olympic movement and sportsmanship. We remain deeply concerned about this incident.'

Kerrigan, fortunately, recovered and was able to skate at Lillehammer. The stage was set, then, for one of the most anticipated events in Olympic history: Harding competing against Kerrigan in the women's figure skating. They even practised together in Lillehammer, under close security and watched by hundreds of the world's media. Kerrigan wore the same white lace dress she had been wearing when attacked.

The attack on Kerrigan and Harding's alleged involvement had led to a media frenzy. In the USA, the television coverage of the first evening of the Olympic skating competition became, at that time, the second most-watched television show in

It was an assault on the basic ideals of the Olympic movement and sportsmanship.

American history. Only the final episode of 'M★A★S★H' had previously been watched by more people.

Harding performed well but, as she set out for her final session, she was involved in further drama. Struggling with a broken shoe-lace, she requested and was allowed to skate later in her group. She eventually finished eighth. Kerrigan, just 50 days after being struck on the knee in Detroit, then went on to give one of the most scintillating performances of her career. She missed out on the gold medal by the narrowest of judging margins in favour of 16 year-old world champion Oksana Baiul from Ukraine. Kerrigan was content with her silver medal: 'I think I skated great. I was smiling. I was happy. How can I complain?'

The Olympics did not mean the end of the saga. Afterwards, the criminal case against Tonya Harding developed.

Eventually, on 16th March, it was Harding's turn to make a plea bargain. She avoided further prosecution and a possible jail sentence by pleading guilty before an Oregon State Court to a charge of hindering the police investigation into the attack on Kerrigan. Harding was sentenced to three years' supervised probation, 500 hours of community service work and a $100,000 fine. She agreed to undergo a psychiatric examination. Asked by the county circuit judge if she had anything to say to the court, Harding said only: 'I'd just like to say I'm really sorry that I interfered.' She continued to maintain her innocence as to any prior involvement in planning or knowledge of the attack. That was the end of the criminal proceedings.

The final episode in the story came six months after the Olympics. The US Figure Skating Association conducted a full investigation. A two-day disciplinary hearing was held in Colorado. Harding did not show up. A five-member disciplinary panel of the Association decided that '*by a preponderance of the evidence*' Harding '*had prior knowledge and was involved prior to the incident*'. The panel acknowledged that this finding was '*based on civil standards, not criminal standards*'. Her conduct had shown '*a clear disregard for fairness, good sportsmanship and ethical behaviour*'. Tonya Harding was stripped of her 1994 US Championship title and banned for life from ice skating competition.

Tonya Harding was subsequently involved in numerous skirmishes with the law for a variety of personal misdemeanours. She actually made a brief comeback to skating, five years later in 1999, when she appeared in the ESPN professional competition, outside the jurisdiction of the US Figure Skating Association, held at Huntingdon, West Virginia. She finished second. In 2002, she appeared as a boxer in a celebrity boxing event against Paula Jones, a name linked with the past of US President Bill Clinton. Harding won. She subsequently competed in various official women's boxing events. She was a pretty good fighter.

4. AYRTON SENNA

Williams team acquitted of culpable homicide

Ayrton Senna was killed after a crash in the San Marino Grand Prix. What was the cause? Was it culpable homicide?

The weekend of the San Marino Grand Prix in 1994 was one of the most harrowing in Formula One history.

The race was being held at Imola's famous Enzo e Dino Ferrari circuit, named after Ferrari's late founder and his son, Dino. Imola, one of the few Formula One circuits to run anti-clockwise, is 30 miles east of Bologna and not far from the nearby state of San Marino – hence the name of the grand prix.

Ayrton Senna was racing for the Williams team that season. The 34 year-old Brazilian was already a legend in Formula One. A triple world champion, he had won the drivers' world championship title in 1988, 1990 and 1991 racing with the McLaren team. After the introduction of restrictions on active suspension and traction controls in Formula One by the racing authorities, Senna had moved from McLaren to the Williams team for the 1994 season in an effort to meet the challenge of the Benetton-Ford racing car of Michael Schumacher. It was Senna's third race for Williams. Despite pole positions in the season's opening two races, he had failed to finish. His Williams Renault FW16 was not yet handling well. Was this to be the breakthrough?

The weekend started dramatically. During Friday's practice, fellow Brazilian Rubens Barrichello hit a kerb and flipped his car onto the top of a tyre barrier. It looked a bad crash but, fortunately, he was not seriously injured. In Saturday's qualifying, however, tragedy struck. Austrian Roland Ratzenberger crashed head-on into a wall after a front wing failure. He was taken to hospital but later died. It was the first fatality in Formula One for 12 years. Senna secured pole position for the next day's race.

Senna was deeply concerned by Ratzenberger's death and led a drivers' meeting the following morning to establish a safety group. He seriously thought of withdrawing from the race. He prophetically remarked: 'There are no small accidents on this circuit.'

Motor racing's governing body, the FIA World Motor Sport Council, and Italian authorities later rejected allegations that Ratzenberger had been killed instantly at the track at Imola. If Ratzenberger's death had been certified at the track on the Saturday, under Italian law Sunday's grand prix would have had to be cancelled.

Sunday, 1st May 1994. The race began. Senna took the lead from his pole position. Back on the grid two drivers, Pedro Lamy and JJ Lehto, were involved in a starting-line accident. Track officials deployed the safety car to slow down the field and enable the debris to be cleared. Senna urged the safety car to go faster, but it would not. On the sixth lap, the safety car left and the race was restarted.

On the seventh lap, Senna was leading with Schumacher just behind. Senna entered the notorious Tamburello corner. It was a flat-out left curve with little room between the track and a concrete wall which protected a creek running behind it. Senna's car entered the corner at 192 mph … and went off the track. His car struck the unprotected concrete barrier. On impacting the wall, the right front wheel of Senna's car was torn off, including a piece of metal suspension. The car bounced back on to the run-off area and came to a halt. It was clear that Senna was seriously injured. The visor in his helmet had been pierced by a piece of metal. Senna had suffered a fatal head injury. A surgeon performed an emergency tracheotomy. Senna was rushed by helicopter to the Maggiore Hospital in Bologna. In the evening, he was declared dead.

'There are no small accidents on this circuit.'

When track officials examined the wreckage of Senna's car, they found a furled, blood-soaked Austrian flag which Senna was going to raise in honour of Ratzenberger at the finishing line.

The 1994 San Marino Grand Prix itself was restarted 37 minutes after Senna's accident. The race was won by Michael Schumacher.

The world of Formula One entered a state of shock and disbelief on news of Senna's death. Three days of national mourning took place in Brazil. Over a million people lined his funeral cortège in his hometown of São Paulo.

Many theories were expounded as to the cause of the accident:
- Was it driver error? Did Senna simply lose control of the car?
- Was there a failure in the power-steering as Senna tried to check over-steer at the corner?
- Was the accident caused, in part, by the fact that the lengthy use of the safety car

meant that tyres were not yet fully warmed up and the car was lower and more vulnerable to bumps on the track coming into the Tamburello corner?
• Was there negligence behind the scenes at Williams?

Inspection by the Italian authorities revealed damage to the steering wheel column. Had it occurred on impact with the concrete wall? Or before Senna left the track? Earlier in the year, the Brazilian had requested that the steering column be modified in order that he could fit more comfortably in the car and have a clearer view of the instrument panel. A new column could not be manufactured before the start of the grand prix season, so the existing column had been cut, welded and reinforced by two metal plates. Had this failed? We shall never know. Unfortunately, in-car videotape footage of the last second or so of Senna's drive, which might have revealed more, has never become publicly available.

The Italian authorities decided to bring a criminal prosecution. It was led by State prosecutor Maurizio Passarini, zealous to make a name for himself. Six people were charged with culpable homicide. Three members of the Williams team were singled out – team principal Frank Williams, technical director Patrick Head and car designer Adrian Newey. Also charged were the FIA circuit director Roland Bruynseraede, the Imola circuit director Giorgio Poggi and the head of the company that operated the Imola track Federico Bendinelli. It seemed that the Italian authorities were determined to blame someone.

Culpable homicide in Italy is a different concept from manslaughter under English law. It can be alleged on the basis of relatively little negligence – certainly not the same level of recklessness required for manslaughter under English law – and prosecutions are not uncommon in Italy after a major accident. Punishment could range up to five years' imprisonment, although a fine was more likely for prosecution after a racing death. To most international observers, however, it sounded the same as manslaughter.

The implications for the individuals charged were considerable. The potential ramifications for motor racing were also major. A guilty verdict, and the risk of prosecutions in the event of any subsequent accidents, would have made it likely that the FIA would withdraw its support for motor racing in Italy. Could there really be no more Formula One racing in the home country of Ferrari?

The trial began in Imola in February 1997, nearly three years after the accident, under Judge Antonio Costanzo. The local courthouse was not big enough, so a ballroom, converted from a Saturday night dance spot, became the venue for what would turn out – with frequent intervals and mini-hearings – to be a 10-month trial.

Prosecutor Passarini contended that a sub-standard

Six people were charged with culpable homicide.

modification had been made to the steering column of Senna's car. 'A modification to the steering column which had been poorly executed caused it to break', he said. The column suffered from metal fatigue as a result of poor workmanship. This led to steering column failure as Senna entered the Tamburello curve. Unable to steer, so the State prosecutor alleged, Senna was unable to brake sufficiently on the track surface. His superb driving skills could not save him.

Engineers from the Williams team, for the defence, said that the problem was most likely over-steer as Senna's car went over a bump on the asphalt surface of the Imola track. They argued that Senna countered by steering away but the car appeared to bump and skid to the right, with the driver unable to brake and hold the line.

Evidence emerged that the steering column in the other Williams car, driven by Britain's Damon Hill, had also been modified in a similar way before the season began. The work was done in March. Both drivers had raced two grand prix events with the modified cars without any problem. Damon Hill himself gave evidence. Whilst some of his recall was rather vague, his opinion was that Senna had been attempting to correct over-steer. After seeing the film, Hill said: 'The steering wheel is exactly the way I would expect to see it to correct over-steer.'

Extraordinarily, neither Patrick Head nor Adrian Newey was allowed to examine the wreck of the car. It remained impounded by the Italian police throughout the trial.

On 7th November, Passarini made his closing submission to the court. He continued to maintain that a defective steering column had been the cause. But without warning, he recommended that all charges against Frank Williams and also officials Bruynseraede, Bendinelli and Poggi should be dropped. Williams merely dealt with the administrative side of the business. Head and Newey were the people, he alleged, ultimately responsible for the design changes made to Senna's car. Defence counsel for the Williams team argued that the prosecution's case simply had no basis in proof. Senna's steering column was the same as Damon Hill's. The case was unfounded.

Judge Antonio Costanzo gave his verdict on 16th December 1997. Not guilty. In a 90-second statement, he cleared all six defendants of culpable homicide in relation to Senna's death.

It was not until June 1998, six months after the verdict, that Judge Costanzo's full written official report was published. This gave the prosecutor, Passarini, zealous to the end, some scope to appeal since Costanzo did cite the breaking of the modified steering column as a cause, although no direct fault could be attributed to the particular defendants. The appeal was heard in Bologna in November 1999. It was short. After three days, the appeal court again absolved the defendants. There was no new evidence. Williams had also appealed on the factual finding and the appeal court said there was insufficient evidence to support the original judge's view that a broken steering column was the cause. The Williams team had been vindicated on all fronts.

We will never know for certain the cause of Senna's death.

Back at Imola, the flat-out Tamburello curve was reshaped as a fourth gear left-right chicane. In 2006, the FIA decided that Imola would not host a Formula One grand prix in 2007 and it has not featured in the calendar since.

5. DUNCAN FERGUSON

Criminal assault at Ibrox?

Duncan Ferguson was seen head-butting an opponent. Should he be prosecuted under the criminal law?

We return to the football field and an incident in April 1994 involving a moment of violence by a well-known participant on a sporting field. Bizarrely, it would later give rise to an orchestral symphony.

The scene was Ibrox, one of the great football stadiums of the world and home of Glasgow Rangers and their fanatical supporters. Rangers, who were destined to be champions that year, were playing Raith Rovers in the Scottish Premier Division. Duncan Ferguson, the home club's main striker and a crowd favourite, always had a fiery temperament. At 6' 4" tall, strongly built and with a competitive nature, he was a centre forward of the old school.

It was a lively first half-hour of the match. Rangers were on the attack again. The ball was crossed by a Rangers player. Ferguson and experienced Raith defender John McStay challenged for it. A tussle took place involving a certain amount of arm-pulling. The referee awarded a free-kick to Raith. Ferguson was not happy. He turned to McStay, grabbed him by his jersey and deliberately head-butted him in the left side of his face. McStay fell to the ground clutching his face. The injury was a flesh wound but not sufficiently serious to prevent him resuming the game.

Ferguson turned to McStay, grabbed him by his jersey and deliberately head-butted him in the left side of his face.

The referee, Kenny Clark, and his linesmen missed the head-butt but the incident was reported to the Scottish FA by the referee supervisor. The Scottish prosecution authorities decided to take a close interest in this incident. They believed that football was not controlling its players and that they should intervene. Ferguson had an existing criminal record. It included two previous, but not football-related, convictions for breach of the peace and assault respectively. Importantly, he was still on probation for one of the offences. Enough was enough. Despite the Scottish FA imposing a 12-match suspension on Ferguson, the police decided to prosecute Ferguson for criminal assault for his challenge on McStay.

Was Ferguson being punished twice for the same offence? The case of Henry Moore, nearly a century earlier, may have made it clear that certain cases such as manslaughter could not be ignored – but should the law intervene with regard to lesser offences on the pitch? The case came before the Sheriff Court in Glasgow.

Legal Question: Should punishment for on-field misconduct be solely a matter for disciplinary bodies within the sport itself? Should Ferguson be found guilty of assault? If so, what should be the punishment?

For: Sport is not above the law. There was no reason why an act of violence which would otherwise constitute criminal behaviour should be exempt simply because it was committed in a sporting context. Violent conduct on the field of play encouraged others (particularly younger players) to follow suit. Ferguson had committed a deliberate assault and should be punished by the criminal law.

Against: Judgments concerning on-field incidents should be left to the disciplinary authorities within the sport. Contact sports inevitably involved a degree of excitable, and sometimes 'over-the-top', behaviour. The disciplinary authorities within the sport were well able to impose serious penalties, fines and suspensions. Introducing the criminal law would be arbitrary, intrusive and unnecessary.

Decision: Ferguson was convicted. He was sentenced to three months' imprisonment by Sheriff Eccles, who said it was *'in the public interest'* and would bring home to Ferguson that such behaviour could not be tolerated.

Ferguson appealed against the sentence to the High Court of Judiciary in Scotland. Ferguson's defence counsel claimed that the incident had happened 'in the heat of the moment', claiming that he 'was a young man now maturing after a period in which he had been less well equipped to handle pressures'.

The appeal was unsuccessful. The court said that it had no wish to intervene in physical contact sports such as professional football but, when acts were done which went well beyond what can be regarded as normal physical contact and an assault was committed, the court had a duty to condemn and punish such conduct. A footballer who assaults another player on the football field is not entitled to expect leniency just because the incident occurs during the course of a match. Indeed, the court said:

Ferguson was the first professional footballer in the UK to be given a prison sentence for an assault on the pitch.

'One of the factors which may indicate the gravity of the offence is the fact that the assault has been committed in public before so many spectators. This fact becomes all the more important where the player is a public figure and the incident occurs during a game which has such a high profile as a league match in the Scottish Premier Division.'

Ferguson was described as having a 'quite appalling record of previous violent offences.' Significantly, he was on probation at the time. The Lord Justice-General summed up: 'The sentence of three months' imprisonment, which was intended to be a deterrent to others, cannot be described as excessive.'

Ferguson was the first professional footballer in the UK to be given a prison sentence for an assault on the pitch. He served 44 days in Glasgow's infamous Barlinnie prison.

This remains a relatively rare case of a criminal prosecution for conduct during a professional football match.

In England, 'off-the-ball' incidents which have attracted the attention of the prosecuting authorities have usually resulted in fines for unlawfully causing bodily harm under the Offences against the Persons Act. There have been numerous prosecutions in amateur rugby and football. In the professional game, Chris Kamara, then of Swindon, was in 1988 the first English professional footballer to be convicted of causing grievous bodily harm after breaking a Shrewsbury Town player's cheekbone in a fracas in the tunnel after the match; he was fined £1,200.

James Cotterill of non-league side Barrow AFC became the first English professional footballer to be given a prison sentence (four months) for an assault during a match – a punch 'off-the-ball' which broke an opponent's jaw during a first-round FA Cup match in November 2006 against Bristol Rovers. The punch, not seen by the referee, was caught by the BBC and shown on *Match of the Day*. The police then intervened.

As for Duncan Ferguson, he was transferred from Glasgow Rangers to Everton before his jail sentence had been completed. His appeal against his 12-match suspension was rejected by the Scottish FA. Following his release from prison and completion of his suspension, Ferguson played his first match – for Everton reserves. These reserve matches rarely attracted more than 1,000 spectators. Ferguson's return attracted a crowd of 10,432. He was saluted by a Scottish pipe band and banners protesting his innocence. Later, the Evertonian terraces could be heard chanting for their new hero, also known as 'Duncan Disorderly'.

Duncan Ferguson's story attracted the attention of one unlikely follower. It inspired a piece of classical music – entitled 'Barlinnie Nine' – by one of Finland's most famous composers, Osmo Tapio Raihala, who happened to be an Everton fan. He said: 'I got the idea for it when [Ferguson] was facing jail and had just become something of a cult figure for Everton. It takes into account the contradictions in him: he has an aggressive side but there is a lyrical undertone to him, as the fact that he keeps pigeons shows.' The night that the orchestral symphony premiered in Helsinki was the same night that Ferguson scored the only goal in an Everton victory against Manchester United.

'There is a lyrical undertone to him, as the fact that he keeps pigeons shows.'

In 2003, Ferguson's 'hard man' image was maintained when he stopped a burglar who was breaking into his house in Formby, Merseyside. The burglar required two days of hospital treatment following the incident.

6. ERIC CANTONA

The Kung Fu kick that shocked football

Should Eric Cantona's Kung Fu attack on a spectator at Selhurst Park be prosecuted as a criminal offence?

Less than a year after Duncan Ferguson's head-butt, English football and the criminal law came together in extraordinary circumstances on 25th January 1995 at Selhurst Park in south London. The Wednesday evening game was a highlight fixture for the capacity Crystal Palace crowd of 18,000, a Premier League match against Manchester United – led by the charismatic but temperamental Eric Cantona. The 28 year-old Frenchman, also captain of his country, was in his pomp and prime.

The incident was triggered just three minutes into the second half of a scrappy game with the score still at 0-0. Little did the crowd realise that one of the unforgettable scenes of football in the 1990s was about to occur. Cantona was in a tussle with Palace defender Richard Shaw, who, unnoticed by the referee, pulled Cantona's shirt. The ball was cleared upfield. Cantona kicked out at Shaw and was sent off.

Little did the crowd realise that one of the unforgettable scenes of football in the 1990s was about to occur.

Matthew Simmons, an unruly 20 year-old Palace fan, ran down 11 rows to the front of the main stand by the touchline to shout at Cantona as he left the field and walked along the touchline in front of the main stand. The words were disputed but they appeared to include: 'F*** off back to France, you French b******'. The red mist descended on Cantona. There followed a scene never before witnessed on a football ground in a top-flight match, a violent attack by a player on a spectator.

Cantona executed, dramatically and perfectly, a Kung Fu kick with both feet into the chest of Simmons in front of the stunned fans. This was followed by punching and fighting. Paul Ince also got involved. Other players and officials attempted to intervene and the brawl was eventually broken up. Cantona was escorted off by ground stewards and the United kit man. The match itself ended 1-1.

The incident made front and back page news. Manchester United took prompt action. The club suspended Cantona for nine months until the end of the season and fined him two weeks' wages. The Football Association also brought disciplinary action, as a result of which he was fined a further £10,000 and banned from playing until October, two months into the following football season. FIFA supported a worldwide ban.

Was this ban, imposed within football's own disciplinary procedures, sufficient? Should Cantona also be punished under the criminal law? The criminal authorities did decide to prosecute. Cantona appeared in March 1995 before the magistrates' court at Croydon.

Legal Question: Should Cantona be convicted of criminal assault? If so, was a custodial sentence appropriate?

For: There is a level of violence which the law cannot tolerate or ignore. The fact that it occurred on a football field was irrelevant. Cantona was a role model for youngsters. The incident could have escalated into major public disorder. A large number of people were horrified by it. A criminal punishment to affirm the role of the criminal law and to deter others was appropriate. The punishment imposed internally by the football authorities was not sufficient. A serious penalty, including a custodial sentence, should be imposed.

Against: The act occurred in the heat of the moment. He had been 'repeatedly and painfully fouled' in the course of the match. The insults and taunts from Simmons added to his frustration. There was considerable racial provocation. No lasting injury was suffered by 'the victim'. The football authorities had acted quickly and efficiently. Their punishment was heavy. The nine-month football ban would have a significant effect on Cantona's ability to play football – his living. The matter had been dealt with adequately within the sport. Any additional penalty under the criminal law was unnecessary.

Decision: Cantona was found guilty of criminal assault. He was initially sentenced to two weeks in prison. The chairman of the bench, Jean Pearch, a retired teacher, told Cantona: *'You are a high profile public figure with undoubted gifts, and as such you are looked up to by many young people. For this reason the only sentence that is appropriate for this offence is two weeks' imprisonment forthwith.'*

Cantona's lawyers immediately lodged an appeal. After three anxious hours in a cell, Cantona was freed on bail. His sentence was reduced on 31st March to 120 hours community service.

The courts have continued to stress that 'the criminal law does not stop at the touchline' or, in this case, the front row of the crowd. At the extremities of behaviour, the criminal law has a role to demonstrate that certain kinds of violence are unacceptable and should result in the sanction of the criminal law. The occurrence of such incidents before a large crowd in a high profile, and often televised, arena undoubtedly influences the authorities in the exercise of their discretion as to whether or not to take action.

There must remain, though, considerable doubt whether the use of the criminal law really acts as a deterrent or, indeed, was a meaningful punishment in these situations. The disciplinary structure within football imposed a serious penalty – one that really hurt. What did such a prosecution and sentence against Cantona really achieve?

Matthew Simmons, a window fitter with a previous conviction for assault, was later convicted of threatening behaviour for his role in the incident. He was fined £500 and banned from all football grounds for one year. In an extraordinary sequel to the original incident, after the verdict was announced at Croydon magistrates' court Simmons leapt over a table and lunged at the prosecution lawyer. He grabbed him by the neck and appeared to kick him in the chest. Six police officers rushed to restrain him. Simmons was jailed for a week for contempt of court but freed after 24 hours.

The original incident, regrettable as it was, did at least provide the opportunity for a memorable press conference after the appeal verdict. Cantona walked in and, referring to the British press, carefully expounded a depth and mystery of philosophy not often encountered in English football: 'When the seagulls follow the trawler, it's because they think sardines will be thrown into the sea.' He then left the room.

> **'When the seagulls follow the trawler, it's because they think sardines will be thrown into the sea.'**

Cantona duly served his community service. This included helping coach schoolchildren and working with juvenile offenders in Salford. In Cantona's absence, Manchester United lost the Premier League title that year by one point to Blackburn.

7. AN OBSESSED TENNIS FATHER

Doping of an opponent: a tragic tale

Would Christophe Fauviau's attempt to help his son to a victory in a local tournament lead to a tragic death – and a manslaughter charge?

Parents of sporting children can be very demanding. Tennis parents can be pushy, intrusive and troublesome for tennis clubs and authorities. Jimmy Connor's mother was pretty outspoken. Mary Pierce's father, Jim, was so abusive he was banned by the Women's Tennis Association from attending tour events. Jelena Dokic's father, Damir, was amongst the most notorious. At Wimbledon in 2000, Dokic was escorted by the police off the grounds after a brawl in which he smashed a journalist's telephone. Later in the year, he was banned from the US Open for unruly behaviour – one incident beginning with his outrage over the price of salmon in the players' cafeteria.

But a story from France went way beyond that level. It ranks as one of the saddest of sporting tales.

The background scene was a tennis club in Dax in south-west France, a sleepy town around 30 miles from Biarritz. It was the summer of 2003. Cristophe Fauviau, a 43 year-old former military officer, had become obsessed with the fortunes of his children as promising tennis players and often practised with them at the Dax club.

His 13 year-old daughter, Valentina, showed real promise and was amongst the highest ranked junior players in France. She had special coaching in Paris and was a junior international player; she later reached the top 500 in the junior world rankings. His son, Maxime, was two years older. He was keen but not as talented as his sister. He was playing a number of local tournaments that summer.

Suspicions of foul play were first aroused in a semi-final of a competition in the nearby village of Bascon. A young player, due to play Maxime, apparently spotted Fauviau senior tampering with his drinks bottle shortly before the match. He decided not to drink from the bottle. He lost but, after the match, still alerted officials about

The first prize was a modest sum of money and a leg of ham.

the father's suspicious behaviour. Then, the following day, Maxime's opponent in the final fell ill after the match (which Maxime won) and was taken to hospital where he was kept for two days. The local police investigated and took away suspect bottles for analysis.

Before detectives had completed their enquiries, the next week's evening tournament in a village near Dax was underway. Maxime was in the quarter-final and due to play Alexandra Lagardère, a popular 25 year-old primary school teacher who was hoping in due course to become a qualified tennis umpire.

Fauviau accompanied his son. It was a muggy July evening. Fauviau offered to get water for the players as they prepared to go on court. After the first set of the match, Lagardère pulled out. He was feeling exhausted with the heat. He had a two-hour nap at a friend's house before driving home at 11pm. He set off. His car left the road, hit a tree and he was killed. There were no skid marks.

Maxime, incidentally, went on to win the tournament. The first prize was a modest sum of money and a leg of ham.

The laboratory tests on the water bottle taken from Maxime Fauviau's previous match revealed traces of Temesta, an anti-anxiety drug that can cause extreme drowsiness. Police then made the link between Fauviau and Lagardère. Post-mortem tests showed that Lagardère's drink also had traces of Temesta.

Fauviau was arrested. He admitted to the drugging of Lagardère. He also admitted to doping the drinks of at least 25 players during matches against his son and daughter over a three-year period. It was never his intention to kill, he said. He realised that he had harmed people and that he would carry the burden of Lagardère's death for the rest of his life. His children had known nothing about their father's activities.

At his jury trial in Mont-de-Marsan in France, Fauviau was found guilty of manslaughter – unintentionally causing death by deliberately administering a toxic substance. He was sentenced to eight years in prison.

8. LEE BOWYER

Brawling with your own team-mate

Lee Bowyer's clash with his own Newcastle team-mate was an unedifying sight – but should the police authorities intervene?

St James' Park, home of Newcastle United, has been the scene of many high points. In April 2005, however, Newcastle were losing 0-3 against Aston Villa before a crowd of 52,000 frustrated spectators. The next few minutes became one of the low points in Newcastle's history.

There were 10 minutes left. Newcastle midfielder Lee Bowyer had (not for the first time) lost his temper. Extraordinarily, he suddenly headed – literally – towards his own team-mate, Kieron Dyer, on the halfway line. Bowyer pushed his head in the direction of Dyer's face. Brawling and punching took place between the two team-mates. Bowyer's frustration had reached boiling point. The reason? Apparently, Dyer had failed to pass to Bowyer when Bowyer thought he was in a good attacking position. Bowyer later described the incident as: 'Just a moment of madness and it happens.'

Both players were sent off. Bowyer was banned by the Football Association (FA) for a further three matches in addition to his automatic four game suspension following his dismissal. He was also fined £30,000 by the FA and six weeks' wages, around £200,000, by Newcastle. Bowyer was a 'bad boy' of football. The media had a field day reporting the latest incident.

Should the criminal authorities also intervene? What would be the purpose?

Well, they did. The case dragged on – partly because Bowyer tried to go to court to get the initial decision to prosecute overturned. Bowyer was eventually brought before Newcastle Magistrates' Court in July 2006, over 12 months after the incident. Although a charge of assault was considered, the Crown Prosecution Service eventually charged Bowyer with the lesser public order offence of using threatening behaviour likely to cause alarm or distress. He was found guilty and fined £600.

Dyer had failed to pass to Bowyer when Bowyer thought he was in a good attacking position.

What was the point? Bowyer's counsel told the court that the prosecution was 'a bewildering response to what was a minor spat in which no one was injured and not one of the 50,000 people at the match complained.' Bowyer had pleaded guilty to avoid a lengthy trial which would have involved a number of his fellow professionals. Gordon Taylor, chief executive of the Professional Footballers' Association, criticised the court action as a 'total waste of public money. The incident, he said, had been blown out of all proportion: 'Far more serious incidents occur almost weekly in sport and go unpunished.'

The police and the Crown Prosecution Service defended the decision to prosecute Bowyer, saying that they had a duty to investigate after receiving complaints. 'The incident was not something arising from competitive contact sport. It was an argument that could just as well have arisen in the street.' The Chief Crown Prosecutor for Northumbria declared publicly after the decision:

'The criminal law doesn't cease to operate once you cross the touchline of a sports field. Neither does being disciplined by an employer or a sport governing body make an athlete immune to the law. It's not only the spectators who have a responsibility to behave themselves, but also the players on the pitch.'

No doubt Bowyer's previous disciplinary record and the high profile of the incident contributed to the decision to prosecute. But did the use of the criminal law really serve any useful purpose? To most, this was simply a waste of time.

In the summer of 2006 Lee Bowyer was transferred from Newcastle to West Ham. In one of football's ironies, West Ham's new manager Alan Curbishley made further signings in August 2007 to build the team. One of his first signings was… Kieron Dyer. Curbishley said: 'I spoke to both players and have been assured that it was a one-off, and they both actually speak to each other regularly.'

It's not only the spectators who have a responsibility to behave themselves, but also the players on the pitch.

Another, more serious, 'team-mate' incident in football concerned Manchester City's Joey Barton. Barton was charged with assaulting City team-mate Ousmane Dabo in a training ground bust-up in May 2007 which left Dabo with injuries to his eye, nose and lip and requiring hospital treatment. This led to a suspended four-month jail sentence and an order to pay £3,000 compensation and work 200 hours of community service. Joey Barton was transferred for £5.8 million in June 2007 … to Newcastle.

9. JOHN TERRY

Watch your f****** language!

A bad-tempered verbal exchange between Chelsea's John Terry and QPR's Anton Ferdinand was spotted on TV and lip-read by an off-duty policeman. Had a crime been committed? What would be the ramifications?.

It came down to three words spoken on the pitch, one of which was 'black'. The incident would trigger the first criminal trial of a professional footballer for racial abuse on the field of play. Its aftershocks would result in three FA disciplinary hearings, the resignation of the England manager and the end of the international career of one of Britain's most famous players. It was John Terry, 32 year-old captain of Chelsea and England, who faced prosecution in Westminster Magistrates' Court.

The televised local derby at Loftus Road between Queens Park Rangers and Chelsea on 23rd October 2011 was a bad-tempered match. Chelsea, the previous year's Premier League champions, were surprisingly losing to an early QPR goal and down to nine men with two players sent off. It was the 84th minute.

Chelsea players, including Terry, surged forward in search of a late equaliser. In a scramble with QPR's centre-half Anton Ferdinand, Terry went down amidst optimistic claims for a penalty. Ferdinand thought Terry had gone down too easily, saying: 'Get up, you're f****** bigger than me.' As he rose, Terry barged into Ferdinand with his shoulder; the latter reciprocated. A free-kick was awarded to QPR. Still close to each other, Terry called Ferdinand 'a c***' and made a gesture across his nose, implying that Ferdinand's breath smelt. As Terry returned to the Chelsea half of the field, Ferdinand followed him shouting abuse and making a fist-pumping gesture - accompanied by remarks recalling

It was an off-duty policeman watching the television coverage who, lip-reading, spotted the words.

Terry's alleged extra-marital affair with a team-mate's partner, saying: 'How can you call me a c***, you shagged your team-mate's missus, you're the c***'. Terry appeared to respond, not elegantly, with the phrase 'f*** off, f*** off, [yeah, yeah and you] f****** black c***, f****** knobhead'. The match ended in a 1-0 win for QPR.

No-one on the pitch actually heard Terry's rant, not even Ferdinand. It was an off-duty policeman watching the television coverage who, lip-reading, spotted the words.

Within hours, broadcast coverage was on *YouTube*. The FA and the police were alerted. John Terry was charged under the Public Order Act that 'he used threatening, abusive or insulting words or behaviour' and that the offence was 'racially aggravated'. The FA decided to postpone any disciplinary proceedings until after the criminal trial.

The consequences off the field were dramatic. The first to go was the England manager. The court (many thought foolishly) decided to postpone the trial for several months until after the summer's European Championships. Should the FA still allow Terry to play for England in the summer's tournament? The FA decreed that he could, but not as captain. England's manager Fabio Capello, disputing the decision, resigned. Roy Hodgson, his successor, selected his squad. It included John Terry but, surprisingly to many, excluded Manchester United's Rio Ferdinand, Anton's brother. England lost in the quarter-finals of the European Championships, on penalties, to Italy.

In July 2012, dressed in a smart blue suit and in the full glare of publicity, John Terry appeared before Chief Magistrate Howard Riddle at Westminster Magistrates' Court. Witnesses included Chelsea's left back, Ashley Cole, who had been near the alleged incident, and the 'victim', Anton Ferdinand. Each said that he had not heard Terry's remarks (although Ferdinand declared that he had been deeply upset when the video footage was reported to him).

There was no dispute that Terry had uttered the words 'f****** black c***'. His somewhat tortuous defence from the beginning was that his words were not uttered by way of abuse or insult. He claimed that Ferdinand, in an earlier fracas, had accused Terry of calling him (Ferdinand) a 'black c***'. Terry denied that he had done so and claimed that, in this later exchange, he was 'repeating, basically, what he's said to me or what I think he's said to me'. Ferdinand, in turn, denied that he had made any such accusation. Chelsea's Ashley Cole gave (somewhat unconvincing) evidence that Ferdinand had used a phrase including a word beginning with 'b' . It could have been 'Bridge' (referring to Terry's team-mate Wayne Bridge) or, according to an amended statement prepared with the aid of a Chelsea official, 'black'.

Lip-reading experts solemnly gave evidence. They agreed that the offensive words were spoken but that they could not expertly determine body language or 'the conversational context' in which the words were spoken. Whilst the prosecution expert opined that Terry had used the words 'yeah and you/ya f****** black c***', there was a possibility that 'you/ya' could have been 'a' or a similar sound, consistent with the defence case that the spoken intonation was a questioning 'f****** black c***?'

On Friday, 13th July the Chief Magistrate issued his verdict. Not guilty. Whilst the prosecution had presented 'a strong case', it had not been made beyond 'reasonable doubt' as required in a criminal trial. He could not be sure that Terry had in fact intended to insult Ferdinand, going on to say: '*Weighing all the evidence together, I think it is highly unlikely that Mr Ferdinand accused Mr Terry on the pitch of calling him 'f****** black c***'. However, I accept that it is possible that Mr Terry believed at the time, and believes now, that such an accusation was made. It is therefore possible that what was said was not intended as an insult, but rather as a challenge to what he believed had been said to him.'* Terry received the benefit of the doubt and walked free from Westminster Magistrates' Court.

The saga turned to farce. *Twitter* took over from *YouTube*. The first to be disciplined was a Ferdinand, Anton's brother Rio, charged by the FA with bringing the game into disrepute by a foolish *Twitter* endorsement, referring to Ashley Cole's testimony, that Cole was a 'choc ice' (a pejorative term generally understood to mean black on the outside, white on the inside). His fine was £45,000.

For John Terry, the story was not over. The FA resumed its own disciplinary investigation. On 27th July it charged Terry with using 'abusive and/or insulting words and/or behaviour' towards Anton Ferdinand, including 'reference to [his] ethnic origin and/or colour and/or race'. This was not that much different from the criminal charge but, importantly, the burden of proof (on the balance of probabilities) was lower before the FA's disciplinary panel than that (beyond reasonable doubt) applicable in the criminal court. Terry angrily claimed that the FA's pursuit of his case made his position in the national side 'untenable'. He announced his retirement from international football: 'It breaks my heart to make this decision.' Jumping before he was pushed?

> **The saga turned to farce. *Twitter* took over from *YouTube*.**

Terry's legal team argued forcibly before the FA's independent disciplinary commission that this was 'double jeopardy' and an abuse of process. The commission disagreed but acknowledged that there must be 'clear and convincing evidence' to overcome the presumption of innocence from the criminal trial. Although there was little new evidence, the commission (chaired by a QC with two members of the FA judicial panel, including former Blackburn player Stuart Ripley) decided, in essence, that it could look at things afresh and arrive at its own judgment. It used 'its collective experience of life and people to judge demeanour'.

Terry did not give evidence in person. He (perhaps foolishly) relied solely on his lawyers and his submissions at the earlier criminal trial. His defence found no favour this time. The commission's damning judgment was that his defence was '*improbable, implausible and contrived*'. '*A much more plausible and likely explanation is that Mr Terry was angry, angry at Mr Ferdinand's taunting and provocation of him, angry at the way the match had gone, and angry at the way in which it seemed likely to end.'* The commission was satisfied, on the balance of probabilities, that the offending words were said by way of insult. Acknowledging that he was not a racist by nature and this was a 'one-off' remark, Terry was banned for just four matches and fined £220,000. He decided, reluctantly, not to appeal.

Will players never learn? Ashley Cole, hearing the commission's criticism of his 'evolving' evidence, promptly attacked the FA on *Twitter* as '#BUNCHOFTWATS'. He was charged by the FA with misconduct and fined £90,000.

At times, during this distasteful and seemingly interminable saga, one didn't know whether to laugh or despair at the crude banality of it all. Yet, at the heart of it all, there was a serious issue. Kicking racism out of football, on and off the pitch, continues to be of the highest priority. Sadly, football's troubles continue but the John Terry saga was over.

Meanwhile, in the Premier League, another season had begun of 'the beautiful game'.

Chapter Two

BETTING, BRIBERY AND CORRUPTION

The criminal law's interest in sport extends beyond acts of violence. More insidious and corrupt behaviour can undermine sport and fall foul of the criminal law.

Many sporting scandals involving betting, bribery and corruption have, over the years, led their perpetrators – or alleged perpetrators – to the criminal courts.

Betting and sport have long been close, but sometimes uncomfortable, companions. The uncertainty of the outcome of a match or competition lies at the heart of sport's excitement. Gambling can, though, lead to temptation – the temptation to find improper ways of reducing that uncertainty, at worst of manipulating the result, for the benefit of the 'insider'. Bribery and corruption are great dangers which threaten the integrity of sport.

10. 1919 CHICAGO WHITE SOX

'Say it ain't so, Joe'

It was baseball's World Series. Was there a fix? The story, if true, would be shattering to the millions of followers of America's national game.

In October 1919, baseball enthusiasm was gripping the American nation after the war. At Redland Field in Cincinnati, more than 30,000 spectators were excitedly awaiting the opening game in the World Series between the Cincinnati Reds and the Chicago White Sox.

The White Sox had one of the best teams ever to play the game, with such players as star pitcher Eddie Cicotte, lead hitter Buck Weaver and one of the greatest players of his era, left-fielder 'Shoeless' Joe Jackson (nicknamed because he once played part of a game in blistered feet without shoes). Chicago were the hot favourites to win the Series. The game was a sell-out.

Cicotte pitched the first ball to Cincinnati's opening batter, Maurice Rath. It was called a strike. The second pitch was wide and hit Rath in the back. Was it deliberate? Was it a pre-arranged sign? Back in the lobby of the Ansonia Hotel in New York, reading the telegraphed play-by-play account of the game, Arnold Rothstein smiled. He was a prominent gambler. He knew the fix for the first game was on. He had financed a scheme involving up to eight Chicago players. They had all been vulnerable to temptation – not only led by greed but also resentment. Although amongst the best players in the game, they were paid less under Chicago's dictatorial owner, Charles Comiskey, than players of many other inferior teams.

With the scores level in the opening game, a fielding error allowed Cincinnati to take the lead. The game ended with a 9-1 victory to the Cincinnati Reds. A similar sequence occurred in the second game. Chicago came back in the third and fourth games of the nine-game series. Was it because the players were unsure that they would be paid? Had the fix come unstuck? Or was it to make the score more respectable? Game five was notable for a throw from left field by Joe Jackson which was intercepted, clumsily, by team-mate Eddie Cicotte, preventing an 'out' and leading to a Cincinnati score. Cincinnati took the lead in the series. The Cincinnati Reds went on to win the World Series 5-3.

Rumours about the fix emerged during the winter months and continued into the 1920 season. The story finally broke publicly during an investigation into alleged match fixing at a lesser league game. A player gave evidence which implicated the 1919 World Series. It created a furore. The American sporting public was stunned. Baseball was the national game and the World Series was its pinnacle. A criminal grand jury investigation commenced. Eddie Cicotte decided to talk. 'Shoeless' Joe Jackson also confessed, in testimony to the grand jury, that he had been involved and that he had been given $5,000. He later asserted that he did not directly participate in any deliberate match fixing.

The second pitch was wide and hit Rath in the back. Was it deliberate? Was it a pre-arranged sign?

On 22nd October 1920, indictments on counts of conspiracy to defraud were named against five gamblers (but not Rothstein) and eight Chicago players – Eddie Cicotte, 'Shoeless' Joe Jackson, Claude 'Lefty' Williams, Oscar Felsch, Arnold Gandil, Fred McMullin, Charles Risberg and Buck Weaver.

The case was heard in July 1921 in the Criminal Court of Cook County in Chicago before Judge Hugo Friend. The prosecution set the scene: 'The spectators wanted to see the great Cicotte pitch a ballgame. Gentlemen, they went to see a ballgame. But what they saw was a con game.'

However, certain of the players' written confessions, including those of Cicotte and Jackson, had mysteriously been stolen or mislaid in the lead-up to the trial. (Many turned up later, after the trial, in the offices of Comiskey's lawyers.) The formal evidence available in court for the prosecution was thin. The trial lasted five weeks.

The jury took only two hours to reach their verdict. Not guilty. Hats and confetti flew in the courtroom from the still faithful supporters.

The consequences of the saga were substantial and wide-ranging. With the game's integrity under severe question following the initial investigation, a new structure for the organisation of US baseball was created with the appointment of the first Commissioner of Baseball, the splendidly-named Judge Kenesaw Mountain Landis. As one of his first acts, Landis announced that, despite the jury verdict, all eight players were barred from organised baseball for life:

'Regardless of the verdict of juries, no player who throws a ball game, no player who undertakes or promises to throw a ball game, no player who sits in confidence with a bunch of crooked ballplayers and gamblers, where the ways and means of throwing a game are discussed and does not promptly tell his club about it, will ever play professional baseball.'

'Gentlemen, they went to see a ballgame. But what they saw was a con game.'

The saga became known as the Black Sox Scandal. To this day, participants in the scandal have been denied entry into the Baseball Hall of Fame.

The innocence of America's great game had been lost. One sad, and probably untrue, story was told in a local newspaper of a youngster going up to 'Shoeless' Joe Jackson on the steps of the courthouse after his grand jury appearance. He was tearful, pleaful, disbelieving, still holding on to his dreams: 'Say it ain't so, Joe. Please say it ain't so.'

'Shoeless' Joe Jackson's career batting average is still one of the highest in baseball history and, although not inducted into the Baseball Hall of Fame, he is still ranked amongst the sport's greatest players. Jackson's last words before his death in 1951 were reportedly: 'I'm about to face the greatest umpire of them all and He knows I am innocent.'

11. SWAN, KAY AND LAYNE

Football's shock sixties' betting scandal

It was a story which, in the 1960s, astonished the footballing public. Could three players from Sheffield Wednesday, a top first division side, be guilty of match fixing?

A conversation took place one morning in late November 1962 over a cup of tea after training at first division side Sheffield Wednesday. It was a conversation which, 15 months later, would lead to the headline: 'THE BIGGEST SPORTS SCANDAL OF THE CENTURY'.

Sheffield Wednesday were then a top-10 side – and had been runners-up two seasons previously, in 1960/61, to the magnificent double-winning Tottenham Hotspur. David 'Bronco' Layne, Wednesday's centre-forward and one of the most prolific goalscorers in English football, led the conversation. He was sitting with Peter Swan and Tony Kay. Swan was the club's centre-half – a strong, talented player, superb in the air, with a trademark look of shorts hitched up at the waist. He was a regular England player; a first-choice member of the squad that travelled to Chile for the World Cup in 1960, although struck down by illness and destined not to play in the tournament. Kay, red-haired, hard-tackling and full of energy, was a highly promising wing-half.

Rumours of match fixing in the lower divisions of the Football League had started to circulate in the early 1960s. There had always been talk of isolated end-of-season promotion or relegation matches being suspect. Now, there were wider allegations and suspicions of more matches being 'fixed' to take advantage of the increase in betting on football – particularly after on-street betting shops were made legal in 1961. Betting firms offered 'fixed odds' for particular matches. A group of three matches, a 'treble', could offer more attractive odds. The bookmakers thought that the risks of a 'treble' of matches being fixed were low. But were they? Despite certain rumours and questioning by the Football League, nothing concrete or widespread had surfaced.

Layne told the others that the previous evening he had been to see a match at his last club, Mansfield. He had bumped into an old team-mate, Jimmy Gauld. Gauld, originally from Scotland, had been around at a number of clubs including Charlton, Everton, Plymouth Argyle, Swindon, St Johnstone and Mansfield. He was a proven goalscorer until his career came to a premature end with a broken leg at Mansfield. It

'Well, we usually lose anyway at Portman Road!'

appeared that he was now using his network of contacts to assist a betting syndicate. Discussing the rumours that were around, Gauld confirmed that there was money to be made out of betting on football – especially 'fixed odds' betting on particular matches. Gauld put a proposal to Layne.

Layne discussed the proposal with Swan and Kay during that tea-break. Gauld had arranged with players to fix matches at two lower-division games which he did not disclose (actually, Lincoln to lose at home against Brentford and York to lose at Oldham). He wanted a treble. No one would suspect a first division match. If Sheffield Wednesday were to lose their forthcoming match against Ipswich at Portman Road, they could make some money. A £50 bet would produce at least twice that sum in winnings.

Layne asked the others what they thought, adding: 'Well, we usually lose anyway at Portman Road!' Each player agreed to stump up £50 for Layne to give Gauld to make the bet.

The first division match against Ipswich took place a few days later on 1st December 1962. Sheffield Wednesday were outplayed and lost 2-0 at Ipswich to two goals from Ray Crawford. Swan later said that he was trying throughout – but he did not know what he would have done if Wednesday had not been losing. Kay was named Wednesday's man-of-the-match by *The People*. The three players thought no more about it. It was a 'one-off' for them.

In 1963 *The People* started running a series of articles about bribes and match fixing in football. They were, though, isolated cases. Three players confessed to throwing a third division match (Bradford Park Avenue against Bristol Rovers) and were each fined £50 at Doncaster Magistrates' Court. One more case, Ken Thomson, of Hartlepool United, was exposed. The series of articles ended and most people thought that was the last of it.

'THE BIGGEST SPORTS SCANDAL OF THE CENTURY.'

Then, on a Sunday in April 1964, the dramatic headline appeared on the front page of *The People*: 'TOP SOCCER STARS BRIBED'. The story featured the strapline: 'THE BIGGEST SPORTS SCANDAL OF THE CENTURY'. The paper had returned to its investigations. Now the paper named players with national reputations, players at the height of their careers in the first division. The unthinkable. *The People* had strong evidence against Gauld, the alleged ringleader. The paper wanted 'big names' for the story. Gauld had decided to go for a last big pay-day. In return for a fee in excess of £7,000, a small fortune in those days, he had told the story of that Sheffield Wednesday first division match and, in 'a shattering exposure', given the paper the top names they wanted.

The newspaper's evidence was handed to the police and the Director of Public Prosecutions. Supporters and footballers throughout the land waited, amidst growing tension and astonishment, to see who would be prosecuted.

Bookmakers had allegedly lost more than £35,000 that December weekend. Swan, Kay, Layne and Gauld were charged with a criminal conspiracy to defraud. All four were found guilty at Nottingham Crown Court. Justice Lawton described Gauld as '*an unpleasant rogue*' and '*the spider in the centre of the web*'. Gauld was sentenced to four years' imprisonment and ordered to pay £5,000 costs. Swan, Kay and Layne were each sentenced to four months in prison and fined £150. Each was subsequently banned for life by the FA from playing football again. Six other players from clubs in the lower divisions, who were more deeply involved in betting activities than the players from Sheffield Wednesday, received sentences ranging from six months to 15 months. The scandal has, nevertheless, always since been associated with the Sheffield Wednesday trio.

It was later revealed that Jimmy Gauld had been one of the players interviewed by the Football League when rumours started in 1961. No concrete evidence emerged, although Football League Secretary Alan Hardaker later remarked: 'Although Gauld denied any knowledge of anything wrong, the firm impression was that he was not telling the truth.' Before sentencing Gauld, Justice Lawton said:

'*Your crime has been great. It is my duty to pass a sentence on you to make it clear to all evil-minded people in all branches of sport that this type of activity is a crime and a serious crime … You are responsible for the ruin of footballers of the distinction of Kay and Swan*'.

The People declared in its inimitable style: 'December 1st 1962 – soccer fans, and all who cherish the good name of British sport, should write that date in bold, black letters. It was the Day of Infamy for British football … the ugly cancer of corruption spread its evil growth right up to the highest strata of soccer.'

Swan, Kay and Layne later played together for Thorp Arch Open Prison football team, much to the delight of the soccer-mad governor.

Swan's ban was lifted by the FA after seven years following support from such figures as Matt Busby and Joe Mercer who wrote to *The Times*. At the age of 36, Swan had one further year at Sheffield Wednesday. He received a great welcome from the crowd on his return against Fulham, a match which Wednesday won 3-0. He then transferred to Bury where he helped them to promotion from the old third division. He later led Matlock Town to the FA Trophy as player-manager.

Kay was transferred in that same 1962 season to Everton for a fee of £60,000. It was a record fee, making him England's most expensive footballer. He played 44 times for Everton, with the club winning the league title in 1962/3, before the exposé broke.

Evidence at the trial included tape-recordings of incriminating conversations with Layne and Kay which Gauld had secretly obtained for the newspaper. This was one of the first times that such taped evidence, obtained in secret, had been used in a criminal court. Kay apparently later spent a day in London explaining – to the notorious underworld Kray twins – how such evidence had been obtained and used.

12. FLOCKTON GREY

A 20-length win, but for which horse?

The grey galloped away to win a two-year handicap race at Leicester. But was the horse a two year-old?

A cold, wet Monday at Leicester was the setting in 1982 for a horse racing 'whodunnit' worthy of a Dick Francis novel.

The Flat season had just begun in March. The first race on the card at Leicester was the Knighton Auction Stakes over five furlongs for two year-olds. One of the 10 runners was *Flockton Grey*. The horse, a gelding by *Dragonara Palace* out of *Misippus*, was entered for his first race as a two year-old.

Flockton Grey was trained by Stephen Wiles, a 34 year-old former jump jockey, at Langley Holmes Stables in Flockton, Yorkshire. Wiles' record as a trainer was undistinguished. He had never had a winner on the Flat. *Flockton Grey* had been bought as a yearling for 1,700 guineas by its current owner, Ken Richardson, a Yorkshireman whose self-made fortune had been founded on a sacks and paper business. Despite the horse's lacklustre background, there seemed to

'This would make a very good book, a good detective story.'

be plenty of betting interest and *Flockton Grey* was surprisingly well-backed at Leicester at a starting price of 10-1.

To even greater surprise, including that of his jockey, *Flockton Grey* galloped away to win the race by 20 lengths. Or did he? The exceptional margin of victory caused suspicion and the Jockey Club launched an investigation. As Judge Henry Bennett QC later addressed the jury in York Crown Court: '... *this case is both curious and fascinating and you may have thought more than once this would make a very good book, a good detective story.*'

George Edmunson, an investigator with a security firm on behalf of the Jockey Club, arrived at Langley Holmes Stables. There was a grey two year-old gelding at the yard. A blood test established, almost certainly, that the horse's blood line was *Dragonara Palace* out of *Misippus*. But it was not the horse that won at Leicester! The 'passport' for the *Flockton Grey* at Leicester described a horse with a conspicuous scar on its off-fore leg below the knee. The grey in Wiles' yard had no such scar.

Wiles told the investigator that *Flockton Grey* was probably at another stables, 70 miles away, owned by Richardson. Another stables to visit. Edmunson drove there. But there was no sign of a grey gelding. *Flockton Grey* had vanished.

Then, a stroke of luck. Subsequent examination of one of the official photographs at Leicester revealed a photograph of the winning horse of the Knighton Auction Stakes with its mouth wide open. Teeth are a distinctive guide to age in a young horse. Veterinary examination of a blown-up photograph of that winning horse indicated that the winner was almost certainly a three year-old horse – not a two year-old. The search was now on for a three year-old with a scar on its off-fore leg!

The search was now on for a three year-old with a scar on its off-fore leg!

Certificates, forms and records were examined in the search for such a horse. Candidates were eliminated – leading to one probable 'suspect'. After further investigation, it was discovered with virtual certainty that the winner at Leicester had been an experienced three year-old grey named *Good Hand*, a horse owned by an associate of Ken Richardson and with a respectable racing record. The mystery was nearly solved. It appeared that a naming form and certificate had been signed, and a passport subsequently issued by Weatherbys in January 1982, for a horse in the name of *Flockton Grey* bearing the markings of *Good Hand* but with a date of birth indicating that the horse was a two year-old. By a complex set of arrangements, the horse racing at Leicester under the name of *Flockton Grey* had not been the unpromising foal but the experienced *Good Hand*. *Good Hand* was eventually traced to a remote field at Glaisdale, near Whitby, eight months after the race.

Further investigations revealed that bets, spread around betting shops in Yorkshire and placed by associates of Richardson, had backed 'the ringer' to win over £200,000.

Richardson, along with his racing manager and his horse-box driver, was charged with conspiracy to defraud. The case rumbled on until a five-week trial at York Crown Court ended in June 1984. Richardson was convicted by a majority verdict of the jury. He was given a suspended nine-month prison sentence and fined £20,000. Following the conviction, the Jockey Club announced that Richardson had been 'warned off' from racing for an unprecedented period of 25 years.

No suspicion was attached to the jockey, Kevin Darley. A former champion apprentice, Darley would surely have won by less than 20 lengths if he had been part of the scam.

Ken Richardson, as many in Doncaster will remember without pleasure, later re-surfaced as the benefactor of Doncaster Rovers Football Club in the 1990s. Although not a director, his friend Ken Haran (who had placed a number of bets earlier for Richardson on *Flockton Grey*) was chairman. Richardson's daughter and niece were directors. His influence at the club was all-pervading. In June 1995 there was a fire in the main stand at Doncaster. Arson was suspected. After a search of the club's offices, Richardson was arrested and charged with conspiracy to burn down the stand in order to collect the insurance money. Sheffield Crown Court was told that Richardson had offered £10,000 to a former SAS soldier to start the fire. Unfortunately for Richardson, his accomplice left his mobile phone at the scene and was easily traced. Richardson was convicted and sentenced to prison for four years.

Extraordinarily, in 2006 – 21 years after his conviction – Richardson obtained leave to appeal the original verdict from the *Flockton Grey* 'ringer' trial. He claimed that the prosecution had failed to disclose evidence which would have cast doubt on the accuracy of the photographs identifying the 'ringer' as *Good Hand*. The Court of Appeal listened but said there was no meaningful new evidence. The conviction stood.

13. FLOODLIGHT PLOT AT THE VALLEY

Strange goings-on at evening matches

Floodlights suddenly failed at matches at Upton Park and then Selhurst Park. Was this a coincidence?

We move to football and an extraordinary tale of floodlights, fixing and an Asian betting syndicate.

The story started at Upton Park, home of West Ham United, in November 1997. An exciting evening match in the Premier League was in progress against relegation-threatened Crystal Palace, who had surprisingly taken a 2-0 lead. West Ham fought their way back to 2-2 with an equaliser in the 64th minute. One minute later, the lights at Upton Park suddenly failed, plunging players and fans into darkness. The referee finally called the match off after a 30-minute wait.

Next, to Selhurst Park in south London later in the same year for another Premier League match. Lowly Wimbledon were playing against Arsenal. A dogged Wimbledon were holding on to a 0-0 scoreline at half-time. Suddenly, just 15 seconds into the second half, the floodlights failed. Despite a restart, they went out again – and the match was abandoned.

Then on to The Valley, again in south London, in February 1999. Charlton Athletic were due to play Liverpool. The police received a tip-off. Three days before the evening match, three men were caught 'red-handed' by the police on the premises at The Valley and were arrested on suspicion of burglary. They were Wai Yuen Liu, from west London, and two Malaysians, Eng Hwa Lim and Chee Kew Ong.

A search of Liu's car and the Malaysian pair's hotel room revealed electrical devices designed to sabotage the floodlights and capable of being triggered by remote control. There was enough equipment to wreck the lights at another eight matches. It now seemed likely that the earlier events at Upton Park and Selhurst Park had been part of a pattern of sabotage.

The earlier floodlight failures at Upton Park and Selhurst Park had almost certainly been part of a plot hatched thousands of miles away in Malaysia.

How had the gang gained access? At The Valley, the criminal gang were assisted by a local security supervisor,

Roger Firth, who was paid £20,000 for letting the saboteurs into the ground. His failed attempt to bribe a fellow security guard led to the uncovering of the plot.

Little did fans in England realise at that time that the earlier floodlight failures at Upton Park and Selhurst Park had almost certainly been part of a plot hatched thousands of miles away in Malaysia. The international popularity of Premier League football as a subject of betting in Asia was becoming apparent. The floodlight plot was a scam by an Asian betting syndicate to fix English Premiership matches.

How did the 'fix' work? Under Malaysian betting custom, the result – and bets made – stood if a match was abandoned at any stage after half-time. This allowed the betting syndicates 'in the know' to rake in huge sums on rigged matches, particularly where a small club was doing well against a large club.

The FA ordered immediate checks of floodlights to be carried out at all Premier League grounds prior to the following weekend's fixtures.

The scale of the crime started to become clearer to the Metropolitan Police Organised Crime Group investigating the case. The insatiable appetite in Asian countries for sports betting, perhaps disillusioned by the blatant match-rigging and corruption in Malaysian football prevalent during the 1990s, had now focused on the Premier League. The police believed that, after the unwelcome publicity of match fixing trials involving Bruce Grobbelaar, Hans Segers and John Fashanu, the efforts of certain Asian gangs had moved to technical sabotage. If the floodlight plot at The Valley had succeeded, it could have netted millions for the criminals.

The saboteurs caught in England, along with the Charlton security guard, were eventually charged with conspiracy to cause a public nuisance. The trial was held at Middlesex Guildhall Crown Court. They were convicted. Ong and Lim were each jailed for four years, Liu for 30 months and Frith for 18 months. Judge Evans told Lim and Ong:

'People who live within the jurisdiction of this court derive much pleasure from following professional sport... You were partners in a highly professional, technical criminal operation for which you were no doubt going to be paid a substantial financial reward.'

The FA, perhaps a little optimistically, declared: 'With the outcome of today's trial, a clear message has been sent to anybody intending to use football as a vehicle for criminal activity.'

In both replayed matches, normal service was resumed. West Ham beat Crystal Palace 4-1 and Wimbledon lost 1-0 against Arsenal. Arsenal went on to become champions that season and Crystal Palace were relegated.

14. HANSIE CRONJE

A fall from grace and cricket's shame

Was it true that a mobile phone call had taken place between Hansie Cronje and an Indian bookmaker? Could it have a shattering effect on the world of cricket?

'Hansie is a god-fearing, intense cricketer. He would never succumb to such a thing. It beggars belief.' Bob Woolmer, then South Africa's coach, expressed the opinion of virtually everyone in cricket.

Rumours of match fixing in cricket had by the late 1990s been circulating for a number of years. Stories proliferated as one-day matches became ever more popular. Many of the rumours involved players or gambling syndicates in the sub-continent of India, Pakistan and Sri Lanka. How much of this was real? How far did match fixing extend in the game?

It was the fifth and final Test of the series between South Africa and England in January 2000 which first raised questions in the minds of some English observers. The match was at Centurion Park, near Pretoria, with South Africa 2-0 up in the series. The Test, with South Africa opening the batting, was badly affected by rain with three days lost. A draw was certain. Before the final day's play, Hansie Cronje, the South African captain, surprisingly offered to declare and forfeit South Africa's second innings if England would correspondingly, in effect, forfeit their first innings. England's captain, Nasser Hussain, accepted the unexpected opportunity to salvage a win. South Africa declared leaving England to chase 249 runs. This was the first time in Test cricket that each side had forfeited an innings. England went on to win the match by two wickets in a dramatic finale. Many applauded Cronje's initiative. Others were not so sure.

Hansie Cronje was one of the most respected men in cricket. Known for his strong religious beliefs, he wore a wristband inscribed with the letters WWJD for 'What Would Jesus Do'. The 30 year-old South African captain was regarded as embodying the true spirit of the game: unrelentingly competitive but always sporting. A shrewd strategist and an inspirational leader, he was a sporting ambassador for post-apartheid South Africa.

Cronje's record as captain was very good. Under his 53 Tests as captain, South Africa won 27 matches and only lost 11. His captaincy of one-day internationals resulted in 99 wins out

This was the first time in Test cricket that each side had forfeited an innings.

of 138 with one match drawn. He had the best win-ratio of all contemporary national captains in one-day internationals during this period. Bob Woolmer, as South African coach, would later say: 'He was the best captain I had the pleasure of working with. He was a real leader of men. They would have walked off Table Mountain for him.'

On 7th April 2000 came the bombshell. Police in Delhi revealed that, after a tip-off, they had taped a mobile phone conversation between Hansie Cronje and an Indian bookmaker, Sanjay Chawla, during the one-day series earlier that year between India and South Africa. The transcript revealed a corrupt plan to 'rig' performances by certain players in one of the matches. The astonishment was not just at the revelation of possible corruption but total disbelief that Cronje could be involved. Delhi police confirmed that three other players, Herschelle Gibbs, Nicky Boje and Pieter Strydom, were also under investigation. Cronje firmly denied the allegations. Ali Bacher, managing director of South Africa's United Cricket Board (UCBSA), backed his captain: Cronje was known 'for his unquestionable integrity and honesty'. Four days later came the defining moment. Cronje called Ali Bacher at 3am to inform him that he had not been 'entirely honest' about his comments and that he had accepted money from an Indian bookmaker for 'providing information and forecasting'. Bacher was shocked to the core.

Cronje was promptly sacked as South African captain. Bacher said: 'We in South African cricket are shattered. We ... have been deceived.'

> **Cronje called Ali Bacher at 3am to inform him that he had not been 'entirely honest'.**

The police investigation in India triggered an international reaction. Over the next weeks and months, numerous enquiries and investigations took place worldwide. Criminal charges were brought against Cronje in Delhi alleging cheating, forgery and criminal conspiracy. The charges were never closed. Back in South Africa, the criminal authorities questioned Cronje. He was granted immunity from criminal prosecution there but only on condition that he told the whole truth about his involvement in the affair.

UCBSA, together with the South African Government, set up a commission to carry out an enquiry into match fixing and related matters affecting South African cricket. The enquiry was led by Judge Edwin King. It was standing-room only in the wood-panelled room as the hearings of the King Commission commenced in June 2000. The next few weeks were sensational. Hansie Cronje read out his statement. He told Judge King that he had 'an unfortunate love of money'. He admitted that he had been talking to bookmakers and others involved in match fixing since 1995 and had accepted around $140,000 from bookmakers over this period. Amongst his confessions:

- He had been asked for match information and had supplied team selections and daily forecasts when India toured South Africa in 1996-97. In the second Test, Cronje had told the bookmakers the score at which South Africa would declare.
- Cronje admitted that in January 2000 he had accepted money (around $7,000) and a gift (a leather jacket) during that fifth Test with England at Centurion Park. Cronje said he had been approached by a bookmaker named 'Marlon' to make an early declaration to ensure the game had an outcome. He was promised a larger sum, to be paid into a charity, but it never materialised.
- He had, during South Africa's 2000 tour, offered bribes to certain players to underperform in a one-day international in India's Nagpur City: Herschelle Gibbs (by scoring less than 20 runs) and Henry Williams (by conceding more than 50 runs as a bowler).

Cronje said that he had 'taken his eyes off Jesus' when Satan approached him. He continued to deny, though, that he had ever fixed a result or deliberately lost a game. Was all revealed to the King Commission? Or was it worse? Was Cronje simply being more honest than most others in his admissions and the scapegoat for more widespread troubles in the game?

In October, Cronje was banned for life by the South African Cricket Board from playing cricket and having any future involvement in cricket-related activities. UCBSA said:

'Hansie Cronje acknowledged accepting money from bookmakers as well as attempting to induce others in his team to underperform. The actions… cut across the foundation of trust placed in a person in such a position of integrity. In our opinion, his actions have harmed the good name of cricket in South Africa.'

President Nelson Mandela met him, saying beforehand: 'It is my duty to say to him "you have made a serious mistake"'.

The only legal action involving Cronje which actually reached the courts was his challenge to this lifetime ban. He argued that it constituted an unreasonable restraint of trade. In September 2001 his campaign to get the life ban overturned opened in the Pretoria High Court. He claimed that he had not been given a fair hearing and that the ban interfered with his attempts to earn a living, including by coaching at grass-roots level. The UCBSA contended that it was perfectly entitled to decide that neither it nor its affiliates would associate with Cronje any longer.

Judge Frank Kirk-Cohen upheld the life ban. However, the court clarified that the ban could not apply to coaching at schools not affiliated to UCBSA. It also confirmed that Cronje was free to attend matches as a spectator and report as a print journalist – although he could be denied media accreditation and associated facilities.

Cronje said that he had 'taken his eyes off Jesus' when Satan approached him.

The effect of the saga on cricket worldwide was great. The game examined its very heart and soul. Investigations were held by the cricket authorities in Pakistan, Australia, India, England, New Zealand, Sri Lanka and the West Indies. Two other former national captains, Mohammed Azharuddin of India and Salim Malik of Pakistan, were also banned for life. Importantly, an Anti-Corruption Unit was set up under Lord Condon by the International Cricket Council (ICC). It reported on 'silence, apathy, ignorance and fear' in the game and gave a wide-ranging and disturbing analysis of corruption in international cricket.

The ICC announced new regulations and potential bans which would apply to any player, umpire, referee, team official or administrator involved in betting on any match in which he takes part or in which his country is represented. Attempting to contrive the result of a match (i.e. match fixing) would result in a life ban.

Wisden summed up the saga simply. Hansie Cronje's *'admission that he took bribes from bookmakers to provide information and fix matches exposed the extent of a corruption scandal that cricket authorities had signally neglected to confront'*.

In June 2002 a light plane, carrying Hansie Cronje as a passenger, crashed during bad weather into a mountain near George in South Africa's Western Cape province. Cronje and the two pilots were killed. Despite conspiracy theories, an inquest eventually judged that the air crash had been due to pilot error.

Nelson Mandela said in a statement: 'Here was a young man courageously and with dignity rebuilding his life… The manner in which he was doing that… promised to make him once more a role model of how one deals with adversity.'

15. ROBERT HOYZER
'The referee's been bribed!'

Questionable decisions helped a German third division side beat Hamburg in the Cup. Had the referee been bribed?

Ante Sapina and his two brothers were well-known at the Café King in Berlin. It was a popular night spot. Sapina, a Croatian, ran a sports betting agency. The police had been keeping an eye on the Sapina family. They were key members of a gambling syndicate suspected of criminal activities. But who was the tall fair-haired man who often joined them for cocktails?

Most football fans have thought it when refereeing decisions go against their team: 'The referee's been bribed.' In 2004 a story broke of actual bribery of a referee at the heart of German football. It was Hamburg's visit to Paderborn which triggered the discovery of the scandal. 21st August 2004 was a big day for Paderborn football club, just a third division side in the German league. Their supporters were looking forward to a first-round cup-tie against Hamburg SV, a leading Bundesliga club. The referee was Robert Hoyzer. 25 year-old Hoyzer, 6ft 5ins tall and a distinctive figure with his fair hair, was one of Germany's best young referees although he had not yet refereed in the top division.

He had received payments of more than €65,000 and an expensive new television set.

The match started predictably. Hamburg pressed forward and swept into an early 2-0 lead. Then, the course of the match changed. Late in the first half, after an innocuous foul, Hoyzer sent off Hamburg's Belgian international striker, Emile Mpenza, for repeatedly protesting the referee's decisions. Spurred on by having an extra man, Paderborn then made a fight-back. Hoyzer awarded them two questionable penalties in the second half. Paderborn went on to record a totally unexpected 4-2 victory, much to the delight of the local fans.

Behind the scenes, Hoyzer's performances had started to arouse questions. Four referees went to officials at the German Football Association with their suspicions. What did enquiries reveal? It was Hoyzer who had been having regular meetings at the Café King in Berlin with Ante Sapina and other members of a Croatian gambling syndicate.

The German FA investigated further. They took the precaution of changing officials for many matches the day before games were due to be played. They discovered that large sums of money had been bet on matches in which Hoyzer had refereed. Certain other referees and players also came under similar suspicion. Hoyzer was questioned.

After initial denials, Hoyzer broke down. He decided to co-operate with both football and criminal investigators. In late January 2005, he admitted to being paid to manipulate a number of games. He had received payments of more than €65,000 and an expensive new television set. In exchange, he had agreed to help the authorities to uncover schemes implicating other officials, players and Croatian-based gamblers. The German FA fined Hoyzer €50,000 and banned him for life from German football.

Criminal action was also taken. Hoyzer was charged and convicted of fraud. The prosecutor sought only a suspended sentence in the light of his co-operation. However, the Berlin court was not impressed. Judge Gerti Kramer sentenced Hoyzer to two years and five months imprisonment, saying: '*It wasn't a youthful misdemeanour but a serious crime.*' Ante Sapina, who was alleged to have made more then €750,000 from Paderborn's victory, was also convicted and given a 35-month sentence. His brothers, Milan and Filip, were given suspended sentences. One other referee, Dominik Marks, was given a suspended 18-month sentence. There would be a few empty seats at the Café King in the months to come.

Hoyzer appealed against his sentence and was supported by the State prosecutor. However, a court in Leipzig did not agree. It confirmed Hoyzer's conviction and length of sentence. The President of the German FA, Theo Zwanziger, commented: '*The threat of two years in prison will make one or two people think before trying to influence a football match.*'

It was Germany's biggest match fixing scandal. The scandal was even more damaging since Germany were due to host the 2006 World Cup a year later. How deep did the rot go? The German FA acted promptly to reassure the public. Berlin prosecutors investigated a total of 25 people. Charges were only brought in respect of matches in the lower leagues. The scandal, it conveniently appeared, did not affect any matches or referees in the Bundesliga.

There would be a few empty seats at the Café King in the months to come.

After review by the German FA, two of the suspect matches were replayed, with one match producing a win for the previously 'victimised' team, but most results were allowed to stand. By the time of discovery of Hoyzer's conduct, Paderborn had already been eliminated from the German Cup. The German FA paid Hamburg €2 million compensation for their loss in the 'rigged' match and agreed, in addition, to hold a friendly international at Hamburg's ground. The German FA later filed a legal claim for damages (initially around €1.8 million) against Hoyzer to recover their legal costs and the settlement paid to Hamburg.

After a hearing before a Berlin court, an out-of-court settlement was reached in 2008. Hoyzer agreed to pay a monthly sum of €700 for 15 years as compensation to the German FA. The amount, adding up to €195,600, is being given to charity by the federation.

All this exposé came too late for the Hamburg coach, Klaus Topmoeller. He was sacked a month or so after Hamburg's defeat at Paderborn.

German supporters quickly adopted a new term of abuse after the scandal. When a referee made a wrong decision, the fans would chant 'Hoyzer!'

16. SERIE A SCANDAL

Calciopoli: a tangled web within Italian football

Secret recordings of conversations between Luciano Moggi, the general manager of Juventus, and refereeing organisations were released by the police. Did they reveal a scandal at the heart of Italian football?

The story broke in May 2006 as Juventus were heading for their 29th Serie A championship title and Italy were preparing for the World Cup. A scandal at the heart of Juventus. A scandal, *calciopoli*, at the heart of Italian football. And at the centre of it all, a balding 69 year-old man with a taste for fine cigars and designer suits.

The scandal was, to a large extent, exposed by chance. The breakthrough came from investigations started by the criminal authorities – but into different allegations. In Naples, inquiries were taking place into an alleged illegal betting ring involving players and referees. Investigating magistrates had ordered phone taps on various people, including a number of mobile phones belonging to Luciano Moggi, general manager of Juventus. In Turin, investigations also involving phone taps were taking place into doping allegations involving players from Juventus. In the meantime, in Rome, magistrates were investigating the affairs of GEA World, a footballing agency with close links to Juventus.

The phone taps revealed conversations between club presidents and executives with representatives of refereeing organisations and with referees themselves. Conversations about appointments of referees for matches, favours to be done, help to be given. It was widespread and sinister. And everyone seemed to be friendly with Luciano Moggi. No club appeared to be more affected or involved than Juventus, the Old Lady of Italian football, the most glamorous and successful team in Italy.

Luciano Moggi had become one of the most powerful figures in Italian football. Having worked as a deputy railway station master in a small Tuscan town in the early 1970s, he had moved into football. His charm, his successful scouting methods for a number of clubs (he is credited with helping to discover Paolo Rossi and Gianfranco Zola) and his good relationships with players and officials had enabled him to move to the top of the game. He was a good friend to have – and an enemy to avoid.

> **At the centre of it all, a balding 69 year-old man with a taste for fine cigars and designer suits.**

Juventus were used to coming first. By 1994, they had won the Italian championship a record 22 times – but, by their standards, they were in a slump with only one championship success in nine seasons. Backed by the influential Agnelli family, owners of Italian car maker Fiat and a major shareholder in the club, Juventus turned to Moggi as new general manager to head up a fresh team to help bring them success. Over the next 11 years, Juventus won six Serie A titles and a Champions League trophy. In May 2006, another Serie A title was just a few days away.

Then, transcripts from the secretly recorded conversations were released to the public by the Italian police. The publication of a conversation between Luciano Moggi and Pierluigi Pairetto, the vice-chairman of UEFA's referees' committee, was a typical and stunning example. It was evidence of a 'Moggi system' more sinister than ever previously imagined, evidence of a system to appoint match referees who would favour Juventus.

Pairetto began: 'I know you've been forgetting about me, but I've been remembering you. I've put in a good referee for the Amsterdam game [against Ajax].'

'Who?'

'Meier.'

'Terrific,' said Moggi.

In alliance with other Juventus officials and key members of the Italian football federation, Moggi appeared to be influencing – and even controlling – the appointment of referees and other match officials for Italian and European matches through a vast network based on influence, pressure and reciprocal favours. He appeared to know about the appointment of some referees before their names were released by the Italian federation. The transcripts of more than 100,000 conversations, over eight months, were to provide the bulk of the evidence in the subsequent trials.

Police investigations in Naples and Turin revealed similar discussions involving other clubs. It became increasingly apparent that this was not just a one-club affair. It was all evidence of a tangled network of relationships between referee organisations and other major Serie A clubs such as AC Milan, Fiorentina and Lazio. The scandal had spread throughout Serie A. The investigating magistrates in Naples described it all as '*a cupola of power marked by alliances between the managers of some big clubs, agents and referees*'. The presiding figure was Moggi.

Naples prosecutors later revealed that another series of telephone calls had been discovered involving Moggi and several referees. During the 24-hour period before one match in 2004, Juventus away at AC Milan, prosecutors discovered a series of 13 telephone calls between Moggi and the referee. The match ended 0-0. Many calls were made using mobile phones with foreign SIM cards – Moggi alone was discovered to have had at least five foreign SIM cards.

The police handed all the evidence to the Italian footballing authorities. The ramifications were wide-ranging, immediate and at the highest level. On 5th May 2006, four referees were suspended. On 8th May, Franco Carraro, President of the Italian Football Federation, resigned. Two days later, his vice-president, Innocenzo Mazzini resigned; next, Tullio Lanese, the President of the Referees' Association. Even the presenter of a TV football show was forced to stand down after it appeared that slow-motion replays had been adjusted to suit Moggi's requests. At club level, the entire board of directors of Juventus resigned on 11th May.

'A cupola of power marked by alliances between the managers of some big clubs, agents and referees.'

Meanwhile, just three days later, Juventus clinched their Serie A title with victory. Joyful celebrations took place amongst the crowd and the players. But it was an uneasy celebration. That same day, a tearful Luciano Moggi resigned and told the press: 'I miss my soul. It has been killed. From this day the world of football is no longer my world.'

On 23rd May, a 76 year-old retired Italian judge, Francesco Borelli, was asked to take over the investigative affairs of the football federation. The criminal investigations continued in Naples, Turin and Rome. Italy was consumed by the scandal, even as the World Cup approached. Media interest was insatiable. Pages and pages were given over to the scandal. To some, the existence of such a web of corruption was not a shock – but, to most, the details of the extent of the network of influence, alliances and corruptive associations were astonishing. Some revelations were almost amusing – including referee Gianluca Papresta being locked in the dressing room by an angry Moggi after failing to award a penalty to Juventus in a match in 2004.

Borelli quickly completed his initial investigations and passed his findings to the sporting public prosecutor, Stefano Palazzi. In Italy, interestingly and effectively, prosecutions in sport are heard by a special sporting tribunal, a court where the level of proof required is less than in a criminal court. The sporting court was presided over by an 81 year-old former judge, Cesare Ruperto.

The sporting trial began in Rome on 29th June 2006, right in the middle of the World Cup in Germany. Palazzi laid out his charges to the court and asked for each of Juventus, AC Milan, Lazio and Fiorentina to be relegated – with Juventus' relegation being not just to Serie B but to Serie C. No witnesses were allowed. Each party argued its case. Each of the clubs professed its innocence, except Juventus who argued that a fair punishment would simply be relegation to Serie B.

In the World Cup, a few hundred miles away, Italy were meanwhile beating Germany in a spectacular semi-final with a winning goal from Alessandro Del Piero – of Juventus

– to set up a final with France in Berlin on 9th July. In the final, with the score at 1-1 at full-time and Zidane sent off for his head-butt on Italy's Materazzi, the match went to penalties. France missed one and it was left to Fabio Grosso to smash in the winning spot kick. Italy had won their fourth World Cup. Captain Fabio Cannavaro – of Juventus, of course – lifted the trophy in his 100th game for Italy. Which league would he be playing in next season?

Just five days later, on a hot Friday evening in Rome, Cesare Ruperto read out the sentences of the trial. The shock was great. Juventus had been stripped of their two Serie A titles for seasons 2004/5 and 2005/6 and relegated to Serie B where they would start with a massive 30-point deduction. Lazio and Fiorentina were also relegated. AC Milan avoided relegation but with a points deduction which removed them from European competition.

The verdict of the court was that this was not a case of match fixing as such. There was, however, a network or system which operated outside of the rules in order to '*alter the impartiality of referees*' and was '*contrary to the spirit of loyalty and integrity*' which should be at the foundation of sport. Juventus were credited with at least getting rid of the culprits and promising a new ethical code. No players were charged.

Each of the clubs appealed against their punishments, first to the football federation's appeal court and subsequently to the Italian Olympic Committee's Court of Arbitration (CONI). The final appeal verdicts were announced. Each of the clubs received better news. The points deduction for AC Milan was reduced and they now qualified for the Champions League. Lazio and Fiorentina were back in Serie A but with heavy point deductions. Juventus, however, remained relegated to Serie B but with a much lower points deduction (nine rather than the original 30). Juventus briefly considered taking a further appeal to the courts but withdrew.

Punishments had been given to around 20 individuals. Luciano Moggi himself was given a five-year ban from football and fined around £50,000 with a further recommendation that he be banned for life from membership of the Italian football federation at any level. Antonio Giraudo (the Juventus chairman) was also given a five-year ban. Pierluigi Pairetto was given a two-and-a-half year ban from football.

Inter Milan were designated champions of Serie A for the 2005/6 season in place of Juventus. The saga was formally over. The Italian football public, most of the nation in other words, had been shocked by the scandal. Football would go on – but speculation would continue. Was all uncovered? Would Serie A recover? Would Juventus return to the top?

The footballing consequences of the saga were considerable. Faced with significantly reduced revenues in Serie B, Juventus could not retain all their best players (or, indeed, their manager). They were forced to transfer such stars as Patrick Vieira, Gianluca Zambrotta, Emerson and Lilian Thuram. Head coach Fabio Capello also resigned and left for Real Madrid as the crisis unfolded – perhaps, but for *calciopoli*, he would not have become available to take over as England's manager at the end of 2007? (Who would then have been appointed? Harry Redknapp?)

The appeal verdict had enabled rivals AC Milan to retain their place in the UEFA Champions League for 2006/7 – and, in one of football's ironies, the club went on to triumph in that competition, beating Liverpool 2-1 in the final. The 2007/8 season ended with Juventus back in the top three in Serie A – and with fresh investigations, and charges, underway into Moggi's activities and those of other teams and officials. Had things really changed in Italian football?

17. KIEREN FALLON

Racing's 'trial of the century': a non-runner

It was an investigation which cast a dark shadow of suspicion over the integrity of British racing. Was six-time champion jockey Kieren Fallon guilty of a conspiracy to defraud?

It was a thrilling finish to the Prix de l'Arc de Triomphe at Longchamp in October 2007. Kieren Fallon showed all his riding skills and determination as he hit the front in the final furlong to win on *Dylan Thomas*. Waving an Irish flag, the man from County Clare received an emotional ovation in the winner's circle. Trainer Aidan O'Brien, for whom it was a first Arc triumph, was delighted: 'Kieren gave him a masterful ride and he is a master in the saddle.'

Less than 24 hours later, on a Monday morning, the 42 year-old Irish jockey was in court 12 of the Old Bailey, London's Central Criminal Court, before Justice Forbes and a 12-person jury, in racing's 'trial of the century'. Fallon, six-time champion on the flat in Britain and widely regarded as one of the finest riders since Lester Piggott, was facing the trial of his life. His co-defendants were two jockeys, Fergal Lynch and Darren Williams, and three members of an alleged betting syndicate led by a professional gambler, Miles Rodgers. They were all charged with a

Fallon, six-time champion on the flat in Britain and widely regarded as one of the finest riders since Lester Piggott, was facing the trial of his life.

conspiracy to defraud – a conspiracy to 'rig' the running of 27 horseraces and defraud punters betting on the online betting exchange, Betfair.

Fallon, perhaps the most talented horseman of his generation, had never been far from controversy. A shy man in public, he seemed to court trouble. He was suspended in 1994 for six months for pulling another jockey, Stuart Webster, from his horse in a race at Beverley. In 1998 he won a successful libel case against *The Sporting Life* over an article questioning his riding of a horse called *Top Cees*. Public splits from leading trainers Henry Cecil and Sir Michael Stoute for personal reasons were to follow. But this was now a trial which could lead to the end of his career – and a trial which threatened the reputation and integrity of racing generally.

It had already been a long-running saga by the time it came to the Old Bailey. In October 2002, a BBC *Panorama* programme on corruption in racing led to investigations by the Jockey Club. Evidence and reports were handed over by the Jockey Club's investigation team to the police. Fallon and others were first arrested in September 2004. A dark cloud of suspicion would hang over British racing for the next three years.

Fallon was released on bail and not formally charged by the Crown Prosecution Service until 3rd July 2006. He was, three days later, suspended by the Horseracing Regulatory Authority (HRA) from racing in Britain. Fallon took his challenge to the High Court. Why not innocent until proved guilty? Having regard to the nature of the charges and the apparent evidence, the High Court decided that the HRA was entitled to conclude that there was sufficient substance to justify the suspension in the light of its *'duty to enhance the public perception of the integrity of the sport'*. It was, with the benefit of hindsight, a hard decision. Fallon could not ride here in Britain – but was free to do so in Ireland and France, which he did with continuing success culminating in his triumph at Longchamp.

––––––––––––––

At the Old Bailey in October 2007, the Crown Prosecution set off. At least the defendants were permitted to sit in the body of the court. A copy of the *Racing Post* was within Fallon's reach. The prosecution's claim was that 27 races were involved in the 'conspiracy' during a period from December 2002 to September 2004 and that a total of £2.12 million had been gambled by the syndicate on these races. Fallon had ridden in 17 of them. A system existed, it was alleged, whereby Fallon, Lynch and Williams would tip-off members of the syndicate and enable bets to be laid, through a large number of Betfair accounts, on specified horses to lose.

The most dramatic race spotlighted by the prosecution was at Lingfield in March 2004. The video was shown to an enthralled jury. Fallon came into the home stretch on *Ballinger Ridge*. He was leading by five or six lengths with two furlongs to go.

Fallon dramatically slowed his momentum, never to recover, allowing another horse to win. Was it a deliberate fix – or an innocent blunder? On the day of the race, it was alleged that Fergal Lynch had been an intermediary for phone calls and text messages between Rodgers and Fallon. Rodgers had placed £74,000 on *Ballinger Ridge* to lose, allegedly winning him £26,599. A stewards' inquiry had later been held and Fallon was suspended for 21 days for easing up.

Other evidence of supposedly rigged rides, and sinister off-course activities, was relayed to the court. There was a story of a plain-clothes officer being spotted one evening by Rodgers, apparently on his way to Fallon's home near Newmarket before changing his course when he thought he was being followed.

On another occasion, associates of Rodgers did visit Fallon shortly after the jockey, allegedly, had made a 'mistake' when he rode *Russian Rhythm* to victory in a prestigious race at Newbury in May 2004. Rodgers had lost over £100,000 which he had laid on six Betfair accounts backing the horse to lose. Fallon's visitors, it was alleged, sought 'a more reliable working arrangement' with Fallon for stopping horses in the future.

Evidence was given of numerous phone calls from Fallon and Lynch on the eve of races to associates of Rodgers and others, many made on mobile phones not registered with the racing authorities as required by rules introduced to protect the integrity of racing. Intriguingly, amongst many others, these included almost daily phone and text messages between Fallon and football star Michael Owen. Was this all evidence to support a conspiracy – or was it, in the later words of Justice Forbes, 'consistent with normal social interchange and innocent transmission of racing tips or information by the jockeys'?

The prosecution case fell apart in three major respects. First, of the 17 races in which Fallon was allegedly involved in a 'fix', Fallon actually won five of them. His win-ratio for these races (29.4 per cent) was higher than his average overall win-rate (19 per cent) during the period of the alleged conspiracy. Fallon's counsel made the most of this: 'The very fact… that the greatest jockey of his generation ends up being unable to help winning more often than when he is trying to win is simply ridiculous.' Rodgers' betting syndicate had actually lost £338,000 over these races! Secondly, there was no evidence that Fallon had himself profited in any personal way from the alleged conspiracy.

Thirdly, and crucially, the evidence of the only expert witness for the prosecution was torn apart. Ray Murrihy, an Australian and chief racing steward in New South Wales, had studied all the videos of the races and determined that the rides were 'suspect'. Under cross-examination by Fallon's counsel, John Kelsey-Fry QC (regarded by most as 'man of the match'), Murrihy admitted that he was not an expert nor knowledgeable in British racing rules, practices and culture. It was the turning-point of the trial. In the words of Justice Forbes:

'This is an extraordinary admission, given that he was purporting to give evidence about twenty-seven races run in the UK according to UK racing rules. In my opinion, that was tantamount to Mr Murrihy disqualifying

The trial, which had cost an estimated £10 million, was over. The case had been thrown out.

himself in giving evidence in relation to the suspect races… It is abundantly clear that his evidence fell far, far short of establishing a prima facie breach of UK racing rules…very little value can be attached to it.'

On 7th December 2007, the 11-week trial collapsed. Justice Forbes formed the view that there was simply *'no case to answer'*. The jury were so instructed and they formally declared Fallon and the other defendants: 'Not guilty'. The trial, which had cost an estimated £10 million, was over. The case had been thrown out. It was a non-runner.

Kieren Fallon, who had been unable to race in Britain for 17 months, expressed his anger but was less ebullient than might have been expected at the press conference that followed: 'I am of course relieved and delighted but outraged. There was never any evidence against me.' Within the day, it was announced that Fallon was in further trouble. It was reported that he had tested positive for cocaine following a race in August at Deauville in France. The B sample was still to be tested. Fallon had previously served a six-month ban in France for a similar offence in June 2006. An 18-month worldwide riding ban still loomed for the 42 year-old jockey.

The investigation had not all been a hardship for the police. Two police officers travelled to Australia to interview Murrihy, the expert witness. 'I remember it was December,' he said. 'They went to Bondi Beach and got sunburn.'

18. MERVYN WESTFIELD

Over to the Old Bailey

The first over from the Essex bowler raised a number of eyebrows. Had the cancer of corruption entered the lower reaches of domestic county cricket?

It was a poor first over. Mervyn Westfield, a 23 year-old right-arm medium-fast bowler, was making a rare appearance for the Essex first team against Durham in a NatWest

Pro40 match at Chester-le-Street in September 2009. It was Westfield's opening spell and the seventh over of the Durham innings. Durham were 30 for 0. The first ball beat the batsman, Ian Blackwell, but went past the off stump. The second delivery passed harmlessly into the slips. The third was declared a wide. The fourth gave an easy half-volley, hit to the boundary. Blackwell played defensively to the fifth. The sixth was a loose delivery, hit comfortably for four. The final ball was played for a single. 10 runs scored off the over. Three years later, Westfield was in front of the criminal court at the Old Bailey – the first cricketer from Britain to be prosecuted for corruption in a domestic county cricket match.

What was the 'fix'? Westfield had agreed to concede at least 12 runs in his opening over. Actually, he failed. (In hindsight, this was in part due to the Durham batsman's failure to take full advantage of some easy deliveries!) But Westfield was still paid £6,000. Discovery of the deal was triggered several weeks later when he showed a team-mate, Tony Palladino, the money he had made for agreeing to 'spot-fix'. Palladino followed the county's anti-corruption guidelines and reported the matter to the Essex hierarchy. The England and Wales Cricket Board (ECB) were informed and the Essex police called in. Westfield was arrested in May 2010 and charged with accepting or obtaining corrupt payments. He admitted the offence.

Westfield had been a promising player. He was awarded a *Daily Telegraph* scholarship in 2003 after being spotted at the Bunbury Festival played at Shrewsbury School, along with three other boys who became county players. A coach recalled: 'He was a good cricketer with a lot of potential. He could bowl quick, he was a good batter and he was athletic in the field.' Westfield did not, though, develop into a regular first team player. He was released by Essex a few weeks after his arrest.

Westfield was the first cricketer from Britain to be prosecuted for corruption in a domestic county cricket match.

The most significant and disturbing feature of the case for most was that it involved an English cricketer. Cases of corruption had arisen in cricket – but, since Hansie Cronje, they had invariably been associated with players from the Asian sub-continent where the murky underworld of major betting syndicates and scams seemed to have its roots. The most high-profile case in England, uncomfortably recent, had been the conviction of three Pakistani Test cricketers (Salman Butt, Mohammed Asif and Mohammad Amir) who were jailed for between six and 30 months for 'spot-fixing' (two of them bowling no-balls at specified times during a Test at Lord's). But spot-fixing in a domestic English county game before a sparse crowd? Why? The link quickly became clear. This was a match being televised by Sky in a broadcast that would be shown on the Indian sub-continent where the principal 'fixers', probably a betting syndicate, were thought to be based and where the corrupt bets were laid. The grasping tentacles of corruption had indeed now spread into the lower reaches of the domestic game in England.

Michael Vaughan, former England captain, voiced the concerns of many: 'This lad's been caught - but how many players out there are getting away with it?'

For the lawyers, the case was also important since it confirmed that spot-fixing was not only a breach of cricket's disciplinary rules, it was a crime under the Prevention of Corruption Act. The ECB declared: 'This case has clearly demonstrated that there can be no complacency with regard to the potential threat posed to all areas and levels of sport, including our domestic game, by corrupt activities. The case sends out a clear message to all players and officials that spot or match fixing is a criminal activity and punishable by law.'

'This lad's been caught – but how many players out there are getting away with it?'

Who was the 'fixer'? Was there a middle-man dealing with Westfield? Westfield was paid £6,000 for his part in the scam. He is thought to have been employed for around £10,000 for the whole season by Essex. Here was the temptation for a vulnerable young player. Sadly, it appears that he was tempted by a senior team-mate acting as a go-between with the principal 'fixer', an Asian bookmaker. The Essex police did not then identify who was responsible for paying Westfield. Ominously, Judge Anthony Morris said that one of the alleged corrupters ('a man who is known to me and to many people interested in cricket') could be named by the prosecution at the hearing prior to sentencing.

The day for sentencing came in February 2012. Westfield was given a four-month jail sentence - the first English cricketer to be jailed for corruption. Named as the 'go-between', knowingly inducing Westfield not to perform, was Danish Kaneria, former Pakistani Test spin bowler and one of that country's record wicket-takers.

An ECB disciplinary panel later handed Kaneria a life-ban from any involvement in cricket under the ECB's jurisdiction, and other countries followed suit. Westfield himself was given a five-year ban from cricket (although he was able to play club cricket after three years). The ECB re-asserted that corruption was 'a cancer which must be rooted out of the game of cricket'.

Chapter Three

SPORTSMEN, CRIME AND PRIVATE LIVES

Sportsmen have high profile lives and yet they are as prone to stray into criminal activities, or to be victims of crime, as any other individuals in their private lives.

Many have found themselves in the criminal courts for private activities unconnected with their sport. Some for assault and other irresponsible acts of violence; some for drunken driving; some for more surprising misdemeanours. A number of offences have deservedly led to jail sentences and are sad and depressing tales.

Here is just a small collection of criminal investigations where high profile sportsmen, some unjustly or unfairly, have over the years made the headlines on the front pages rather than the back pages – including the story of St Leger Goold, the Wimbledon trunk murderer; a false claim of theft against Bobby Moore which threatened England's World Cup chances; and a group of sportsmen challenging for 'the oddest crime of all'.

19. THOMAS ST LEGER GOOLD

A Wimbledon finalist and the trunk murder

It was a gory tale: a dismembered body in a trunk at a railway station in Marseilles. And the murderer? A former Wimbledon finalist.

In August 1907, the dramatic headline appeared in *The Times*: 'A WOMAN'S BODY IN A TRUNK'. It was reported that Vere Thomas St Leger Goold had been arrested for murder. He was later convicted. Who was he?

Twenty-eight years earlier, Goold, or St Leger as he was known, had been a finalist in the third year of the Wimbledon Championships. The younger son of an Irish baron from Waterford in County Cork, St Leger was a popular player with flamboyant shots and an attacking style which appealed to spectators. As inaugural Irish champion earlier in the year, he entered Wimbledon for the 1879 Championships, then held at grounds off Worple Road, and made a strong impact. He won his way through to the All-Comers' Final losing, a little tamely, 6-2 6-4 6-2 to the Reverend John Hartley.

Hartley had only just made it through his semi-final. He was the vicar in a Yorkshire village and, expecting to lose earlier in the tournament, he had not arranged a replacement to take Sunday services before his Monday semi-final. So, he had to travel back to Yorkshire on Saturday, take Sunday services, breakfast early on the Monday, ride by horse to Thirsk station, travel by train to King's Cross, London and take a horse-drawn cab to get him to Wimbledon by 2pm for his semi-final. Somewhat tired, a rain-break refreshed him and his win put him in good shape for his final against St Leger the following day. Perhaps life for St Leger would have been very different if Hartley had not won that semi-final.

St Leger disappeared from the tennis scene in the early 1880s. He married Marie Violet Giraudin, a French woman, in 1891. It was her third marriage. They emigrated to Montreal in Canada but returned to Britain in 1903 where they started a laundry business in Liverpool. The business failed and they found themselves in financial trouble.

It was the move to Monte Carlo which really proved their undoing. The couple apparently assumed the title of Sir Vere and Lady Goold.

When the trunk and bag were opened, the police found the dismembered remains of a woman.

Trying to make their fortune on the gaming tables, they sunk even more heavily into debt. They came across Emma Liven, a wealthy Danish widow and a frequent gambler at the tables. One evening, she turned up at the Goold apartment. It is unclear whether she had lent the Goolds money which she wanted back or whether the Goolds invited her over knowing her penchant for wearing expensive jewellery.

The following day, the Goolds caught the 5.38am train from Monaco to Marseilles. They left a trunk and a large bag in the station cloakroom at Marseilles and asked a railway porter to send the luggage on to London. The porter noticed a 'terrible stench' from the luggage. The police were informed. When the trunk and bag were opened, the police found the dismembered remains of a woman – the victim was Emma Liven.

The Goolds were arrested. They pleaded innocence at first, saying that the victim had been killed by her lover and they had panicked to avoid being implicated in the crime. But the story did not stand up. St Leger confessed to the crime. Protecting his wife, he claimed that 'he alone was the murderer and he alone had dismembered the body'. His wife denied actually being involved in the killing, but there were too many stab wounds for one person alone to inflict.

The murder trial was held in Monte Carlo before presiding judge Baron de Rolland. Both of the Goolds were convicted. St Leger was sentenced to penal servitude for life. Marie was initially condemned to death but, on appeal, this was reduced to life imprisonment. She was sent to jail in Montpellier where she died six years later. St Leger was sent to Devil's Island, the notorious French penal colony off the coast of South America. Aged 55, he died one year later – 30 years after being a finalist at Wimbledon.

20. BOBBY MOORE IS INNOCENT, OK!

The case of the stolen bracelet in Bogota

Bobby Moore was arrested in Bogota. Was it a conspiracy to prejudice England's chances of retaining the World Cup?

There was disbelief and concern throughout the nation. Even the Prime Minister felt that he should intervene. England's preparations for the World Cup were thrust into turmoil. It was a criminal investigation that dominated the front page headlines.

Bobby Moore, England's captain, the man who four years earlier had lifted the World Cup at Wembley, had been arrested.

The incident happened in Bogota, the capital of Colombia, in May 1970. The England team were due to play a friendly match against Colombia later in the day as part of their preparations for the World Cup finals soon to be held in Mexico. Bobby Moore and Bobby Charlton, two of England's greatest players, were in the Fuego Verde (Green Fire) jewellery shop off the foyer at the Tequendama Hotel in Bogota where the team were staying. They were looking for a present for Bobby Charlton's wife, Norma.

Even the Prime Minister felt that he should intervene.

Moore and Charlton left the shop and sat a few yards away in the foyer of the hotel. Suddenly, the shop assistant, Clara Padilla, came out and accused Bobby Moore of stealing an emerald and diamond bracelet then worth around £600 (around £9,000 in today's money). The police were called and statements taken. Moore and Charlton offered to be searched but this was not taken up. Manager Alf Ramsey, not known for his diplomatic skills, was called. He spoke to the players and then to the police. The matter appeared to have been resolved.

Moore and Charlton rejoined their team colleagues. England went on to beat Colombia 4-0 in the friendly, with two goals from Martin Peters and one each from Alan Ball and Bobby Charlton.

The England party then flew to Quito for another friendly, against Ecuador, to gain further experience playing at altitude. After beating Ecuador 2-0, they headed off to Mexico for the start of England's defence of the World Cup – but via Bogota because there was no direct flight. They returned to the Tequendama Hotel. Moore and other team members were watching a film in the hotel, *Shenandoah*, when he was tapped on the shoulder. The police had come to arrest him.

After diplomatic discussions involving the local British Chargés d'Affaires, Moore agreed voluntarily to go later in the day to a police station to make a further statement. After hours of questioning, Moore was formally arrested. He was about to be placed in jail when the Colombian government intervened. Moore was, instead, placed under more civilised house arrest at the home of Alfonso Senior, the Director of Colombian Football. He was accompanied by two armed guards.

Moore and other team members were watching a film in the hotel, *Shenandoah*, when he was tapped on the shoulder.

The following day, a reconstruction was held at the jewellery shop. Moore was dressed in the England jacket which he had been wearing at the time of the alleged incident. Part of the shop assistant's evidence was that Moore had taken the bracelet and put it in his inside-left pocket. Moore demonstrated to the judge that there was no such pocket.

After the reconstruction, Moore returned to Alfonso Senior's house and asked if he could go training. Accompanied by his guards, he used a public playing field nearby – much to the delight of a crowd of local boys who were soon organised by Moore, as if marshalling his defence, into two teams along with the guards.

Moore was held under house arrest for four days. More diplomatic pleas and interventions were tried – including from Britain's Prime Minister, Harold Wilson. They were finally successful. On 29th May, Moore was released and allowed on a flight to Mexico, subject to a promise to return if required.

England's opening match in the World Cup was four days later in Guadalajara against Romania which, in sweltering heat, England won 1-0 with a goal from Geoff Hurst. In the next game, just nine days after his release, Moore played in the classic 0-1 encounter against Brazil in one of the greatest games of Moore's career. His famous tackle, cleanly sweeping the ball away from Jairzinho, was a defining example of defensive skill. The photograph of Moore and Pelé swapping shirts at the end of the match remains an iconic image.

England qualified for the next stage but went out 2-3 in extra time to West Germany in the quarter-finals in Léon after holding a 2-0 lead with little more than 20 minutes left.

The case against Bobby Moore lingered on. In November 1972 a Colombian judge decided that the charges against Moore were to be shelved, but the case was re-opened in 1973. On 2nd December 1975 Moore was finally sent a letter by the UK Foreign Office stating that the case had been closed.

A further twist to the story occurred nearly 30 years later. A UK Foreign Office document released by the Public Record Office in March 2003 revealed that even the head of Colombia's police had believed all along that Moore was not guilty. In June 1970, within weeks of Moore's arrest and four days after Moore's legendary display against Brazil, a British Embassy official had reported in writing to the Foreign Office that the police in Colombia had traced the bracelet, which had been 'hawked around the underworld during the previous week'. The police had also 'established the identity of the thief, a woman, and hoped to make an arrest shortly'. The background of the jeweller and the witnesses had been thoroughly scrutinised and 'some suspicious circumstances established'.

Why was Moore placed under arrest? Was there a conspiracy to hamper England's chances of retaining the World Cup? Was it simply a case of mistaken identity? We will never know, but Moore's legacy remains firmly intact.

21. LESTER PIGGOTT

Centaur brings down Britain's greatest jockey

Lester Piggott had failed to declare substantial amounts of riding and bloodstock income to the Inland Revenue. Exposed by an investigation codenamed 'Centaur', was a jail sentence awaiting one of Britain's greatest jockeys?

Lester Piggott remained stony-faced as Justice Farquharson delivered his sentence at Ipswich Crown Court in 1987. The 51 year-old former champion jockey, one of the greatest figures of British sport, had been found guilty of a tax fraud involving over £3 million of undeclared income.

Memories were still fresh of his fabulous racing record. He had retired as a jockey just two years earlier. A winner all over the world with 30 Classic victories to his name in England, including nine in the Epsom Derby where, as an 18 year-old in 1954 on *Never Say Die*, he had been the youngest ever jockey to win the event. His rides on horses such as *Sir Ivor*, *Nijinsky*, *Roberto* and *The Minstrel* were the stuff of sporting legend. He rode 5,300 victories in more than 30 countries during his unparalleled career. He was awarded the OBE in 1975.

It was at that time the largest individual tax evasion charge to be prosecuted in England.

But Piggott had failed to declare income from the fruits of his success to the Inland Revenue. It was alleged that he had signed false declarations during three successive investigations into his tax affairs by the Inland Revenue between 1970 and 1985. The largest sum on the charge sheet related to non-disclosure of £1.3 million or more of riding income. Another charge alleged that, during a period of 14 years, he had omitted to declare over £1 million of income from bloodstock operations. The prosecution claimed that he had used different names to channel his earnings to secret bank accounts in Switzerland, the Bahamas, Singapore and the Cayman Islands.

Piggott was charged following a joint investigation by HM Customs and the Inland Revenue codenamed 'Centaur' after the half-man, half-horse beast of mythology.

The sentence delivered by Justice Farquharson was severe. Three years' imprisonment. It was at that time the largest individual tax evasion charge to be prosecuted in England, and the heaviest sentence to be passed for a personal tax fraud. Appeals for leniency were rejected. The judge said that he could not ignore the scale of Piggott's tax evasion without an invitation to others to cheat.

Piggott was stripped of his OBE in 1988 following his conviction.

Lester Piggott served 366 days in prison – first in Norwich and then a prison near Haverhill, about 10 miles from Newmarket. He received the *Racing Post* each day. Many had questioned his ability to cope. But the taciturn demeanour he always had in public, attributable in part to partial deafness and a minor speech impediment, served him well. 'I kept my nose clean and stayed out of trouble. The year passed.'

Two other sporting figures have been stripped of honours following criminal misdemeanours. Boxer 'Prince' Naseem Hamed was stripped of his MBE in December 2006 following his 15-month prison sentence for dangerous driving. The world darts champion, Phil Taylor, was also relieved of his MBE in 2006 after being convicted of an assault on two female fans.

As for Lester Piggott, he thrillingly returned as a jockey in 1990 at the age of 54. Less than two weeks after picking up the racing reins again, he won a famous victory on *Royal Academy* in the Breeders' Cup Mile at Belmont Park, one of the most prestigious races in America. It was a second coming. The flair, the skill and the drive were undiminished by time. Even Lester Piggott, once described as having a face 'like a well-kept grave', found a smile.

22. ROSCOE TANNER

The fall of the fastest serve in tennis

Roscoe Tanner was a Wimbledon finalist in 1979. Twenty years later, it had become a sorry tale of fraud, debt and jail.

Roscoe Tanner, the left-hander from Chattanooga, Tennessee, had the fastest serve in tennis in the 1970s. Winner of the Australian Open in 1977, the American was a Wimbledon finalist in 1979 and gave Bjorn Borg a serious fright before Borg won his fourth title in a five-set thriller 6-7, 6-1, 3-6, 6-3, 6-4.

What happened to Tanner afterwards? His former coach at Stanford University, Dick Gould, summed it up: 'It's a sad, sad story. He always saw his glass as overflowing. He just kept screwing things up.'

Tanner seemed unable to adapt to an ordinary life. 'He just doesn't understand money', said his former coach. His first marriage ended in a bitter divorce. He fathered a child by Connie Romano, an artist, whom he met when she was working for an escort service. He agreed a large lump sum payment to support the child. He failed to pay. During a senior tennis event in Naples, Florida in 1997, he was arrested after failing to show up before a New Jersey court and was jailed for the first time.

'It's a sad, sad story. He always saw his glass as overflowing. He just kept screwing things up.'

Four years later, deep in debt, he was arrested again during a senior tournament in Atlanta and jailed for failing to pay agreed monthly amounts to his second wife, Charlotte, with whom he had two daughters.

Worse was to come. A year previously, in 2000, he had bought – none of the reports tell us why – a 32ft yacht in Florida from a man named Gene Gammon for $39,000. Tanner handed over a deposit and paid a cheque for $35,595. It bounced. Tanner then used the boat to secure a personal loan.

Several years later, in 2003, Gammon tracked Tanner down after the latter had gone, with his third wife, to Germany to earn some money playing club tennis there. The US government sought an extradition order against Tanner, who was jailed in Karlsruhe, Germany before being transferred to a jail in Florida, and later New Jersey, for nine months. In November 2003, undertaking to mend his ways, he was sentenced to 10 years' probation for the earlier yacht fraud in 2000. He failed again to make agreed payments to Gammon and, this time, in 2006 was arrested and sentenced in Clearwater, Florida to two years in prison for violating his probation.

Tanner, when asked how it all went wrong, said: *'It was a multitude of things. When I was in jail, I was thinking about all the things I had been blessed with and given, and wondered: how did I end up in this spot? I'm not proud of what I've done. I made a lot of money, but I also made some bad deals and had some unfortunate marriages and liaisons. I was broke, but I was still trying to put up the front as a successful guy.'*

In 2010, it all began again. Another arrest warrant was issued on charges of writing a worthless cheque for boat repairs, which Tanner evaded until January 2012. In March 2013 came a further arrest in Florida and a sentence of restitution and probation. In November 2014, another arrest – this time for driving with a suspended licence – and a 10-day jail sentence. He is, at the time of writing, believed still to be wanted on a charge of contempt of court in Georgia in connection with unpaid child support.

23. ANDRÉS ESCOBAR

'Goooooool'

Could an own goal in the World Cup lead to tragic consequences and one of football's saddest tales?

Andrés Escobar, the Colombian footballer, was with his girlfriend as they left the El Indio bar in a suburb of Medillín, his hometown, and went to the car park. There was an altercation with some 'supporters'. Suddenly, he was shot and killed by 12 bullets fired in sequence. After each bullet, the killer is said to have shouted 'Goooooool'. It was surely the most tragic case of a sporting victim of crime.

Twenty-seven year-old Escobar had been a regular international player for the successful, if unpredictable, Colombian national side. He played in both the 1990 and 1994 World Cup sides. He is remembered in England for his goal in the 1-1 draw at Wembley in 1988. He was a gentlemanly player, nicknamed 'El Cabellero del Futbol' (the Knight of Football) in Colombia.

The 1994 World Cup campaign augered well for Colombia. They were playing exciting football, including an astonishing 5-0 win over Argentina in their South American qualifying group. Players such as Asprilla (later remembered well at Newcastle), Valderrama and Rincón were adding spark and dazzle to the team. The footballing world was taking notice. Many experts fancied them to do well in the World Cup in America. But their preparations were conducted against a backdrop of rumours of South American betting syndicates and drug cartels. Coach Hernán Gomez was reported to have received death threats.

The opening match against Romania was a shocker for Colombia. They looked edgy and uncertain. It was a surprising, and deflating, 3-1 defeat to begin their campaign. Worse was to follow in the second match against the USA before a 93,000 crowd in the Rose Bowl in Los Angeles.

For Escobar, he was desperately unfortunate in the 34th minute of the match against the USA. A cross came over from the left and, positioned around the penalty spot, Escobar stretched out his leg towards the goal to cut out the cross. The ball caught his boot and deflected firmly towards the near post of the Colombian goal. The goalkeeper was wrong-footed. The own goal set the USA on the path to a surprise 2-1 win and the Colombians were out of the World Cup in the first group round.

Just 10 days later, back in Colombia, Escobar was shot. His murder was widely believed to be a retribution for the own goal.

Subsequently charged, and convicted a year later, was Humberto Muñioz Castro. He was sentenced to 43 years in prison. This was later reduced and he was eventually released in 2005 after serving approximately 11 years. It has never been established whether he acted alone or at the direction of one of the gambling syndicates.

South America's passion for football as more than just a sport has triggered other excitable and dramatic consequences in the past. Notably, riots in a match between El Salvador and Honduras in June 1969 came at a time of deteriorating diplomatic relations between the two countries over immigration and border disputes. This led two weeks later to open warfare between the two countries with many casualties. It became known as the 'Soccer War'.

It was surely the most tragic case of a sporting victim of crime.

The tragic tale of Andrés Escobar must, though, be the saddest individual story.

24. BOB WOOLMER

An open verdict

Bob Woolmer, Pakistan's cricket coach, was found dead the morning after the team's shock exit from the World Cup. Was it death by natural causes – or murder?

Bob Woolmer, Pakistan's 58 year-old cricket coach, could scarcely believe his eyes. Pakistan, ranked fourth in the world in one-day internationals, had lost to unfancied Ireland. It was one of the biggest upsets in cricket history. Pakistan were out of the 2007 World Cup at the initial group stage.

Woolmer attended the post-match media conference. He spoke of the stresses of the job: 'Doing it internationally, it takes a toll on you – the endless travelling and the non-stop living out of hotels.' He went back, around 8.30pm, to his room on the 12th floor of the Pegasus Hotel in Kingston, Jamaica. Perhaps he thought about the past and how he had arrived here. Almost certainly he thought about the future and his family back in England. Should he resign?

Born in India to English parents, cricket had always been in Woolmer's blood. He developed into a fine all-rounder for Kent and then for England – remembered for

A maid entered his room to find Woolmer's body – he was a big man – sprawled on the floor by the bathroom door.

his six-and-a-half-hour defence against Lillee and Thomson in an innings of 149 runs in his second Test for England at the Oval in 1975. Not averse to controversy, he had joined the rebel 'Packer Circus'. Although he continued to play for England, he never really recovered his form of the 1970s and retired as a player in 1984.

He became an innovative and well-respected coach. It had become his life. Appointed to coach South Africa in 1994, he had many successful years working closely with captain Hansie Cronje and his team. He had also, his reputation untouched, been through the turmoil of the betting and bribery crisis. After a brief return to England, the travelling began again when, in 2004 and to the surprise of many, he accepted an offer to coach the Pakistan team. He had experienced many highs and lows in that role, including the ball-tampering disputes and now this shock World Cup defeat. He knew that the reaction back in Pakistan to the team's performance would be highly critical. He sent an email to his wife saying he was 'a little depressed… our batting performance was abysmal. I could tell the players were for some reason not able to fire themselves up.'

At 10.45am. the following morning, a Sunday, a maid entered his room to find Woolmer's body – he was a big man – sprawled on the floor by the bathroom door. Blood and vomit were on the walls. Woolmer was taken to the University of the West Indies Hospital but pronounced dead. Speculation was immediate and unconstrained. Natural causes? Suicide? Murder? The following days and weeks would rank amongst cricket's darkest times.

The Jamaican police, headed by deputy police commissioner Mark Shields, investigated. An early autopsy report was given by government pathologist, Dr Ere Seshaiah. A spokesman announced the dramatic news on 22nd March:

'The pathologist's report states that Mr Woolmer's death was due to asphyxiation as a result of manual strangulation. In these circumstances, the matter is now being treated by the Jamaican police as a case of murder.'

Theories and speculation abounded throughout the press and the cricket world:

- There was no sign of any forced entry into the room. He must have known his assailant. There were rumours of arguments with members of the Pakistan team.
- There was 'very little' sign of a struggle. Had he first been drugged or poisoned? Rumours of a snake venom and, later, traces of a weedkiller in his stomach started to circulate.
- Had Woolmer been murdered as retribution for the World Cup defeat?
- Was he killed at the direction of a gambling syndicate? Rumours continued of

match fixing and dubious 'hangers-on' in Jamaica from the ubiquitous Asian betting world. The spectre of corruption in cricket loomed again.

• Was he about to write a book recording 'secrets' of his time with South Africa and Pakistan which others did not want to become public? Barry Richards, one of South Africa's greatest cricketers and best man at Woolmer's wedding, remarked: 'There was a feeling around that Bob was going to expose something. There is a dark side to cricket. Bob was passionate about the game. Perhaps too passionate.'

Should the World Cup be cancelled? These were sad, mysterious and troubled days. The Pakistani team were finger-printed and interviewed. Many were outraged by their treatment and the innuendo of suspicion. Others called for a major review of cricket. The World Cup continued, but under a dark cloud of disinterest, accusations and chaos.

The Jamaican authorities struggled to cope with an investigation in the spotlight of the world's media. It had all become front-page news, worldwide. Representatives from Scotland Yard and a British pathologist were invited at the end of March to assist in the investigation.

No real leads emerged to solve the 'crime' and doubts gathered as to the correctness of the original autopsy report. The weeks passed. On 12th June, the Jamaican police declared that, after all, it was not a case of murder. South African and Canadian pathologists had also joined the medical team and concurred with a finding by the British forensic team: '*Mr Woolmer died of natural causes.*' In later toxicology tests '*no substance was found to indicate that Bob Woolmer was poisoned*'.

That was not, however, the end of proceedings. A coroner's inquest had been ordered in Jamaica back in April and the process was still to be completed. Investigations continued. Several members of the Pakistan team had refused to travel to Jamaica for the inquest, including captain Inzamam-ul-Haq. There was still lingering resentment at some of the accusations and treatment directed at the Pakistan team in those initial days.

The inquest in Kingston finally concluded in November 2007. It had heard from over 50 witnesses. Coroner Patrick Murphy gave his final summation. He listed several possible verdicts available to the jury – death by natural causes, accidental death, suicide, murder and involuntary or voluntary manslaughter.

The verdict was inconclusive. The 11-member jury decided that there was insufficient evidence of either a criminal act or death by natural causes. They were unable to decide an outcome. It was an 'open verdict'. The jury's foreman was reported as saying: '*We had no choice. We came to an open verdict because the evidence was too weak. There were too many what-ifs and loopholes.*'

The inquest therefore did not rule out the controversial strangulation theory of the Jamaican government's pathologist. But the Jamaican police decided that it was the end of their investigation: 'We do not intend to go any further with these investigations,' said deputy police commissioner Mark Shields.

The saga was at an end. Shocking, sad and disturbing for all concerned – for Bob Woolmer's family and for the world of cricket. For a time, a long time, they had seemed cricket's darkest hours. Many of cricket's troubles, prejudices and potentially destructive influences had surfaced again menacingly. The crime that never was? Probably death by natural causes of a much-travelled, big man of cricket suffering from diabetes and stress. But, in the end, an open verdict.

25. A 'LAGS' SOCCER TEAM

And the oddest crime of all?

Could a British all-international team be assembled from footballers who have spent time in jail? Which footballer has committed the strangest crime of all?

Sportsmen (and indeed they do all seem to have been men) have been caught in some pretty odd activities in their private lives which have fallen foul of the criminal law.

There have been some unpleasant and sad tales. Footballers have been prominent and a strong football team could be assembled from players who have served a jail sentence. A British 'lags' soccer team, playing a fluid 4-3-3 formation, could have a starting line-up of the following international players (number of caps in brackets):

???

Gary Charles (2, England)   Terry Fenwick (20, England)
      Tony Adams (Capt) (66, England)   Peter Swan (19, England)

                  Dennis Wise (21, England)
Peter Storey (19, England)   Graham Rix (17, England)

George Best (37, N Ireland)   Mickey Thomas (51, Wales)
            Ian Wright (33, England)

(It is fair to point out that Dennis Wise, initially jailed on an assault charge, was later acquitted, and also that Ian Wright's 14 days in prison for non-payment of motoring fines came, as a 19 year-old, before his league career began.)

There was some speculation that the midfield in our theoretical team could become even stronger when, in 2008, Steven Gerrard was up before the Liverpool Crown Court on a charge of affray, but he was found not guilty. The prospect of Harry Redknapp being available as manager also faded when, in 2012, he was acquitted of tax evasion – so Tony Adams would have to double-up as player/manager. Principal substitutes for the 'lags' team would, in midfield and defence, be Joey Barton (1 cap, England) and Tony Kay (1 cap, England). In attack, those also qualified include David Partridge (7 caps, Wales), Ched Evans (13 caps, Wales), Kerry Dixon (8 caps, England) and Duncan Ferguson (7 caps, Scotland). Dixon is the latest qualifier after a jail sentence in June 2015 for assault. Others (uncapped but experienced) could include Lee Hughes, Jermaine Pennant and Micky Quinn.

'So, Roy Keane is on 50 grand a week. Mind you, I was on 50 grand a week until the police found my printing machine!'

The goalkeeper position is a problem. In order to complete a full all-international team, one overseas player would have to be fielded - goalkeeper René Higuita of Colombia. Famed for his 'scorpion' kick at Wembley against England in 1995, he was later imprisoned for seven months (but later released) in Colombia for his involvement as a go-between in a kidnapping.

As for the challenge for the strangest crime of all, Mickey Thomas is a strong contender. The long-haired ex-Welsh international winger was a popular player in the 1970s and 80s with clubs such as Wrexham, Manchester United, Everton and Chelsea. In 1993, Thomas found himself in court before Justice Gareth Edwards on a charge of passing counterfeit £10 and £20 notes to trainees at Wrexham when he was a player there. Despite his illustrious Welsh name, the judge had little sympathy for Thomas. The judge thought Thomas was a 'flash and dashing adventurer' and decided to make an example of him. Perhaps he had heard Thomas joking with reporters as he arrived at court: 'Anyone got change of a tenner for the phone?'

Thomas was sentenced to 18 months in jail, spent in Walton prison in Liverpool. It did not subdue Thomas, who later became popular as a pundit and after-dinner speaker: 'So, Roy Keane is on 50 grand a week. Mind you, I was on 50 grand a week until the police found my printing machine!'

For a collection of unusual offences, Peter Storey, the hard-tackling midfielder for Arsenal's double-winning side in 1971 and holder of 19 England international caps,

A rugby league star had been arrested for an alleged fight with Father Christmas in the early hours of Christmas Day!

had a distinctive and unenviable record. In 1979 he was fined £700 and given a six month suspended jail sentence for running a brothel in east London. A year later, he was jailed for three years for involvement in a plot to counterfeit gold coins. In 1990 he completed his collection with a 28-day jail sentence for attempting to import 20 pornographic videos from Europe which he had hidden in a spare tyre.

A new contender for the most unusual offence by a sportsman appeared in January 2012 with a newspaper report that a rugby league star had been arrested for an alleged fight with Father Christmas in the early hours of Christmas Day! Closer study revealed that the incident did not take place in Lapland but outside a pub in Pontrefract. Castleford's full-back, Richie Owen, was arrested on suspicion of assault after a late night punch-up involving a gang of men dressed in Father Christmas costumes. Facts are hazy. He was fined two weeks' wages at a club disciplinary hearing. It appears that the West Yorkshire police did not pursue a formal charge.

The award of 'the oddest crime of all' continues, though, to rest with footballer Glen Johnson for an incident in January 2007. An England international left-back, and reportedly earning £30,000 a week, 22 year-old Johnson was then on loan from Chelsea to Portsmouth. An extraordinary report appeared. Glen Johnson had been arrested by the Kent police on suspicion of stealing a toilet seat and tap fittings from a B&Q store in Dartford, Kent.

Johnson and fellow footballer Ben May, a striker on loan at Millwall from Chelsea, were seen on CCTV putting the toilet seat in a box marked with a cheaper price tag and hiding the taps underneath a sink at the check-out to avoid paying for them. They were spotted by a 74 year-old security guard at the DIY store. Police were called and both Johnson and May were given on-the-spot £80 fixed penalty fines.

A worker at the B&Q store told reporters: 'We all recognised Johnson. No one could quite believe a bloke like him, with all that money, would be moronic enough to nick a toilet seat. They seemed to find the whole thing funny.'

The following week, Johnson turned up for training at Portsmouth. He found two toilet seats on his peg in the changing room put there by his team-mates. 'He's taken a lot of stick but he took it all in good heart,' one of them said.

26. LEWIS HAMILTON

Behaving like a hoon

A Mercedes sports car was fish-tailing, amidst clouds of smoke, along a suburban street in Melbourne. Who was the driver?

Who was that driving like an idiot? Constable Scott Woodford and his colleague in a patrol car watched in astonishment in March 2010 as a high-powered Mercedes sports car accelerated and 'fish-tailed', its rear wheels skidding and generating clouds of smoke in a 'burn-out' across the tarmac in a suburban street just outside the Albert Park racing circuit in south-east Melbourne. The police officers intervened. A 'gentleman who resides in Switzerland' was interviewed for half-an-hour and arrested. His car was impounded and he was escorted back to his hotel.

Lewis Hamilton, the 2008 Formula One World Driver's Champion who earlier in that afternoon had set the fastest time in the first practice session for the Australian Grand Prix, would now face a charge before the local Magistrates' Court. Driving from the racing circuit to the McLaren team's hotel just after 9pm, he had decided 'to entertain' his fans but failed to spot the nearby police car. Hamilton quickly admitted that he had been 'very silly' and 'driving in an over-exuberant manner'. He later pleaded guilty before the Melbourne Magistrates' Court to a count of 'driving a vehicle causing loss of traction'.

Hamilton's counsel (in the driver's absence preparing for the Belgian Grand Prix) told the court that his client had suffered embarrassment and humiliation over the incident. It was a 'momentary lapse of judgment' and Hamilton recognised that he had a 'duty to act as a role model'. Magistrate Clive Alsop was not sympathetic. Imposing the maximum fine of A$500, he declared that Hamilton had abused his high-profile position: *'He didn't show the level of responsibility and maturity that he must use every day on the racetrack.'*

Australians are plain-speaking people. Tim Pallas, the Victoria State Roads Minister who had just launched a road safety campaign under the strapline 'Don't be a dickhead', was asked whether Hamilton met that description. The Minister initially called him a 'very silly young man' but, when pressed, continued:
'OK, I'll say it. He's a dickhead.'

Magistrate Alsop had put it a different way in court: *'This is somebody in a responsible position behaving*

'This is somebody in a responsible position behaving like a hoon.'

like a hoon.' (A 'hoon', for the British reader, is an informal word used (according to the Oxford Dictionary) in Australia and New Zealand meaning 'a lout or hooligan, especially a young man who drives recklessly'.)

Hamilton finished sixth in the Australian Grand Prix. His luxury silver Mercedes AMG C63 sports car, with just 343 miles on the clock, was later auctioned for charity by a local dealership. The winning bidder also received a copy of the police report filed after the embarrassing incident.

Lewis Hamilton was not the only world-class sportsman in 2008 to be in trouble with the law for careless driving. Four months earlier, the Florida Highway Patrol issued golfer Tiger Woods with a citation for careless driving. Woods, hurriedly driving his SUV out of his driveway in the early hours of the morning, had smashed into a fire hydrant at the edge of his neighbour's property and damaged the trunk of an oak tree. There had been reports of a domestic incident. His then wife, Elin Nordegren, had used a golf club to break the rear window – apparently in an attempt to help free an injured Woods from the car. It is not known what club she used. Woods paid his US $164 fine.

27. HARRY'S GAME

Rosie's bank account in Monaco

Harry Redknapp was pleased with his signing of Peter Crouch for Portsmouth and his subsequent transfer at a profit for the club of £3.25 million - especially since he would get a share of the profit. Did he receive more than his formally agreed share? Was there a scheme to evade tax?

It was a bad 24 hours for Harry Redknapp. On Sunday, 22nd January 2010, the 64 year-old Tottenham Hotspur manager saw his team's title hopes suffer with a 3-2 defeat at Manchester City after a last-minute penalty from City's Mario Balotelli. The following morning, the people's favourite to become the next manager of England was in the dock in Court 6 at Southwark Crown Court, behind a glass screen with his co-defendant, football club owner Milan Mandaric, facing a two-week trial on charges of tax fraud.

Football's transfer dealings had been attracting the attention of the Inland Revenue for many years. Harry Redknapp was known as an astute and active operator in the transfer markets. An earlier investigation into his tax affairs had cleared him, but only after a badly-handled early morning raid by the City of London Police on Redknapp's luxury home in Sandbanks, Dorset. Enraged at the incident, he sued. The High Court ruled that the police raid was illegal and awarded Redknapp £1,000 in damages.

It was Rosie who revived the tax authority's interest – or, more particularly, an account opened in Monaco in the name of Rosie47, the name of one of Redknapp's pedigree bulldogs coupled with his year of birth. Early evidence revealed Redknapp's affection for Rosie (sadly, no longer alive). 'I loved her to bits', he said, adding: 'If a man had a wife as nice as Rosie, they have got a good wife. I still don't like calling her a dog, she was so much better than that.'

Redknapp (after a seven-year reign as manager of West Ham) had joined Portsmouth as director of football in June 2001 on a contract that included payment of commission of 10 per cent on net transfer profits. One of his first signings was Peter Crouch for £1.25 million from Queens Park Rangers. Despite the doubts of Pompey's owner Milan Mandaric (dismissing Crouch as a 'basketball player'), Harry was confident: 'Crouchy at 6ft 7ins was not exactly Milan's cup of tea … I said he's young, he's developing, he's getting taller.' In March 2002 Redknapp was appointed full-time manager and, as part of his new contract, his commission on transfers was reduced to five per cent. (For many observers, it was astonishing that a manager, whose job was to develop the best team for his club, could be encouraged to have such a potential conflict of interest in selling players.)

Nine days later, Crouch was sold to Aston Villa for £4.5 million, a profit of £3.25 million. Redknapp was paid a five per cent bonus of £115,473 (with tax duly deducted) but considered that 'morally' he should get his full 10 per cent. Four days after receiving his contractual payment, Redknapp flew with his wife Sandra to Monaco and opened the Rosie47 account at a branch of HSBC Private Bank. 'It would be a

The following morning, the people's favourite to become the next manager of England was in the dock in Court 6 at Southwark Crown Court.

waste of time giving me any forms because I would most probably have left it on the deckchair where me and Sandra were sitting.'

A first payment of US$145,000 was paid by Mandaric into the account in June 2002. Early the following year, upon a request form signed by Redknapp, US$100,000 was transferred from the account to a company in Miami called First Star International, linked with Mandaric. (Redknapp could later offer little explanation: 'All I was thinking about was marking David Beckham.') A further US$150,000 from the Milan Mandaric Revocable Trust was paid into the Rosie47 account in April 2004. In February 2008 the Rosie47 account was closed and the balance of US$202,000 transferred to Redknapp's London HSBC account. Was this all a scheme to pay a 'bung' to Redknapp in a way which deliberately aimed at evading UK tax and National Insurance on payments that were really taxable remuneration?

It was only in November 2009, during another enquiry into corruption in football led by Lord Stevens, the former Metropolitan Commissioner, that Rosie's bank account came to light. Later questioned by a *News of the World* journalist, Rob Beasley, Redknapp said that US$145,000 paid into the account was 'a bonus for selling Peter Crouch' and part of his cut of the profit. The conversation had secretly been recorded on tape. In Southwark Crown Court, the prosecution argued that the statement 'condemns [Redknapp] from his own mouth'. Redknapp countered that he lied to Beasley 'just to get him off my back' while he concentrated on the following day's Carling Cup Final between Spurs and Manchester United (United won 4–1 on penalties).

'I write like a two year-old and can't spell... I'm a fantastic football manager, not a hard-headed businessman.'

Redknapp had talked his way into trouble. He would have to talk his way out of it. Wearing a dark blue suit and heavy rimmed glasses (were they new for the court hearing?), the happy-go-lucky character entertained the jury with his easy wit and simple charm. He was 'Arry from the East End. 'I am completely and utterly disorganised. I write like a two year-old and can't spell. I can't work a computer, I don't know what an email is, I have never sent a fax and I've never even sent a text message.' (Perhaps, in retrospect, not the best advocacy if he wanted to become manager of England, but present needs were greater.) 'I don't look at my contracts, I don't read one word, I sign at the bottom. Then my accountant rings up and says, "Harry you've got a £500,000 bonus [on qualifying for] the Champions League". I'm a fantastic football manager, not a hard-headed businessman.' He was generous and had always paid his taxes. It was unbelievable, he said, that two men who had paid millions of pounds in tax would have concocted such a fiddle to save a relatively small amount of tax. A mobile phone went off in the public gallery with a ring-tone claiming 'Glory Glory Tottenham Hotspur'.

Co-defendant Milan Mandaric, asked about his relationship with Redknapp, said: 'Do you mean when I want to strangle him or when I love him?' Explaining the payments, he said: 'I want to do something special for Harry because he means more to me than as a football manager. This was something as a friend.' It was 'seed money' for an investment portfolio with Redknapp.

There were moments of nostalgia. Defence lawyers even recalled an old court case involving Redknapp's former West Ham colleagues, Bobby Moore and Geoff Hurst. The FA had paid a bonus of £1,000 to each member of the World Cup-winning squad in 1966. The Inland Revenue, not overlooking an opportunity, had sought to tax this as remuneration. The court decided that the payments had the 'quality of a testimonial or accolade rather than the quality of remuneration for services rendered' and were therefore tax-free. Redknapp's lawyers (led by John Kelsey-Fry QC, who had successfully defended Keiren Fallon and would again play a star role) argued that the payments here should likewise be viewed as 'gifts' that 'were not linked to quality of services'.

Eleven days of evidence had amused and, one suspected, bemused the jury. The judge, Anthony Leonard QC, summed up. Were Mandaric and Redknapp deliberately aiming to evade tax? '*Football is an emotive subject, stirring in an individual anything from deep passion to resentment,*' he declared with feeling. The eight men and four women were warned '*to ignore footballing matters in their deliberations*'. (Perhaps the prosecution had made a mistake in asking the jury to 'keep their eye on the ball' when considering their verdicts.)

The jury deliberated for nearly four hours but failed to reach a verdict before being sent home. The judge made it clear that he wanted a unanimous verdict. The following morning, 8th February, the verdict was declared: 'Not guilty'.

Just a few hours later, over at the FA's offices in Wembley, Fabio Capello unexpectedly resigned as England manager. Harry Redknapp was instantly installed as the bookmakers' favourite to be his successor. Tottenham's next match was at home against Newcastle. It was a 5-0 win. Harry was back.

After months of speculation, however, it was Roy Hodgson who was appointed England manager. Harry Redknapp was replaced as Tottenham manager in 2012. He would, though, still enjoy his walks on the Dorset coast with Buster, Rosie's former companion.

Chapter Four

NEGLIGENCE AND PERSONAL INJURY

Injuries occur, sadly but inevitably, in the course of sport. Potential causes of accidents are varied and numerous.

They include a dangerous sliding tackle in football, a collapsing scrum or head-high challenge in rugby, a badly sliced golf shot, reckless horse-riding or a defective grandstand. Serious injuries can result – not only to participants but also to spectators.

Who should bear the risk of injury? Should the principle of liability for negligence apply to injuries in the course of sport? If so, what level of care is required? Who can potentially be liable – players, referees, event organisers, club owners, spectators, governing bodies within sport, the police? A wide range of disputes have come before the courts which have explored these questions, particularly during the last 20 years or so – and we see how major court decisions have significantly shaped the law in this area.

Sporting accidents included in this chapter have occurred at such famous and varied sporting venues as Brooklands race-track, White City Stadium, White Hart Lane, Anfield, Buckpool Golf Club, Llanharan rugby ground and Hexham racecourse.

28. BROOKLANDS

Spectacular crash along the finishing straight

An extraordinary accident during a race at Brooklands resulted in death and injury to spectators. Were the track operators liable?

The Talbot racing car was thrown high into the air before crashing into the crowd. The accident, in 1930, was of a kind never before seen at Brooklands. It became a first for the courts: were the track operators, the Brooklands Automobile Racing Club (BARC), liable to spectators for injuries arising from the sporting action?

The famous Brooklands racetrack in Surrey, just 20 miles south-west of London, had been associated with motor racing since 1907. It was the birthplace of British motorsport. Constructed by wealthy landowner Hugh Locke King, it was the world's first purpose-built motor racing circuit and in 1926 was the scene of the first ever British grand prix. The two-and-a-half mile circuit, with its massive and distinctive concrete banking on two sides, captured the public's imagination. It represented the epitome of speed.

The track was oval in shape. There was a long straight stretch, the finishing straight, which was more than 100ft wide and bounded on its outer side by a six-inch high cement kerb and, beyond that, iron railings 4ft 6ins high. Spectators could view from stands higher up, but many preferred to be much closer to the track and stand by the railings.

The race meeting in May 1930 was held under the auspices of the Junior Car Club, an established and distinguished racing club. It was a long-distance race under handicap, the JCC Double-12 hours event, with the two 12-hour races being held on consecutive days. Christopher Hall was a student at the Royal Naval College at Greenwich. He went excitedly with some friends to see the racing on the first day. Being an enthusiast, he had taken up a viewing position close to the railings towards the end of the finishing straight.

It was just after 6pm and the day's racing was in its closing stages. A small Austin came along the straight at around 85mph. Gaining on it, and about to lap it, were three larger cars racing at around 100mph. One was an Alfa Romeo which was followed just behind, on each side, by two Talbots (number 22 was a car's length behind on the left and number 21 was on the right, in effect 'slip-streaming' the Alfa Romeo).

Hall watched keenly. At the end of the straight, tightly packed, the group of cars came to a sharp left-hand bend which was best approached from the right side of the straight. Talbot 22, driven by Colonel Rabagliati on the left of the group, appeared to swerve its course to the right. The hub of its left rear wheel touched the hub of the near front wheel of the Talbot 21. The blow, startlingly, threw the Talbot 22 high into the air.

The blow, startlingly, threw the Talbot 22 high into the air.

The car struck the top of the railings, turned upside down and rolled into the crowd of spectators. Some managed to flee but most were struck before they could move. No accident of this kind had occurred before at Brooklands.

Two people died, one being the riding mechanic accompanying the driver in the Talbot 22 and the other a spectator. Twenty other spectators were injured, some seriously, and were taken to the Weybridge cottage hospital. One of injured was Christopher Hall, who suffered scalp wounds and contusions.

At the inquest four days later, the jury concluded that the deaths were by misadventure. The clerk of the course said that 'nothing less than fortification' would have withstood the impetus of a car weighing a ton and going at 80mph. The coroner remarked, nevertheless, that arrangements should be made to keep the spectators further back.

Christopher Hall subsequently brought a claim to get compensation for his injuries. No negligence was alleged against the driver of the Talbot but Hall instead sued the BARC, lessees and operators of the track, for negligence. He alleged that the BARC had provided insufficient protection for spectators watching such a highly dangerous sport or had, at the least, not given sufficient warnings of danger.

This was the first time that the courts had been called upon to consider the duties of a sports event organiser or venue owner to spectators arising out of the actual sporting action itself – rather than, for instance, the more obvious physical risks of a defective grandstand.

Legal Question: What was the extent of the duty owed by an event organiser or venue owner to paying spectators? Should the BARC be liable to compensate the injured spectators?

For: Motor racing was known to be a dangerous sport. Accidents could occur. The track operators should have ensured that paying spectators were kept a safe distance from the track or, at least, that sufficient warnings were given. It was an implied term in the contract of admission that the event organiser should use reasonable care to ensure safety of spectators. The railings were not strong enough to resist such a collision at high speed. The kerb was useless. Reasonable care for the safety of spectators had not been taken.

Against: This was the first time, since the racetrack at Brooklands had opened, that any spectator had been injured by a car leaving the track. No car had ever before gone through the railings. A spectator must appreciate that there was a risk of an accident inherent in motor sport notwithstanding that all usual precautions were taken. A spectator voluntarily took that risk. The duty was simply to use reasonable care. It was not an absolute warranty of safety.

Decision: Hall lost his claim. He won in the lower court but the case went to appeal. The Court of Appeal decided that the operators of the racetrack, the BARC, were not liable. They were not '*insurers*' against accidents '*which no reasonable diligence could foresee, or against dangers inherent in a sport of which a reasonable spectator takes the risk*'. Lord Justice Greer summed up:

'*I do not think the defendants are under any obligation to provide safety under all circumstances, but only to provide against damage to spectators which any reasonable occupier in their position would have anticipated as likely to happen.*'

There is a certain level of risk, inherent in many sports, which a spectator must accept. The sports event organiser owes a duty of 'reasonable care' not an absolute guarantee of safety.

In relation to its facts, this is a decision of an earlier age. The modern-day compensation culture had not yet taken root. The level of 'reasonable' care expected of an event organiser has moved with the times. It is undoubtedly the case that, today, the interests of safety of spectators would require a higher standard of care from an event organiser than those accepted in the early days at Brooklands. It is a useful reminder, though, that the law does not impose an

This was the first time that the courts had to consider the duties of a sports event organiser or venue owner to spectators arising out of the actual sporting action itself.

absolute guarantee of safety. Motor sport is dangerous. Attending a sports event is not 'risk-free'.

In January 1946, the circuit at Brooklands was sold. The Junior Car Club absorbed the Brooklands Automobile Racing Club. It changed its name, retaining the same initials as the latter, and became the British Automobile Racing Club.

29. CHEETHAM CRICKET CLUB

A straight six and a surprised pedestrian

Bessie Stone, peacefully standing outside her house, was unexpectedly struck by a cricket ball. Was the local cricket club liable?

In August 1947 post-war Britain was enjoying a hot summer. In cricket, Denis Compton was in glorious form for England and his swashbuckling style was captivating the sporting nation. Locally, cricket was being played at Cheetham cricket ground on the outskirts of Manchester. It was a typical scene repeated throughout the country.

The cricket club at Cheetham had been in existence, and matches played regularly on its ground, since around 1864. The ground was bounded at one end by Beckenham Road, which was built in 1910. At that time, a small strip of land was given up by the cricket club in exchange for a strip at the other end, so that the Beckenham Road end was a few yards nearer the batsman than the opposite end. The cricket field was protected by a seven-feet high fence which, in effect, was even higher above the pitch because of the sloping ground.

Bessie Stone lived at 10 Beckenham Road, near the cricket ground. She had stepped from her garden onto the pavement. She was suddenly hit on the head by a cricket ball – a huge six struck straight down the ground by a player on the visiting team during a game against the Cheetham 2nd XI. Miss Stone was injured. She had been standing not far short of 100 yards from where the cricket ball was struck by the batsman.

A neighbour, at 11 Beckenham Road which was slightly nearer the pitch, said that balls had hit his house, or come into his yard, a number of times over the previous few years. Others said balls had been hit out of the ground only about six times over 30 years. Bessie Stone claimed damages against the cricket club to compensate her for her injury. It became a major issue. Another first for the courts. The case was fought all the way up to the House of Lords.

She was suddenly hit on the head by a cricket ball – a huge six.

Legal Question: What was the duty of a sports event organiser or club to prevent balls escaping and causing injury? Should the cricket club be found guilty of negligence in failing to take sufficient precautions to prevent cricket balls being hit out of the ground?

For: When the boundary was altered in 1910, the club should have taken into account the increased risk of balls being hit out of the ground. Cricket balls were not hit out of the ground accidentally. If a motorist on the road had been hit, it could have resulted in serious injury or death. The pitch should have been moved further away from the Beckenham Road end or the fence at that end should have been raised.

Against: Cricket was a lawful game. Every person using the highway must accept some risk from the lawful activities of others on their own property. The cricket club did not have to guard against every conceivable risk but only those which were reasonably probable or foreseeable. It was not necessary to provide against an extraordinary or exceptional stroke. One must stay in the realm of practical life and common sense. The club should not be liable to pay damages.

Decision: Bessie Stone lost her claim. A first judge dismissed her case at the Manchester Assizes but she was successful on appeal to the Court of Appeal. A majority of that court decided that the cricket club (which, since it was an unincorporated club, meant that the persons responsible were the members of the club committee) had been negligent since they were aware of the potential risk.

The House of Lords came to the cricket club's rescue. The Lords concluded that Bessie Stone had no claim after all. The hitting of a cricket ball out of that ground was an event which could have been foreseen and it was a conceivable possibility that a person might be injured. In order for liability in negligence to arise, however, the court declared: '*There must not only be a reasonable possibility of its happening but also of injury being caused.*'

In this case, the risk of injury had been so remote that a reasonable person would not have anticipated it. Lord Normand concluded: '*It is not the law that precautions must be taken against every peril that can be foreseen by the timorous.*'

Lord Normand, one suspects a cricket fan, set out the ultimate dilemma which would have faced the club: '*The only practical way in which the possibility of danger could have been avoided would have been to stop playing cricket on this ground.*' Implicitly, such a step was too extreme to contemplate at this time in the context of a cricket-loving nation.

Cheetham cricket club were more fortunate with the court's judgment than many golf clubs – including St Augustine's Links in Ebbsfleet, Kent where a passer-by in 1922 was struck by a golf ball driven from the 13th tee while he was driving on a road adjacent to the course. The golf club was held liable. The court was influenced by the fact that balls had for some time, and frequently, been sliced on to the road. Or were our post-war judges more pre-disposed in favour of cricket than golf?

30. WORK OF ART

An accident at the National Horse Show

A photographer was injured by a horse galloping off course during a competition at the White City. Should the rider be held liable for negligence?

The heavyweight horse galloped dramatically towards a photographer and his companion. The horse's rider had lost control. The unfortunate, if bizarre, accident in 1959 at the White City Stadium raised another first for the courts: what liability does a player or other sporting participant have for an injury to a spectator?

The stadium at White City had been built for the London Olympic Games in 1908. The running track was the site in 1954 of Chris Chataway's famous win over Vladimir Kuts to break the world 5,000 metres record. Five years later, White City was the arena not for an athletics event but for the National Horse Show organised by the British Horse Society.

Although the equestrian arena was over 100 yards long and 70 yards wide, it was quite tight for the gallop. The famous running track surrounded the equestrian arena. The competitors entered at one end. At the other, they rounded a bend and turned right into a straight which then ran in front of a bandstand. The competition this time at the National Horse Show was for heavyweight hunters.

One of the leading horses was *Work of Art*, owned by Hugh Sumner and ridden by an experienced horseman, Ron Holladay. For this competition, the horses were required to walk, trot, canter and gallop. The gallop was the strength of *Work of Art* and Holladay was anxious to display his horse's abilities to the full. He started his round. *Work of Art* took the bend at the far end at a fast pace – too fast. Holladay tried to straighten him but lost control. A few feet off line, *Work of Art* set off down the straight on a course towards a set of flower tubs on the edge of the arena by the running track.

Edmund Wooldridge was a photographer for the event. He had, with permission, taken up position with his camera and tripod close to a bench seat between two of the flower tubs – towards which *Work of Art* was now hurtling at speed. Unfamiliar with horses, Wooldridge took fright at the approach of the galloping heavyweight horse. He was particularly concerned, gallantly, for the safety of Miss Smallwood,

He was particularly concerned, gallantly, for the safety of Miss Smallwood.

a director of the company which employed him, who was sitting on the bench near him. Wooldridge attempted to pull Miss Smallwood off the bench out of the line of the horse. As he did so, he stepped or fell back onto the cinder running track. Unfortunately, this was directly into the path of the galloping *Work of Art*. The horse had veered to the left on to the cinder running track and past the bench where Wooldridge had been standing, rather than to the right on to the grass arena. Wooldridge was knocked down and severely injured.

Wooldridge later brought a legal claim against Holladay for negligence in the riding of *Work of Art*. The courts had not previously been called upon to consider the liability of a participant to a spectator. Eric Cantona had not yet made his appearance! The Court of Appeal wrestled with the arguments.

Legal Question: What was the extent of the duty which a competitor in a sporting event owed for the safety of spectators? Should Wooldridge be entitled to recover damages from Holladay, to compensate for his injury, on the grounds of negligence?

For: Holladay had ridden his horse too fast round the corner of the arena. Trying to bring it back in line, he carried the horse too close to the bench seats where he knew people were positioned. He knew, or should have known, that this would be likely to endanger them. The fact that Holladay was participating in a sporting competition was irrelevant to the underlying duty to take reasonable care not to injure others – and that included injury to spectators.

Against: Allowance must be made for the sporting context. It was not the same as a motoring accident. The duty of care which a competitor in a sporting event owed to spectators was no greater than that owed by him to other competitors. He must not act recklessly but, short of reckless disregard, he should not be held liable for an accident which occurred in the course of sporting competition. A horse was an unpredictable animal. A spectator voluntarily assumed such risks as there might be inherent in a competition.

Decision: Edmund Wooldridge lost. The Court of Appeal decided that Ron Holladay was not negligent and was not liable to compensate the injured photographer.

By riding too fast around the bend in these circumstances, Holladay might have been guilty of an error of judgment in '*the agony of the moment*' but this did not amount to negligence. In the sporting context, a higher threshold was required before liability arose for negligence. The court concluded that a spectator attending a game or competition took the risk of an act of a participant causing injury to him even if this involved an error of judgment or lapse of skill.

Lord Justice Diplock summed up:

'*A person attending a game or competition takes the risk of any damage caused to him by any act of a participant done in the course of the game ... unless the participant's conduct is such as to evince a reckless disregard of the spectator's safety ... The most that can be said against Holladay is that he was guilty of an error of judgment or a lapse of skill ... That is not enough to constitute a breach of the duty of reasonable care which a participant owes to a spectator.*'

The court upheld the general principle that everyone, organisers and participants, should use reasonable care not to cause injury. However, the courts would be reluctant to find that the threshold had been crossed, giving rise to liability, unless the act of carelessness had reached a level tantamount to reckless disregard for safety. An error of judgment 'in the heat of battle' or in 'the flurry or excitement of the competition' is not sufficient.

Ron Holladay, although he had apparently been unconscious for a short time after the accident, returned to the arena to ride again on *Work of Art* and triumphed to become champion in class on the same horse later in the evening.

31. BRADFORD FIRE DISASTER

Litter, fire and tragedy at Valley Parade

The dreadful fire tragedy at Bradford City resulted In the death of 56 spectators. Was there liability for negligence?

It was a hot, sultry day with a light, but gusty, wind blowing. Saturday, 11th May 1985. The day should have been a celebration. It became a tragedy.

Bradford City, already assured of the Third Division Championship, were playing their final match of the season, against Lincoln City. 11,076 fans were at Valley Parade, the club's home ground, to see locally-born captain Peter Jackson presented with the championship trophy before the kick-off. It marked City's promotion to the second tier of English football for the first time since before the Second World War.

At 3.40pm, shortly before half-time, the first signs of a fire were noticed beneath the wooden bench seats at the Kop End in Block G of the antiquated Main Stand, built in 1909 in a golden era for the football club. The stand was holding 2,150 supporters.

According to later forensic investigation, the likely cause of the fire was the accidental dropping of a match or a cigarette stubbed out in a polystyrene cup and setting light to rubbish and debris under the stand. Within a few minutes, flames were clearly visible and the police began to evacuate people. The match referee, Dan Shaw, stopped play three minutes before half-time with the score still 0-0.

Although onsite fire equipment was brought into action immediately, the blaze engulfed and destroyed the wooden structure of the Main Stand within a few terrible minutes. Supporters at the front spilled on to the pitch. Others towards the back were trapped by the locked gates. There were many acts of heroism. Numerous police officers and supporters later received bravery awards. But 56 supporters tragically lost their lives and approximately 265 people were injured.

A cruel irony was that steel to replace the wooden roof of the stand was lying in a car park behind the stand for erection the following week.

Amongst the dead were John Fletcher and his son Andrew. Subsequently, John's wife, Susan Fletcher, brought an action for negligence against Bradford City FC and the West Yorkshire County Council. The purpose of the claim was primarily for the respective insurance companies of the two defendants to be able to apportion liability for the compensation costs between them.

The club had been warned of the dangers of a build-up of litter under the stand.

Evidence emerged at the High Court that an inspector for the Health and Safety Executive had written to the club several years earlier in which he had warned of the dangers of a build-up of litter under the stand seating. Firemen searching through the charred remains of the wooden grandstand found newspapers dating back to the late 1960s.

An earlier visit from a representative of the county council's engineers department, in connection with an application for an improvement grant, had resulted in a written warning to the club about the potential fire risk of a carelessly discarded cigarette. Also contributing to the loss of life were locked exit doors and turnstiles and the absence of an emergency evacuation system. The council's fire department received significant criticism during the court hearing. Any warning letters received by them appeared to have been filed with no action being taken. The court concluded that *'either the letter was not considered at all or ... an irresponsible decision was made without proper consideration'*. Who should bear the liability?

The claim was brought before the High Court in 1986. The High Court decided, after a three-week hearing, that both Bradford City FC and the West Yorkshire County Council were negligent. The club should be apportioned with two-thirds of the blame and one-third of the liability should be borne by the West Yorkshire County Council.

The tragedy itself had very significant consequences for football – and for all sports grounds throughout the country. An inquiry into Crowd Safety and Control at Sports Grounds, set up by the government, was chaired by Sir Oliver Popplewell. The inquiry also took into account the events at the Heysel Stadium in Belgium, just 18 days after the Bradford fire, in the European Cup final between Liverpool and Juventus. The final Popplewell Report was published in 1986.

Its recommendations resulted directly in new legislation governing safety at sports grounds across the UK, principally the Fire Safety and Safety of Places of Sport Act 1987. Any stand at a sports ground, with covered accommodation for 500 or more spectators, would now need a Safety Certificate from the local authority. A complete revision took place of the Green Guide issued by the Home Office regarding safety measures at sports grounds. In 1990 came the terrible tragedy at Sheffield's Hillsborough Stadium during the FA Cup semi-final between Liverpool and Nottingham Forest. Lord Justice Taylor's subsequent Report into the tragedy made further, major recommendations to improve safety at football grounds. Football stadia could never be the same again after these disasters.

Bradford City played all their 'home' fixtures for the 1985/6 season and the first half of the following season at adopted grounds – at Bradford Northern Rugby League Club (Odsal Garden), Huddersfield Town (Leeds Road) and Leeds United (Elland Road).

In 2015, the 30th anniversary of the tragedy, a retired police officer revealed in a BBC documentary that a man (no longer alive) had admitted to dropping the cigarette that probably caused the fire. He went to stamp it out but it fell through a knothole in the timber floor. The police decided, apparently, not to release his name at the time.

32. A GOLFER'S NIGHTMARE

A badly-sliced drive at the fifth

It was a golf society day at Buckpool golf club. During the afternoon round, a badly sliced drive by John Shipley injured another golfer. Was he liable for negligence?

The links golf course at Buckpool lies close to the fishing town of Buckie in the north-east of Scotland. It is, for many, one of Scottish golf's best kept secrets. Folklore has it that Robbie Burns, Scotland's national poet, must have crossed the land, where Buckpool's course is now set out, in order to reach the welcoming inn where, as declared in one of his poems, he enjoyed the good ale of Lady Onlie:

'Lady Onlie, honest Lucky
Brews gude ale at shore o' Bucky.
I wish her sale for her gude ale.
The best on a' the shore o' Bucky.'

There are wonderful views from the golf course across the Moray Firth towards the hills of Caithness. Sea breezes whip up from the Firth between shots and add to the test. Built on sand, Buckpool has fast rolling fairways, often lined by tall mature gorse bushes. It is a challenging course. Paul Lawrie, later an Open Champion in 1999 at Carnoustie, had his first professional win at Buckpool in 1986 and has played the course several times.

In September 1987 the local cricket club had a golf society day at Buckpool. The morning round was completed without incident. A good lunch was followed by an afternoon round; a very common scene at golf clubs around the land.

Thirty-two year-old John Shipley was an occasional player and a 24-handicapper. He had been playing well by his standards. Having holed out at the long par 4 fourth, Shipley's group moved to the fifth tee. It was aptly named 'Morven' since the distinctive hill on the north side of the Moray Firth dominated the skyline as the golfers stood on the elevated tee. It was a slight dogleg to the right, with a row of four bunkers to the right of the fairway and gorse and broom to the left. The ideal line for the drive was to the left of the bunkers.

As Shipley's group prepared to drive off, Paul Lewis and his group reached the fourth green. For golfers playing from the fifth tee, the fourth green was forward and to the right. The nearest part of the fourth green was around 20 yards away; the furthest part around 50 yards. One member of Shipley's group drove off down the fifth fairway. Shipley went next. Shipley took his stance and drove. Unfortunately, the ball came off the toe of the club and went at an angle of 30 degrees to the right. It struck Paul Lewis as he reached the fourth green and injured him.

Lewis later claimed damages from Shipley. The case was heard, on appeal, by the Sheriff Court at Elgin in the Scottish Grampians.

Legal Question: What is the extent of the duty which a golfer owes to fellow golfers on the course? Should Lewis be entitled to claim against Shipley for negligence?

For: Shipley was negligent in driving off while Lewis and his group were on the fourth green. He could see that they were within range of a ball driven in that direction. As a 24-handicapper, Shipley knew or should have known that there was a real risk when he hit the ball that it would not go straight down the fairway but at an angle towards the fourth green. It was an accident which it was reasonably forseeable could occur.

Against: None of the players involved thought that there was a real risk. One of Shipley's group had driven off immediately before him without mishap. Shipley had not previously that day mishit a shot by 'shanking' or striking the ball with the toe of the club. Although the layout of the fourth and fifth holes had been unchanged for 60 years, there was no record of any similar incident having happened. The risk of being hit by a golf ball in the circumstances of the accident was simply a risk Lewis impliedly accepted by playing the game of golf.

Decision: Lewis won his claim. The Scottish court decided that Shipley was negligent in driving off in these circumstances. A reasonably careful player, conscious of some lack of skill and aware of a real risk that he might mishit the ball and cause injury, would have delayed before driving off.

A good lunch was followed by an afternoon round; a very common scene at golf clubs around the land.

The court declared: *'If there is a real risk that the event will happen, as distinct from a mere possibility which would never influence the mind of a reasonable man, it is negligent to neglect such a risk if it can be avoided without difficulty.'*

Golfers beware! Court decisions are unpredictable. The message for most golfers is clear: taking out injury and liability insurance is sensible.

33. MICHAEL WATSON

A tragic night for boxing

Michael Watson suffered a brain haemorrhage at the end of a boxing title fight. Was the British Boxing Board of Control liable to him for not ensuring better medical support?

It was a tragic and unforgettable evening in 1991 at White Hart Lane in north London. It was an evening which would have a profound effect on boxing and serious implications for the legal responsibilities of all sports governing bodies.

Normally the home of Tottenham Hotspur, White Hart Lane on that September night was the setting for a WBO super-middleweight title bout, an all-British fight between Michael Watson and Chris Eubank. It was a cool evening, with a blustery autumn breeze, for the open air fight. The boxers arrived to a ringside atmosphere which was intense and partisan.

Twenty-six year-old Michael Watson was a popular, classy boxer from London. His fights with Nigel Benn and then Chris Eubank had excited fans and TV audiences throughout Britain. Just over three months earlier, he had fought a classic encounter with Eubank at Earl's Court for the WBO world middleweight title. Eubank, born in England but brought up in Jamaica and later in New York, retained his title although most observers thought Watson, the 'people's champion', had done enough to win. This was the re-match. It would turn out to be a night that would change boxing.

It was a savage fight, tough but fair. Eubank was behind on most scorecards until, shortly before the end of the 11th round, a fierce uppercut from Eubank caught Watson square on the chin and threw him back against the ropes seconds before the end of the round. It was clear that Watson was in difficulty. Less than a minute into the 12th and final round, he appeared unable to defend himself. The referee, Roy Francis, stopped the fight. Watson had in fact suffered a brain haemorrhage and, returning to his stool, he lapsed into unconsciousness.

Chaos erupted in and outside the ring. Seven minutes elapsed before Watson was examined by one of

Watson had in fact suffered a brain haemorrhage.

the doctors in attendance. He was taken by ambulance to North Middlesex Hospital. Nearly 30 minutes elapsed between the end of the fight and Watson reaching the hospital. He could then be given oxygen and blood – but had to be transferred to St Bartholomew's Hospital in central London for treatment in its neurological department. By this time, Watson had sustained serious brain damage. He sadly remained in a coma on a life-support machine for 40 days and underwent multiple surgeries to remove two blood clots from his brain. He was paralysed down his left side and suffered other physical and mental disabilities. His neurosurgeon, Peter Hamlyn, doubted that Watson would ever be able to walk again.

Watson later claimed damages against the British Boxing Board of Control for negligence on the grounds, he alleged, that there had been an inadequate level of medical support. It was the first time a claim for damages had been brought against a sports governing body for injury sustained by a competitor in the course of the sport. The case went to the Court of Appeal.

Legal Question: Should the British Boxing Board of Control (BBBC), as the regulatory body responsible for boxing in the UK, be liable for negligence in not regulating for better medical support at such a boxing event?

For: The fight had taken place in accordance with the rules of the BBBC. The resuscitation treatment received at the hospital should have been available at the ringside. If it had been, Watson would not have sustained such serious brain damage. The Board, as governing body, had regulatory control over a sport where physical injury was foreseeable The Board failed in its duty of care to see that all reasonable steps were taken to ensure that a boxer received immediate and effective attention if injured during a fight.

Against: The Board was a non-profit making body. It did not itself organise boxing contests or employ medical staff at contests. Indeed, the fight was organised by the World Boxing Organisation (WBO). The Board was simply a UK regulatory body. There was no evidence of any other boxing authority in the world imposing regulations requiring the degree of medical support contemplated. There had in fact been an ambulance close to the ringside staffed by an adequately trained paramedic. The BBBC should not be liable in negligence for Watson's injury.

Decision: Watson won his claim. The Court of Appeal decided that the BBBC was liable. The Board was the regulatory body for boxing in Britain. The court, in haunting words for sports governing bodies, said that:

'[T]he Board was in a position to determine … the measures that were taken in boxing to protect and promote health and safety … of professional boxers at fights held in the UK. This gave rise to a duty of reasonable care owed by the Board to each boxer. The Board had access to specialist learning in the field. A reasonable standard of care required the availability of resuscitation facilities at the ringside and of medical staff who knew how to use them. If they had been available, the outcome would probably have been different.'

Watson was subsequently awarded damages of around £750,000.

This was truly a landmark case, the first in which a governing body had been judged negligent for failing to regulate properly for the safety of participants – even though it had no direct role in the organisation of the contest itself. It was a decision which really made sports governing bodies sit up and take notice of their potential legal liabilities. Governing bodies, generally, have become much more alert to their potential liabilities to participants as well as spectators.

The plight of Watson forced the sport to introduce a number of safety measures which have since helped to save other fighters. Indeed, many believe that British boxing has now probably the best safety procedures in the world of boxing, including a requirement to have an ambulance available with the necessary resuscitation equipment at the venue and trained teams of paramedics at the ringside.

This was truly a landmark case for sports governing bodies.

For the BBBC itself, the case was a financial disaster. The Board was a non-profit organisation and inadequately insured. It had thought liability insurance 'too expensive and inappropriate'. Facing legal costs of around £300,000 and the prospect of substantial compensation to be paid to Watson, the BBBC was placed into administration in 1999 in a bid to secure its long-term survival as the regulatory body of the sport. Two partners of an accounting firm, Hacker Young & Partners, were appointed joint administrators. The BBBC eventually sold its London headquarters to finance the damages settlement and is now headquartered in Cardiff.

In 2003, 12 years after his accident, the sporting world was uplifted at the sight of Michael Watson walking the London Marathon. He completed the 26.2 mile course in just over six days, raising funds for the Brain and Spine Foundation. Watson's neurosurgeon described it as 'one of the greatest physical achievements the marathon has ever seen'. He was joined for the final mile by Chris Eubank.

Michael Watson was awarded an MBE in the New Year honours list in 2004 for his work for disabled sport.

34. DEAN SAUNDERS

A career-ending tackle at Anfield

A clash between Dean Saunders and Paul Elliott led to the end of Elliott's playing career. Did a claim lie in negligence against Saunders?

Liverpool were at home at Anfield against Chelsea in September 1992. Two fiercely competitive teams. A nasty clash early in the game led to a first for the courts. Could a professional player sue another player if he was injured as a result of a bad tackle?

The score was 0-0 after 10 minutes. The ball was played out of the Chelsea half into open space near the halfway line. Dean Saunders, a Liverpool striker and Welsh international, ran toward the ball – as, from a different direction, did Chelsea's highly regarded defender, Paul Elliott. Saunders was just favourite to reach the ball. Elliott made a leap towards the ball with his right leg forward in a kind of scissors action. Saunders saw this and, a brief fraction of a second later, responded by jumping with both feet off the ground. Saunders' feet landed on Elliott's outstretched leg in the area of the knee. Elliott was seriously injured; the cruciate ligaments in his knee were severed. The incident, in effect, brought Elliott's playing career to an end.

It was the first legal claim by one professional footballer against another for damages based on an alleged negligent tackle during a match.

The match ended in a 2-1 win for Liverpool.

Elliott later brought a legal claim for damages against Saunders for negligence. It was the first legal claim by one professional footballer against another for damages based on an alleged negligent tackle during a match. The case came before the High Court.

Legal Question: What is the duty of care owed by a professional footballer in making a challenge during a match at the level of the Premier League? Was Dean Saunders guilty of negligence by making a challenge which intentionally or recklessly risked serious injury?

For: The video evidence suggested that Saunders jumped at Elliott rather than the ball. He appeared to have changed his mind, checked and slowed down, waiting for an opportunity to jump at Elliott. Saunders could have taken evasive action to avoid the collision. He acted recklessly in going 'over-the-top' at the man rather than the ball.

Against: Saunders claimed that he was always going for the ball. His actions in that moment were governed by instinct rather than careful thought. He jumped to avoid injury without intending to land on Elliott's outstretched leg. His eyes were focused on the ball. The referee had a good view of the incident and, in fact, gave a foul against Elliott for dangerous play.

Decision: Paul Elliott lost his claim. Justice Drake observed: *'Dry legal language hides the drama which has led to the appearance in this court of two top ranking professional footballers who, with numerous supporting witnesses, have over a period of about nine days, replayed an incident which, in real life, lasted less than a second.'*

The court acknowledged that *'there is a lot of popular support for the view that the law should be kept away from sport'*. It reaffirmed nevertheless that the law of negligence did apply to injuries on the sporting field. The question was: did Dean Saunders break the standard of care required?

On the basis of the evidence, particularly from the officials in charge of the game, Justice Drake had little difficulty in reaching the judgment that Elliott had failed to prove that Saunders was in breach of his duty of care. Saunders was not guilty of dangerous or reckless play.

The evidence given during the case appeared at times to be a lengthy edition of *Match of the Day*. A series of well-known players and commentators gave their views. As the judge remarked, they brought *'their individual colour into the witness box'*. Much of the witness evidence, on both sides, was based on study and analysis of the slow motion video replay.

In the witness team put out by Paul Elliott were such illustrious figures as Dennis Wise, Dave Beasant, John Hollins, Don Howe, former eminent referee Ken Aston and reporters Brian Glanville and Patrick Barclay. Even Ken Bates, Chelsea's colourful chairman, gave evidence based on the video replay. All suggested that Dean Saunders had paused momentarily and, recklessly or intentionally, jumped in a way which went 'over-the-top' at the man rather than for the ball. Some purported to have a view from the pitch, including Dennis Wise who was about 20 yards away and said that he had not seen many worse tackles than this one by Saunders. Justice Drake did not, however, find Wise *'reliable as an eye-witness'*.

Chelsea's formidable midfielder Vinnie Jones was a reluctant witness. Officially recognised by Justice Drake as 'a player with a considerable reputation as the hard man of football', Jones in the end could not say for certain that Saunders deliberately went over-the-top: 'The whole thing took place at lightning speed... football is a man's game and people can get hurt.' Justice Drake was impressed by Jones as *'a very good reliable and honest witness'*.

As the judge remarked, they brought 'their individual colour into the witness box'.

Lined up as witnesses for the defence of Saunders were former players Larry Lloyd, Garry Birtles and Geoff Hurst. Hurst thought that, once committed, Saunders could not avoid Elliott's challenge and acted reasonably in jumping as he did. Saunders himself said: 'Instinct told me to get my feet off the floor and that was the only way I was going to get the ball without getting seriously hurt.'

The strongest evidence came, in the end, from the officials themselves. The referee, John Key, was only about 10 yards from the incident. He thought Saunders was attempting to play the ball. He awarded a free kick not against Saunders but against Chelsea because of Elliott's dangerous play. The nearest linesman raised his flag for the same reason. Journalist Brian Glanville said the referee was 'inept', but the Football League referee assessor at the match thought the referee's decision to penalise Elliott was correct.

It would be another day before a professional player would succeed in a claim for negligence against a fellow player.

The first successful claim by a professional footballer was in 1996 when Stockport County's Brian McCord was awarded £250,000 in damages against Swansea's John Cornforth after a career-ending high tackle. This was followed by Gordon Watson's claim after playing for Bradford City and suffering a double leg fracture in a clash with Huddersfield defender Kevin Gray in a division one game in 1997. Watson was awarded over £950,000 – importantly, not only against Gray but also Huddersfield Town FC as his employer.

Clubs beware! For several years, the courts became reluctant to impose liability for on-the-ball incidents. But the potential liability of an 'employer' for the misdeeds of its players took a significant turn in 2008. First, Redruth Rugby Club was ordered by the Court of Appeal to pay £8,550 in damages (plus substantial legal costs) when one of its players, second row forward Richard Carroll, hit and injured an opponent after '*a melée of the kind which frequently occurs during rugby matches*'. The incident was, the court said, sufficiently connected with his employment for the club to be liable – even if deliberate and he was only a part-time employee. Clubs must be encouraged to '*eradicate, at least minimise, the risk of foul play which might cause injury*'.

Later in 2008, Ben Collett, a young, promising Manchester United player (described by Sir Alex Ferguson as an 'A-class' player with an 'outstanding chance' of being awarded a professional contract), succeeded in a claim after his career had been ended by a reckless 'over-the-ball' tackle by a Middlesbrough player in a reserve match. His damages? An extraordinary, and record £4.3 million, which had to be met by

Middlesbrough or, more particularly, the club's insurers. Many clubs – and lawyers – wonder where all this will lead. Insurance premiums have risen significantly.

As for Paul Elliott, he served for a number of years on the disciplinary panel of the Football Association. He was awarded the CBE in 2012 for services to equality and diversity.

35. ADRIAN MAGUIRE

Injury in a two-mile hurdle at Hexham

It's not just football or rugby where players cause accidents. Careless riding in a race at Hexham by leading jockey Adrian Maguire led to an injury to a jockey on a following horse. Could a claim of negligence be brought against Maguire?

Hexham racecourse is in a lovely country setting, perched on Yarridge Heights high above the historic market town of Hexham. It has been the home of National Hunt racing in Northumberland for more than a century.

A two-mile novice hurdle race at Hexham in September 1994 involved 23 year-old Adrian Maguire, one of the country's leading jump jockeys. The Irishman had, in 1992, won a stirring victory in the Cheltenham Gold Cup aboard *Cool Ground* and then, the following year, the King George VI Chase on *Barton Bank*. In the two-mile hurdle at Hexham he was on *Master Hyde*. Grand National winner, Mick Fitzgerald, was riding *Mr Bean* and Derek Byrne was on *Royal Citizen*.

It was a close race. These three horses were together as they jumped the second last hurdle. *Royal Citizen*, on the inside, jumped badly. Ahead, they approached a left hand bend. *Mr Bean* and *Master Hyde* pulled three-quarters of a length ahead of *Royal Citizen*.

Both Maguire and Fitzgerald moved their horses inside, taking a line which left Derek Byrne on *Royal Citizen* no room on the bend. Byrne, though, was seeking to make up the lost ground and was urging *Royal Citizen* forward between the rail on his near side and *Mr Bean*. *Royal Citizen* shied away from the closing gap and veered to the right behind *Mr Bean* and *Master Hyde*. This manoeuvre unseated Byrne.

Byrne's fall brought down the immediately following horse, *Fion Corn*, ridden by jockey Peter Caldwell. Caldwell fell to the ground and suffered serious injury, breaking his back.

A stewards' inquiry was held following the race. The stewards found that Maguire and Fitzgerald had been guilty of careless riding on the grounds that they had left insufficient room for Byrne to come along the inside rail on *Royal Citizen*. Each jockey was suspended for three days.

Later, Caldwell brought a claim in the courts against Maguire and also Fitzgerald, on the grounds of negligence, to recover damages to compensate for his injuries. It was the first case of its kind in horse racing. The case eventually went to the Court of Appeal.

Legal Question: How high is the standard of care owed by a participant in competitive sport to other participants? Should Maguire be found guilty of negligence and liable to pay damages to Caldwell?

For: Maguire and Fitzgerald were guilty of careless riding under the rules of racing. Both jockeys should have looked to check that *Royal Citizen* was no longer in contention as they moved inside. They had not satisfied the standard of care required in the circumstances. It was foreseeable that injury could result to a jockey on a following horse if they failed in that duty. They should be liable for damages in respect of the injuries caused by that negligence.

Against: Account must be taken of the special circumstances of competitive sport. Decisions are taken in the heat of the moment. Accidents and misjudgements inevitably occur. Careless riding was a relatively common offence in racing. The threshold before a legal claim could be brought in the courts for negligence should be much higher than a mere error of judgment or lapse of skill. The standard should be equivalent to deliberate or reckless disregard of the consequences. Maguire and Fitzgerald were not guilty on that test.

Decision: The courts decided in favour of Maguire and Fitzgerald. Caldwell's claim for negligence failed.

In the High Court, evidence was given – including by fellow jockey John Francombe – that they should not have taken the inside line unless and until they were one length clear of *Royal Citizen*. Double Grand National winner Carl Llewellyn was also called as an expert witness. He agreed that the two jockeys should have known Byrne was on their inside, but said: 'It happens every day of the week. These things happen all the time.'

In the High Court, the judge decided that the riding of the two jockeys had not been reckless or negligent: '*This incident reflected the cut and thrust of serious horse racing. In theory avoidable but in practice something that is bound to occur from time to time, no matter how careful is the standard of riding.*'

On appeal, the Court of Appeal was of a similar view. The test for negligence, in this context, must take into account the circumstances of competitive sport including the inherent dangers, customs and conventions of that sport and the skills and standards reasonably to be expected of participants in a fast-moving horse-race. Lord Justice Tuckey summed up:

' ... *participants in competitive sport owe one another a duty of care ... [but] it is not possible to characterise momentary carelessness as negligence. [There should be] no liability for errors of judgment, oversights or lapses of which any participant might be guilty in the context of a fast-moving contest. Something more serious is required.'*

Maguire and Fitzgerald had not broken that level of duty.

Adrian Maguire had, unwillingly, helped to clarify the law. This was an important judgment. The decision reaffirmed that civil claims between playing participants in a competitive sport can only be brought in extreme circumstances. The law makes considerable allowance for the 'rough and tumble' of competitive sport. The courts will be reluctant to support a civil claim for damages for accidental injury unless the defendant has, in effect, been guilty of a level of recklessness which is outside the 'playing culture' of the sport.

Adrian Maguire narrowly lost out to Richard Dunwoody in the race for champion jump jockey in that 1993/4 season – 194 winners to Dunwoody's 197. Maguire later became one of the elite group of jump jockeys to ride over 1,000 winners in his career.

36. WHO'D BE A REFEREE?

A collapsing scrum at Daisy Field

A tragic incident in an amateur Welsh rugby match gave rise to an important question. Does a referee owe the players a duty of care for their safety?

Daisy Field, home of Llanharan rugby football club in south Wales, was the scene of a tragic incident late in an amateur match in 1998. It gave rise to another first for the courts: could an amateur referee be liable for injuries suffered by a player in an adult match?

Llanharan moved to Daisy Field in 1990. The ground was so called because of the adjacent milk processing plant which closed in the late 1960s after more than 50 years.

It was the first time a claim had been brought against a referee for negligence in an adult match.

In January 1998 a local derby match was being played between the amateur Llanharan 2nd XV and neighbouring Tondu 2nd XV. It was a hard-fought match on a boggy pitch.

After half-an-hour's play, Llanharan lost their loose-head prop forward through injury. They had no trained front row player on the bench or the field to replace him. The referee, David Evans, told the Llanharan captain that they could provide a replacement from within the scrum forwards or, if they wished, opt for non-contestable scrums. If they opted for the latter and won the match, the points would not count towards the league competition.

Llanharan flanker, Chris Jones, said that he would 'give it a go' as front row forward. He was not asked by the referee about his experience for that position. When the match resumed, set scrummaging deteriorated and the scrum collapsed a number of times. The lack of technique and experience of Jones as a prop forward was a significant factor.

The match moved into the final minute. Llanharan were leading 3-0 but Tondu were attacking strongly. There were a number of set scrums five metres from the Llanharan line. Tondu were looking for a pushover try which, if converted, would have enabled them to snatch victory.

There was a final scrum. The Llanharan pack did not crouch as a unit. Twenty-four year-old Richard Vowles was the Llanharan hooker. The front rows failed to engage properly. The referee blew his whistle. As the scrum parted, Vowles collapsed to the ground. It was clear that it was a serious injury. The referee brought the match to an end. Vowles was taken by ambulance to hospital. He had suffered a dislocated neck which led to paralysis.

Confined to a wheelchair following the injury, Vowles later brought a legal claim for negligence against the referee, David Evans, and the Welsh Rugby Union (WRU) who appointed him. The basis of the claim was that Evans, the referee, ironically a practising solicitor, had breached his duty to safeguard the safety of the players. It was the first time a claim had been brought against a referee for negligence in an adult match (one earlier claim against a referee had been made following an accident in a youth match).

It was the first time a claim had been brought against a referee for negligence in an adult match.

Legal Question: Did an amateur referee owe the players a duty of care? Should Evans have satisfied himself that Jones was sufficiently trained or experienced to be tried in the front row?

For: One of the responsibilities of a referee is to safeguard the safety of the players. He should apply the laws of the game with this in mind. The evidence suggested that Evans did not satisfy himself that Jones was suitably trained or experienced for the front row. He abdicated responsibility by simply leaving it to the Llanharan captain to elect whether or not to proceed with non-contestable scrums. This constituted a breach of his duty.

Against: Evans was an amateur referee. It was not fair or reasonable to expose such a referee to the risk of ruinous legal liability. If referees were to become potentially liable for damages claims, the supply of amateur referees might well diminish significantly – contrary to the interests of the game. If a referee is to be held liable, the threshold for liability should be very high and not simply an error of judgment. A finding of negligence would be excessive.

Decision: Richard Vowles won his claim for damages in the Swansea County Court. The court recognised that it was making an important judgment in the context of amateur officials. Justice Morland nevertheless said: ' … *it is just and reasonable that the law should impose upon an amateur referee of an amateur rugby match a duty of care towards the safety of the players.*'

The Court of Appeal confirmed the finding of the lower court that the referee, David Evans, had been guilty of negligence and was liable to compensate Vowles for his severe injury. The court concluded that a primary cause of the accident to Vowles was that the referee, in breach of the laws of the game and negligently, had permitted a player who lacked suitable training and experience to play in the Llanharan front row. Lord Phillips stated: '*Mr Evans abdicated … responsibility … of deciding whether … to insist upon non-contestable scrummages. This constituted a breach of his duty to exercise reasonable care for the safety of the players.*'

The court emphasised that the referee's decision was made when play had stopped. Very different considerations would apply where it was alleged that a referee was negligent because of a decision made during active play itself. Lord Phillips was aware of the implications of the decision:

'*In my judgement when rugby is funded not only by gate receipts but also by lucrative television contracts I can see no reason why the Welsh Rugby Union should not insure itself and its referees against claims and the risk of a finding of a breach of duty of care by a referee where the threshold of liability is a high one which will not easily be crossed … Insurance cover for referees would be a cost spread across the whole game.*'

This was another landmark case. It was the first time that an amateur referee in any sport had been held liable for injuries arising in an adult amateur game.

The WRU accepted responsibility for the referee whom they had appointed and therefore became liable for payment of the damages to Vowles.

The decision caused deep concern in many quarters. It seems a very hard decision on the facts – and undoubtedly influenced by the fact that the WRU was known to be standing behind the individual referee for payment of any damages. Who would be a referee? Many fears were expressed that the decision could have a serious effect on the willingness of amateurs to referee matches and, indeed, on coaches, teachers and volunteers of all kinds who assist in amateur sport.

The court's decision had a particularly serious effect on the finances of the WRU which only held limited insurance cover. Subsequently, the WRU's insurers insisted that only qualified referees should referee in matches at all levels. This led to the cancellation of many matches in Wales the following season. The WRU were given a grant by the Sports Council to assist in increasing the number of trained referees in Wales.

Better times in Llanharan's history occurred in 2003/4 when, under the off-pitch leadership of Welsh legend Gareth Edwards, the club's first team won a thrilling race to win the first division championship and earn the club a place in the top tier of Welsh club rugby.

Chapter Five

REFEREES, UMPIRES AND THE OLYMPICS

We move to the heart of the competitive action. Referees, judges, umpires and panels are constantly making decisions in the course of play (or, sometimes, at the end of play) which are crucial to the outcome of the match or competition.

The ordinary courts are, rightly, very reluctant to become involved in reviewing purely 'field of play' decisions. But when should a court or arbitral tribunal intervene to correct a proven mistake or apparent injustice?

The Court of Arbitration for Sport (CAS), with its headquarters in Lausanne, Switzerland, has become the most important arbitral tribunal in sport. It was set up in 1984 by the International Olympic Committee (IOC) with the objective that the growing number of sports-related disputes should be resolved 'within the family of sport' rather than the more hostile and costly environment of litigation in the traditional courts. A large number of international and national sporting bodies provide for CAS to be the ultimate appeal body for disputes under that body's jurisdiction.

CAS has developed a special role in the Olympic Games. A panel of arbitrators is available at short notice to hear any disputes which need resolution during the Games. Whilst its decisions only apply to the particular dispute before it, principles expressed by CAS are widely respected and influential in future sports' cases worldwide.

This chapter takes us to challenges before CAS in a wide range of sports, including disputes challenging the results in the 20 kilometre walk, the marathon, gymnastics, equestrian eventing at the Olympics and a wheelchair race in the Paralympics.

37. CHRISTOPHE MENDY

A hit below the belt?

Could Christophe Mendy use video evidence to get a referee's decision to disqualify him overturned and his Olympic boxing bout re-held?

'I've sacrificed years of my life for this. Why stop that fight? Why?' A heavyweight boxing contest was the setting for a major controversy at the 1996 Olympic Games in Atlanta. It was a quarter-final bout between Christophe Mendy, a 25 year-old highly fancied French boxer, and Canadian David Defiagbon. The winner was assured of at least a bronze medal.

Mendy was much admired in the boxing world. He was a bronze medal winner at the 1995 World Amateur Championships when he narrowly lost to reigning Olympic champion Félix Savón from Cuba. A stylish boxer, Mendy was the strong favourite against Defiagbon and regarded by many experts as the most likely challenger to the legendary Savón, who was seeking to retain his Olympic title. Defiagbon, born in Nigeria, was an All-African champion who fled to Canada for political reasons in 1992 and obtained citizenship.

The fight was closer than expected. Mendy led after the first round and well into the second. Defiagbon then recovered to take a 10-8 lead on the judges' scores by the end of the second round. The third round started. Mendy attacked strongly, boring in on Defiagbon and slinging punches as Defiagbon was pinned to the ropes. Mendy was now just one point behind. There were nearly two minutes left for Mendy to assert his superiority.

Then, after a punch to the body from Mendy, Defiagbon suddenly dropped to the canvas as if his legs had been removed from under him. He rolled on the floor, clawing at his groin with his glove and claiming a low blow. Mendy looked down in disbelief. Defiagbon continued writhing, his face contorted with pain for several minutes.

'This is sacrilegious. This is dishonest. Why stop that fight? Why?'

A doctor was called. He examined Defiagbon in the ring and accepted the Canadian's word that he was unable to continue. Mendy was disqualified by the referee, Abduk Samad. The fight was over. Mendy was astonished, angry and near to tears.

The French team were outraged. Mendy, through an interpreter, made his plea: 'This is sacrilegious. This is dishonest. Why stop that fight? Why?' The French team leader made a written protest and delivered a videotape of the fight to officials, claiming that Mendy should not have been disqualified. It was not a low blow but a legitimate punch to the liver. Defiagbon could in any event have continued.

Should videotape evidence be used to alter the referee's decision and the result? The Amateur International Boxing Association (AIBA) rejected the protest. The French team persisted and appealed to the ad hoc panel of CAS available at the Olympics. The panel met before the semi-final round.

Legal Question: Should CAS review the decision made by the referee that the punch was below the belt and that Mendy should be disqualified?

For: The French team argued that the videotape indicated that the blow was not low. Defiagbon was in any event greatly exaggerating the effect of the blow. He could have continued. A clear injustice had occurred and the decision of the AIBA to reject the protest should be overturned.

Against: The referee's decision made at the time, on the application of technical 'game rules' to the circumstances, must be treated as final. This was an essential element of sport. The protest had in any event been considered by the appropriate body within the AIBA. It would be wrong for it to be reviewed or overturned by an outside arbitral tribunal.

Decision: Mendy lost again. CAS decided that, although it did have power to review the case, it would not intervene.

It was the first time that a claim to review a referee's decision had come before CAS. CAS laid down the fundamental principle. It was not appropriate for an arbitral panel to review a referee's decision regarding the application of a technical rule specific to the sport concerned. Such decisions were the responsibility of the referee or the federation concerned. CAS declared:

'... the referee's decision ... is a purely technical one pertaining to the rules which are the responsibility of the federation concerned. It is not for the ad hoc Panel to review the application of those rules.'

The arbitral panel was less well placed to decide than the referee in the ring or the ring judges. Intervention with a referee's decision should only be considered if there is evidence of an error of law or of a malicious act. It was for each sport to decide to what extent, and how, within its own rules a player or team should be able to challenge a refereeing or sporting decision. CAS would not, in the absence of evidence of bad faith, go beyond that and itself hear again or review a 'field of play' decision of a referee or umpire.

There has been no reported case in England of a legal challenge to a referee's decision aimed at altering the actual result of the game or competition itself – as opposed to a disciplinary consequence of a referee's decision, such as a sending off. In the Paul Elliot/Dean Saunders case (see Chapter 4), the court affirmed: '*Unless and until video is introduced by the governing body of a sport as an aid to the referee or umpire [as part of the game's rules], his decisions on the field must be final as regards what happens during the game.*' The English courts would almost certainly take the same line as CAS and not interfere with any 'field of play' decision unless bad faith or fraud is demonstrated.

Defiagbon went through to the semi-final – which he won and so became assured of at least the silver medal. In the final, he was well-beaten, 2-20, by the great Félix Savón.

38. BERNARDO SEGURA

Mexican outrage at 'Olympic robbery'

Could Bernardo Segura claim that his disqualification was contrary to the rules and that his Olympic marathon gold medal should be re-instated?

It was a warm September evening. The Olympic Stadium in Sydney would be the scene of many dramatic finishes during the 2000 Olympics. None more so than in the first track event, the 20 kilometre walk. Who was the winner?

The spectators in the stadium were excitedly awaiting the climax as the walkers entered the stadium for the final lap. The crowd had followed the race on the large television screens. It was going to be the closest finish ever in Olympic race walking. The race had been at a fast pace throughout. An Olympic record was in prospect.

Thirty year-old Mexican Bernardo Segura, holder of the world record, was making a challenge for the lead. Just in front were the reigning 50 kilometre walk Olympic champion, Poland's Robert Korzeniowski, and another Mexican Noé Hernández. They were 10 metres ahead when Segura began his challenge to overtake the two leaders as they left the loop around the stadium and began to enter the long tunnel into the stadium itself.

In race walking, at least one foot must remain in contact with the ground throughout. Competitors are assessed by highly experienced judges at many points along the race. A judge may give either a caution directly to a competitor or an official warning. The same judge may only give one warning. Warnings are not given to a competitor but are posted on a signboard and the competitor does not know which judge has given a warning. If a competitor receives two official warnings, a third warning leads to disqualification. Disqualifications can, however, only be notified by the chief judge. A disqualification must, under the rules of the sport, be given as soon as practical during the race or 'immediately' after the finish.

> **Segura conducted his victory celebrations, draped in the Mexican flag.**

Segura knew that he had already received one warning, after 1 hour 51 minutes of the race. His second warning, of which he was apparently unaware, came eight minutes later as he left the loop outside the stadium for the final time and began accelerating to catch the leaders. Then, as Segura entered the tunnel into the Olympic Stadium and just four minutes and 400 metres from the finish, another judge spotted a further loss of contact.

Segura and the crowd were completely unaware of the situation and its implications. Segura pressed forward to finish ahead of Korzeniowski by just two seconds in a dramatic neck-and-neck finish. It was a new Olympic record. Mexico rejoiced. Segura conducted his victory celebrations, draped in the Mexican flag. He was interviewed by television. With the cameras rolling, he received a congratulatory telephone call from President Ernesto Zedillo of Mexico.

Then, a full 15 minutes after he had crossed the line, the chief judge interrupted. He showed an astonished Segura a red card for disqualification. Mexican officials launched an official protest, but it was rejected. They felt victimised. A further appeal against the disqualification was made by the Mexican officials to the Court of Arbitration for Sport (CAS). The matter was heard at short notice by the ad hoc panel of CAS which sat at the Olympics.

Legal Question: Should Segura's disqualification be set aside on the basis that it was not given 'immediately' after the finish as required by the rules?

For: The rules must be interpreted strictly where a disqualification is concerned. 'Immediately' means promptly after the finish of the race. In an event as important as the Olympic final, it was known that any disqualification would dramatically affect the result and that victory celebrations would be televised worldwide. In these circumstances, it was vital that the rule should be strictly interpreted.

Against: Segura had been judged to have lost contact on three occasions. Official warnings had been given in accordance with the rules. At the finish, the chief judge was engaged in giving a warning to another competitor still racing. Discretion was then exercised not to interrupt the televised interview which Segura was giving (until it went on longer than anticipated). The delay was unfortunate but the disqualification should stand.

Decision: Segura's disqualification was confirmed by CAS.

The three warnings had been duly given. 'Immediately' must be read as qualified by a notion of 'reasonable under the circumstances'. There was no evidence of malice or bad faith by the judges. The arbitrators stressed that it would be unfair on the other competitors if the result was altered:

'The panel must have regard to the interest of competitors who did not infringe the rules ... The undoubted disappointment and embarrassment suffered by Mr Segura do not begin to outweigh the fact that he merited disqualification under the applicable rules; his competitors are entitled not to be deprived of their places.'

The delay was unfortunate but the disqualification must stand. Arbitrators should be very reluctant to review a determination made 'on the playing field' by officials charged with applying the rules of the game unless the rules are applied in bad faith. It would be unfair on all competitors who had abided by the rules if the result was altered. The panel ruled that the disqualification must stand.

Robert Korzeniowski was confirmed as the winner of the gold medal.

This was another clear example of the reluctance of courts or tribunals to intervene in decisions made by referees, umpires, judges or panels 'on the playing field' when applying the rules of the game. Any other decision would have been unfair on other competitors who had raced in compliance with the rules. Even if the manner of disqualification was unsatisfactory, the underlying substance must prevail. The interest of maintaining the integrity of sporting competition led inexorably to the 'fairness' of disqualification.

The decision did little to quell the sense of outrage amongst the Mexicans. Feelings were so great in Mexico itself that the Australian embassy in Mexico City even felt compelled to issue a statement denying any official conspiracy by the Australian government. One of Mexico's leading daily newspapers described it as 'an Olympic robbery'.

39. CHANTAL PETITCLERC

Collision in the wheelchair 800 metres

Could Chantal Petitclerc overturn a chief referee's decision ordering a wheelchair race in the Paralympics to be re-run after a crash earlier in the race?

Kylie Minogue sang to the crowd. Australia embraced the 2000 Paralympics with the same enthusiasm as the summer Olympics earlier in the year. An audience of 87,000 spectators enjoyed a party atmosphere at the opening ceremony with the parade of nations involving 4,000 athletes from more than 120 countries. But competition was as fierce as in the summer Games. None more so than in the women's 800 metres wheelchair race.

The Paralympic flame was ignited at the opening ceremony by one of Australia's best-known wheelchair athletes, Louise Savage. The reigning World Sportsperson of the Year with a Disability, Savage had won seven gold medals at the previous Barcelona and Atlanta Games. She had not been beaten in a wheelchair race for eight years.

Savage's great rival for the women's 800 metres was Canada's top wheelchair racer, 31 year-old Chantal Petitclerc. After an accident in 1983 had left her with paraplegia, Petitclerc had turned to sport. Her intense dedication and skill had won her universal recognition. In 1999 she was honoured for her contribution to the advancement of women in track and field by the International Amateur Athletics Federation (IAAF). Petitclerc had already won silver medals in both the 100 and 200 metres at the Sydney Paralympics. She was looking forward to the 800 metres and her race with Savage. 'I have dreamt about Louise more than I have about my boyfriend,' she said.

The racers were ready. It was a fast start. Petitclerc and Savage were soon in the leading group as they fought for the lead. Further back, a collision occurred after 198 metres between three athletes. Under the rules of the IAAF and the International Paralympic Committee, the starter had entire control of the start. He could choose to 'stop the race within the first 200 metres if a collision takes place'. The official starter allowed the race to continue. Out at the front, Petitclerc and Savage fought a thrilling battle. In a dramatic finish, Petitclerc held on to beat Savage and win the gold. A famous victory. Or was it?

'I have dreamt about Louise more than I have about my boyfriend.'

A protest was made after the race by one of the

other competitors, Wakacho Tsuchida of Japan, who was bounced out of her chair in the earlier collision. She felt that, but for the collision, she would have had a chance of a bronze medal. The chief referee, considering the protest, decided to disqualify an Irish athlete who caused the collision. More significantly, he ordered the race to be reheld the following Thursday. The Canadian Paralympic Committee protested. Petitclerc's victory, they argued, should stand: 'Chantal won that race. She won it fairly. We will go to all lengths to ensure that Chantal is treated justly.'

> **The chief referee had no power under the rules to overturn the starter's decision.**

The Canadians argued that the starter's decision at the time to continue the race was the official decision and should stand. The race should not be re-held. The Canadian team appealed to the ad hoc panel of the Court of Arbitration for Sport (CAS), who heard the case just two days after the original race.

Legal Question: Should the decision of the chief referee to order a re-race be overturned? Should the decision of the starter to allow the race to continue be upheld? Should Petitclerc retain her gold?

For: The collision occurred within the first 200 metres. The starter had, under the rules, the sole power to decide whether or not to stop the race. He decided not to stop it. The leading pack were ahead of the collision and the starter judged it right to let them continue. It was not within the power of the chief referee to overrule the starter's decision.

Against: The race had ceased to be within the first 200 metres when the leading group were beyond that mark. It was within the chief referee's power to decide whether or not to order the race to be re-held. It could not be certain where innocent racers, affected by the collision, might have finished. The chief referee properly exercised his power to order a re-race.

Decision: Petitclerc won her case. CAS decided that, for the purposes of the rules: ' ... *a race is within the first 200 metres if some athletes are within 200 metres of the start even though some ... are beyond the 200 metres.*' The starter should have been the sole judge, under those rules, whether or not the race should be stopped when there was a collision within the first 200 metres. The chief referee had no power under the rules to overturn the starter's decision.

The decision of CAS was not a case of subsequent intervention in a 'playing decision'. It was a case of upholding the rules and the decision of the 'field of play' official who, under those rules, had the responsibility for making the decision. Louise Savage accepted the decision gracefully: 'The court's decision is fine. I had nothing to do with it. We didn't disagree with anything that happened. That's the way it goes.'

Petitclerc retained her victory and the 800 metres gold.

The two great rivals met again later in the 2000 Paralympics in the wheelchair 1,500 metres. Savage gained her revenge, winning gold with a fine tactical race. Petitclerc came fifth.

In 2005 Chantal Petitclerc was named Canada's female athlete of the year – as well as being given the prestigious Laureus Award by sports journalists around the world to the disabled athlete of the year. She won a further five gold medals at the Beijing Paralympics in 2008.

40. OLYMPIC 'SKATEGATE' SCANDAL

The French judge and the second mark

Could the Canadian skating pair get the Olympic decision overturned on the grounds that one of the judges had unfairly prejudged the result?

It promised to be a great night. The Russian, Canadian and Chinese pairs were amongst the most talented ever assembled in competition. The capacity 17,000 spectators in the high, imposing stands of the Salt Lake Ice Center were excitedly anticipating the finals of the pairs figure skating event at the 2002 Winter Olympic Games. It became one of the most controversial events in Olympic history.

Russian skaters had long dominated this high profile event in world skating. The Russian pair, the graceful Yelena Berezhnaya and Anton Sikharulidze, were in the lead after the short programme. Not far behind in the scoring were the crowd favourites, Canada's pair of Jamie Salé and David Pelletier. The scene was set for the all-important long or 'free' programmes.

For the nine judges, this was their own Olympic final. It was the pinnacle of their careers. The youngest was judge number four, Marie-Reine Le Gougne from France.

With her striking red hair and stylish glasses, she looked sophisticated and very French. This was her second Olympics. She was one of the rising stars of her generation of judges and already a candidate for appointment to the prestigious technical committee of the International Skating Union (ISU). She looked a little nervous.

Berezhnaya and Sikharulidze went first. The Russian pair moved with awesome grace and power. Their programme was one of the most difficult ever attempted, with dramatic throws and advanced choreography. But they were prone to minor mistakes. It was clear that they stumbled during their double axel. The judges' marks (potentially up to 6.0) for technical merit were good but included some 5.7s and 5.8s. The second marks, for presentation, were high, including seven 5.9s. The door to gold was nevertheless open for Salé and Pelletier if the Canadian pair could skate a 'clean' programme.

She looked a little nervous.

The Canadian pair set off. They were not as fast or powerful as the Russian pair but there was an easy, fluent feel to their skating programme. They were a couple on and off the skating rink. They glided movingly to the music from the film *Love Story*. Although skating a slightly less difficult programme than the Russians, the Canadians performed flawlessly. The crowd adored them and clapped in time to the music. They were given a standing ovation. Most expert commentators thought they had done enough to win.

The judges' marks went up.

There was clear disbelief and astonishment from the crowd.

The marks for technical merit were good but six of the nine scores were 5.8s. Slightly ahead. It all depended on the second mark for presentation. The scores went up. There were only four 5.9s and no 6.0s. The scoreboard flashed: second place. The crowd erupted in boos. David Pelletier described the second mark as a 'punch to the stomach'.

Monitors then revealed that judges from the United States, Canada, Germany and Japan had scored the Canadians higher. Judges favouring the Russian pair were from Russia, the People's Republic of China, Poland, Ukraine … and, to complete a 5-4 split in favour of the Russians, the judge from France. There was clear disbelief and astonishment from the crowd. Salé and Pelletier accepted their silver medal with disappointment.

Then the story started to unravel. After the event, Marie-Reine Le Gougne, the French judge, walked into her hotel. Waiting for her was the head of the ISU's technical committee, Sally Stapleford, who gave her an angry look and spoke about integrity and honesty. Le Gougne began to cry. Two other members of the technical committee joined her. They left convinced that the French Federation had forced Le Gougne to vote as she did as part of a deal with the Russians to help their pair and, in exchange, get support for the French dance team which had a good chance of the gold medal the following week.

A judges' event review was held the following day. The referee told the judges that those who had voted for the Russians had made a serious mistake. It had been a miscarriage of justice. Le Gougne broke down again. Sobbing, she said that her federation president, Didier Gailhaguet, had pressured her to vote for the Russians and that it was not her own choice. She pleaded that the ISU must 'help us' break free from the pressure of the federations.

Events moved swiftly. The ISU president, in a press conference, admitted that the referee had received an allegation of misconduct. The Canadians officially appealed the decision in the pairs event. They formally proposed that Salé and Pelletier should have a dual gold medal with the Russians. If not, the Canadians would go forward with an appeal to the Court of Arbitration for Sport (CAS).

Although the original decision of the judges was not challenged in court or before an arbitral tribunal, the situation revealed a type of bad faith or corruption which would surely justify intervention with the 'playing decision' of a referee or judge in accordance with the guidelines for intervention pronounced from time to time by CAS. The ISU and the International Olympic Committeee (IOC) acted without this being necessary.

The ISU Council met and voted to declare Le Gougne's vote void. The pairs event was declared a tie and, with the approval of the IOC, a gold medal was given to Salé and Pelletier at a second awards ceremony. The Canadians dropped their appeal to CAS.

For skating, the saga had significant consequences. The ISU substantially changed the judging rules for figure skating. Under the new system, a more complex and objective system for awarding marks for each skating element was introduced. Each judge's mark is anonymous; the scoreboard hides their identities. Importantly in this context, the panel of judges has been increased to 12 — but marks are averaged by randomly selecting nine judges, discarding the highest and lowest marks, and averaging the remaining seven. 'Nobbling' a single judge is now far less likely to be effective.

Two months after the Olympics, the ISU Council held an internal disciplinary hearing in relation to Marie-Reine Le Gougne and Didier Gailhaguet. With the exception of Le Gougne, none of the judges who voted for the Russians were present. Le Gougne claimed that she had made her confession while in an overwrought emotional state. Le Gougne and Gailhaguet were found guilty of prejudging the Olympic pairs event.

Each received just a three-year suspension and a prohibition from taking part in the 2006 Olympics.

In May 2003, Didier Gailhaguet easily won re-election for another year to the presidency of the French ice skating federation.

Both the Canadian and Russian pairs retired from amateur competition shortly after the 2002 Games and embarked on a professional career. In December 2005, Jamie Salé and David Pelletier were married in Banff, Canada.

41. YANG TAE YOUNG

A judge's mistake on the parallel bars

Could Yang Tae Young overturn the result of the gymnastics final which had been reached after a clear error had been made by the judges?

The men's individual all-round gymnastics final in Athens in August 2004 was destined to be the closest men's all-round competition in Olympics history – and the most controversial. An error was made by the judges, *bona fide* but crucial to the result. Could it be corrected?

Judging in gymnastics is complex. One group of judges assess the start value, the technical difficulty of the routine. Another group of judges assess the execution, the performance of that routine. The combined marks, according to an appropriate formula, determine a competitor's final score for that event.

After the first four events in Athens, several gymnasts were in contention as they entered the parallel bars routine which was the penultimate session of the six-rotation event. Twenty-four year-old Yang Tae Young was the hope of South Korea. Lying in third place, the parallel bars was one of his major strengths. Yang performed strongly on the parallel bars and received a high mark overall. In fact, he took the lead in the overall competition after that event. It should, though, have been an even higher mark. Yang's routine on the parallel bars, it later transpired, was given a start value of 9.9 rather than a 10, which was technically correct under the rules of the International Gymnastics Federation (FIG). (For the expert, it appears that the judges had failed to spot that Yang had performed a Belle in his routine rather than the less difficult Morisue.) Yang had been given a 10 for the identical routine earlier in both the team qualifying and team finals sessions at the Olympics.

This error was not noticed at the time of the competition. Meanwhile, the USA's leading gymnast, Paul Hamm, had moved into close contention and, with a sensational performance in the sixth and final routine on the high bar, Hamm became the winner of the gold medal. Yang came third for the bronze.

The earlier judging error was then discovered after a videotape review. FIG officials confirmed that one-tenth of a point had been wrongly deducted from the difficulty value of Yang's routine. Yang should have been awarded a start value of 10. He had scored 9.712 points on the parallel bars but, with the higher start value, he would have finished the overall competition with 57.874 points and defeated Hamm by 0.051 points. FIG suspended the three judges involved.

'We want this obvious misjudgment to be corrected. We want fairness and justice.'

The South Korean delegation formally protested: 'We want this obvious misjudgment to be corrected. We want fairness and justice.' Yang claimed that the result should be corrected and that he should win the gold medal or, at least, receive a shared gold medal with Hamm.

Bruno Grandi, the president of FIG, personally supported this claim and actually wrote to Paul Hamm in the week after the event. The score had been miscalculated, Grandi wrote: 'The true winner of the all-round competition is Yang Tae Young.' He suggested that Hamm should give up his Olympic title, saying that he would view the gesture as the 'ultimate demonstration of fair play'. Neither the US team nor the International Olympic Committee (IOC) agreed. Yang and the South Korean federation took their claim to the Court of Arbitration for Sport (CAS). The hearing lasted nearly 12 hours and CAS deliberated over this difficult case for several months.

Legal Question: Was this is a circumstance where a court or arbitral tribunal should review an error made by judges 'on the playing field'? Should the error of the judges be corrected, the result changed and the gold medal awarded to Yang?

For: The error by the judges was clear. If the error had not been made, Yang's overall score would have been greater than Hamm's. The president of the International Gymnastics Federation himself acknowledged that Yang was 'the true winner'. This was a case where it was right to correct the result.

Against: The formal protest by the Korean federation was not made until after the competition had ended. If it had been made earlier, a mechanism existed within the rules of the sport for reviewing the result. After the event, it was not appropriate for a court or tribunal to review retrospectively decisions made by officials on 'the field of play'.

Decision: Yang's claim failed. CAS decided that the result should not be changed. The rules of the competition, in the view of CAS, did not permit a challenge after the event. Even if it had jurisdiction, a court or tribunal should only interfere with an official's 'field of play' decision if it was tainted with fraud, arbitrariness or corruption. The panel should abstain from correcting the results of simply an admitted error by an official.

In addition and crucially, CAS stressed that there was no certainty that Yang would have gone on to win. The reactions of leading competitors under pressure in the final event could have been different if the score or competitive circumstances had been different. Any solution or method for dealing with a judging error should be left to mechanisms within the framework of that sport's own rules. The considered judgment of CAS clearly set out this fundamental position:

'An error identified with the benefit of hindsight ... cannot be a ground for reversing a result of a competition. We can all recall occasions where a video replay of a football match, studied at leisure, can show that a goal was given when it should have been disallowed (the Germans may still hold that view about England's critical third goal in the World Cup Final in 1966), or vice versa or where in a tennis match a critical line call was mistaken...

For a court to change the result would on this basis still involve interfering with a field of play decision. Each sport may have within it a mechanism for utilising modern technology to ensure a correct decision is made in the first place (e.g. cricket with run outs) or for immediately subjecting a controversial decision to a process of review (e.g. gymnastics) but the solution for error ... lies within the framework of the sport's own rules; it does not license judicial or arbitral interference thereafter.'

Hamm kept his gold medal.

Forward, in contrast, to the 2008 Beijing Olympics. There were just seconds to go in the quarter-final of the taekwondo event when the judges missed a clear points-winning kick to the head by Britain's Sarah Stevenson against a Chinese opponent. An immediate and exceptional appeal was, after discussion, not contested by the Chinese federation. Stevenson was awarded the bronze medal.

As for Yang Tae Young, he was still treated like a champion in his own country. The Korean Olympic Committee awarded him a symbolic gold medal. Their president said: 'The Korean Olympic Committee has decided to treat Yang Tae Young as a gold medalist – regardless of the verdict of the Court of Arbitration for Sport.'

42. BETTINA HOY

A false start in Athens

Could the French and British equestrian teams overturn a successful appeal decision which awarded Olympic gold medals to Bettina Hoy and the German team?

It was astonishing. The gold medal seemed to be changing hands by the hour. The 2004 Olympic Games in Athens provided one of the most thrilling equestrian eventing competitions in Olympic history – and chaotic.

Equestrian eventing comprises three events: dressage, cross country and showjumping. The final showjumping phase at the Markopoulo Olympic Equestrian Centre on the outskirts of the capital was coming to its climax. France were ahead in the team event and top French rider Nicolas Touzaint was leading in the individual event. Poor rides in the jumping by the French team, however, then left Germany with a strong chance of the team gold medal.

The leading German equestrian rider was 41 year-old Bettina Hoy. Her next round, if a clear round, could clinch the team event. It would also count towards the individual event and set her up with the prospect of a personal gold.

Bettina Hoy set off on her grey gelding, *Ringwood Cockatoo*. Under the rules of the International Equestrian Federation (FEI), she had 45 seconds to reach the start line and then 90 seconds to complete the course after crossing the start line. The bell rang. Hoy started her warm-up circle. She unintentionally crossed the start line, well within the initial 45 second time limit. Unknown to her, this automatically triggered the computerised timing device for the start of her round. But the stadium clock, visible to the competitors, did not re-start.

Hoy, still apparently thinking she was in her warm-up circle and with time in hand, made a wide turn shortly before the first fence and this brought her once again behind the start line for her 'real' round. As she crossed the start line this time, the stadium clock re-started. It was a glorious clear round. Hoy, judging her timing by the stadium clock, completed the triumphant round two seconds inside the 90 second time requirement. Germany celebrated the team gold medal.

With tears of joy, Bettina Hoy fell into the arms of her Australian husband, Andrew, who was competing for his home country. They were a rare married couple, competing for different countries in the same event. There were more tears to follow as the saga unfolded.

It was discovered that, during Hoy's round, the computerised timing device had continued to measure her time from the first crossing of the start line. The timing device indicated a total time which was 12.61 seconds over the 90 second limit. The French team formally protested. After deliberations, the stewards of the Ground Jury ruled that Hoy should be penalised with 14 time penalties. The team gold medal was gone. The German team slipped from gold back to fourth place outside the medals. The French had now won the team medal.

Chaos ensued. Hoy and the German team appealed instantly to the FEI Appeals Committee – who met promptly and decided on the grounds of 'fair play' that Hoy should not suffer because of a timekeeping mistake by the organisers. 'Bettina Hoy had no way to believe that her round had started,' explained a member of the Appeals Committee, 'as the clock was re-started when she crossed the line for the second time. When errors occur in the management of a competition, it is right to make sure the rider doesn't pay the consequences.' The Appeals Committee rescinded the time penalties imposed earlier by the Ground Jury. The team gold medal had been won again by Germany. Win, loss, win – all within the same day.

> **With tears of joy, Bettina Hoy fell into the arms of her Australian husband… There were more tears to follow as the saga unfolded.**

After the chaotic finish of the team event, the best-placed riders overall had a final round of jumping to decide the individual gold. There was still a sense of turmoil. Was Hoy now going for a double gold or was her earlier ride still in doubt? Hoy on *Ringwood Cockatoo* had one rail down in the final round and, assuming the earlier round stood, was in second place, awaiting the final round of the leading 24 year-old French rider, Nicolas Touzaint, who could afford one error. Dramatically, Touzaint knocked down a pole at the first jump, then another, and another. Britain's Leslie Law moved into second place. Hoy had won the individual gold … or had she?

The medal ceremony went ahead. The medals were presented by HRH Princess Royal, an IOC member and a former Olympian in eventing. Hoy and Germany proudly celebrated. Nevertheless, it was now the turn of representatives of the French, British and American teams to object. The chaotic issue was referred to the ad hoc panel of the Court of Arbitration for Sport (CAS).

Leagl Question: Should the decision of the FEI Appeals Committee be over-ruled and the time penalties imposed by the Ground Jury on Hoy be reinstated?

For: Hoy crossed the start line and the timing of the round should commence from that first crossing. The computerised timing device should be the prevailing mechanism. The Ground Jury was the body set up under the FEI rules with authority to settle all problems within its jurisdiction. Appeal bodies, such as the FEI Appeals Committee and indeed CAS, should not interfere with the initial 'field of play' decision of the Ground Jury.

Against: By any test, Hoy was the fastest individual rider in the competition. She had seen the stadium clock and had clearly been misled by the timing shown by it. Hoy should not suffer because the starting procedures of the organisers were at fault. The FEI Appeals Committee was not second-guessing the facts but interpreting the rules. It was authorised to apply a principle of fairness. The gold medals should remain with Hoy and Germany.

Decision: Hoy and the German team lost. CAS decided, three days after the event itself, that neither it nor the FEI Appeals Committeee should interfere with the judgment of the Ground Jury. This was the '*field of play*' decision made by the official body on the spot. The FEI Committee '*had no jurisdiction to entertain the appeal*'. Its decision was '*null and void*' and '*the decision of the Ground Jury is reinstated*'. The time penalty on Hoy should stand. France won the team gold medal, not Germany. Leslie Law of Great Britain won the individual gold medal, not Hoy.

Bettina Hoy was aboard a flight from Athens to Germany, with her gold medals safely packed, before she learnt of CAS's decision taking them away for the second time in three days. As for Leslie Law, he was competing in horse trails in Solihull when he heard that he had become Britain's first eventing gold medallist since 1972. He was so shocked he withdrew from the competition. 'My concentration level was zero.'

In one sense, this was a narrow decision based on the specific rules of the FEI which, in the view of CAS, left the matter to be decided by the Ground Jury and not the FEI Appeals Committee. In a more fundamental sense, this was another important example of the reluctance of courts and tribunals to interfere with 'field of play' decisions. In most sports, there is a decision of the referee or umpire during the course of play. Here, as in a number of other sports, it is the judgment of officials made immediately after the competition. In either case, the hurdle for challenging decisions made by referees, judges or panels at the 'field of play' in sport is great. It will always depend on the rules of the particular sport but intervention is very rare.

And yet there is a lingering feeling in this case that, although the right decision was reached on the merits and the computerised time device should have prevailed, this was indeed an issue of interpretation of the rules which could properly have been decided 'within the sport' by the FEI Appeals Committee.

After the 2004 Olympics had ended, a small gold-plated statue of Bettina Hoy was modelled to mark her success and can be seen in the city hall of her birth-town of Rheine in Northern Westphalia. The FEI said: 'The FEI wishes to emphasise that the decision taken by its Appeals Committee was based on fair play and the best interest of the sport, as well as a different interpretation of the rules.'

43. VANDERLEI DE LIMA
The Olympic marathon and the Irish priest

Could Vanderlei de Lima claim a joint gold medal after being stopped by an interloper when leading the Olympic marathon?

It was the last day of the summer Olympic Games in Athens 2004. The men's marathon was in progress. No one could have foreseen the extraordinary incident which would take place. How would the intervention of a former Irish priest affect the result?

The marathon, in line with the historical setting of the 2004 Games, was due to finish in the 108 year-old marble Panathinaiko Stadium where the first modern Olympics were held in 1896. Beginning in the town of Marathon, the race followed a steep and difficult course. Legend has it that this was the course along which the Greek messenger, Pheidippides, carried the news in 490 BC that the Greeks had defeated the Persians … and then dropped dead after delivering it.

The leader in 2004 was Vanderlei de Lima from Brazil, an experienced marathon runner and winner of the 2003 Pan American Games. Just 5ft 6ins tall, he was attempting to become the first Brazilian to win an Olympic gold in the men's marathon. De Lima had been in the leading pack throughout the race and had held a clear lead since the halfway mark, at times almost by a full minute. After 35 kilometres and with less than 10 kilometres to the finish, de Lima still held a lead of 48 seconds over his closest pursuers, Italy's Stefano Baldini and America's Meb Keflezighi. Was glory beckoning for the Brazilian?

Suddenly, an interloper appeared, dressed extraordinarily in a kilt, green beret and wearing knee-high socks. He was later identified as Cornelius Horan, a former Irish Catholic priest. Horan, originally from County Kerry but living near London, was an established troublemaker. The previous year he had been jailed for running on to the track and disrupting the British Grand Prix at Silverstone. This time, in Athens, he was bearing a placard declaring: 'THE SECOND COMING IS NEAR SAYS THE BIBLE GRAND PRIX PRIEST'.

Horan hurled himself at de Lima, shoving him sideways into the kerbside and the adjacent crowd. It was fully 15 seconds before de Lima, stunned beyond belief and helped by a spectator, could struggle free to start again. With his rhythm badly shaken and slightly dazed, de Lima gathered himself and continued – joined by a posse of police motorcycle outriders. His lead had been cut to around 10 seconds. Within minutes, he was passed by Baldini and Keflezighi. Baldini went on to cross the line first and win the gold.

When de Lima entered the Panathinaiko Stadium, it was to great acclaim from the 70,000 strong crowd who had been watching the earlier incident in amazement on the large television screens in the stadium. De Lima sprinted joyously to the line, smiling broadly, spreading his arms and blowing a kiss to the crowd, to take the bronze medal. His time was 77 seconds behind Baldini.

Suddenly, an interloper appeared, dressed extraordinarily in a kilt, green beret and wearing knee-high socks.

The Brazilian track foundation launched an official appeal, claiming that a second gold medal should be awarded to de Lima. De Lima himself said afterwards about the incident: 'I was scared, because I didn't know what was going to happen to me… If you stop in a marathon, you struggle the next three or four kilometres. It's hard to get your rhythm back. I don't know if I could have won, but things would have been different.'

The International Association of Athletics Federations (IAAF) rejected the appeal. The Brazilian Olympic Committee and de Lima appealed to the Court of Arbitration for Sport (CAS).

Legal Question: De Lima was clearly hampered. Should the result be altered or, at least, a second gold medal awarded to de Lima?

For: De Lima was still in a clear lead. He was physically and seriously affected by an event beyond his control – and one which the race and security authorities might have done more to prevent. He could have held on to his lead and won. The Olympic ideals should recognise the special circumstances and award a second medal to de Lima.

Against: It was impossible to calculate how much energy and momentum was lost by the attack. There was no certainty, or indeed probability, that de Lima would have won. It was an act of 'force majeure' which had to be accepted. The result could not be changed under the rules.

Decision: De Lima failed in his claim. CAS decided that the result could not be changed. It had '*no power to remedy his legitimate frustration*'. The circumstances were unfortunate, but it could not change the results of a sporting event unless there was evidence of bad faith or arbitrariness. '*The results of the marathon race of the Athens Olympic Games must stand.*'

Baldini kept his gold medal and de Lima his bronze.

Should CAS have attempted to impose a 'fair' solution? Unless the rules of competition give an appeal body scope to impose, retrospectively, a 'fair' solution, then neither the IAAF nor CAS could do so. 'Rules are rules.' But what if, theoretically, de Lima had been within yards of the finishing line? Would a different decision have been reached?

Considerable sympathy was felt for de Lima. He was later asked why he was so joyous when he crossed the line at the end of the race. Through an interpreter, he explained: 'It is a festive moment. It is a unique moment. Most athletes never have this moment, very few have the privilege to live such moments.'

At the closing ceremony of the Games, the International Olympic Committee gave de Lima a medal named after the founder of the modern Games, Pierre de Coubertin, in recognition of his 'exceptional demonstration of fair play and Olympic values'.

As for Cornelius Horan, he was taken to the General Police Division in Attica and held overnight. He was later given a 12-month suspended jail sentence.

Chapter Six

DOPING AND CHEATING

FROM MATCH FIXING TO MURDER

All competitive sports have rules requiring minimum standards of conduct from the participants. These rules seek to establish 'a level playing field' for competitors. Cheating can take many forms, from doping to industrial espionage - and even to faking a blood injury.

Anti-doping rules, in particular, aim to ensure that participants do not cheat by gaining artificial advantage over others through the use of drugs. Decisions of disciplinary bodies (not always 'men in blazers') who enforce these rules can seriously affect the livelihood of a player or athlete and his or her opportunity to win medals, prizes or competitions – and, in a team sport, a ban may affect the fortunes of a team deprived of a star player.

This is fertile ground for legal challenge. Sporting bodies strain to keep such challenges to a minimum, strongly preferring that these issues should be settled 'within the sport' and not the law courts. Many appeals, under the rules of sport governing bodies, now make their way to specialist tribunals or ultimately to the Court of Arbitration for Sport (CAS) – but many have also found their way to the ordinary courts.

In this chapter, we visit a kaleidoscope of different sporting events and venues, including athletic stadiums in Seoul, Sydney and Lisbon, horse racing at Epsom and long distance swimming in Brazil.

44. BEN JOHNSON

First in Seoul and then in Montreal

Could Ben Johnson successfully challenge his lifetime ban on the grounds of being an unreasonable restraint of trade?

The Olympics 100 metres final in Seoul, South Korea on 24th September 1988 was the showdown between Ben Johnson and Carl Lewis.

Ben Johnson, the 26 year-old Jamaican-born Canadian, was the 1987 World Champion and current 100 metres world record holder. Carl Lewis, America's golden athlete, held the 1984 Olympic 100 metres title amongst his glittering array. There was no love lost between Lewis and Johnson. Their rivalry will go down in athletics history. Millions around the world turned on their television sets, many of us in the Western world in the middle of the night, to witness the most anticipated sprint race in history.

With a sensational start, Johnson led from the starting blocks to the finish, destroying the field and clocking a new world record of 9.79 seconds. Forty-six strides; the fastest man in history. He later remarked that the time would have been even faster had he not, in that iconic gesture, raised his hand in triumph just before the finish. A race that all spectators and viewers will never forget.

And yet it became the race when athletics lost its innocence. The integrity of sport at the highest level was shattered. Previously, in public perception, the problem of drugs abuse had largely been confined to weightlifting and other field events. Now, it was centre stage – in one of the signature events of the Olympic Games.

The telephone call came to Johnson in the early hours of 27th September. His urine sample after the race had been found to contain traces of Stanozolol, a prohibited anabolic steroid. He was disqualified and his gold medal was forfeited by the International Olympics Committee (IOC). He was sent home in disgrace. The gold medal was awarded to Carl Lewis.

It became the race when athletics lost its innocence.

Johnson was subsequently banned by the International Amateur Athletics Federation (IAAF) for two years.

The story started to unfold more fully. An in-depth Canadian governmental investigation in 1989, the 'Dubin Inquiry' under Chief Justice Charles Dubin, heard hours of testimony about the use of performance-enhancing drugs by athletes. It appeared that the use of drugs was widespread. Johnson was not alone. He was just one of the first to be caught. Charlie Francis, Johnson's coach and also Canada's national sprint coach for nine years, told the inquiry that Johnson himself had been taking steroids since 1981. Johnson's 1987 world record was annulled in the light of this investigation.

After his two-year ban ended in 1990, Johnson was re-instated. He started competing again but never recovered his former speed. Indeed, he took part in the 1992 Olympics in Barcelona as a member of the Canadian team, but failed to make the 100 metres final.

After his comeback, he was tested after every race in which he participated. All was well on that front until January 1993 when he competed in an indoor event in Montreal. His urine samples, following a test at that event, revealed a level of testosterone greater than the permitted level. Hearings took place. Time for appeal ran out. In April 1993, Johnson was advised that he was now banned by the IAAF from competition for life. It was this decision that led to the court case before a three-judge panel of the Ontario Appeal Court.

The public had a right 'to know that the race involves only an athlete's own skill, his own strength, his own spirit and not his pharmacologist'.

Johnson challenged the decision on the grounds that a lifetime ban from competition was an unlawful restraint of trade.

Legal Question: Should Johnson succeed in overturning a lifetime ban?

For: The ban restricted Johnson from carrying on his livelihood as a runner. It was a restraint of trade. A lifetime ban was more than was reasonably necessary to protect the public interest. It was excessive and unlawful.

Against: The ban, even if technically a restraint of trade, was reasonable in all the circumstances. It was necessary to protect not only Johnson himself but, importantly, the public interest in fair competition. The integrity of the sport must be protected. The influence of elite performers on young athletes should also not be ignored. Most major sports impose a lifetime ban for a second offence.

Decision: Johnson lost again. The Ontario Appeal Court held that, even though the ban was a restraint of trade, a lifetime ban was reasonable and lawful in the circumstances. The interests of the parties and the public required the maintenance of integrity in the sport. As the defence counsel put it vividly: 'The public had a right 'to know that the race involves only an athlete's own skill, his own strength, his own spirit and not his pharmacologist'. The court's function was not to review the merits of decisions reached by tribunals in specialised fields. Johnson's lifetime ban was upheld.

To many, the sport of athletics has never recovered since that race in Seoul.

Johnson would never race again. Whilst he admitted to the extensive use of steroids, Johnson later maintained that his test at Seoul in 1988 was sabotaged by a 'third party' as part of a conspiracy against him. He says that Stanozolol was not a steroid that he used.

In 2006, Johnson appeared in an advertisement in the USA for an energy drink, Cheetah Power Surge. In a mock interview, Johnson was asked: 'Ben, when you run, do you Cheetah?' Johnson replied: 'Absolutely. I Cheetah all the time.'

45. DIANE MODAHL

A remedy for being innocent?

Could Diane Modahl sue for damages when suspended by the governing body for a doping offence for which she was subsequently exonerated?

Diane Modahl was one of Britain's leading athletes, and 1994 promised to be a great year for her. The women's 800 metres champion in the 1990 Commonwealth Games, the 27 year-old was a leading contender to retain her title at the forthcoming Games in Victoria, Canada. No one could have foreseen that the year would end in high controversy and that British athletics would be set on a path to bankruptcy.

In June 1994 Modahl was competing in an athletics meeting at the Lisbon University Stadium in Portugal shortly before the Commonwealth Games. She was asked, under the doping control procedures of the International Amateur Athletics Federation (IAAF), to provide a routine urine sample. Part of the sample, the A sample, was tested by a laboratory in Lisbon. It reported a level of testosterone well above any permissible level. Modahl was, by this time, in Canada. She was informed of the result and asked to return to Lisbon. The B sample, tested by the same laboratory, later showed similar results. She was suspended from the Commonwealth Games.

Modahl was the first British woman athlete to have tested positive in a drugs test.

It was a high profile case. Modahl was the first British woman athlete to have tested positive in a drugs test.

An initial hearing in December, before a five-man disciplinary committee of the British Athletics Federation (BAF), concluded that she had committed a doping offence and banned her from competition for four years – the length of sentence applicable under the rules adopted by the BAF and the IAAF at that time. Modahl strongly protested her innocence and appealed.

Before the appeal body, Modahl claimed that the initial committee proceedings had been biased against her. Backed by scientific advisers, she was also able to produce new evidence that mishandling of the samples at the Portuguese laboratory may have led to contamination. Delayed refrigeration of the sample could have kick-started a bacterial growth in the urine, a by-product of which could have been an increased level of testosterone in the sample. The appeal body decided in Modahl's favour and lifted the ban in July 1995. It was not until March 1996, though, that the IAAF also accepted the report and cleared her to compete internationally.

Modahl was still angry. She had been unable to compete internationally for nearly two years at the peak of her career. She brought a legal claim for damages against the BAF. Modahl alleged that the initial disciplinary panel had been biased against her since certain members had publicly presumed her to be guilty. This bias had prevented a fair and impartial hearing. This was, she alleged, a breach by the BAF of its contractual duty to her to conduct a fair and impartial hearing.

She claimed almost £1 million in damages, legal and medical costs. This was the first time that an athlete had sued a governing body in Britain for damages as a result of a disciplinary decision. Modahl's claim resulted in much complex litigation lasting many years. Eventually, it came before the Court of Appeal.

Legal Question: Should Diane Modahl be entitled to recover damages from the BAF to compensate for the period of the ban which resulted from the initial disciplinary hearing and which was subsequently overturned?

For: As a member of an athletics club affiliated to the BAF and as a competitor in BAF-governed events, Modahl was bound to abide by the governing body's disciplinary procedures. On the part of the governing body, there was an implied contractual obligation to administer those rules through disciplinary proceedings which were fair and impartial. In this case, two members of the initial disciplinary committee were either biased or appeared to be biased. It was this faulty hearing that resulted in Modahl's disqualification – which lasted until the ban was lifted internationally by the IAAF in March 1996. Modahl was entitled to damages as a normal remedy for breach of contract.

Against: Athletes accept the disciplinary jurisdiction of the BAF simply by competing and not through a formal contractual relationship. In any event, there was no evidence that members of the original disciplinary committee were actually biased. The difference between the first disciplinary hearing and the appeal, at which Modahl was cleared, was the new scientific evidence that the samples could have been degraded through the handling procedures at the Lisbon laboratory. A fair result had been reached. Modahl was cleared. A governing body should not be liable in damages if the eventual result was fair.

Decision: Diane Modahl lost her claim.

The Court of Appeal decided that, where '*a sensible appeal structure*' has been put in place by a governing body, the parties must '*accept what in the end is a fair decision*'. In fact, the court decided that there was no actual bias in this case – and that the apparent bias of one member did not taint the process or influence the decision. It did not amount to a breach of the obligation to provide a fair hearing overall. '*The test is to ask whether, having regard to the course of the proceedings, there has been a fair result.*' The principal reason for the change in the decision at the appeal stage was the new scientific evidence available.

So, no monetary compensation for Modahl.

At the sporting level, a highly important consequence of the Modahl case was the tightening-up of criteria for accreditation of laboratories for drug testing in sport, together with more rigorous procedures for taking samples and their subsequent laboratory analysis.

For sports governing bodies generally, this was a wake-up call. It stressed the importance of having fair disciplinary procedures. This was the first time in the UK that an athlete had brought a legal claim against a governing body for damages following a disciplinary decision. In the US, American Harry 'Butch' Reynolds, the 400 metres world record holder, had brought an $18 million claim for damages against the US athletics governing body when his suspension for a drugs offence was lifted. After extended litigation, he failed in his claim.

She claimed almost £1 million in damages, legal and medical costs.

For the governing body, the BAF, the high cost of

litigation proved overwhelming. Effectively bankrupted, after a period of turmoil, the BAF went into administration and was later re-incarnated as UK Athletics. The potential threat of litigation, these days, is never far away. All sports governing bodies must now take extra care to ensure that their disciplinary processes are fair and properly conducted.

Diane Modahl returned to competition in 1996 and won a bronze medal in the 800 metres at the Commonwealth Games in Kuala Lumpur. But she never recovered her previous best form. In 2004, following the example of her cousin, boxer Chris Eubank, Modahl appeared in the reality TV show *I'm a Celebrity, Get Me Out of Here!*

46. ALAIN BAXTER

A nasal inhaler and a bronze skiing medal

Should Alain Baxter be disqualified if doping was accidental and not sufficient in quantity to be performance-enhancing?

People knew when Alain Baxter was around at the 2002 Winter Olympics in Salt Lake City in Minnesota, USA. Proud of his Scottish background, 28 year-old Baxter sparked some early controversy at the Games by dying his hair blue and white in the cross of St Andrew, the flag of Scotland. The British Olympic Association, wanting to project an image of 'Britishness', asked him to remove it.

Baxter, from Aviemore in Scotland and known as 'the Highlander', was Britain's best alpine skier. Named after the 1970s French skiing star, Alain Penz, Baxter first represented Britain in 1991 and had steadily moved up the world rankings. He was looking forward to the challenge of the 2002 Winter Olympics in Salt Lake City.

Baxter frequently suffered from nasal congestion, a long-standing medical condition. In the UK, he normally used a non-prescription Vicks vapour inhaler for relieving the congestion. The inhaler was a permitted substance under UK athletic anti-doping rules. There had never been any issue.

His nasal problem resurfaced in Salt Lake City. He asked his coach, Christian Schwaiger, to pick up a Vicks inhaler when he was out shopping. He came back, instead, with a liquid Sinex recommended by the British team doctor, but Baxter found that this did not work satisfactorily.

Baxter then crashed during training and took the next day off – and went shopping in nearby Park City where he was staying. Looking around, he spotted a Vicks vapour inhaler in the chemist section of the supermarket. 'I saw the inhaler that I wanted Christian to buy in the first place because I had been using it since I was a kid.' He bought it, not consulting the team doctor or reading the back of the package, since it appeared to be exactly the same product as the one he regularly used in the UK.

When competition began, on the slopes at the Olympics, Baxter was in excellent form in the slalom. He performed well on his first run, finishing in eighth place. On his second, Baxter had a brilliant run and moved into second position. There were a number of skiers left to complete their second runs. Would Baxter's time be sufficient for a medal? One by one, the remaining competitors struggled on an increasingly rutted and difficult course.

Finally, with only American home favourite, Bode Miller, and first-run leader, Jean-Pierre Vidal of France, left to go, Baxter was assured of at least fourth place. Then Miller sensationally crashed and Baxter was certain of a medal – which became a bronze when Vidal clinched the gold for France. Baxter and the British team were ecstatic. This was the first ever alpine skiing medal for Britain at an Olympics.

As a medallist, Baxter then underwent a routine doping test for which he submitted a urine sample. He returned to Scotland the following morning and received a hero's welcome. The next day, as Baxter was celebrating in his home village of Aviemore, the shock telephone call came. The laboratory report had revealed a very small trace of methamphetamine, a prohibited substance under the IAAF anti-doping rules. A disciplinary hearing was held and reported to the

This was the first ever alpine skiing medal for Britain at an Olympics.

International Olympic Committee (IOC) Executive Board. A month later, in March, it was announced that Baxter had been disqualified from the men's alpine skiing slalom and had lost his medal. He was banned from competition for three months.

How did this occur? It transpired that the composition of the US version of the Vicks inhaler which Baxter had bought was slightly different from the version sold in the UK and included a level of levmetamphetamine, a form of the prohibited substance methamphetamine. It was accepted by all, though, that the minimal quantity was not sufficient to be in any way a performance-enhancing stimulant. It made no difference to the result. Baxter challenged the decision and the matter was referred to the Court of Arbitration for Sport (CAS).

Legal Question: Should Baxter be entitled to his bronze medal, and the disqualification be lifted?

For: Baxter did not take the drug intentionally. His use was consistent with the medication he had always taken in the UK. The levels of levmetamphetamine were so low that it would not have had any stimulant effect on athletic performance. The IOC doping rules failed adequately to distinguish between the different types of methamphetamines as prohibited substances. Disqualification and suspension was a disproportionate remedy in the circumstances.

Against: Levmetamphetamine was within the scope of substances prohibited under the IOC rules. Athletes are strictly responsible for substances placed in their body. Results achieved by a 'doped athlete' at a competition must be cancelled irrespective of guilt. The level was also irrelevant. It was simply a question of whether it was a prohibited substance or not under the rules. The fight against drugs, and fairness to all athletes, required that the rules be strictly enforced. Baxter should, of course, have read the back of the package and was not entirely without fault.

Decision: Baxter lost. CAS dismissed his claim. The drug was a prohibited substance under the rules of the IAAF. Disqualification was the minimum sanction under the rules, irrespective of whether ingestion of the substance was intentional or negligent or entirely innocent. Disqualification applied irrespective of whether or not the actual dosage in fact had any performance-enhancing effect.

Rules were rules. CAS confirmed that the rules could not be ignored unless '*they were so overtly wrong that they would run counter to every principle of fairness in sport*'. That was not the case here.

The panel accepted that Baxter was 'a sincere and honest man' who did not intend to obtain a competitive advantage in the race. However, the consequence of this doping violation must be disqualification and the loss of his bronze medal.

The case brought home to the British sporting public the severity of the anti-doping laws at the Olympics. Were they too severe?

The fight against doping in sport requires tough laws. Each athlete must be responsible for any substance which enters his body – irrespective of whether it has been taken knowingly or innocently. Was it inevitable that there would be a few 'hard' cases in the cause of ensuring tough and effective laws to 'clean' the sport? Or did this case go too far?

There should surely be a burden on the anti-doping authorities to ensure that substances are only prohibited at a level which genuinely leads to a 'performance-enhancing'

'The consequence of this doping violation must be disqualification and the loss of his bronze medal.'

advantage for a competitor or is a substance harmful to the health of the athlete. The doping regulations should have distinguished between the different types of methamphetamines. If a substance exceeds the prohibited level, then the fairness of 'a level playing field' for all competitors almost certainly means that disqualification is inevitable. But any subsequent suspension of an athlete from competing or additional penalty for the offence must surely be proportionate to the offence? A ban was too much.

Baxter was very unlucky. This was a 'hard' case.

47. THE BALCO SCANDAL
Walkin' Fish, a syringe and a sporting earthquake

A syringe turned up, anonymously, at the US anti-doping agency. It contained a 'clear' substance. What was in it? Would it trigger a sporting earthquake?

It was a simple plastic syringe. It arrived, in June 2003, at the US Anti-Doping Agency (USADA) from an anonymous source. The sender described himself over the phone as a high profile track coach. He said the syringe contained a drug given to a number of leading US athletes. He named the owner of the Bay Area Laboratory Co-Operative (BALCO), Victor Conte, as the source of the steroid in the syringe. It started a sporting earthquake and its tremors were felt worldwide for years.

Who was Victor Conte? He was a session musician for many years, playing bass guitar. With a laid-back style earning him the nickname 'Walkin' Fish', he played in a few bands around the San Francisco area. One was a trio calling themselves, ironically, the Pure Food & Drug Act. The most successful was the horn-based soul and rock band Tower of Power, with whom he appeared for a few years in the late 1970s – he played on the cult band's 1978 album *Come Play With Me*. He would later say that he 'was one of the few band members who weren't on drugs'.

Conte had big ideas. He became a self-taught pharmacist. Developing contacts in sport, he saw an opportunity to make money by providing nutritional supplements to swimmers and athletes. He founded in 1984 the Bay Area Laboratory Co-Operative (BALCO). The obscure nutrition laboratory off US Highway 101, near

San Francisco Airport, initially offered blood and urine tests for athletes and supplied nutritional supplements for them, particularly a zinc and magnesium replacement supplement which Conte termed ZMA. Many top athletes and baseball players became clients and advertised the (perfectly legal) product. He termed them his 'ZMA track club'.

They were the 'golden couple' of world athletics.

One of his key clients was US sprint star Marion Jones, coached by Trevor Graham, the former Jamaican sprinter. Jones became the triumphant athlete of the 2000 Sydney Olympics – her 'Drive for Five' resulted in gold medals in the 100 metres, the 200 metres and the 4x400 metres relay, as well as bronze medals in the long jump and the 4x100 metres relay. Five medals – a feat never before achieved by a female athlete. After divorcing her first husband (and college coach), shot-putter CJ Hunter, she became attached to promising US sprinter Tim Montgomery. In September 2002, at the IAAF Grand Prix finals in Paris, Montgomery stepped into the public limelight himself when he sensationally broke the 100 metres world record with a time of 9.78 seconds. They were the 'golden couple' of world athletics.

Marion Jones gave birth to a son by Montgomery in June 2003. It was the same month that the plastic syringe arrived at USADA.

The syringe was half-full of a 'clear' substance. USADA arranged for scientists at the Olympic drug-testing laboratory in Los Angeles to determine its chemical structure. It turned out to be a steroid – tetrahydrogestrinone or THG – previously undetectable in drug screening tests. The term 'designer drug' entered the sporting lexicon.

Then came a critical step. Four months later, in September 2003, a joint raid on the offices of BALCO was made by government agencies with powers of criminal prosecution – the San Mateo County Narcotics Task Force, the Food and Drug Administration, representatives of USADA and agents of the Internal Revenue Service. At an off-site storage facility, they found numerous vials and containers of steroids, human growth hormone and testosterone. Computers and documents were seized, listing athletes who had been clients. BALCO had been exposed.

Criminal prosecutions followed. Damning evidence of the scale of BALCO's operations emerged during grand jury and other pre-trial

BALCO had been exposed.

investigations under the US criminal system. Numerous witnesses from the world of athletics and baseball testified before the grand jury. It was evidence which would provide the basis for later criminal trials – including charges of perjury.

In February 2004, the US Attorney General announced a 42-count indictment against four men (the BALCO four): founder Victor Conte, the mastermind behind the scheme; executive James Valente; track coach Remi Korchemny; and trainer Greg Anderson. Among the charges were conspiracy to distribute anabolic steroids, conspiracy to defraud through misbranded drugs and money laundering.

Victor Conte chose his only escape route and agreed to a plea bargain with the US federal prosecutors. He pleaded guilty to steroid distribution and money laundering in a deal to help the prosecutors with their investigations. He was sentenced in July 2005 to just four months in prison and four months of house arrest. James Valente, BALCO's vice-president, received probation. Greg Anderson, long-time friend and trainer of US baseball star Barry Bonds, received a six-month prison sentence. Conte has since described his sentence as 'the wrist slap heard round the world'.

The effects of the BALCO scandal were devastating. It became the biggest drugs scandal in sport. New drug screening tests for athletes were developed and past samples reviewed. The roll call of athletes caught up in the aftermath of the scandal has been extensive. Amongst notable athletes caught within the early trawl for THG or a similar drug, modafinil, were world title holder for the women's 100 and 200 metres, Kelli White, and Britain's leading sprinter, Dwain Chambers. Chambers was banned for two years.

But who sent the syringe that triggered all the investigations into BALCO?

In the second half of 2005, the spotlight fell on Tim Montgomery. He was found guilty of taking performance-enhancing drugs and banned by the Court of Arbitration for Sport (CAS) for two years. Importantly, the ban was based on evidence gathered during the BALCO criminal investigation and not on a positive drugs test at an athletics event. Montgomery's results since 31st March 2001, including the 100 metre world record he once held, were nullified from the record books. The 100 metres world record seemed cursed.

A continuing escapee was Marion Jones. She continued to assert that she was drug-free and threatened to sue if the US anti-doping agency imposed a sanction that was based on anything other than a failed drug test. In her autobiography, she said: 'I am against performance-enhancing drugs. I have never taken them and I never will.'

But who sent the syringe that triggered all the investigations into BALCO? Who had the knowledge?

Jamaican-born athletics coach, Trevor Graham, was later identified as the man involved. Was he acting for the good of the sport – or was it simply to gain revenge on Conte? He had once worked closely with athletes supplied by BALCO, including Marion Jones and, for a time, Tim Montgomery. There appears to have been a major row in 2002 between Graham, Conte and Montgomery, probably about money. After Montgomery broke the world record in Paris, many track observers noted that Graham's move to congratulate him at the track was rebuffed; a bitter argument was heard between them, with Montgomery saying it 'was nothing to do with' Graham.

Where did the syringe come from? Graham said later that he was given it by CJ Hunter, who was trying to get a job as a coach with Graham at the latter's own Sprint Capitol track training and advisory clinic in Raleigh, North Carolina. CJ Hunter apparently said the syringe came from BALCO, from whom he had now split. We will probably never know the truth.

In June 2006, another 100 metres world record holder had fallen. Olympic and world champion sprinter, Justin Gatlin, tested positive for THG. Gatlin was trained by … Trevor Graham. Already having one offence on his record, Gatlin attempted to avoid a lifetime ban by helping anti-doping officials in their continuing investigations. An initial eight-year ban was reduced, on appeal, to four years. Now it was Graham's turn to be under the spotlight. Was Graham really thinking it through when he sent the syringe to USADA? Did he not realise that the investigation would eventually get round to his own camp of athletes?

Perjury is the charge which trapped them; perjury arising out of evidence under oath at the grand jury trial into the BALCO four in 2003. Graham now faced criminal charges. Similar charges of perjury were made against a number of others, including Marion Jones and baseball's Barry Bonds, who in 2007 broke past Hank Aaron's career record for home-runs in major league baseball – one of America's iconic sporting records. The tremors from the BALCO affair showed no sign of ending.

In October 2007 came the news that many had suspected. Marion Jones was facing criminal charges of perjury – lying to the BALCO grand jury in 2003 that she had not taken performance-enhancing drugs and, separately, to federal investigators in a cheque fraud case involving her former boyfriend, Tim Montgomery. She finally broke down. She confessed that she had taken performance-enhancing drugs before, during and after the 2000 Sydney Olympics: 'I have let my family down. I have let my country down and I have let myself down.' She blamed her choice of men in her life. She claimed at first that she did not take the drug knowingly and was told that it was just a supplement called 'flaxseed oil'. She accepted a two-year ban from US Track and Field, although she promptly retired from athletics. All her results since September 2000 have been nullified. Jones has been stripped of her five Olympic titles and she has handed back the five medals from the 2000 Olympics.

In January 2008 Marion Jones was sentenced by US District Judge Karas to six months in prison for perjury.

Jones, who 'survived' more than 160 drug tests (what does that say about the effectiveness of these drug tests?), became the first athlete to be convicted of a criminal offence for her role in the BALCO saga.

With hindsight, perhaps early signs were there. As a 16 year-old at high school, Marion Jones escaped punishment after missing a drugs test. She was defended by Johnnie Cochran, the lawyer who later successfully defended OJ Simpson.

The BALCO affair became the biggest drugs scandal in sport. Sports bodies and governments were forced to face the truth that elite athletes have routinely used steroids, growth hormone and other banned substances in their quest to succeed. BALCO educated the world about doping and stimulated the biggest worldwide shake-up in sport's drug-testing regulations, testing and investigative procedures. It underlined the International Olympic Committee's requirement that all nations wishing to participate in the Olympics must have signed up to the World Anti-Doping Code promulgated by the World Anti-Doping Agency (WADA).

'I have let my family down. I have let my country down and I have let myself down.'

In May 2008, Trevor Graham was found guilty in San Francisco on one count of perjury, lying to federal agents investigating BALCO. A lifetime ban from athletics and a sentence of one year's house arrest lay ahead.

Victor 'Walkin' Fish' Conte himself is back in his laboratory in California running a successful business again selling and distributing nutritional supplements through his new company, Scientific Nutrition for Advanced Conditioning. Astonishingly, he even turned up at the London 2012 Olympics and was photographed alongside US female boxer, Marlen Esparaza, who won a bronze medal. (Another medallist at the Games was Justin Gatlin who (re-instated after his ban) won a bronze in the 100 metres.)

The tremors from the BALCO affair continue to rumble. All triggered by a plastic syringe turning up anonymously in the post.

48. DAVID MECA-MEDINA

A case of doping or a diet of wild boar?

Marathon swimming was the background. The issue? Are disciplinary rules liable to challenge under European competition laws or does a 'sporting exception' apply?

David Meca-Medina was a professional long distance swimmer. In open water, the Spaniard was the world's best. Ranked number one, he started 1999 in fine form. He won the opening event of the FINA Marathon Swimming World Cup held in January 1999 at Salvador de Bahia in Brazil. Then ... trouble. But was his diet to blame?

Triumph turned quickly to disaster for Meca-Medina and second-placed Igor Majcen from Slovenia. They tested positive for nandrolone, a prohibited substance under the rules of the International Swimming Federation (FINA).

Meca-Medina's tests revealed a nandrolone level of 9.7 nanograms per millilitre – substantially in excess of the permitted level of two nanograms under the anti-doping code. He joined a long list of athletes who have crossed the line with this substance. FINA's anti-doping panel suspended both Meca-Medina and Majcen for a period of four years in accordance with FINA's then penalty regime for a first offence.

In January 2000, Meca-Medina saw an escape route. Scientific experiments appeared to show that nandrolone could be produced endogenously within the human body (and therefore innocently) up to a level which could exceed the doping threshold of two nanograms per millilitre – particularly when certain foods, such as wild boar meat, have been consumed. Meca-Medina claimed that this could have been the case here; he had been eating a Brazillian speciality, sarapatel, a stew often based on wild boar meat.

Meca-Medina and Majcen appealed to the Court of Arbitration for Sport (CAS) for a review of FINA's penalty. They were partially successful. The penalty was reduced to two years suspension.

This was not enough for Meca-Medina and Majcen. They were determined to challenge the penalty further. They took the matter to the European Commission. They claimed that the permitted two nanogram level for nandrolone was too low and could catch innocent athletes. The penalties were excessive. FINA's anti-doping rules were generally anti-competitive and violated the European community rules on competition and freedom to provide services.

He had been eating a Brazillian speciality, sarapatel, a stew often based on wild boar meat.

This was a new claim. This was the first time that the legality of anti-doping rules in sport had been challenged directly under European competition law. The European Commission itself had previously refused to intervene in sport's anti-doping measures on the basis that this was a matter for sport itself. But Meca-Medina and Majcen were persistent. They eventually brought an action before the European Court of Justice.

Legal Question: Were FINA's anti-doping rules contrary to European competition law? Were the penalties on the swimmers excessive and open to legal challenge as not being proportionate to the particular offence?

For: Anti-doping rules, even if based on sporting objectives of fair play, were capable of having a significant economic impact on the participants. They must therefore comply with European laws relating to competition. The rules and restrictions must be reasonable and proportionate. These were not. The permitted threshold of nandrolone fixed by FINA's anti-doping rules was set at an excessively low level which was not founded on any scientifically safe criteria.

Against: Anti-doping rules were based purely on sporting considerations of integrity and fair play. They had nothing to do with economic activity. The rules should therefore not come within the scope of the European competition and economic freedom laws. The 'sporting exception' applied. Nandrolone was a substance which, in an athlete's body, was capable of improving performance and compromising the fairness of a sporting event. FINA's rules were in accord with the WADA Code. The two-year ban was accordingly justified in the light of the objective of anti-doping rules.

Decision: The European Court dismissed the claims of the two swimmers. Importantly, though, the European Court did agree that the anti-doping rules and penalties fell within the scrutiny of European competition law. Although the rules were based on sporting factors 'in order for competitive sport to be conducted fairly ... and to safeguard equal chances for athletes', they could have economic consequences. This was sufficient for the European competition laws to apply. The court concluded:

'The penal nature of the anti-doping rules at issue and the magnitude of the penalties applicable if they are breached are capable of producing adverse effects on competition because, if penalties were ultimately to prove unjustified, [they could] result in an athlete's unwarranted exclusion from sporting events ...'

Their operation was not excluded because of a 'sporting exception'. Restrictions must be reasonable and penalties must be proportionate.

However, the court was of the view that the anti-doping rules and penalties in this case were not disproportionate. The evidence at the time the rule was applied was that the minimum endogenous production of nandrolone by the human body was substantially lower than the two-nanogram threshold set by the anti-doping rules. The length of the bans would not be overturned. Meca-Medina won the skirmish but not the battle.

This was one for the lawyers. Although the European Court rejected the swimmers' claim, it established that anti-doping rules, previously thought to be outside the scope of competition law, did fall within the ever-pervasive jurisdiction of European law. Any restrictions on competition imposed by sporting bodies must be shown to be inherent in the pursuit of sporting objectives and proportionate to those objectives.

Meca-Medina won the skirmish but not the battle.

Many fear that the law of sport has been changed by a further, and unnecessary, encroachment of European law into sport. The 'sporting exception' would appear to apply only in exceedingly narrow circumstances. European competition law hangs again, Bosman-like, over rules and decisions of sporting bodies – particularly disciplinary decisions.

In public protest at his original FINA ban and with an eye for drama, David Meca-Medina once swam – with his feet in shackles – from the former prison island of Alcatraz across San Francisco Bay to the city. It took him 36 minutes.

49. TOUR DE FRANCE

Floyd Landis, Lance Armstrong and yet another scandal

Floyd Landis, after an extraordinary recovery on a mountain climb, was the 'winner' of the 2006 Tour de France. He became the first cyclist to be stripped of his Tour title in his year of victory. Then came revelations about previous seven-time winner Lance Armstrong. The credibility of cycling, and of its most famous race, was hanging by a thread.

The Tour de France has a history riddled with drugs. It is a sporting event which calls upon human reserves of stamina, strength and endurance perhaps beyond any other. The saying even developed: 'No dope, no hope.'

The problem was first brought to the world's attention, sadly and dramatically, when

Britain's Tommy Simpson died during the 1967 Tour. During stage 13, on a beating hot July day during a climb up Mont Ventoux and about two kilometres from the summit, Simpson began to zigzag across the road before collapsing. Two empty tubes and a third full of amphetamines were found

It was regarded as one of the most spectacular single-day performances in the history of the Tour.

in the pocket of his jersey. He, tragically, was so doped that he did not know he had reached the human level of endurance.

In 1978, glory became farce. Having just claimed the leader's yellow jersey on a mountain stage, the Belgian Michael Pollentier and another rider went missing when they should have provided a urine sample. They turned up two hours later. One doctor was suspicious and tugged at Pollentier's shorts – revealing a tube linked to a rubber condom of pre-prepared urine under his armpit. Pollentier was thrown off the Tour.

Before the 1998 Tour, one of the managers of the leading Festina team, Willy Voet, drove across the Belgian-French border early one morning. A routine, but unexpected, examination of his official Fiat estate car by French customs officials revealed it to be full of illegal prescription drugs, erythropoietin (EPO), growth hormones, testosterone and amphetamines. At first, he said that they were for his 'own personal use'. French police raided the Festina team's hotel. The Festina team were just the first of seven to withdraw from the 1998 race as ever-increasing evidence was found and criminal arrests were made. Use of drugs was still, clearly, widespread in professional cycling.

Rules were tightened and a more optimistic view was taken that the sport had become 'clean'. Lance Armstrong, overcoming testicular cancer, became a seven-time winner and a legend of the sport, retiring after his victory in 2005. Surely there would be no further scandal in 2006?

It was stage 17 of the 2006 Tour de France which stunned the cycling world. Experts described it as one of the most epic days of cycling ever seen.

Floyd Landis, the 30 year-old American who had been a close team-mate of Lance Armstrong at the end of his winning reign, had led the Tour overall by 10 seconds after stage 15. The next phase, stage 16, was a disaster for Landis. He suffered badly on the last hill climb and, shoulders slumped, rider after rider passed him. He fell back from first to 11th place overall and a full eight minutes behind the new leader, Spaniard Oscar Pereiro. His chances of winning the coveted title, with just three stages left, now seemed to be over.

The following day's stage was the last mountain climb of the Tour. Landis, leader of the Phonak team, had a bold plan. He decided to make an individual breakaway attack from the very first climb, fully 130 kilometres from the finish, and with four further tough climbs to follow during the gruelling stage. Landis broke the field as the chasing pack failed to react. He was the 'master of the mountains'. It was regarded as one of the most spectacular single-day performances in the history of the Tour. Landis eventually won the stage by nearly six minutes, a massive distance. He punched the air ecstatically in triumph. He had closed the gap with Pereiro by more than seven minutes and was now back in third place overall with a renewed chance of the title.

Indeed, Landis succeeded in making up the gap with the leader in the following two days' final stages. He proudly crossed the finish line, on the elegant cobbles of the Champs Elysées in Paris, a triumphant winner of the world's greatest cycling race. He was presented with the final yellow jersey.

The euphoria of victory drained away when, three days, later, it was reported that an 'adverse analytical finding' had resulted from a drugs test after stage 17. No name was given but the president of the International Cycling Union (UCI) said that it was the 'worst possible outcome'.

Why would he do it? How could he be so stupid as to get caught?

On 27th July 2006 came the announcement from the Phonak team. It was Floyd Landis. He had tested positive after stage 17 for an excessive level of the hormone testosterone – the ratio of testosterone to epitestosterone (the T/E ratio) was apparently 11:1 and far above the maximum permitted ratio of 4:1. Past samples of Landis during the Tour were also tested. A number, but not all, revealed similar results.

First reactions were of bemusement. Why would he do it? How could he be so stupid as to get caught? It did not seem to make sense. Tests on Landis two days before and two days after stage 17 had shown no adverse findings. How did testosterone, a drug for developing muscle growth, really aid short-term recovery in the circumstances of the Tour? It was not blood manipulation or use of an oxygen enhancer, such as EPO. Or had he been taking something more regularly which had previously been 'masked'?

Testosterone is a difficult substance for the testers since it is naturally produced within the body. A variety of tests have to establish whether its presence is endogenous (naturally produced) or exogenous (synthetically produced) – is it from 'the body' or 'the bottle'? Landis denied cheating and said high levels of testosterone must have occurred naturally in the body. For months afterwards – and well into 2008 – Landis sustained a vigorous and public attack on the procedures for testing at the LNDD laboratory.

Landis was charged with a doping violation by the US anti-doping agency (USADA) in September 2006. The case went to arbitration in Malibu, California in May 2007 under the auspices of the American Arbitration Association. Landis mounted a highly sophisticated, detailed and seemingly never-ending challenge. He even developed his defence, through a website, by publicly appealing for 'the collective resources of cycling fans', particularly in relation to the deficiencies of the LNDD. It became known as the 'Wikipedia defence'.

In September 2007 the American arbitration panel decided, by a 2-1 majority, that Landis was guilty of a doping offence. His defence, costing an estimated $2 million had failed. The panel acknowledged that: 'The practises of the [LNDD] in training its employees appear to lack the vigor the panel would expect … given the enormous consequences to athletes.' However, the panel by a majority did conclude that the charge of 'exogenous testosterone being found in the sample' was established and this was an anti-doping violation. The UCI president commented: 'He got a highly qualified legal team who tried to baffle everybody with science and public relations, and in the end the facts stood up.'

Landis was banned for two years as from 30th January 2007. The UCI stripped him of his 2006 Tour de France title. He was the first 'winner' of the Tour de France to be stripped of his title because of a doping offence. The title was awarded to Spain's Oscar Pereiro.

The saga of Floyd Landis was still not over. Landis appealed further to the Court of Arbitration for Sport (CAS). A cynical, and exhausted, public awaited the final verdict. It came in July 2008. CAS dismissed Landis' claim. The laboratory had used some '*less than ideal laboratory practices but not lies, fraud, forgery or cover-ups*' as Landis had contended. CAS concluded:

'*The Panel finds that the presence of exogenous testosterone … proves that [he] engaged in doping… Accordingly, [his] result at the 2006 Tour is disqualified.*'

Were the trials and tribulations of the Tour de France now over? No. The curse continued. The winner in 2010 was the great Spanish rider, Alberto Contador. He became the subject of another drugs investigation and a long legal wrangle up to CAS. The result? He too was stripped of his title. Could there be more?

Then, in 2012, coinciding with the opening day of the Tour, after rumours and allegations, the USADA announced formal charges against past seven-time Tour winner, legend of the sport, Lance Armstrong, for use of illegal performance-enhancing substances and methods. Little by little, the case had developed. A confession by Floyd Landis in 2012 had broken the wall of silence that teammates had built around Armstrong. It led to the revelation that Armstrong and his US Postal Services team had engaged in what anti-doping officials described as the most sophisticated doping programme in history. Armstrong was given a

Landis was the first 'winner' of the Tour de France to be stripped of his title because of a doping offence.

lifetime ban. The International Cycling Union (ICU) supported USADA's ruling and formally stripped Armstrong of his seven Tour de France titles.

In January 2013, after a decade of obstruction, obfuscation and denials, Lance Armstrong finally confessed his use of performance-enhancing drugs during a US televised interview with Oprah Winfrey.

Lawsuits, investigations and trials continue. In March 2015 an arbitration panel decided that SCA Promotions, an insurance company and one of the sponsors of Armstrong and his US Postal Service team, was entitled to recover $10 million from Armstrong for past payments. The panel declared that Armstrong had engaged in '*an unparalleled pageant of international perjury, fraud and conspiracy*'.

How widespread was drug use in professional cycling? In March 2015 also, a 227-page report was published by the Cycling Independent Reform Commission (CIRC). Although clearing the leadership of the UCI of outright corruption, it criticised the former UCI bosses of many failings - worst, that the UCI did not really want to catch cheats and therefore turned a blind eye to anything but the worst excesses. The report concluded with a raft of recommendations to prevent cycling returning to the dark days. There is, however, a long road ahead.

Lance Armstrong continued to claim that that he had been treated differently from others and that his ban should be reduced. The current ICU president, Brian Cookson, remarked: 'I think it's fair to say that Lance was given exceptional treatment but then again he was an exceptional offender.'

It was almost light relief to learn that Armstrong had avoided another court appearance in February 2015 – pleading guilty to careless driving and hitting two parked cars in icy conditions after a party in Aspen, Colorado.

50. MCLAREN AND 'SPYGATE'

Allegations of espionage in Formula One

Nearly 800 pages of technical information, derived from Ferrari, were found in the possession of a senior McLaren engineer. What would be McLaren's penalty?

It was a visit to a photocopying shop in Walton-on-Thames that triggered it all.

Months later, the McLaren racing team and Lewis Hamilton waited nervously for the judgment of the FIA World Motor Sport Council (WMSC). Would the British-based McLaren team be banned from racing for the remainder of 2007, or indeed for 2008? Would Hamilton retain his lead in the individual drivers' championship or would McLaren team drivers be docked points and Hamilton's chances of sensationally winning the title in his 'rookie' year be dashed?

Ferrari and McLaren were the two top teams in Formula One during 2007.

It was Ferrari, no doubt unwittingly, who started the saga. Nigel Stepney, the team's test and technical manager, had been with Ferrari since 1992. He was part of the 'dream team', with driver Michael Schumacher, credited with the success of Ferrari in the late 1990s. But Ferrari announced a change in team structure in February 2007. Stepney was not happy and thought about getting away from Ferrari. There were allegations of a 'white powder' and sabotage of a Ferrari car at the Monaco grand prix. Stepney was dismissed by Ferrari on 3rd July 2007.

The scope of the story dramatically widened. Ferrari announced, on the same day, that it was taking action in the High Court against an engineer from the McLaren team – later named as Mike Coughlan, their chief designer. A search warrant had been obtained. Coughlan's home in the UK had been searched. He was found to be in possession of 780 pages of Ferrari technical documentation and two computer discs on to which the documents had been copied. The material originated from Ferrari's Maranello factory. Where did the lead come from? Coughlan's wife, Trudy, had taken the material to a photocopying shop in nearby Walton-on-Thames. An observant employee at the shop had spotted that the documents were marked 'confidential' and appeared to belong to Ferrari. He decided to contact the team's headquarters in Italy.

A few days after the announcement, Ferrari dropped its action against Coughlan in return for a promise of full disclosure and co-operation. With a senior engineer at McLaren knowingly in possession of detailed confidential information relating to Ferrari, they had McLaren in their sights instead. Finding out as much as possible about rival car designs, studying race photographs and videos and listening to gossip were everyday occurrences. But had McLaren overstepped the mark? Were they, in effect, guilty of industrial espionage?

McLaren team boss Ron Dennis, fighting for his reputation for integrity and fair play, announced that a full investigation had taken place and asserted: 'No Ferrari intellectual property has been passed to any other members of the team or incorporated into [our] cars'. Coughlan, he said, had acted without their knowledge and on his own. Indeed, there was a strong suspicion that Stepney and Coughlan were colluding not to benefit McLaren but to offer themselves to another team. Honda had even interviewed both of them.

After an internal hearing in Paris, the FIA's WMSC found that McLaren had been in possession of confidential Ferrari information and therefore were technically in breach of motor racing's International Sporting Code – but, since there was no evidence that they had actually used the information, no punishment was levied. The FIA reserved, however, the right to reconvene if any new evidence emerged.

———————————

Ferrari were furious: 'Ferrari find it incomprehensible that violating the fundamental principle of sporting honesty does not have, as a logical and inevitable consequence, the application of a sanction.'

And then came another critical moment. A disaffected employee entered the story – none other than McLaren's own twice-world champion, Fernando Alonso, who was in open conflict with Ron Dennis since he thought Britain's Lewis Hamilton was now getting favoured driver's treatment at McLaren. An angry exchange took place between Alonso and Dennis during qualifying at the Hungarian grand prix Alonso threw in a verbal grenade. He threatened to send to the FIA details of certain email exchanges between himself and Pedro de la Rosa, McLaren's test driver, clearly linking the two drivers with information provided by Mike Coughlan.

'No Ferrari intellectual property has been passed to any other members of the team or incorporated into [our] cars.'

Was this the 'smoking gun'? Ron Dennis himself called FIA chief, Max Mosley, and informed him of the exchanges. He claimed that there was nothing in them – but was this an indication that disclosure, and possible use, of the Ferrari information had gone further into the McLaren organisation than previously imagined?

The FIA decided to reopen its investigation. The three McLaren drivers (Alonso, Hamilton and de la Rosa) were asked to provide evidence against an assurance that, if there was full disclosure, no action would be taken against the drivers personally. Mobile phone records were examined. These revealed that, during the period from 11th March to 3rd July, no fewer than 288 text and email messages and 35 telephone calls were exchanged between Coughlan and Stepney. Some information was passed on to de la Rosa and Alonso. It was clear, as the World Motor Council later stated, that both drivers *knew that this information was confidential Ferrari information and was being received by Coughlan from Nigel Stepney.*

The data received by McLaren covered such detailed matters as Ferrari's brakes, weight distribution, aerodynamic balance and tyre pressures. There was an exchange, for instance, in which de la Rosa asked Coughlan if he knew the weight distribution of the Ferrari because he wanted to test it in McLaren's simulator. But did de la Rosa know about the specific Ferrari documents – or simply that Coughlan and Stepney spoke together as long-term friends?

McLaren were charged again under motor racing's International Sporting Code which made it an offence to commit 'any fraudulent conduct or any act prejudicial to the interests of any competition, or to the interests of motor sport'. There was no requirement that a party must have been advantaged by the use of documents – although this would undoubtedly aggravate the offence. However, did the integrity of the sport require a severe penalty?

McLaren were found guilty by the FIA's WMSC. An extraordinary meeting of the WMSC was held in Paris in September. They concluded that '*some degree of sporting advantage was obtained, though it may forever be impossible to quantify that advantage in concrete terms*'. What would be the penalty? The WMSC decided to inflict a heavy punishment on McLaren because '*there was an intention on the part of a number of McLaren personnel to use some of the Ferrari confidential information in its own testing*'.

The WMSC announced that McLaren would lose all points in the 2007 constructors' championship – but not in the drivers' championship. Hamilton retained his three-point lead in the title race. The team would also be open to examination to prove that there was no Ferrari 'intellectual property' in their cars next year before racing.

In addition, to initial gasps, McLaren were fined $100 million. It was the largest fine ever imposed in sporting history.

Bernie Ecclestone later said that McLaren were 'minutes away' from being thrown out of the World Championships of 2007 and 2008. 'A few of us sort of battled on and campaigned for the fine instead.' Conscious, no doubt, that Hamilton's success and the dramatic battle for the drivers' title were of enormous commercial value to Formula One as a sport.

To many, including former champion Jackie Stewart, the punishment did indeed seem harsh when weighed against the fact that there was no concrete evidence that McLaren benefited in any significant way from the Ferrari information. And why weren't Ferrari also to blame for the actions of Stepney, who disclosed the information in the first place? But sport's ability to decide for itself in its own best interests is what the 'autonomy of sport' means. This was a classic case of a disciplinary issue being dealt with 'within the sport'.

Legally, the punishment could have been challenged if it was clearly disproportionate. McLaren claimed that it was and threatened to appeal. Ron Dennis could 'not accept that we

It was the largest fine ever imposed in sporting history.

deserve to be penalised or our reputation damaged in this way'. After a few days, McLaren announced that it would not do so, saying that further actions and hearings would be damaging to the sport. The show should go on – on the track.

In 2008 racing resumed on the track. Ferrari and McLaren settled their differences. The parties 'agreed to bring the various disputes between them in relation to this matter to a final conclusion'.

The drivers' world championship in 2007 went to the last grand prix of the season in Brazil. By an irony (or was it justice?) the championship was won by Ferrari's Kimi Raikkonen, who won the last two races to clinch the title by one point ahead of McLaren's Lewis Hamilton and Fernando Alonso.

51. DWAIN CHAMBERS AND CHRISTINE OHURUOGU

Two British runners, bans and Beijing

Two British athletes returned from bans for drug-related offences. Two potential medal contenders. Could Christine Ohuruogu or Dwain Chambers overturn the lifetime eligibility ban imposed by the British Olympic Association and go to the Olympics in Beijing?

Dwain Chambers settled into his starting blocks for the 100 metres final at the British Olympic trials in July 2008. This was his chance. Ten seconds later came his victory roar amid the sound of the crowd. Ten seconds dead, well within the Olympic qualifying time of 10.21 seconds for the 100 metres. He was Britain's top-ranked sprinter again and was a potential medal contender. But would he be going to Beijing?

The British Olympic Association (BOA) said: 'No'. Chairman Colin Moynihan was adamant: 'There will be no room for cheats in the British team as long as I am involved with the BOA.'

'There will be no room for cheats in the British team as long as I am involved with the BOA.'

The governing rule was bye-law 45 of the National Olympic Committee of the BOA, a bye-law first introduced in March 1992 under the chairmanship of Arthur Gold and promoted by Britain's leading athletes as 'Gold's law'. The BOA had failed to persuade the International Olympic Committee (IOC) to adopt the rule generally. Britain would , though, carry on with its rule:

'Any person who has been found guilty of a doping offence… shall not… thereafter be eligible for consideration as a member of a Team GB… in relation to any Olympic Games.'

An exception could be made if the offence was 'minor' or there were 'significant mitigating circumstances'. There were none here. Chambers could only beat the ban by fighting it in court. Within the following year, two leading British athletes would stand before courts or tribunals challenging the BOA in their pursuit of places in Beijing.

First, Christine Ohuruogu. Born in east London and pride of Newham and Essex Beagles, her breakthrough came as a 21 year-old at the 2006 Commonwealth Games in Melbourne when she stormed past the Olympic and World champion, Tonique Williams, to win a stunning gold in the 400 metres. Triumph turned to personal disaster later in the same year.

She fell foul of the random 'out-of-competition' drug testing rules introduced by the International Association of Athletics Federations (IAAF). Athletes registered in the testing pool with the IAAF were now obliged to provide 'whereabouts information' for one hour a day, five days a week – a measure to counter the activities of 'cheats' (athletes like Dwain Chambers himself in his BALCO days) whose use of drugs was designed to be out of the athlete's system by the day of competition itself. Three missed tests and severe sanctions apply.

Not difficult? Twice within a period of nine months during 2005 and 2006, a doping control officer from UK Sport had turned up at the location scheduled that day for Ohuruogu's training. She had been training elsewhere and had forgotten to update her schedule. Two missed tests.

Ohuruogu's bad luck (or neglect) continued in July 2006. The Mile End Stadium was the declared location for her training that day between 11am and 12 noon. But there was a school sports day! Her coach had called early that morning to say she would have to train at the Crystal Palace stadium instead. The doping officer turned up at the Mile End Stadium to conduct a test. It was a third missed test. She was in trouble.

Ohuruogu was called before the disciplinary committee of UK Athletics and found guilty of an anti-doping violation. She was suspended from competition for one year, which was the fixed penalty for this offence under the rules of the IAAF.

Christine Ohuruogu was deeply upset. Her career was in jeopardy. She complained that the penalty was unfair. Britain's world triathlon champion, Tim Don, had received only a three-month ban in 2006 under the triathlon association's rules for his missed tests. A one-year ban for Ohuruogu was disproportionate. It should be struck down. She appealed to the Court of Arbitration for Sport (CAS) to over-rule, or at least reduce, this ban. Should she succeed?

CAS upheld the one-year ban. The IAAF rules were clear and one year was within the range of punishment permitted by the World Anti-Doping Agency (WADA) Code. CAS added that there was no suggestion that Ohuruogu was guilty of taking drugs to enhance her performance: '*This case can be viewed in all the circumstances as a busy young athlete being forgetful.*' Nevertheless, the suspension '*was proportionate and should not be disturbed*'. It should serve:

'*... as a warning to all athletes that the relevant authorities take the provision of 'whereabouts' information extremely seriously as they are a vital part in the ongoing fight against drugs in the sport.*'

Christine Ohuruogu was 'totally stunned by the decision'. (Echoes of Rio Ferdinand's reaction to the penalty imposed on him for missing a drugs test at Manchester United while shopping at Harvey Nichols.) Ohuruogo's dream of going to Beijing was in tatters.

Ohuruogu served her one-year ban. She returned to athletic competition in August 2007 ... and promptly caused a major upset when, in only her second meeting since the ban, she sensationally won the 400 metres at the World Championships in Osaka. The dream of Beijing was still there – except for the major obstacle of the continuing lifetime ban imposed by the BOA on athletes found guilty of a doping offence. So, back to a tribunal.

She appealed to an independent BOA Panel chaired by Nicholas Stewart QC. Could she show that there were 'significant mitigating circumstances'? Surely there was a difference between an offence for, innocently, missing tests compared with actually being a drug cheat? Indeed, there had been a record of successful appeals – at least 25 athletes (including Tim Don) had previously satisfied the 'minor' or 'mitigating circumstances' criteria. But an offence carrying a one-year ban was of a different order.

The Appeals Panel decided: 'Yes'. There had been no intent to avoid the rules. This, however, was not enough on its own to support her appeal. The Appeals Panel nevertheless thought that, with hindsight, more could have been done to train and instruct athletes as to the vital role of 'out-of-competition' testing. It would be very difficult in future for any athlete to claim the benefit of 'teething problems'.

Christine Ohuruogu was fortunate. By such fine margins can sporting fortunes turn. She was free to race in Beijing. One suspects that the BOA were secretly relieved.

It was indeed 'the full enchilada' of performance-enhancing drugs.

Thirty year-old Islington-born Dwain Chambers knew that his case was more difficult. He had been a drug cheat. Former world junior record holder and bronze medallist in the 1999 World Championships, his talent was undoubted. But he had struggled to fulfil his enormous potential at the highest level. He moved to California and in 2002 joined up with a new coach, veteran Remi Korchemny, the Ukranian who coached Valery Borsov to double Olympic sprint glory in 1972. And then Chambers became involved with nutritionist Victor Conte at BALCO ... and a positive test for THG was exposed in August 2003.

The IAAF mandatory ban for a first offence was then two years. (It had formerly been four years but was reduced, primarily for consistency with other sporting bodies, to two by the IAAF in 1997. It has, since 2015, now reverted to four years for most offences in line with the revised WADA Code.)

Chambers had served his two-year ban by August 2005. His first athletics comeback had mixed fortunes. He needed to earn money. He dabbled, unsuccessfully, as an American football player and then, for a bizarre period early in 2008, had a month's trial as a rugby league player with Castleford Tigers. He now wanted to re-establish himself in top-class athletics. His performance at the British Olympic trials, and earlier in the World Indoor Championships, had proven that he was fast enough.

He was also reformed and wanted to help in the campaign against drugs. He persuaded Victor Conte to detail his drugs regime. John Scott, head of UK Sport's anti-drug unit, was enthusiastic: 'This is priceless information. What Dwain is giving us is a unique, detailed and honest account of exactly how sophisticated drug use in athletics has become. The manual of a drug cheat.'

What did it show? Not only had Chambers taken THG but a whole cocktail of performance-enhancing drugs including also: a testosterone/epitestosterone cream, blood-boosting drug EPO, human growth hormone, insulin, a 'wakefulness agent' called modafinil and liothyronine, a synthetic form of thyroid hormone. It was indeed 'the full enchilada' of performance-enhancing drugs. Conte also explained how athletes were continuing to use 'duck and dodge' tactics to get away with cheating.

Sympathy for Chambers was low. For people like Sir Steve Redgrave, the position was clear: 'Every athlete that competes for Great Britain knows the BOA's rules. If an athlete takes the risk of cheating they have to accept the penalties that go with this.'

And yet there was disquiet in some circles. Dick Pound, former president of the World Anti-Doping Agency and noted 'hard man', expressed his concern:

'The sanction for a first offence is a two-year suspension. Chambers has served his ban and I think, depending on your view of criminal justice, if you serve the penalty that was deemed appropriate – for whatever the offence was – you are entitled to be reintegrated into society. The additional penalty of never representing Britain again can be seen as a sanction that is over and above what is in the [World Anti-Doping] Code.'

Emotions ran high. Many of the comments seemed personal to Chambers, fuelled by some of his less diplomatic remarks. To side with Chambers' case was to appear 'soft on drugs'.

Chambers finally made his move. He initiated proceedings on 3rd July 2008. His High Court hearing came on 16th July, four days after his victory in the British Olympic trials and just days before the BOA's final nomination of the team for Beijing. He sought a temporary injunction requiring the BOA to suspend its eligibility rule. Should Dwain Chambers succeed?

Justice McKay gave his judgment on 18th July. The issues were complex and there were arguments on both sides. A full hearing could be held in March 2009, after Beijing. But, in short, Chambers had left it too late. He could have made his legal challenge much earlier than the '11th hour' and enabled the court to assimilate more fully the difficult arguments. On the evidence, he had not yet proved an unreasonable restraint of trade. Justice McKay summed up:

'Many people both inside and outside sport would see this bye-law as unlawful. In my judgment, it would take a much better case than the claimant has presented to persuade me to overturn the status quo at this stage and compel his selection for the Games.' Chambers looked across at his legal counsel who mouthed simply: 'We've lost.' Chambers would not be going to Beijing.

Immediate reaction to the High Court decision was triumphant. Nobody wants to be 'soft' on drugs. But a suspicion remained that the door was still open for a sustained legal challenge to the bye-law. It would come in 2012 after the case involving LaShawn Merritt (see below).

If Dwain Chambers had been in Beijing and run 10.00 in the final, he would have come seventh – well behind Usain Bolt's stunning world record of 9.69 seconds.

As for Christine Ohuruogu, there was Olympic glory in the 400 metres. Her thrilling, surging finish clinched Great Britain's only track victory in Beijing. The gold medal was presented to her by Lord Coe.

52. BLOODGATE AT THE STOOP

Did the wink give it away?

Harlequins were losing against Leinster in the quarter-final of the Heineken Cup. The minutes ticked away. Last ditch efforts were called for, but would this be an unscrupulous step too far? At the centre of the scandal was a legend of English rugby.

From capsule to cover-up; was it a tragedy or a farce? The fake blood capsule was, fittingly, bought from a joke shop – a party store in Clapham offering a packet of 'realistic' liquid blood capsules 'for a bloody mouth' for £3.99. Its use would cost Harlequins a fine of more than £250,000, lead to resignations of the club's chairman and director of rugby (an icon of the sport), result in career-threatening bans and damage deeply the reputation of rugby union.

At the centre of the storm was Dean Richards, former policeman with the Leicester Constabulary but better known for his 48 caps for England during the 1980s and 1990s as one of all-time great number eights – six times a player with the British Lions, stalwart of Leicester Tigers and now the Harlequins' director of rugby.

It was the wink that gave it away. Harlequins were losing 5-6 to Leinster at the Stoop in the Heineken Cup quarter-final in April 2009. Tom Williams, a second-half substitute for the Quins, came off with 'blood' around his mouth and with 10 minutes of the game left. Fly-half Nick

As he left the field, Williams gave a wink in the direction of his teammates on the bench. Was there something dodgy going on here?

Evans, previously substituted for an injury, was able to return to the field as a 'blood substitute'. He was a specialist goal kicker. It gave Harlequins a chance of kicking a drop-goal or penalty to win the match. As he left the field, Williams gave a wink in the direction of his teammates on the bench. It was caught by a watching TV camera. Was there something dodgy going on here?

Quite simply, Harlequins had cheated. There it was on the TV footage. Williams, during a break of play, had gone down on one knee, reached to take something out of his sock and put it into his mouth. Then he dropped it! He picked it up, bit and suddenly 'blood' appeared around his mouth – just as it said on the packet. He was escorted from the pitch by the club's physiotherapist, Steph Brennan.

Events after the match moved from farce to a disturbing, and dangerous, cover-up. A Leinster official was heard to exclaim: 'That's not real blood!' Williams went with the club's match-day doctor, Wendy Chapman, to the physio's room. Match officials attempted to have a look at Williams as Chapman indicated that he had an injury to one of his teeth. One of the officials wiped some drops that had fallen onto Williams' leg and said it was not blood. Left alone with Chapman and panicking that the 'fake' would be exposed, Williams pressed the doctor to cut his lip and produce real blood. Chapman hesitated but did the deed, using a stitch-cutting knife. She later told the tribunal that, when she first examined his mouth, 'there was bleeding' and 'active oozing' of blood from a 'jagged-edged wound'.

Amidst allegations of misconduct, a first hearing of the European Cup Rugby (ERC) disciplinary committee was held in July. Harlequins and Williams concealed the extent of the cover-up and Richards denied any involvement. Williams was banned for a year for fabricating a wound or blood injury. Harlequins were fined €250,000 but payment of one-half of the fine was suspended for two years. The committee found that misconduct claims against Dean Richards, Wendy Chapman and Steph Brennan had not been proven.

The furore continued amidst suspicions of a wider conspiracy and cover-up. Pages of newsprint reported and analysed the 'bloodgate' scandal. Both Williams and the ERC disciplinary officer appealed to the ERC Appeals Committee. Still the full extent of the story and the cover-up was concealed by Harlequins. The club offered to pay Williams 'compensation' for the damage it had caused him and proposed an extended contract. The club's chairman and chief executive outlined the likely consequences for the club of full disclosure. They could be severe, worse than relegation. But Williams was no longer going to keep quiet. 'I felt badly let down by the club,' he said. The following morning, chairman Charles Jillings announced that Dean Richards would be resigning.

The ERC Appeals Committee reported in August 2009 after a 14-hour hearing in Glasgow, chaired by Rod McKenzie. Williams told the full story. He admitted lying at the original hearing. Dean Richards had called him over during the match and said that 'he would be coming off for blood'. Williams was given the blood capsule by Brennan on the field during a break in play. 'I had no real choice in the matter. If I had refused to bite the capsule, Dean might refuse to play me again.'

It was a damning 99-page report by the Appeals Committee. Dean Richards was identified as the '*directing mind*' having '*central control of everything that happened*'. He was *'prepared to try and cheat Leinster out of victory'*. He *'orchestrated'* the cover-up. A three-year ban from participating in any capacity in ERC tournaments was imposed on Richards (and this was later confirmed as a worldwide ban by the International Rugby Board). The reputation of one of the iconic figures of English rugby was, in the words of his counsel, 'burnt to cinders'.

> **The reputation of one of the iconic figures of English rugby was, in the words of his counsel, 'burnt to cinders'.**

In addition to the cover-up, it was revealed that there were four previous occasions in non-ERC tournaments in which Richards and Brennan had fabricated a wound or blood injury. The level of misconduct by its employees 'was of a greater magnitude' than had been established in the original hearing. The fine on Harlequins was increased to €300,000 and made payable in full. Harlequins escaped, however, suspension from the following year's Heineken Cup.

Tom Williams benefited from his decision to 'tell all'. His appeal was upheld and his ban reduced to four months.

The reputation of rugby had fallen to the depths. Even a headline in the *Daily Telegraph* now implored: 'Rugby authorities must act to halt slide into abyss.' It was less than 15 years since rugby union had gone 'professional'. Were the worst fears of opponents of professionalism justified? Is this where a 'win at all costs' philosophy would lead?

Some would ask: how different was this from the deliberate foul, the knowingly false appeal, the deceitful dive to get a penalty, the use of the unseen hand to get the ball illegally out of a ruck or (in football) to score? Was cheating now endemic in professional sport? Yet, for most, the physical use of the knife and the deliberate, pre-meditated plan of deceit, rather than a 'heat of the moment' reaction on the field, were distinguishing features that cast this case into a different category of cheating - let alone the cover-up and lying to a tribunal which could never be justified.

Rugby union seemed at its lowest ebb in 2009, but sport has a remarkable way of recovering from scandals. Sporting excitement and the thrill of competition soon again came to the fore of the public's attention. The 'bloodgate' saga was a tragedy for the individuals involved and would be woven into the history of a famous club - but, already, the lasting memory is of a farce; a farce where the key 'prop' came from a joke shop in Clapham.

Perhaps there was some kind of sporting justice. Coming on to the pitch in place of Williams in that fateful match against Leinster, Nick Evans missed his attempt at a drop-goal and Harlequins lost the quarter-final. Leinster went on to win the Heineken Cup.

53. RICHARD GASQUET

A kiss with Pamela

Richard Gasquet, France's leading tennis player, enjoyed a night out in Miami. Would a kiss have surprising and unfortunate consequences?

Richard Gasquet would remember his night out in Miami in March 2009. The 23 year-old, ranked number one in France, was one of the world's leading tennis players. Tennis fans recalled his epic match at Wimbledon in 2008 with Andy Murray when the Scot came back from two-sets down to win an enthralling contest on Centre Court. The following March, the top men's circuit had moved to Miami. Gasquet's every move that night would later be subject to scrutiny in the Court of Arbitration for Sport (CAS).

The Frenchman had developed a shoulder injury and, after a scan, decided that he should withdraw from the Miami Masters tournament. He made, in retrospect, a foolish decision not to complete the withdrawal formalities that evening (and take any drug test then). Instead, he chose to go out. He would deal with the formalities the following day.

There was a popular French DJ in town, Bob Sinclair, and Gasquet had an invitation to go and see him perform at the *Set* night club. First, Gasquet went with his coach and a colleague to an Italian restaurant, *Vita*, and shared a table with the owner. They eyed a group of four young women on a nearby table and recognised one of them, Francesca Antionitti, a French sports news presenter. Later, they joined the women. Gasquet spoke particularly with a woman known throughout the saga as 'Pamela'. She came from Paris and was on holiday in Miami with two friends. She was also going on to *Set*.

Around midnight, they all went off by foot to the club. They were invited to join Bob Sinclair's table. They stood around talking, drinking and listening to the music. Open jugs of mixed drinks and apple juice were on the table as well as a bottle of vodka and bottles of water. Gasquet drank a glass of vodka and apple juice mixed for him, and later some more apple juice and a bottle of water. He also ordered another vodka and apple juice from the bar. He was attracted to Pamela and spent much of the time with her. At one point, they went upstairs and kissed on a sofa. On their way downstairs, they kissed again. The tribunal later declared that: 'In total, they kissed mouth to mouth about 7 times, each kiss lasting about 5 to 10 seconds.' (Unlikely, so

The tribunal later declared that: 'In total, they kissed mouth to mouth about 7 times, each kiss lasting about 5 to 10 seconds.'

far, to be a story that would have interested the *News of the World*.) Would he regret it all in the morning?

Around 4am, Gasquet was feeling tired but was persuaded by Pamela to go, with the group, to another club, *Goldrush*, where a friend of hers was performing. They went in two taxis, Gasquet sharing with Pamela. *Goldrush* was a strip club. Gasquet decided not to stay long. Before they left, Pamela went to the toilet where she was an unusually long time. When she returned, she had 'replenished her make-up and re-arranged her hair'. Gasquet and Pamela said their goodbyes, including a kiss on the mouth for two or three seconds, and Gasquet caught a taxi, went back to his hotel and slept. In the afternoon, he formally withdrew from the Miami tournament and took a standard urine drug test.

The tennis circuit moved to Europe. In April, he was playing in Barcelona and Rome, and playing well. Then came the letter from the International Tennis Federation (ITF) and the shock. His urine sample in Miami had revealed a very small amount of benzoylecgonine, a cocaine metabolite. It was a doping offence. This was serious. It would be an automatic two-year suspension, for a first offence, unless Gasquet could show no or no significant fault or negligence. How did it happen?

At first, it seemed an extraordinary explanation. Yet, as Sherlock Holmes would say: 'When you have eliminated the impossible, whatever remains, however improbable, must be the truth.' It seemed that Gasquet's contact with Pamela must have been the cause. Subsequent testing, in France, of Pamela's hair by the police revealed evidence of regular use of cocaine (although Pamela denied any use that night in Miami). Although the missing link could not be proved beyond doubt, the ITF Anti-Doping Tribunal decided that: '*it was more likely than not that Pamela's kisses were the source of the player's contamination*'. In the unusual circumstances, Gasquet's suspension was reduced to two-and-a half-months. Both the ITF and Gasquet appealed. It would be for CAS to scrutinise further Gasquet's night in Miami.

The CAS panel met in Lausanne. The ITF pressed for a strict approach to the doping laws. Gasquet, they argued, was not free from fault. He was drinking from open bottles. He went to a club for an event that was known for suspected drug use amongst its audience. There were a number of possible contamination explanations.

Gasquet argued his innocence. The CAS tribunal was satisfied that, due to the minute portion of cocaine, it was unlikely that his drinks had been 'spiked' or that the contamination had resulted from his own recreational use. The most likely explanation was that Pamela was the source. It was probable that, as a regular user, she had taken cocaine at some stage that night. Contamination could have arisen in two ways: transfer of saliva, or transfer of loose particles of cocaine powder clinging on the lips or around the nose for some time after the use of the substance.

The anti-doping programme 'could not impose an obligation on an athlete not to go out to a restaurant where he might meet an attractive stranger whom he might later be tempted to kiss'.

But was Gasquet entirely free from blame? The CAS panel adopted an understanding approach – far more understanding than that shown by its predecessor in the Alain Baxter case. When he met Pamela at the *Vita* restaurant, Gasquet did not know that she would be going to the *Set* nightclub. Members of the panel would not have believed, without the expert evidence now before them, that a kiss could be a means of contamination. Perhaps remembering their own youth, the panel declared that the anti-doping programme: '… *could not impose an obligation on an athlete not to go out to a restaurant where he might meet an attractive stranger whom he might later be tempted to kiss.*' Under the given circumstances, even exercising the utmost caution, Gasquet '*could not have been aware of the consequences of kissing a girl whom he had met in a totally unsuspicious environment. The player therefore acted without fault or negligence.*' His suspension was lifted.

Gasquet regained his form and his top 20 ranking, reaching the Wimbledon semi-finals in 2015. It is not known if he has re-visited the *Set* night club when he played again in Miami – but it seems unlikely. It was a kiss he would remember.

54. LASHAWN MERRITT
Performance enhancement and the Olympics

LaShawn Merritt, world-class US athlete, unexpectedly failed a doping test. Could a male enhancement product really be the cause? Would he cease to be eligible for the Olympic Games?

LaShawn Merritt, world 400 metre champion, was anxious to improve his performance – but not, on this occasion, his athletic performance. He purchased a product, ExtenZe, advertised to enhance a man's sexual prowess. It seemed to work for him. It would, though, lead to a ban under the anti-doping rules – and a major challenge to the

International Olympic Committee (IOC). In Britain, the British Olympic Association (BOA) and Dwain Chambers followed proceedings keenly.

Merritt, from Virginia in the USA, was a promising junior whose senior career matured into gold with victory in the 400 metres at the 2008 Olympic Games in Beijing, together with another gold medal for the US in the 400 metres relay. Successor to Michael Johnson, he confirmed his status at the pinnacle of his event by winning the 2009 World Championships in Berlin. Now, though, he was in his off-season. Time for the 25 year-old to relax.

After an evening at a night club in October 2009, he went into a local 7-Eleven store. He had seen the commercials claiming that ExtenZe helped you 'last longer and stay firmer'. He sought those qualities when dating his girlfriend. Content with the outcome, he bought the product on a number of occasions over the next few months. A witness at one 7-Eleven store recalled that Merritt's habit was typically to purchase 'a lottery ticket and jungle juice' before purchasing condoms and ExtenZe. All seemed well in Merritt's life.

Until March 2010, when an out-of-competition test by the US Anti-Doping Agency (USADA) unexpectedly proved positive. Merritt had been drug-tested extensively throughout his career and all tests previously had been negative. His first reaction was that the problem must have been caused by a skin cream that he had recently started using for acne. He shared this information with USADA but a sample tested negative. It then occurred to Merritt that the cause might just possibly have been ExtenZe. He bought another 4-pill packet, looked at the label and his heart sank. The listed ingredients included DHEA and pregnelone, both steroid derivatives and the 'offending' drugs revealed by his test.

What would be his penalty? Would it be the maximum two-year ban for a first offence then applicable under the World Anti-Doping Code (WADA)? Somewhat embarrassed and humiliated, Merritt faced the North American Court of Arbitration for Sport Panel. The panel had some sympathy. It decided that the penalty should be reduced to 21 months of ineligibility. Merritt was negligent (in not looking at the label) but not significantly negligent in the circumstances. There was no intention to dope. He was not attempting to enhance sport performance and no competitive advantage was gained.

A major question remained for Merritt. Would he now be ineligible to retain his title at the Olympic Games in 2012? His 21-month suspension would end in July 2011 - but he fell squarely within the rule passed by the IOC in June 2008 in Osaka, Japan (known as Rule 45 or the Osaka rule) to the effect that an athlete banned for more than six months by any anti-doping organisation for a doping violation would not be eligible for the following Olympic Games in his/her sport. Was the rule invalid as being in excess of the maximum ban under the WADA Code? It was vital issue – both for Merritt and for Olympic sport. The issue escalated to a challenge between the US Olympic Committee (USOC) and the IOC before the full Court of Arbitration for Sport (CAS) in 2011.

Legal Question: Was IOC's Rule 45, making an athlete ineligible for the following Olympic Games, invalid and unenforceable if the purported ineligibility went beyond the maximum two-year ban prescribed by the WADA Code?

For: USOC (on Merritt's behalf)) argued strongly that Rule 45 constituted a sanction on athletes and was not simply an eligibility rule. It was contrary to the WADA Code (which all signatories had agreed to observe) because, going beyond a maximum two-year ban, it constituted a substantive change to the Code which had not been agreed in accordance with the Code. It also violated the principle of 'double jeopardy'.

Against: The IOC appealed to higher values. As a unique institution, it promoted the universal values and principles of Olympism. It had a social mission that transcended the governance of sport and aimed to educate the youth of the world. Rule 45 was an eligibility and not a disciplinary rule. It pursued a different purpose from an anti-doping sanction. It was appropriate given the special nature of the Olympics.

Decision: The CAS Panel gave its verdict. Rule 45 was *invalid and unenforceable*. The Panel was satisfied that the Rule had the nature and inherent characteristics of a sanction:

'Being prevented from participating in the Olympic Games, having already served a period of suspension, certainly has the effect of further penalising the athlete and extending that suspension.'

Or, as the North American court had put it: 'If it looks like a duck, walks like a duck and quacks like a duck, it is a duck. ' As a signatory to the WADA Code, the IOC was obliged to observe its terms. The rule constituted an (unagreed) substantive change because the period of ineligibility for a first offence now became more than two years. If the IOC wanted to maintain this rule, it should propose an amendment to the WADA Code which could then be considered in that context. Incorporation in the Code would also remove any claim of 'double jeopardy'.

LaShawn Merritt was reprieved; he was eligible to compete in the London 2012 Games.

Where did this leave Dwain Chambers and the BOA's more severe rule that athletes banned (for more than six months) for a doping offence would not be eligible to

Or, as the North American court had put it: 'If it looks like a duck, walks like a duck and quacks like a duck, it is a duck.'

represent Britain in any future Games? Surely the BOA's lifetime ban was similarly invalid? By a convoluted process, the issue came before CAS in early 2012 following a challenge by WADA that the BOA's rule was non-compliant with the agreed WADA Code.

The BOA's legal team argued, nobly, that there were distinctions between the BOA rule compared with the Merritt case. The BOA rule (taken with its in-built appeal process) meant that it caught only athletes who had been deliberate cheats (such as Dwain Chambers) and not accidental violations (such as Merritt's). It was, moreover, a selection policy by an autonomous national body rather than a generally applicable sanction flowing from the doping conviction. All now hopelessly in vain. The three-man CAS Panel was identical to that which had decided the Merritt case. CAS unsurprisingly held that the BOA rule was 'in substance' an additional sanction and therefore an unagreed change to the WADA Code.

The CAS Panel again left open the door that a sanction of non-eligibility for one or more Olympic Games might be possible, but would have to be incorporated in the WADA Code by agreement of the signatories and not stand outside the WADA Code. Defeat for the BOA was inevitable. (Both the IOC and the BOA said that they would be pressing for increased sanctions during the then next revision of the WADA Code.)

Dwain Chambers joined LaShawn Merritt, and several others, as eligible for the London 2012 Games. LaShawn Merritt would now be concentrating on his athletic performance.

In the London 2012 Olympics, Dwain Chambers qualified for the 100 metres semi-finals but failed to make the final. LaShawn Merritt failed in defence of his 400 metres title, limping away with a hamstring strain in his heat.

Chapter Seven

SPORT AND BUSINESS

Business and sport, particularly professional sport, have become inextricably linked.

Leading companies spend substantial sums on promoting their products or corporate image through an association with major sporting events, teams or personalities. Significant commercial arrangements are made including television and other broadcasting deals, sponsorship and official supplier arrangements, licensing and merchandising contracts. Corporate hospitality has become a significant source of income. Individual sporting stars have become 'hot property', able to exploit their reputation and image through profitable sponsorship, product endorsement and merchandising deals.

This explosion of commercial activity has inevitably led to numerous legal disputes which have been fought in the courts. Our journey takes us to an evocative range of sporting events, including horse racing in Australia, Formula One motor racing, Euro 2000 football in Holland, souvenir selling outside Highbury stadium and golf at Augusta.

55. AN OUTSIDE RADIO BROADCAST

An unusual horse racing commentary position

Should a racecourse owner be entitled to prevent broadcasting from private land opposite the course?

George Taylor lived on a road opposite the Victoria Park racecourse on the outskirts of Sydney. His front lawn was the unlikely scene for a dispute in 1937, in the early days of sports broadcasting, which would significantly affect the legal basis for the commercialisation of sport.

The course at Victoria Park had been opened in 1908 by Sir James John Joynton Smith, a keen sportsman. Built on reclaimed land, it had become a leading centre for horse and pony racing with significantly better facilities than those at the previously disreputable pony tracks. Prior to the 1930s, Victoria Park had also been the scene of historic aviation activity. In December 1909, an Englishman, Colin Defries, made an attempt there at the first powered air flight although his flight only reached an altitude of 15 feet. It ended in a crash landing after 100 yards when he lost control grabbing for his hat blown off in the wind.

Most of the racecourse at Victoria Park was, in 1937, surrounded by an 11-foot high weatherboard fence. It was bounded on the east side by Dowling Street. George Taylor owned a cottage and land on Dowling Street on the opposite side from the racecourse. With a canny eye on some useful income, Taylor allowed a broadcasting company, the Commonwealth Broadcasting Corporation, to build a platform on scaffolding, about 16 feet high, on his front lawn.

From the platform on Taylor's land, a person could see the whole of the racetrack – including the notice boards showing the names and positions of the competing horses. An employee of the broadcasting company watched the races through his field glasses and gave a running commentary into a microphone connected with a transmission station. The commentary, mingled with advertisements, was broadcast 'live' to the public in Sydney and surrounding districts.

Taylor allowed a broadcasting company to build a platform on scaffolding, about 16 feet high, on his front lawn.

The racecourse owners of Victoria Park

were outraged. No permission had been given for this broadcast. They did not want any outside broadcasting from the course. It encouraged betting to take place off course rather than at the track. Plus it could seriously damage spectator attendances at the racecourse and admission receipts. It violated their 'rights'. But what rights?

The racecourse owners brought a legal action to stop this broadcasting from Taylor's land. It became a major case and it would go to the High Court of Australia.

Legal Question: Should the racecourse owners be entitled to prevent broadcasting taking place from facilities constructed outside the territory of the racecourse itself?

For: No permission had been given for the broadcasting. It could prejudicially affect the owner's business at the racecourse. Attendances were likely to be affected. The activity, which was not a natural use of Taylor's residential property, interfered with the proper use and enjoyment of the racecourse. The racecourse owners had spent considerable sums building up the business and goodwill in the racecourse as a sporting venue. The activities on Taylor's land violated the rights which the racecourse owners had in the business and its commercial exploitation.

Against: The construction of the platform on Taylor's land and its use were perfectly lawful. There was no exclusive right or property in the races, or any of the information being displayed, which prevented an outsider simply describing what he could see. There was no trespass onto the racecourse. It was simply exploitation by Taylor of his own land. The broadcasting should be allowed to continue.

Decision: The court decided in George Taylor's favour. He could not be stopped.

The activities of Taylor and the broadcasting company had not infringed any legal right of the racecourse owners. There was no wrong in describing what took place on the racecourse. Chief Justice Latham set out the position succinctly: '*I am unable to see that any right of the plaintiff has been violated or any wrong done to him.*' He added, critically: '*A 'spectacle' cannot be 'owned' in any ordinary sense of the word.*' There was no proprietary right in a sporting event.

George Taylor could continue with his activities. The owners of the Victoria Park racecourse would have to build a higher fence.

This case arose in the early days of broadcasting and the commercialisation of sport. It was an important decision since it denied any general 'property' right in a sporting event as such. English and Commonwealth law was forced to take a different direction from that taken in certain other countries – including the USA where the courts have been much readier to establish rights for sports events organisers.

As a result, a sports event organiser in the UK can only create valuable 'rights' by a series of measures mostly centred on the right to control entry to the venue itself and the contract conditions which apply to those who do enter – whether spectators, participants, broadcasters, sponsors or others. For instance, it is only by the contract of admission, the all-important ticket, that spectators and others can be restricted from unauthorised broadcasting, photography, sponsorship activity and merchandise selling.

> 'A 'spectacle' cannot be 'owned' in any ordinary sense of the word.' There was no proprietary right in a sporting event.

Would the analysis in 1937 have been different if the court could have foreseen the explosion in sports broadcasting which would take place later in the century? Little did George Taylor know that he was shaping the law of sport.

56. THE PGA

Hospitality at the Ryder Cup

Could the PGA prevent an unauthorised company using the term 'Ryder Cup Hospitality Village' to cash in on the event?

The Ryder Cup has become one of the great sporting events of the world. The golf competition is held on a biennial basis between professional golfers from the USA and Europe and involves many of the best players in the world.

The Ryder Cup at Muirfield Village golf course in Columbus, Ohio in 1987 had seen the first victory for Europe on American soil. The next match was due to be held in September 1989 at the Belfry course near Birmingham in England. The tournament was being organised by the Professional Golfers Association (PGA). Interest in the event had never been greater.

Hospitality at the Ryder Cup, as with other major sports events, was much in demand. As the High Court later noted, long gone were the days when 'a cup of hot soup on a cold wet day and perhaps some shelter at midday' was all that was required. Hospitality operations and services offered to customers had become extensive: food, refreshment, seating and marquees along with highly-prized admission tickets. The provision of hospitality had become a profitable business activity. The PGA had appointed Keith

Prowse to be the sole agent for the provision of hospitality on the course and for the sale of tickets for the 1989 match at the Belfry.

Brochures, however, started in early 1988 to be issued by another company, Ryder Cup Hospitality (RCH), founded by Marcus Evans. These offered tickets to potential customers and

Long gone were the days when 'a cup of hot soup on a cold wet day and perhaps some shelter at midday' was all that was required.

advertised special facilities in what was described as 'the Ryder Cup Hospitality Village' located at a 'prime course site location'. Potential customers were invited to enquire at the 'Ryder Cup Hospitality sales office'.

The PGA and Keith Prowse, alarmed at these advertisements, brought legal action in an attempt to prevent RCH from using the expression 'Ryder Cup Hospitality' in their promotional offerings. They alleged that RCH were, in effect, parasitically taking advantage of the business goodwill built up by the PGA in the Ryder Cup. It was a form of what has since been termed 'ambush marketing'.

Legal Question: Should the PGA be able to prevent the use of 'Ryder Cup Hospitality' by RCH in its advertisements?

For: The provision of hospitality was part of the business of the PGA in staging the Ryder Cup. It had built up substantial goodwill in that business. RCH's brochure was deliberately suggesting an 'official' association with the tournament and so take advantage of the PGA's goodwill. It was misleading and potentially harmful to the official hospitality providers, Keith Prowse, who could lose business and reputation. The PGA should be able to take action to protect the exclusivity which it offered its official suppliers.

Against: 'Ryder Cup' was not a registered trademark. It was simply a description of the event. There was nothing to prevent RCH providing hospitality facilities at a location alongside the course. It was not breaching any condition of entry on to the course.

Decision: The PGA won. A preliminary injunction was granted by the court to restrain Evans and RCH from using the name 'Ryder Cup Hospitality Village' in their promotions. The court was satisfied that the use of these terms would create '*a serious risk that the hospitality services offered will be associated by those to whom they are addressed with [the PGA] and Keith Prowse*'. There was a material risk of potential customers being confused or misled. This is the kernel of what the lawyers quaintly call 'passing off'.

Evans and RCH were also stopped from reselling tickets in breach of the original ticket conditions.

Keith Prowse and the PGA were happy. The match at the Belfry was another great contest, resulting in a 14–14 tie. Europe retained the Ryder Cup.

'Ambush marketing' can take a variety of forms and on many occasions it is difficult to assert that it is wrongful. Sports event organisers try to protect against unauthorised activity of third parties by registering trademarks and by use of copyright logos and designs. Enforcement is then easier. 'Ryder Cup' itself was not then a registered mark (it now is). Although this was only a temporary injunction pending a full trial, this decision was important. It did demonstrate a willingness of the courts to intervene to prevent 'ambush marketing' where it crossed the line.

The remedy, though, is not quick or certain. As far as the London 2012 Olympics were concerned, legislation was introduced to give stronger and more specific protection. An exceptional 'London Olympics Association Right' was created. Broad in scope, this prohibited the use of any visual or verbal representation in a manner likely to create in the mind of the public an association with the 2012 London Olympics. It covered, specifically, use of words such as 'games', '2012', 'gold' and 'medals'. Many other major events would greatly welcome similar protection.

Event owners must constantly be wary and vigilant. At the Ryder Cup in 2010 at Celtic Manor in Wales, bookmaker Paddy Power attempted to 'ambush' the event with a 270ft promotional Hollywood-type sign on a hillside overlooking the course, a stunt in which they had succeeded at the Cheltenham Festival earlier that year. Celtic Manor owner Terry Matthews said: 'It's just disgraceful that genuine backers of the event can be usurped in such a fashion.' An injunction brought by the local council on planning grounds forced the betting firm to take down the sign.

57. TIGER WOODS

A Master of Augusta

Should Tiger Woods be entitled to prevent the commercial sale of a painting exploiting his image at Augusta?

The fairways of Augusta National were their usual glorious emerald green in April 1997 for The Masters. The course was set majestically, the cathedral in the pines.

As ever, a sense of history pervaded this event – the first of the golf majors and the one where the previous winners of the coveted 'green jacket' are invited to return each year. This was destined to be Tiger Woods' year.

Eldrick 'Tiger' Woods, aged 21, was playing for the third time in The Masters. After a glittering amateur career, Woods was marked out for sporting greatness. The previous year, his first as a professional, he had failed to make the halfway cut. In 1997, however, he was a sensation. After a shaky start, he played superb golf over the last three-and-a-half rounds and destroyed the field – winning by 12 shots over his nearest rival. He became the youngest ever winner. His score of 270 was the lowest in the history of the tournament (now tied with Jordan Speith's similar score in 2015).

———

Rick Rush is an artist from Alabama. He became known as 'America's Sports Artist'. In 1998, he produced a painting commemorating Woods' 1997 victory. Entitled 'The Masters of Augusta', the painting consisted of three distinctive perspectives of Woods in front of the Augusta National clubhouse. Depicted against a light blue background were shadowy images of Arnold Palmer, Sam Snead, Jack Nicklaus and other previous great winners of The Masters. Behind them could be seen The Masters' leaderboard. The painting was to be sold commercially as a limited edition print including a set of 5,000 lithographs. The narrative accompanying the print said that the painting featured Tiger Woods 'displaying that awesome swing' and 'flanked by his caddie and final round player partner's caddie'.

What should the law favour? Protection of the rights of a sportsman against the unauthorised commercial exploitation of his image or freedom of expression?

Woods had not been involved in any of this. He had not given permission for any painting. Were any of his rights infringed? Woods' licensing company, ETW Corp, complained that the painting, without Woods' permission, wrongfully exploited the rights of Woods in his image or his right of publicity under Ohio law. They sought to prevent any commercial sale of the painting.

It became a classic case. It encapsulated a significant, and difficult, issue. What should the law favour? Protection of the rights of a sportsman against the unauthorised commercial exploitation of his image or freedom of expression? One of the world's richest sportsmen and his commercial machine against the 'little' man, the creative, small town painter.

Rick Rush said: 'I believe these events are in the public domain. I want to capture the sporting lifestyle.' Media organisations lined up to back the artist. 'Mr Woods' extraordinary accomplishments give rise to many benefits and a few burdens. One of the burdens … is having to see himself depicted in words and pictures by people who have things to say about him.'

Lawyers for Woods countered: 'When a painting is done and hung on the wall, that may be acceptable but when you commercialise that person's image, you cross the line.' What should prevail?

The issue was fought, ultimately, in the US Court of Appeals in Cincinnati.

Legal Question: Should Tiger Woods be able to prevent the commercial sale of a painting which exploited his image?

For: The painting depended on the image of Woods for its basic subject matter. It used the name of Tiger Woods in the accompanying description to assist the selling of the painting. The painting was for commercial sale, designed to produce a financial benefit utilising the image of Woods. The financial benefits would be solely for the publishers and the painter, not Woods. This should not be permitted without his consent.

Against: This was an artistic work. Woods had no copyright in the painting. That belonged to the artist. The use of his name was a description and not use as a trademark. The concept of a sportsperson's 'image rights' did not extend to prevent all commercial use of his image. Any such concept should not override the general principle of freedom of expression, particularly for an artistic work.

Decision: Woods lost. The US Court of Appeals decided, by a 2-1 majority, against Woods. Woods could not assert trademark rights in every photograph and image of himself. He had no 'image rights' which outweighed the freedom of artistic expression which was a principle of US law. Judge James Graham concluded:

'After balancing the societal and personal interests embodied in the First Amendment against Woods' property rights, we conclude that the effect of limiting Wood's right of publicity in this case is negligible and significantly outweighed by society's interest in the freedom of artistic expression.'

Rick Rush could sell his paintings.

This decision, controversial in many quarters, was based specifically and narrowly on US law which emphasised the priority of the First Amendment to the US Constitution over the 'rights of publicity' of an individual under Ohio law. However, it was significant because the law in most US States has a more developed concept of a 'right of publicity', an exclusive right of a celebrity to exploit commercially his or her image, than exists under English law.

58. BSKYB'S BID FOR MANCHESTER UNITED

A marriage of broadcasting and football?

What could stop Rupert Murdoch's BSkyB from acquiring Manchester United?

Sport attracts investment by 'big business'. Football clubs, in particular, have since the early 1990s been a magnet for the attention and money of major investors – both individual and corporate. And there is no bigger club than Manchester United.

Perhaps Rupert Murdoch envied the position of Italy's Silvio Berlusconi, head of his own television and media empire and majority owner of AC Milan. Or possibly Murdoch's thoughts were first stirred by the memory of Michael Knighton on the pitch at Old Trafford in 1989 celebrating, he thought, a successful deal with Martin Edwards to acquire Manchester United for £20 million.

With hindsight, if it had gone through, Knighton's bid would have been the deal of the century. It failed. Manchester United's shares were instead floated publicly on the London Stock Exchange in 1991. The club had entered the world of high finance, stock exchange regulation and exposure to a potential takeover bid. The duties of the parent company's directors were now to enhance 'shareholder value'. Manchester United was no longer simply a football club.

In 1998, Murdoch spotted his opportunity. As principal shareholder in News Corporation which in turn owned BSkyB, Murdoch recognised clearly how the fortunes of football and subscription television were closely connected. The Premier League, founded in 1992, was enjoying the revenues from its TV broadcasting deal with BSkyB which was thriving on the millions of subscribers attracted to its packages by the 'battering ram' of its exclusive TV access to live premier football.

Manchester United was no longer simply a football club.

On 7th September 1998, to an unprepared and astonished sporting world, BSkyB and Manchester United announced that they were involved in takeover talks. Two days later, Manchester United's board of directors announced that they were recommending the acceptance of BSkyB's bid of £623 million to its shareholders. The offer was too good to refuse.

Murdoch was, to many outside observers, being as shrewd as ever. BSkyB already had the exclusive rights to live screenings of Premier League matches until 2001. Ownership of Manchester United would strengthen BSkyB's

The bid for Manchester United appeared to be a classic 'each-way bet' for BSkyB.

influence and position in any future negotiations with the Premier League for the sale of its broadcasting rights. Indeed, as owner of Manchester United, BSkyB would share directly in a proportion – a relatively significant proportion – of the revenues which it itself paid for the rights!

In addition, there was a real possibility that the system of collective sale by Premier League clubs of broadcasting rights centrally through the Premier League might be broken up – in favour of each club being free to negotiate independently the sale of broadcasting rights to its own home matches. The system was being reviewed by the then Office of Fair Trading and the Restrictive Trade Practices Court. If the decision went against the collective sale system established by the existing rules, what better position for BSkyB to be in than owner and controller of the rights to Manchester United, the club with the greatest support and commercial reach in the country? The bid for Manchester United appeared to be a classic 'each-way bet' for BSkyB.

The press, and the fans, reacted with astonishment – many with considerable anger and fury. Protests mounted. The club's fans attempted to campaign through the Independent Manchester United Supporters' Association. But it was now in the world of corporate takeovers. What could effectively be done to stop the sale? A majority of the shareholders seemed to favour the bid which the board were recommending. Success of the bid appeared certain.

Then, to the surprise of many, the UK Government decided to intervene through the Secretary of State for Trade, Peter Mandelson. He used powers under legislation which enabled significant acquisitions and mergers to be referred to a body then called the Monopolies and Mergers Commission (MMC) and, if necessary, blocked on the grounds of the public interest. During the next four-and-a-half months, the panel of the MMC investigated the proposed acquisition, taking evidence from more than 350 parties.

Issue: Should BSkyB's proposed acquisition of Manchester United be blocked on the grounds of the public interest?

For: If successful, the bid would consolidate BSkyB's already dominant position in the market for live football broadcasting. It would become more difficult for others to make inroads into the industry. In addition, Manchester United's decisions might no longer be based principally on footballing considerations. The club would become a bargaining and marketing tool for a broadcasting company intent on enhancing its dominant position in the pay-TV market.

Against: Manchester United's shareholders should be free to decide what was in their own best interests. The risk of a takeover bid (and the opportunity for shareholders to realise value from a sale of their shares) was an inevitable consequence of the club being listed on the Stock Exchange. BSkyB's acquisition would substantially strengthen the club's financial position and ability to buy players and compete as a football club. The market should be allowed to operate freely.

Decision: The MMC reported in March 1999. They concluded that the proposed merger might reduce competition for the purchase of broadcasting rights to Premier League matches. This would lead to less choice for the Premier League. It would reduce competition in the market for sports premium television channels. On the wider front, the MMC judged that:

'... *the merger would reinforce the existing trend towards greater inequality of wealth between clubs, weakening the smaller ones. The merger would give BSkyB additional influence over Premier League decisions relating to the organisation of football. On both counts, the merger could have an adverse effect on English football. This adverse effect would be more pronounced if the merger led to other mergers between broadcasters and Premier League clubs.'*

The only way of dealing with the full range of public interest concerns, in the view of the MMC, was to prohibit the merger.

Four weeks later, the Secretary of State, by now Stephen Byers, accepted in full the findings and recommendation of the MMC. The takeover was stopped. Murdoch had been foiled at the last minute.

Who would have thought Peter Mandelson and Stephen Byers would be heroes in the homes of Manchester United supporters up and down the country?

Who would have thought Peter Mandelson and Stephen Byers would be heroes in the homes of Manchester United supporters up and down the country?

BSkyB and other broadcasting companies might have been prevented from building up controlling interests but the dynamics of football club ownership were changing. Entrepreneurs and wealthy investors from across the world have taken an increasing interest in the financial prospects of owning Premier League clubs. More than half of the clubs in the Premier League are now under foreign ownership.

Manchester United itself fell into the hands of the family of Texan oil billionaire, Malcolm Glazer, for £790 million in 2005.

59. EDDIE IRVINE

A radio and a doctored photograph

Could Eddie Irvine, leading motor racing driver, stop a radio station using a photograph doctored to suggest he was using its service?

Eddie Irvine was a shrewd businessman. Evidence before the court – in a dispute over a cheeky commercial promotion – suggested that he 'would not get out of bed for less than £25,000'. The decision would have a major effect on a sportsman's 'image rights' in the UK.

The Ulsterman was one of the characters of Formula One racing. In only his second grand prix, he was lapped by the great Ayrton Senna in his McClaren – and, deciding that Senna was then going too slow as Irvine was chasing another back-runner, Irvine overtook Senna and unlapped himself. Senna later let Irvine know that he was not amused! By 1999 Irvine had become a major force in Formula One in the 1990s and was partnering Michael Schumacher at Ferrari. Irvine enjoyed the limelight and it was his most successful racing season. He won four grand prix races and was destined to finish a close second to Mika Hakkinen in Formula One's drivers' championship.

This challenge before the courts, though, was not about a race at Monaco or Monza but a leaflet distributed during that 1999 season by Talk Radio to potential advertisers. Talk Radio, later to become talkSPORT and a not infrequent visitor to the courts, was a commercial radio station whose chairman and chief executive was Kelvin McKenzie, former editor of *The Sun*. It was beginning to make its mark and had acquired radio broadcasting rights to a number of major sporting events, including the Formula One championship. It was trying to build its profile. McKenzie was not afraid of lively marketing techniques.

Talk Radio sent a promotional pack to around 1,000 advertising executives. It was intended to be humorous in nature. Each pack included, for instance, a pair of boxer shorts with a skid mark of the kind a racing car might make. An accompanying

In the 'doctored' version, Irvine appeared to be listening to a radio bearing the words 'Talk Radio' and the company's logo.

leaflet contained pictures of a number of grand prix drivers – and the front cover featured a photograph of Eddie Irvine. The photograph had been obtained legitimately. There was no breach of copyright in the use of the photograph.

But the photograph had been 'doctored'. In the 'doctored' version, instead of holding a mobile phone to his ear, Irvine appeared to be listening to a radio bearing the words 'Talk Radio' and the company's logo. The strapline was 'we've got it covered'.

Irvine complained. The original photograph was of him with a mobile phone. He had not agreed any commercial deal with Talk Radio. The misleading and unauthorised use of his image was wrongful. Talk Radio agreed not to distribute any more of the 'doctored' leaflets, but that was not enough for Irvine. He proceeded to bring a legal action against Talk Radio seeking damages. The claim came before the High Court.

Was it just simple, innocent fun? Or was Talk Radio wrongfully taking advantage of Irvine's reputation for its own commercial use?

Legal Question: Should Talk Radio be liable to pay damages to Irvine on the grounds that the leaflet wrongfully implied that he was endorsing the Talk Radio service? If so, what should be the amount?

For: Irvine had built up valuable goodwill and reputation in his name and image. He had various existing commercial deals to endorse certain products. Talk Radio's leaflet was designed to deceive members of the public to whom it was sent into believing that Irvine was endorsing Talk Radio. This constituted 'passing off' (the legal term for commercial misrepresentation). As to damages, Irvine produced evidence that his endorsement fee, whilst depending on the size of the deal, would normally be substantial; he 'would not get out of bed for less than £25,000'.

Against: The photograph had been lawfully obtained. Its publication was not in breach of copyright. It was clearly a humorous promotion. The leaflet was only sent to a very limited number of recipients. There was no evidence that it would have any effect on Irvine's reputation or his ability to enter into other endorsement deals. In any event, no-one would have paid more than £500 for such a small campaign. It was inappropriate to base damages, if any, on 'fancy' sums which Irvine might secure in commercial endorsement deal.

Decision: Eddie Irvine won. The High Court decided in his favour. The promotional leaflet was a form of misrepresentation, implying wrongfully that Irvine was endorsing

Talk Radio. The court, however, initially awarded just £2,000 in damages. On appeal, Irvine was more successful. The Court of Appeal agreed that £25,000 was the appropriate measure based on Irvine's other endorsement deals. What mattered was the fee which Talk Radio *'would have had to pay to obtain lawfully that which it in fact obtained unlawfully'* – and, possibly, Irvine's assertion as to the amount required to get him out of bed.

The amount of money at stake may have been relatively small, but this was a breakthrough case in sporting law. It gave sportsmen stronger rights to prevent or get money from product advertisements which 'wrongfully' implied their endorsement or an association with a sporting star.

One of the first sportsmen to take advantage of the 'new' right was Ian Botham who sued Diageo over an advertising campaign during the cricket World Cup for Guinness which (without his consent) as a backdrop featured images of Botham's exploits. Botham reportedly obtained a substantial payment in settlement. Boris Becker won a similar claim for damages in Germany following a product advertisement using his image. More indirectly, Oliver Khan and Michael Ballack brought a legal action against a German sex toy manufacturer for unauthorised promotion of 'Olli K' and 'Michael B' sextoys. There was a 'David B' version but the England player decided not to sue after he apparently 'saw the funny side of things'.

In the meantime, Talk Radio had changed its name to talkSPORT. It was soon back in the courts.

60. EURO 2000

talkSPORT and an Amsterdam hotel room

Could the BBC stop talkSPORT from broadcasting a 'live' match at Euro 2000 from a hotel room?

Back to broadcasting and a lively court case involving a broadcaster's attempt to protect its 'exclusive' commercial position. And a reappearance in the courts of the innovative, but somewhat provocative, talkSPORT (to which Talk Radio had changed its name). The setting was Euro 2000 – or was it an Amsterdam hotel bedroom?

The European football championships were taking place in Belgium and the

Netherlands. England were playing Portugal, a key first round match in Group A. The match was being played in Eindhoven. Millions of English fans were watching on television or listening on the radio. Most were tuned into the BBC.

Many, though, were listening to talkSPORT, a UK radio broadcaster focusing heavily on sports coverage. The commentator described the gripping action – Paul Scholes scoring for England after just three minutes but England going down in a dramatic 3-2 win for Portugal. Listeners heard the noise of a football crowd and the ambient sounds of the match.

The commentator was not in the stadium. He was not even in Eindhoven.

The BBC was up in arms at this coverage. Why? Unlike the BBC, Talksport was not an authorised broadcaster in the stadium itself. talkSPORT was operating 'off tube'. The commentator was not in the stadium. He was not even in Eindhoven – but simply commentating from the television footage, transmitted by another broadcaster, shown in an Amsterdam hotel room which had become talkSPORT's studio for the tournament. The ambient crowd sound was not from the match itself. Every 10 minutes or so, an announcement was made: 'This is talkSPORT, not the BBC, with unofficial full match commentary on Portugal v England on talkSPORT, courtesy of our TV monitors at the talkSPORT Amsterdam studio.'

The BBC strongly objected to talkSPORT advertising its Euro 2000 coverage as being 'live'. The BBC, as the only UK radio broadcaster authorised by Euro 2000 in the stadium, argued that the occasional disclaimers did not bring home to listeners that the commentators were located many miles from the action. The BBC brought a legal action in the English courts to stop talkSPORT describing itself as providing 'live' coverage. The dispute came before the High Court.

Was this just a domestic spat? Or did it raise a serious issue? When a broadcaster is appointed by an event organiser and pays substantial sums for 'exclusive' rights, can it prevent an 'off tube' broadcaster from muscling in on the event?

Legal Question: Should the BBC be entitled to prevent talkSPORT describing itself as producing 'live' coverage? Should the BBC be able to claim damages for this misrepresentation by talkSPORT?

For: The BBC was the UK radio broadcaster 'authorised' by Euro 2000. The talkSPORT coverage was misleading. Listeners did not really appreciate that the commentators were not at the ground. The BBC had a long-established reputation as a broadcaster of live sporting events. talkSPORT's claim that its coverage was 'live' devalued the reputation of live coverage of sporting events and could cause damage to authorised

Tonya Harding *(right)* and Nancy Kerrigan avoid each other during practice before the 1994 Winter Olympics in Lillehammer, six weeks after a physical attack on Kerrigan in Detroit. Harding was alleged to have links with the attack. (Case 3)

Newcastle's Lee Bowyer brawls with team-mate Kieron Dyer during a match at St James' Park in 2005. Dyer had not passed the ball to Bowyer. Team-mate Stephen Carr and Aston Villa's Gareth Barry try to stop them. (Case 8)

John Terry arrives at Westminster Magistrates Court in July 2012 to stand trial for alleged racial abuse during a Chelsea match. (Case 9)

England captain Bobby Moore at Mexico City airport in 1970. Moore had been released from house arrest in Bogota. (Case 20)

(Above) Colombian defender Andrés Escobar lies on the ground after scoring an own goal in the World Cup match against the USA in 1994. Ten days later he was shot dead. (Case 23)

The Pakistan cricket team in silence during the 2007 World Cup after the unexplained death of coach Bob Woolmer. (Case 24)

Brazil's Vanderlei de Lima is pushed into the crowd by an interloper, a former Irish priest, when leading the 2004 Olympic marathon. Did it rob him of gold? (Case 43)

Tom Williams of Harlequins walks off (with physio Steph Brennan) to be replaced as 'blood' pours from his mouth during the 2009 Heineken Cup quarter-final against Leinster. (Case 52)

(Above) Manchester United
fans protest against the
board's deal with Rupert
Murdoch's BSkyB, whose bid
looked unstoppable. (Case 58)

London marathon race director
Dave Bedford in his running days.
He was surprised, along with many
others, in 2003 to see runners
advertising the 118 118 telephone
enquiry service. (Case 63)

Renée Richards playing at the US Open after her sex-reassignment surgery. It had been a difficult case for the New York courts. (Case 75)

Jane Couch, the 'Fleetwood Assassin'. She won the WBF lightweight world title at the David Lloyd Club in Raynes Park, London in 1999 ... after becoming the first licensed professional female boxer in Britain. (Case 78)

Darrell Hair, accompanied by co-umpire Billy Doctrove, examines the suspect ball with Pakistan captain, Inzamam-ul-Haq, at the Oval Test in 2006. (Case 80)

Ian Botham and his wife, Kathy, leave the high court during his libel case with Imran Khan in 1996. (Case 89)

Scotland kick off, and celebrate victory after three seconds, in an unusual World Cup qualifying match in Estonia in 1996. (Case 95)

FIFA president Sepp Blatter taps the shoulder of Chuck Blazer at the start of the 2011 FIFA congress at which Blatter was again re-elected. Within six months Blazer would become an informant for the American FBI, leading to the arrests in May 2015 of several FIFA officials. (Case 101)

broadcasters, such as the BBC, who were providing a superior and proper live coverage. The BBC might also lose listeners in due course as a result.

Against: 'Live' simply meant coverage at the same time as the event. The disclaimer made it clear that talkSPORT was coming from its Amsterdam studio. In any event, the BBC had no separate interest which was being damaged. It was simply describing its own activities as a broadcaster. There was no separate goodwill which the law should protect. There was no real risk of financial damage to the BBC.

Decision: The court rejected the BBC's action. It would not intervene. The court did not condone talkSPORT's coverage. It considered that the coverage was '*deceptive*', although it did in a literal sense provide a blow-by-blow account of what was going on at the scene of play. Importantly, however, the court decided that the BBC had no separate interest or goodwill to support an action of this kind. Whilst the BBC has '*a widespread and long established reputation as a broadcaster of live sporting events*', the court did not consider there was '*any protectable goodwill simply in what it does*' to found an action. In addition, there was no real risk of financial damage to the BBC. Any such claim seemed '*fanciful*'. The court decided that the BBC's claim was not sufficient to justify the court's intervention.

In a sense, this was a narrow point. The claim was technically an application for injunctive relief which was always in the court's discretion. More generally, however, this case illustrates again the hurdles which event organisers have to overcome in order to protect 'exclusivity' for their authorised licensees. Authorised licensees demand properly protected exclusivity if they are to pay significant sums for these rights.

For talkSPORT, the case provided some excellent publicity.

61. UP THE GUNNERS!

Matthew Reed and his Arsenal merchandise

Matthew Reed had sold his 'unofficial' souvenirs and merchandise on the street outside Highbury for over 30 years. Could Arsenal stop him now?

Highbury stadium, in north London, was the home of Arsenal FC until 2006. The club had a tradition and following as strong as any club in London. Highbury was the home of 'the Gunners'. It was also the site of Matthew Reed's trading stall.

Reed had been a lifelong supporter. He was also a street trader, one of many lining the streets outside Highbury on match days. He had worked his pitch there for more than 30 years, selling hats, scarves, shirts and other football merchandise.

He had celebrated through his merchandise the great Arsenal stars and triumphs. A number of the scarves and other items bore the legend 'Arsenal', 'Arsenal Gunners' and the club's distinctive shield and cannon design. All part and parcel of the football stadia scene on match days?

Reed had a large sign on his market stall stating that his goods were 'unofficial goods'. The sign went on to state:

'The words or logos … are used solely to adorn the products and do not imply or indicate any affiliation or relationship with the manufacturer or distributor of any other products. Only goods with official Arsenal merchandise tags are official Arsenal merchandise.'

Obviously written by a lawyer!

Arsenal were unhappy with this type of activity. 'Arsenal', 'Arsenal Gunners' and the shield and cannon design were registered in 1989 as trademarks of Arsenal FC. Most of Reed's products, however, were not manufactured by any authorised licensee of Arsenal. The club decided to crack down on sellers of 'unofficial' merchandise such as Matthew Reed. It wanted to exercise full control over the sale of 'Arsenal' merchandise. In January 1999 Arsenal started proceedings against him.

But Reed was stubborn. He strenuously fought the action. 'I might as well go all the way as this will affect a lot of small traders around the country,' said Reed. Indeed, the dispute occupied the time and attention of numerous courts including, extraordinarily, the European Court of Justice. The contest swung to and fro, the result uncertain until the end.

Legal Question: Should Arsenal be entitled to prevent Matthew Reed trading, without permission, in souvenir goods bearing the marks 'Arsenal' and the registered shield and cannon design?

For: The merchandise sold by Reed used the registered marks and logos of Arsenal. The products were not manufactured or sold by any 'official' licensee of Arsenal. They could mislead buyers into thinking that they were buying 'official' merchandise with the approval of Arsenal (and that some of the funds would find their way back to the benefit of the football club). They were not manufactured by any person authorised to use the trademarks. It was as simple as that. Reed, and other offending traders, should stop.

Against: Matthew Reed had been trading outside Highbury for more than 30 years. Customers did not buy the goods because they thought the Arsenal club was the origin of manufacture. They bought them solely because of their support and allegiance to the club. The marks were simply a 'badge of allegiance'. In legal terms, this was not 'trademark use'. Also, Reed had a placard clearly informing people that the goods were not 'official' merchandise. Arsenal made millions of pounds out of merchandising; this was a pin-prick in terms of revenue.

Decision: Losing initially in the UK courts, Arsenal were heading for defeat until rescued by a surprising late goal in the European Court. The court decided that the type of use by Reed could constitute an infringement of Arsenal's trademark. Whilst the court admitted that the use of the marks in this case may not strictly indicate source or origin of manufacture, a number of potential buyers may be confused. Over time, the confusion could damage the marks and weaken their ultimate function as an indication of origin.

The final result in Europe was a victory for Arsenal. But there was still 'extra time' to be played back in the UK courts. One judge thought that the European Court had exceeded its remit. But the Court of Appeal disagreed. It followed the European Court's guidance. Reed's type of use of the marks on his merchandise was an infringement and should be stopped.

This was an important decision, a verdict welcomed by major football clubs and sportswear manufacturers. It gave football clubs and other sporting event organisers control over the sale of merchandise bearing 'official' marks. It indicated a move by the courts to prevent this form of 'ambush marketing'. The case has, however, its limitations. It only applies to the use of official marks. It does not extend to use of marks or indicia which have not been registered – where a claimant has to overcome the stricter tests of 'passing off'. Event organisers and clubs still have much work to do to prevent forms of 'ambush' marketing which benefit from an association with the club or event but which do not employ the use of registered marks or copyright material.

> **Some commentators remarked that Arsenal had been more successful in the courts of Europe than the club's recent campaigns in Europe on the football field.**

Some commentators remarked that Arsenal had been more successful in the courts of Europe than the club's recent campaigns in Europe on the football field.

62. THE FOOTBALL LEAGUE

ITV Digital and the pot of gold

When its TV broadcaster went bust, could the Football League sue the broadcaster's parent shareholders, Granada and Carlton?

Commercial deals relating to sport, as in other fields of business life, depend – or at least their enforcement depends – on contracts. The Football League would discover, much to its cost, that contracts are very important.

No source of revenue is more lucrative to football than the sale of TV broadcasting rights. The fortunes of the Premier League were founded on the vast sums paid by Rupert Murdoch's BSkyB. In 2000, there was growing competition in the market for subscription TV. The Football League, comprising the 72 clubs in the English first, second and third divisions outside the Premier League, was keen to increase its broadcasting income. It was attracted by the prospect of enjoying some of 'the pot of gold'.

The Football League put its broadcasting rights out to tender in 2000. It was excited by the interest shown, particularly by ONdigital. ONdigital (later branded as ITV Digital) had been launched with great fanfare in 1998. It was jointly owned by two major media companies, Granada and Carlton Communications, with each having a 50 per cent share. ONdigital was seeking to challenge BSkyB. As with its rival, it saw football as being a major attraction to pull in subscribers and it hoped in due course to get rights to show Premier League matches. In the meantime, it was prepared to bid high to secure TV rights to the Football League. Very high.

In April 2000, ONdigital proposed an initial bid of around £80 million a year for the TV rights to the Football League. Further discussions took place. On 7th June a bid document, expressed to be 'subject to contract', was submitted by ONdigital with a bid worth around £240 million for a three-year deal. The non-binding bid document included a statement that 'ONdigital and its shareholders will guarantee all funding to the FL [Football League] outlined in this document'.

The tendering process intensified. The Football League thought it could get even more. More negotiations took place. Eventually a deal was done later in June. A binding contract (the June Contract) was entered into with ONdigital – a three-year deal worth, in total, around £315 million: the payments were £12 million on signature; £35.25 million payable within three months; and three annual payments of £89.25 million. The Football League and its member clubs were overjoyed. It did seem that they had found, in effect, a 'pot of gold'. The June Contract did not include any guarantee by the two shareholders, Granada and Carlton.

The commercial world can be tough. The ITV Digital service never really took off. Subscribers could not be found or retained in sufficient numbers. The sums payable for the Football League broadcasting rights were crippling for the new company. It had overpaid and the plug had to be pulled. ITV Digital (as now named) went into administration in April 2002. It gave up its broadcasting licence and payments to the Football League ceased.

Where did that leave the Football League? Chasing the money, fruitlessly.

The Football League and its member clubs were overjoyed. It did seem that they had found, in effect, a 'pot of gold'.

Mitigating its loss, the Football League managed to sign up a replacement deal with BSkyB worth £95 million over four years – substantially less than the deal with ITV Digital. The Football League sought compensatory payments from ITV Digital's two shareholders. Granada and Carlton reluctantly offered a compromise £74 million. The Football League rejected it. The League argued that Granada and Carlton were liable, as guarantors, to pay the full amount – in effect, a claim to recover the Football League's 'loss' of £178.5 million being the additional sums which would have been received by the Football League if the ITV Digital contract had lasted. The Football League decided to take legal action against Granada and Carlton before the High Court. Would the Football League succeed or was it a major tactical error?

The High Court dismissed the Football League's claim. There was no guarantee. The original bid document was clearly made 'subject to contract'. There had been extensive subsequent negotiations. The June Contract did not contain a guarantee and neither Granada nor Carlton were parties. Granada and Carlton were not liable to pay the Football League. Justice Langley was withering in his comments: '*In my judgment the Football League's case remains just as unpromising at the finish as it looked at the start.*'

The Football League was left to count the substantial cost.

The consequences of the ITV Digital collapse were significant. Many clubs in the Football League had overspent in the first year of the deal – using funds expected to be received as their share of the ITV Digital deal which had not yet arrived. Many came close to going out of business. Hundreds of players were transfer-listed across all clubs in an effort, particularly, to reduce wage bills. The Football League – along, no doubt, with other sporting bodies watching the League's precedent – had learnt a tough commercial and legal lesson. Commercial deals can only be enforced if there is a binding contract. And companies can go bust!

The Football League tried to sue its lawyers and recover some of its loss. It claimed damages of £150 million – one of the biggest professional negligence claims ever. It lost. The judge found two minor breaches of duty and awarded damages of just £4, with the Football League being held liable for virtually all legal costs.

The Football League – along, no doubt, with other sporting bodies watching the League's precedent – had learnt a tough commercial and legal lesson.

Heads rolled at the Football League. Although not in office at the time of the original deal, both the chairman (Keith Harris) and the chief executive (David Burns) resigned in August 2002. They paid the price for the way the case had gone. The new chairman was Lord Mawhinney. He remarked simply: 'The collapse of ITV Digital marked a watershed for the Football League and its clubs.'

63. DAVE BEDFORD

'I've got your number'

To the surprise of many, advertisements appeared in 2003 featuring two comic runners bearing a close resemblance to the figure of Dave Bedford, an athlete of the 1970s. Could Bedford stop them?

Dave Bedford was one of Britain's most colourful athletes of the 1970s. No one would have predicted that in 2003, 30 years after his heyday, he would find himself in a challenge to protect his 'image rights'.

A fine middle distance runner, Bedford once held three British records over three different distances. He set a world record for the 10,000 metres in 1973 at Crystal Palace – a record which had been reduced by barely more than one minute over the intervening 30-year period. With lengthy black hair and sporting a drooping moustache, the London-born athlete was a distinctive figure on the running tracks of the world and on television. He frequently wore red socks, sky blue shorts with gold braiding and a running vest with two hoops.

Forward to 2003. The UK Government had opened up to the private sector the telephone directory enquiry service previously run by BT. One of the new licensees, The Number, operated under the number '118 118'. To the surprise of many, on advertising hoardings and television screens around the UK suddenly appeared two runners, in rather comic strip and actions, advertising the service – and bearing, to those with memories of the 1970s, a close resemblance to the figure of Dave Bedford as remembered by many: the hairstyle, the drooping moustache and similar running kit.

On advertising hoardings and television screens suddenly appeared two runners, in rather comic strip and actions, bearing, to those with memories of the 1970s, a close resemblance to the figure of Dave Bedford.

The Number claimed that the advertisements were not specifically based on Bedford: 'During the Seventies all the runners had moustaches and long hair, even the footballers did.' A great many felt, nevertheless, that the figures did deliberately represent a caricature of him. Bedford was unhappy. He had certainly not been consulted or approved the advertisements.

The route Bedford chose to make his challenge was not a direct legal action against The Number but to make a formal complaint that the commercials contravened the Advertising Standards Code. The Independent Television Commission upheld Bedford's complaint. The Number appealed to Ofcom, the regulatory body which ultimately supervised the Code.

Legal Question: Could Bedford claim that his image rights were being infringed and stop the use of the advertisements?

For: The advertisements clearly bore a close resemblance to the distinctive figure of Dave Bedford, with his drooping moustache and running kit. They were taking commercial advantage of his 'image'. The fact that it was an amusing caricature should make no difference. Bedford's consent was required before such an advertising campaign could be run.

Against: The advertisements were not directly based on Bedford. They were a caricature of runners at that time, not a copy of his image. There was no suggestion that Bedford was endorsing the service. Bedford had not suffered any financial harm.

Decision: Ofcom decided that the 118 118 advertising campaign did '... *caricature Bedford by way of a comically exaggerated representation of him looking as he did in the 1970s sporting a hairstyle and facial hair like his at the time'*.

Since the caricature was published without Bedford's consent, it constituted a breach of the Code.

It was, though, a doubtful victory for Bedford. Ofcom did not ban the adverts. Bedford had delayed for about six months before making a complaint and The Number had committed itself to substantial expenditure in continuing the successful advertisements for the 118 118 service and its brand image. There was no evidence that Bedford had suffered any financial harm as a result of the caricature. Ofcom decided, on balance, that to ban the advertisements *'would be disproportionately damaging to The Number compared with any harm to the feelings or reputation of David Bedford as a result of the advertisements'*.

This harm could be addressed by an announcement that there had been a breach and, importantly, that Bedford had not endorsed the 118 118 service.

Many observers were critical of Ofcom's decision not to punish the breach of the Code by banning the advertisements. This did not as such prevent Bedford from trying to bring a personal claim in the courts – but he did not do so and it is doubtful whether such a claim would have been successful under current English law.

After the decision, The Number subtly changed the appearance of the comic runners. They developed a new image. The 1970s look was gone. The runners kept their moustaches but their hair became shorter and restyled in a somewhat more contemporary look.

Dave Bedford, who was Race Director of the London Marathon until 2012, said that he was not seeking 'greedy' damages. He was pleased that Ofcom had vindicated his claim that The Number had 'ripped off my image'. He said he had decided eventually to pursue the matter when he 'would go into pubs and people would shout: "I've got your number"'.

64. SKY AND A SOUTHSEA PUBLADY

Cheers at The Red, White & Blue

Customers in a Southsea pub enjoyed the televised matches from the Premier League, even if the commentary was in Greek. Had Sky been out-smarted? A long saga in the courts would follow.

There was a good crowd in the bar at The Red, White & Blue, a pub not far from Portsmouth's ground at Fratton Park. It was a Saturday afternoon in August 2006 and the large television screen was showing Bolton Wanderers v Tottenham Hotspur on the first day of the Premier League season. The pub's 41 year-old landlady Karen Murphy was happy. Little did she realise that six years of court proceedings would lie ahead.

'I think it's unjust. I think it's a greedy private company trying to dictate to the small people what they can or cannot do, purely for profit.'

Yorkshire-born Murphy had recently taken over the pub and she was determined to make a go of it. Football attracted the punters, even though she admitted the game 'bored her to tears'. The trouble was the cost. BSkyB (Sky) held the exclusive right from the Premier League to broadcast matches in the United Kingdom but she refused to pay the high subscription demanded by Sky. The cost for pubs was much higher than that for individuals. Instead, on the recommendation of the brewery (then Gales), Murphy discovered a much cheaper way – nearly 10 times cheaper – than the 'official' subscription. She acquired a decoder and decoder card by subscription from NOVA Supersport, a Greek satellite company, which gave access to matches (including the Premier League) originally intended for television broadcast in Greece. The Greek 'footprint' was large enough to be viewed, with the right decoder, in Britain.

A growing number of other publicans were using the same system. This also enabled viewers to watch matches intended for screening (outside the UK) during the 'black-out' period from 3pm when matches could not be screened in the UK under the rules of the Premier League. A double whammy.

Sky (and the Premier League) did not like this at all. It cut across their regime of country-by-country sale of rights. The broadcaster wished to stamp out this type of unauthorised or 'pirate' activity on the grounds that it was illegal and could undermine the full commercial value of the rights for which it had paid very substantial sums to the Premier League (£1.2 billion over three years). The Premier League was fearful that such activity could, if it grew, affect the future price broadcasters may be willing to pay for not-so-exclusive rights. Karen Murphy was unimpressed: 'I think it's unjust. I think it's a greedy private company trying to dictate to the small people what they can or cannot do, purely for profit.'

What did the Premier League do? Through its 'enforcers' (an agency called Media Protection Services), it brought a prosecution under the criminal law against Karen Murphy, the pub landlady at The Red, White & Blue. This would be a 'show trial'. The prosecution was technically brought under s297(1) of the Copyright, Designs and Patents Act 1989 whereby an offence is committed if a person 'dishonestly receives a programme included in a broadcasting service provided from a place in the United

Kingdom with intent to avoid payment of any charge applicable to the reception of the system'. Murphy knew that Sky had the exclusive right in the UK to charge for reception of its services and, the prosecution argued, Murphy was therefore dishonestly intending to avoid this payment.

Proceedings began in the Portsmouth Magistrates' Court. Karen Murphy started well. Indeed, the first time she was prosecuted, she was acquitted. Judge Arnold had sympathy since Murphy had originally been acting on the recommendation of the brewery and 'not acting dishonestly'. 1-0 to Murphy. When she persisted in using the NOVA system and came before Judge Arnold a second time, the court was no longer sympathetic. She was now acting 'dishonestly'. Convicted, a fine of £8,000 was imposed. 1-1. The enforcers were now on a roll. Murphy appealed but her conviction was upheld by the Portsmouth Crown Court. 2-1 to Sky/Premier League.

Murphy (supported by the other publicans and the European Satellite Operators Association) was still determined to fight the Goliath broadcaster and appealed to the High Court. It was all getting pretty serious. A somewhat esoteric and technical debate took place amongst the lawyers and experts in the High Court – in particular, as to whether (using the NOVA system) 'a broadcasting service' was being provided 'from a place in the United Kingdom' for the purpose of the Act. The court said 'Yes' and upheld Murphy's conviction – subject only to a separate hearing on certain European (EU) law issues which Murphy's defence had raised. Such claims under EU law were generally regarded as the last vestige of misplaced hope of a failing litigant. Lord Justices Pumfrey and Burnton even said: '*It is unclear to us how there can be a relevant free movement case.*' Sky was confident and issued a public statement: 'We hope that licensees and others will now heed the advice of the courts and accept that the use of foreign satellite systems to screen Premier League football in the UK is copyright theft, pure and simple.' 3-1 to Sky/Premier League.

Sky, however, had been over-confident. The court proceedings turned out, in football parlance, to be 'a match of two halves'.

The High Court met again to hear the arguments under EU law (after some delay because one of the judges, versed in the case, had died). The arguments were complex and, even for lawyers, obscure. The case had now become high profile and joined, on issues of free movement of goods and services under EU law, with another case involving a civil action against a European satellite provider. The High Court found it difficult and declared that it needed to refer the issues to be considered by the European Court of Justice. Murphy still had a chance of victory. 3-2.

Sky, however, had been over-confident. The court proceedings turned out, in football parlance, to be 'a match of two halves'. The European Court of Justice (ECJ) went into deep deliberation. The interaction between the protection and exploitation of intellectual property rights which encourage innovation (such as copyright) and EU rules promoting the 'single market' causes tension and difficulties for the law. Eventually, the ECJ opined in October 2011. The judgment came as a shock to many. The court declared that national laws which prohibit the import, sale or use of foreign decoders are contrary to an EU broadcaster's freedom to provide goods and services cross-border within the EU. Whilst rights holders are entitled to 'appropriate' remuneration, the prohibition on use of foreign decoders in these circumstances went beyond what was necessary to ensure 'appropriate' remuneration for rights holders.

3-3 and the momentum was now with Murphy.

The criminal proceedings still needed to be resolved. Back to the High Court in February 2012 and to Lord Justice Burnton, sitting with Justice Barling. The prosecution was in retreat. They admitted that, in the light of the ECJ judgment, Murphy was not guilty of 'intent' to avoid a reception charge. It was conceded that she had been wrongly convicted. Karen Murphy's conviction was formally quashed. 4-3 to Murphy at full-time.

Drinks all round at The Red, White & Blue. The NOVA system was reinstated. Karen Murphy declared that she 'was over the moon'. She planned to drink to her success : 'I shall go off to have the largest sambuca in the world.'

Was this the end of Sky's ability to operate a territorial system of licensing? Would the value of sports broadcasting rights be diminished? Or was this just a 'phyrric' victory with the might of Sky still able to win the war?

The ECJ judgment was not all bad news for Sky and the Premier League. It acknowledged that copyright continued in important elements of the broadcast. The opening sequence, the Premier League anthem, pre-recorded films showing highlights of recent Premier League matches and various graphics were all 'works' which could be protected by copyright in each country separate from the broadcast of the match itself. Enforcement against an armchair viewer in a private home would not be feasible (but who, in a private home, wants to hear commentary and analysis solely in Greek?) but transmission in a pub of a broadcast containing such protected works still appeared to require the authority of the copyright holder.

The legal battles continue. The Premier League has embarked on a further series of actions, now civil actions based on breach of copyright, against pubs in selected parts of the country. The landlord of one, 'The Rhyddings' in Swansea, is appealing to the Court of Appeal. More still to come.

Karen Murphy's success does not, seem to have diminished the value of sports broadcasting rights. In June 2012 the Premier League announced that the sale of broadcast rights in the UK covering Premier League matches for three seasons commencing in 2013 would raise more than £3 billion, an increase of 70 per cent over the previous deal. And in the latest deal, for the three seasons from 2016/17, the figure has increased by a similar percentage to £5.1 billion. Sky alone will be paying over £4.1 billion.

Karen Murphy declared that she 'was over the moon'. She planned to drink to her success : 'I shall go off to have the largest sambuca in the world.'

Back on the south coast, The Red, White & Blue still offers 'great beer and good old-fashioned service' and Karen Murphy is a heroine.

65. RORY MCILROY

An expensive Christmas party

Twenty-two year-old Rory McIlroy was one of the world's most exciting young golfers. Courted by Horizon, an Irish sports management agency, he met up with them on the day of their Christmas office party. Would he later regret it?

Office parties can involve situations where an experienced, charismatic individual encourages a younger person to take a step he or she may later regret. Wednesday, 21st December 2011 was the day of the Christmas office party of Horizon Sports Management led by Irishman Conor Ridge. The planned liaison? A commercial agreement, a formal Representation Agreement, to be concluded by the management company with young Irish golfer Rory McIlroy, one of the most exciting and talented players in the game. The Agreement was signed amidst handshakes and humour. The liaison, after an acrimonious split, ended before the High Court in Dublin in March 2015.

Conor Ridge, Galway-born, was ambitious. For leading sportsmen, the financial rewards can be great – and big business for their agents. In 2005 Ridge set up his own agency, Horizon, based in Dublin. His breakthrough was signing Ulster-born Graeme McDowell ('G-Mac' in the golfing world) who left Andrew 'Chubby' Chandler's International

Sports Management (ISM) to join Horizon at the end of 2007. A marvellous win in the 2010 US Open changed McDowell's career – and Horizon's. Conor Ridge was there at the final green at Pebble Beach celebrating alongside McDowell's father, Kenny: 'It has upped the stakes and put the company on a new level.'

Could Rory McIlroy, born in Holywood in County Down, be his next target? McIlroy, just 22 years-old, won his first major in June 2011 at the US Open, neatly following his friend and fellow-countryman's win the previous year. With his fluent swing and prodigious talent, the young Irishman's commercial potential was huge. McIlroy decided to leave Chubby Chandler's ISM camp in October 2011. One of his main reasons was, apparently, ISM's unwillingness to encourage McIlroy to engage fully with the PGA Tour in the USA.

Conor Ridge knew this was his opportunity. McIlroy was courted. The golfer was assured, he claimed, that the commercial terms would be the same as for McDowell. On the day of Horizon's office party in Dublin in December 2011, the deal was concluded in a solicitor's office in circumstances, McIlroy would later declare, 'of great informality'. The Representation Agreement was signed. McIlroy was not accompanied by any lawyer. He, apparently, had not seen any earlier draft of the Agreement. The commission rates payable to Horizon, it is reported, were five per cent of pre-tax 'on course' prize winnings and 20 per cent of 'off course' sponsorship and appearances money (reducing to 15 per cent if McIlroy agreed to extend the term of the Agreement in due course). Ridge had got his man. McIlroy's arrival transformed Horizon into a serious player on the world golf stage.

The liaison, after an acrimonious split, ended before the High Court in Dublin in March 2015.

The 'honeymoon' period of the relationship seemed, at least on the surface, to go well. Off the course, Conor Ridge joined Rory McIlroy at a banquet at the White House in March 2012 as guests of US President Barack Obama and Britain's Prime Minister David Cameron. On the course, McIlroy confirmed his standing as golf's most exciting young talent. He won his second major at the USPGA championship in August 2012.

McIlroy's existing sponsorship portfolio was revised. Most dramatically, Horizon secured a new five-year sponsorship/equipment deal for McIlroy with Nike in January 2013 – at a staggering fee for McIlroy of, reportedly, more than $100 million over the five-year term. Other deals were concluded with Omega and Bose. McIlroy was now one of sport's very highest earners. He signed a further agreement with Horizon in March 2013, extending the firm's representation until the end of 2017. But was the relationship really sound? Was there friction underneath?

The early months of 2013 were difficult on the course for McIlroy. Based now in Florida, his golf form had dipped. He seemed to be having difficulty, especially off the tee, adapting to the new Nike clubs – or was there more? He withdrew controversially in the middle of one tournament citing a wisdom tooth problem – without much support from Horizon. ('He's not sick, he's not injured, and he won't answer the phone … so I don't know', Ridge was quoted as saying.)

Simmering was a growing resentment by McIlroy at the size of the sums he was paying Horizon. He thought they were 'creaming off' too much. He strongly suspected that he was paying higher commission rates than Graeme McDowell – a position made more sensitive by McIlroy's discovery that McDowell owned a small shareholding in Horizon itself so that he benefited from the overall success of Horizon (including McIlroy's money). Other aspects of Horizon's behaviour annoyed him: a €166,000 donation was made to UNICEF without his knowledge or consent; and a first-class flight to Abu Dhabi, paid for in McIlroy's name, was changed to benefit a member of Horizon's staff.

In April 2013, McIlroy announced that he was terminating his arrangement with Conor Ridge's Horizon. He intended to move on and form his own company. McIlroy's father would play a more prominent role. It was not until September that the real depth of the dispute with Horizon became apparent. McIlroy filed a legal suit on the day before McDowell's wedding (which McIlroy did not attend). Horizon counter-sued. Tens of millions of pounds were at stake.

McIlroy (whose address was now given as Avenue Princess Grace in Monaco) claimed that he was entitled to rescind the Agreement with Horizon on the grounds that:
- It was invalid and unenforceable. He had been co-erced by 'undue influence' into signing an 'unconscionable' agreement providing for 'unreasonable' fee rates.
- McIlroy was inexperienced and, known to Horizon, did not receive independent legal advice. He had trusted Horizon to charge the appropriate rates since they had represented that they would be the same as those for Graeme McDowell. Horizon owed a fiduciary duty to be open and fair. McIlroy claimed that the rates applied to him were those reserved for 'an inexperienced or unproven golfer' and were 'markedly inferior' to those for McDowell.
- Horizon, he argued, were 'primarily concerned with maximising their own share of any commission'. McIlroy claimed repayment of over $6 million in 'excessive' commission payments.

Horizon counter-sued, claiming that McIlroy was simply reneging on a binding commercial agreement. They wanted over $9 million in unpaid commission since April 2013 together with substantial damages. They argued that:

- McIlroy was not entitled to terminate the Agreement. Horizon were entitled to damages equal to the commission they would have earned over the remainder of the contractual five-year term. They estimated that McIlroy would earn around £100 million in endorsements from existing contracts over that period.
- Horizon had also been denied other opportunities – such as negotiating the lucrative branding rights to McIlroy's golf bag to the corporate market. More formally, they had planned to continue 'building McIlroy's global commercial model' in accordance with an 'agreed long term brand strategy'.
- Horizon's work had 'played a significant role in the securing of [his] portfolio of lucrative sponsorship agreements, the activation of which now forms the bedrock of his global brand value and marketability as an athlete'.

The legal process took a lengthy and bitter course. McIlroy's lawyers sought detailed discovery of McDowell's contractual arrangements with Horizon which the latter's lawyers opposed. In turn, they sought access to McIlroy's mobile phone records and those of key members of his team, alleging that several phones had been wiped clean that might have contained information relevant to the case. McIlroy said that he periodically changed and re-set his phones in order to keep a distance from journalists and fans who obtain his number. It all became, in McIlroy's words, a 'nasty' and 'tedious' business. What would need to be disclosed in open court? Was it worth it?

On the course, ironically, McIlroy appeared to be liberated. 2014 became a golden year for the talented golfer. In a sustained spell of brilliance, he won a number of tournaments including two majors, winning at Hoylake in The Open and then at Valhalla in the USPGA championship. He was now clearly the world's number one golfer. At Gleneagles in Scotland in September both McIlroy and McDowell starred in Europe's Ryder Cup win. The mutual hug of congratulation and friendship between McIlroy and McDowell was a heartening sight.

Off the course, the legal battle between McIlroy and Horizon went on. A High Court judge ordered the parties to engage in formal mediation discussions. The parties remained intransigent after two days of talks. A likely eight-week and ugly court case seemed inevitable with each party's financial details, and more, being made public. McIlroy declared: 'It's not a nice process, it is a shame that it has gone this far but it's hard when two sides sort of see things completely differently the only way to sort it out is to get a judge in to tell us what to do.'

> **It all became, in McIlroy's words, a 'nasty' and 'tedious' business.**

He would be very careful in future what he signed on the day of a Christmas party.

The court date was set. Fresh from a three shot-winning victory at the weekend in the Dubai Desert Classic, McIlroy arrived on Tuesday, 3rd February 2015 at the High Court in Dublin. Dark-haired, wearing black-rimmed glasses and with suit and tie in place, perhaps wiser of the business world and its ways, the 25 year-old faced the court and the world's media. The galleries were packed. After a brief opening of less than a minute, hearings on the case were deferred during the day. There followed hours of last ditch negotiations. McIlroy stayed in the court building until 9pm.

The following day, there was no sign of McIlroy. He was already on a flight to Florida to prepare for the Honda Classic tournament. His counsel told the court: 'The entire matter has been resolved.' Judge Brian Cregan congratulated the parties for settling what he said would be 'a long case' if it went ahead. A brief press release was issued: '*The legal dispute between Rory McIlroy and Horizon Sports Management has been settled to the satisfaction of both parties who wish each other well for the future. The parties will be making no further comment.*' Neither side would confirm any details about the size of the settlement. Reports suggest that, in the end, McIlroy paid around $25 million.

Law scholars may have been disappointed that the court no longer had this chance to opine on the law of 'unconscionable' contracts – a relatively rare doctrine usually reserved to protect the vulnerable or the elderly (although sometimes assisting naive young pop stars 'taken for a ride' in lengthy management contracts) but probably a step too far in this case. The prurient were deprived of the spectacle of one of the world's leading sportsmen being questioned under oath on intricate financial matters.

For the golfing world, there was simply widespread relief that Rory McIlroy could change out of his suit into his golfing gear and concentrate fully on the build-up to the season's first major tournament, The Masters at Augusta in April. He finished fourth. He was soon winning tournaments again and confirming his ranking as the world's leading player.

He would, however, be very careful in future what he signed on the day of a Christmas party.

Chapter Eight

LEAGUES, COMPETITIONS AND TEAMS

Competitive sport requires the framework of a league, tournament or other competition in which teams or individuals can compete against each other – with the outcome of the competition depending upon the results of each match or contest.

It is the significance of the result within the context of the particular league or competition, coupled with the prior uncertainty of that result, which provides sport with much of its excitement, fervour and tension – both for players and spectators. Success leads to rewards for participants (individuals or teams) and their managers and owners.

Major sporting disputes have come before courts or tribunals involving the organisation of leagues and competitions and the right of individuals and teams to participate in them. Many have centred on the formation, or attempted formation, of new leagues or competitions and their potential effect on the 'old order'. Deep conflicts in the organisation of cricket, football, snooker and darts have led to disputes before the courts. Many have been critical to the future of the particular sport. Some of the decisions have changed the face of sport in this country.

66. TONY GREIG AND KERRY PACKER

Starting a revolution in cricket

Kerry Packer, with the support of Tony Greig and many leading test players, was planning a new 'World Series' cricket tour. Could it be stopped by the established cricket authorities?

The Centenary Test Match between England and Australia was being played at the Melbourne Cricket Ground in March 1977. The enthusiastic spectators were enjoying a classic encounter. Extraordinarily, the result was exactly the same as that first Test 100 years previously, Australia winning by 45 runs. In the background, however, a thunderous political storm was brewing.

Tony Greig was the England captain. The 6ft 7ins all-rounder loved being at the centre of the action. Born in South Africa to a South African mother and a Scottish father, he moved to England aged 20 and qualified to play for Sussex. Now 30 years-old, he was not only thinking about the match, he was also thinking of his future. He hoped to play Test cricket for a few more years but, planning ahead, some work as a television commentator would be welcome. Greig had arranged to meet Kerry Packer at his home in Sydney on 20th March.

Packer put forward a striking, and secret, proposition to Greig.

The Australian broadcaster was an ambitious and forceful character. He had a strong interest in Australian sport, particularly cricket. One of his channels was the Channel 9 Network, which Packer had taken over after the death of his father. He was determined to turn around the fortunes of the network with an aggressive strategy centred on more sports programming. He had already secured the rights to the Australian golf open and Packer wanted to acquire the exclusive rights to televise Test matches in Australia. He made a strong bid. Despite Packer's higher offer, the Australian Cricket Board stayed loyal to their existing broadcaster. Packer was deeply upset by the decision. He planned his next move.

Packer and Greig met. Packer put forward a striking, and secret, proposition to Greig. He said he planned to launch a new tour, a 'world series' cricket tour to be held in Australia from 1st September to 30th March. It would be televised exclusively on Channel 9. Offering significant financial reward, Packer had already secured the promised participation of many of the leading Australian cricketers. He wanted Greig to join and help build the new tour.

Just five days later, on 25th March, Greig signed a three-year contract with Packer's organisation: 'It was a purely financial decision, and a very easy one to make.' Greig, he said, planned to continue playing cricket in England in the summer but, along with the other recruits, he committed to Packer's programme. More than that, he undertook to assist in the recruitment of other top-class players. Recruits already signed up included Sussex's former England fast bowler John Snow and Gloucestershire's captain and world class South African all-rounder Mike Proctor, as well as many of the existing Australian Test team. The duration of their individual contracts varied from one to three years. All had been recruited amidst 'cloak and dagger' secrecy.

It was not until 9th May that the news of Packer's plans became public – and then only after some loose remarks at a press conference when the Australian team were visiting England. The news caused immediate consternation among the cricket governing bodies of all the Test-playing countries. Their fear was that the well-paid 'private' series run by Packer would greatly damage the structure of Test cricket which had historically been the foundation of the sport. The condemnation was severe.

Tony Greig was sacked as England captain for his role in the new tour. A spokesman pronounced: 'This was considered to be a breach of the normal trust which is expected between the captain and the England team and the authorities.' Steps to fight the rebel organisation were initiated by 'the establishment'. It was civil war. Two constitutional measures, in particular, were enacted:

- On 26th July, the International Cricket Council (ICC) passed a resolution changing the qualification rules for playing in Test matches. In effect, any person who played in the 'Packer Circus' after 1st October 1977 would be disqualified from playing Test cricket unless specific consent was given by the ICC.
- Shortly afterwards, the Test and County Cricket Board (TCCB) imposed an even more drastic resolution applicable to English county cricket (where many overseas players, such as Mike Proctor, played during their winter months). Any player who was subject to an ICC Test ban would be disqualified for two years from playing in any competitive English county cricket match.

The Packer 'rebels' would be ostracised. The battle for the future of cricket was on and the battleground moved to the courts.

Tony Greig, John Snow and Mike Proctor, as representatives of the new 'World Series' contract players, brought a legal action in the English courts to declare invalid the resolutions of the ICC and TCCB. They alleged that the resolutions were an unlawful restraint of trade. Each of them wanted to continue to play county and, if selected, Test cricket. The outcome of the litigation would be critical to the future of World Series Cricket (WSC). If they lost, the 'old order' would prevail. The case began in September 1977 before Justice Slade in the High Court.

Legal Question: Should the resolutions of the ICC and TCCB be declared invalid on the grounds that they were unreasonably in restraint of trade – by unjustifiably restricting the ability of professional cricketers to earn their living? Should Greig, Snow and Proctor be entitled to overturn the ban which would otherwise apply to them?

For: The immediate threat to the Test-playing countries was exaggerated. Players would still be available to play in English county cricket. The impact of World Series Cricket would be to stimulate greater general interest in cricket and thereby bring financial benefits to the game. The ban would apply to players (like Greig) who had already signed contracts with Packer – as well as being a disincentive to prevent other players 'deserting' in future. This retrospective application of bans to players who had already signed contracts was indiscriminate, unfair and unjustifiable.

Against: The ICC and TCCB were entitled to protect the long-term interests of Test and county cricket. World Series Cricket constituted a very grave threat to the economic viability of Test cricket throughout the world. WSC was, in effect, a parasitic organisation 'creaming off' star players from conventional first-class cricket when it had incurred no expense in training and preparing them for stardom. Television viewers might well watch WSC matches and diminish the future viewing of official Test matches. Retrospective application of the ban was necessary in order to give credibility and act as a deterrent in order to prevent WSC ruining existing Test and county cricket.

Decision: Evidence was given, on both sides, by leading figures in the game of cricket. Erudite legal submissions were made. After seven weeks of evidence and argument, the High Court made its decision. Greig and the WSC won this vital battle. The High Court decided that both bans were unreasonable and unlawful.

Justice Slade recognised that: '*Cricket has traditionally been regarded by many as embodying some of the highest professional standards in sport.*' However, the ban deprived professional cricketers of the opportunity to make their living. The resolutions were retrospective in effect. They were designed to encourage players to withdraw from or breach their existing contracts with WSC. This was the major flaw. Justice Slade found it:

'... impossible to see how resolutions in this extended and wider form [could] be adequately justified on any rational and objective grounds To deprive, by a form of retrospective legislation, a professional cricketer of the opportunity of making his living in a very important field of his professional life is ... both a serious and unjust step to take.'

The ban was contrary to the public interest since the public would be deprived of a great deal of pleasure and the opportunity to watch these talented cricketers – including in the many official Test matches which would not clash with World Series Cricket. The ICC had not discharged the burden on it to show that its resolution was reasonable.

Greig and the WSC won this vital battle. The High Court decided that both bans were unreasonable and unlawful.

The TCCB resolution was, in the view of the High Court, even more unreasonable since it prevented players from playing county cricket – the principal means by which players could supplement their incomes outside Test cricket. It would deprive the cricket-going public in England from seeing talented players like Greig, Snow and Proctor in first-class cricket.

The Test and county bans on the players could not be implemented. Players were free to join Packer's organisation and they did so – in numbers. Greig and Packer had won on all fronts. The World Series Cricket would go ahead. It was a vital victory.

The first WSC match, between the Australians and the West Indians, was held at VFL Park, an Australian rules football stadium in Melbourne, on 2nd December 1977.

For lawyers, this was an important decision. A rule of a sports governing body had again been struck down on the grounds of restraint of trade. This had become a major legal weapon with which to attack the rules and decisions of sporting bodies and tribunals.

For cricket, this was an even more momentous decision. Greig himself, following Packer's death in 2007, summed up the impact of Packer's revolution: 'Packer was a colossal man, wonderful Australian and, of course, a great friend of cricket.' He applauded the role Packer played in changing the face of cricket:

'The most important thing, I suppose, was night cricket – that got cricket to a wider audience. The second most important thing is that cricketers are paid what they should be paid. Every cricketer would be grateful, I am sure, for the involvement of World Series Cricket, because it got them a better deal. Also, he certainly improved cricket on television beyond recognition. He just took it to another level. Associated with that was the one-day game, played at night, which required a white ball and if you have a white ball you need coloured clothing. All sorts of things like that were directly as a result of Kerry Packer.'

The chairman of Cricket Australia added: 'One-day international cricket is now an international phenomena as a result of Kerry Packer. He has left a lasting legacy in the way the game is played, administered and presented to the public.'

More than 30 years later, echoes of the Packer case reverberate as the ECB and other cricket authorities respond nervously to the heady financial attractions being offered to players to participate in the Indian Premier League.

67. THE AMERICA'S CUP

The saga of the big boat and the catamaran

Tradition and custom were being set aside by a New Zealand club's proposal to fight the America's Cup with a 90ft boat. It was an extraordinary challenge. How would the San Diego Yacht Club react?

It should have been a friendly lunch. The Commodore of the San Diego Yacht Club, the holders of the America's Cup, was entertaining Michael Fay from New Zealand's Mercury Bay Boating Club on his visit to San Diego in July 1987. Then, over coffee, came the challenge.

The America's Cup is one of the most prestigious sports events in the world – and one of the oldest. The competition is named after the New York Yacht Club's schooner *America* which won the trophy, an ornate, silver cup, offered to the winner after defeating 15 British yachts in a race around the Isle of Wight in 1851. The race was watched by Queen Victoria and held in conjunction with Prince Albert's Great London Exhibition. Queen Victoria asked: 'Who is first?' '*America* has won,' she was told. 'Who is second?' asked the Queen. The famous reply came back: 'Your Majesty, there is no second.'

The America's Cup became the most sought-after trophy in international sail boat racing. It is a competition which has involved many protests, court actions and arbitral proceedings. But no dispute has been bigger than the one triggered by that lunch in 1987.

First, a little more background. The cup was donated to the New York Yacht Club on the terms of a Deed of Gift drafted in 1857 – a two-page trust deed which, although amended in part over the years, still formed the underlying basis for the competition. The trophy was to be 'preserved as a perpetual Challenge Cup for friendly competition between foreign countries'. It set out the terms for challenges to be made against the defending club, generally thought to favour the defending club. Indeed, for over 100 years until the 1960s, the competition became a series of failed attempts by the British to gain the Cup from the New York Yacht Club. Then, the Australians joined in.

In 1983, the Royal Perth Yacht Club of Australia, financed by Alan Bond and led by skipper John Bertrand, won the Cup with their famous winged-keel yacht. The America's Cup left America for the first time. In 1987, skippered by Dennis Connor, the Cup was reclaimed for America by the San Diego Yacht Club. San Diego were preparing for their first defence – anticipating a race in 1991, since the Cup was now usually held every four years with a prior qualifying competition for challengers from many nations.

Then, at that lunch in July 1987 came the dramatic surprise. Michael Fay said that the San Diego Yacht Club would be receiving a challenge from New Zealand's Mercury Bay Boating Club. Michael Fay, a boyish, bespectacled, millionaire banker, was, in the words of American Dennis Connor, planning a 'backdoor assault' on the Cup: 'If the America's Cup is sport's most contentious contest, this had to be its singular most combative act.'

Fay and his legal advisers had read closely the terms of the Deed of Gift under which the trophy was originally donated. No-one else had for years. Mercury Bay's challenge broke with tradition in three major respects. First, they challenged for a race on just 10 month's notice. Secondly, it was to be a single challenge without the now customary pre-Cup qualifying race between multiple challengers. Thirdly, and most significantly of all, Fay specified a challenge with a giant sailing vessel with a length of 90ft at the water line. Although the original Deed of Gift referred to a maximum water line length of 90ft, the race had by mutual consent and tradition for nearly 30 years been run with 12-metre boats about 44ft long at the water line. Mercury Bay had already been working on its design of a challenger boat.

No dispute has been bigger than the one triggered by that lunch in 1987.

San Diego promptly rejected a challenge involving 'a big boat', a boat more than twice the traditional size. There was no way that, on just 10 month's notice, they could design, finance and build a similar long boat even if they were prepared to change the traditional format of the race. It was clear that the longer the boat, the greater would be the sail area and the faster it would go. San Diego considered it a rogue challenge.

Mercury Bay pressed ahead. They went to the courts. Eleven weeks later, in August, they sought a declaration from the New York Supreme Court that the challenge was valid under the terms of the Deed of Gift and that the race should proceed. Mercury Bay won their claim before Justice Carmen Beauchamp Ciparick (another splendidly named US judge). ' … *Mercury Bay Boating Club has tendered a valid challenge and … San Diego Yacht Club must treat it as such in accordance with the terms of the Deed.*' The race was on.

> **Dramatically, San Diego responded with an announcement that they would defend by racing with a 60ft catamaran.**

What could San Diego do? If Mercury were going to play 'clever' by the rules, so were they. Dramatically, San Diego responded with an announcement that they would defend by racing with a 60ft catamaran. As Dennis Connor would later say: 'It was an alley fight. He jumped us, and I turned round and decided to fight to the death.' Sometimes termed 'biker boats', it was well-known that a catamaran, a multihull boat, would be faster than a monohull, however big. Mercury Bay realised that they no longer stood a chance of winning the Cup at sea if this went ahead.

So, back to the courts. Mercury Bay brought a second action, claiming that sailing a multihull catamaran against a monohull would no longer be a 'match' under the Deed of Gift and should be prohibited. They argued that San Diego's actions amounted to a contempt of court following Mercury Bay's previously successful legal action. Justice Ciparick refused, however, to hear the case at that time, deferring the hearing until after the end of the Cup. The race would go ahead.

The race was held on 7th and 9th September 1988 in the waters off San Diego. The result was predictable. It was a strange duel. Connor's catamaran *Stars & Stripes '88* easily won the first two races with victory margins of 18 and 21 minutes respectively over Mercury Bay's giant sloop *New Zealand KZ1*. Connor was reported to have gone slowly so as not to make the victory margin even greater. It was a gross mismatch.

Michael Fay and Mercury Bay returned to the courts in New York. The issue came first before the same Justice Ciparick. How would the court decide?

Legal Question: Had the use of a catamaran by San Diego been unsportsmanlike and contrary to the basic concept of a 'friendly competition between foreign countries'? Had San Diego's actions broken the 'spirit and intent' of the Deed of Gift?

For: The Deed of Gift contemplated a 'match'. Mercury Bay's original challenge was within the rules and had been recognised as such by the courts. A catamaran was completely different. It was no longer a 'match' within the terms or spirit of the Deed.

Against: Use of a catamaran was within the specification permitted by the Deed of Gift. If Mercury Bay could use the literal terms of the Deed with a 90ft boat, San Diego could respond by also employing a literal approach.

Decision: Justice Ciparick decided in favour of Mercury Bay. It had not been a 'match' as contemplated by the Deed of Gift. San Diego forfeited the Cup.

But that was not the end of the litigation. It rarely is in America. San Diego lodged an appeal to the Appellate Division of the Supreme Court. This court, by a bare majority, took a different view and decided in favour of San Diego. There was no provision, or implied term, in the Deed of Gift that multihulls should be prohibited. Chief Judge Wachtler stressed:

'This case ... has caught the public eye like few cases in this court's history. Much of the reason ... is the supposition that here at stake are grand principles – sportsmanship and tradition – pitted against the greed, commercialism and zealotry that threaten to vulgarise sport. In the end, however, the outcome of the case is dictated by elemental legal principles.'

The Deed did not require that vessels be evenly matched or raced with 'like or similar' boats. The Cup was re-awarded to San Diego.

Mercury Bay tried once more by appealing further to the Court of Appeals of the State of New York. This final appeal was heard in April 1990. Was there to be a further twist in the saga? No, by a majority, the court upheld the decision that San Diego's catamaran was a valid defence. It criticised heavily *'...the most distasteful innovation of all – resolution of the competition in court.'* The court continued: *'No one wishes to see the competition debased by commercialism and greed. But if the traditions and ideals of the sport are dependent on judicial coercion, that battle is already lost.'*

The America's Cup stayed in San Diego. The 1988 contest and the litigation were finally over.

San Diego successfully defended the Cup three times before losing it in 1995 – to New Zealand's Royal New Zealand Yacht Squadron.

For a 'friendly competition between two countries' the America's Cup has seen more than its share of litigation in recent years. The challenge for the 33rd competition found itself first in the New York State Court of Appeals and once more before Justice Ciparick. This time the esoteric question was: did the eligibility criteria in the Deed of Gift for a challenger, 'having for its annual regatta an ocean water course on the sea', require a yacht club to have held a regatta on the sea prior to issuing its challenge? The court decided it did. This opened the door for the Golden Gate Yacht Club to become the valid challenger and winner of the Cup in 2010. Justice Ciparick must have thought: what next?

68. FA PREMIER LEAGUE

FA and Football League fight over the birth of a new league

The FA was supporting the breakaway of the first division clubs into a new Premier League. Could it be stopped by the Football League?

The years 1990 and 1991 were turbulent for football. Sir Bert Millichip, the genial chairman of the Football Association (FA), and Graham Kelly, his chief executive, had many uneasy moments in the offices of the FA at Lancaster Gate in London as they considered the future.

At that time, the first division was simply one of the four divisions within the Football League. The major first division clubs, led by the 'big five' (Manchester United, Liverpool, Arsenal, Tottenham and Everton), were threatening to break away and form a 'super league'. Convinced that they were the major attraction for the growing commercial interest in the game, the leading clubs believed they were entitled to a greater share of the ever-increasing revenues available from broadcasting and sponsorship. They also wanted a greater say in the running of their own league and associated affairs. Sir Bert was under pressure. How should the FA react to the increasing pressures for change? Was the structure of professional football in England about to break apart?

Was the structure of professional football in England about to break apart?

The Football League, founded in 1888, sought valiantly to keep its current structure together. The Football League was, along with around 2,000 other leagues and competitions in England, formally run under the ultimate sanction and authority of the FA, the governing body and rule-making authority for football in England. The Football League applied annually for the sanction of the FA to run its league. It had always been a formality.

The Football League's leaders were very concerned. Broadcasting revenues were presently shared, in agreed proportions, between all members of the League. Income for the lower clubs in the Football League would be vastly reduced if the major clubs left. Worried by the threat of a total breakaway by the top clubs, the Football League had in 1988 adopted a regulation requiring any club to give at least three full seasons' notice if it intended to leave the Football League. The time period was actually inconsistent with the FA's own regulations which provided for annual renewal, but nothing was said by the FA until 1991 – when they decided to act.

Sir Bert Millichip and Graham Kelly decided that a breakaway in some form by the top clubs was inevitable. The FA published its own *Blueprint for the Future of Football* in June 1991. The FA considered that it would be in the best interests of football if the new league was created with substantial autonomy for the clubs but still kept under the auspices of the FA. Plans were developed with the major clubs for the formation of the FA Premier League.

Events moved quickly to pave the way for the new league. The FA decided in May 1991 to amend its conditions for sanctioning leagues. The revised condition said that any rule of a league which required a member club to give longer notice to leave than that required under the FA's own rules

It was a last-ditch attempt to prevent the formation of the FA Premier League.

would not be acceptable. The league would not be sanctioned. This condition would enable the first division clubs to leave the Football League at the end of that season and the new FA Premier League to commence in the 1992/3 season.

The Football League continued to fight. They brought a legal action to challenge and overturn the FA's amended rule. It was a last-ditch attempt to prevent the formation of the FA Premier League. If the Football League succeeded, the FA Premier League could not proceed – certainly not in the proposed form or timescale. The matter was heard urgently in the High Court in July 1991.

Legal Question: Should the FA's decision, in effect to impose new conditions on the sanctioning of the Football League and to facilitate the birth of the FA Premier League the following season, be open to legal challenge?

For: The FA was a body which regulated an important aspect of national life. Its decisions should be open to judicial review in the same way as other government and administrative bodies. It was obliged to act impartially, as a regulatory body, but it would have a serious potential conflict of interest if it entered into competition with the Football League by running its own league. The new rule also had the effect of inducing a breach of contract between the Football League and its clubs since the three-year notice rule was well-known to the FA. Changing the rules was an abuse of power by the FA.

Against: The FA was a domestic body and its decisions should not be open to legal challenge in the same way as a government department. Its role was *bona fide* to make decisions in the best interests of the game, which it was doing. Its role was also not simply a supervisory one. It already ran the FA Cup and was involved in commercial matters. Its role in relation to the FA Premier league would not result in a conflict of interest. The Football League's requirement for three years' notice for a club to leave the league was inconsistent with the scheme of annual sanctioning of leagues. There was nothing to prevent the FA from insisting on compliance with its rule for the following season as a condition of sanctioning the Football League.

Decision: The Football League lost. Justice Rose stressed that: '*it is no part of my job to decide whether the creation of a premier League will or will not be a good thing for English football.*' He then decided that the FA was not a body susceptible to legal challenge in this way. It was a domestic body and the issue was simply a matter of private law between the FA and the Football League based on the contractual terms of the annual sanctioning of the Football League. The court would not intervene.

Even if the FA's decision were open to judicial review as a governmental-type body, the court expressed the view that it would still not have intervened. '*The challenge mounted would, in my view, fail,*' said Justice Rose. The FA's decision was fairly within the scope of its function to govern football in England.

The Football League's resistance was quashed. The formation of the FA Premier League could go ahead.

This was a momentous decision for football. It cleared the way for the birth, in the following 1992/3 season, of the Premier League - more formally entitled 'The Football Association Premier League'. On 20th February 1992 all first division clubs gave notice en masse of their resignation from the Football League at the end of the 1991/2 season. Each of the clubs in the new Premier League became a shareholder in the company which would run the Premier League. The FA held a 'special share' with certain supervisory rights in relation to the England team and the FA Cup.

> **The Football League's resistance was quashed. The formation of the FA Premier League could go ahead.**

Although transitional payments were established to soften the blow for the remaining clubs in the Football League, the die was cast. The Premier League opened the way for the leading clubs to benefit from the explosion in commercial revenues, led significantly by the television revenues from BSkyB. Football in England would never be the same again.

The first matches in the new Premier League were held on 15th August 1992, with the first goal being scored by Brian Deane of Sheffield United in a 2-1 win over Manchester United. The sale by the Premier League of UK live broadcasting rights to Sky Sports and BT Sport for the three-year period, 2016-2019, will raise £5.136 billion.

69. THE GREAT DARTS DIVIDE

A bitter battle

Phil Taylor, Eric Bristow and other leading players were threatening to break away to form a new organisation. Could the British Darts Organisation prevent a major split in darts?

The Embassy World Darts Championships final in 1992 between Phil Taylor and Mike Gregory at the Lakeside Country Club, Frimley Green, was one of the finest darts matches ever played, a classic encounter which went right down to a tie-break in the final set of the match. Phil Taylor won his second title and was beginning an ascendancy which would lead commentator Sid Waddell later to remark: 'If we'd had Phil Taylor at Hastings against the Normans, they'd have gone home!' The standard of darts had never been higher. And yet, behind the scenes, a deep division was developing within the sport.

A year later, at the 1993 Embassy Championships, the division had become apparent. There was heavy political tension in the air. John Lowe was destined to be the last winner of a unified world championship. A bitter dispute was coming to the boil. Darts would be split into two factions and there would be two separate world championships. How did this all come about?

The background was a declining popularity in darts from its high point of the early 1980s. Some attributed this in part to image. Players drinking alcohol and smoking cigarettes during matches had not helped the reputation of the game. Many sponsors had dropped out. The number of televised events in the UK had virtually ceased except for the Embassy Championships. Many players who had earlier turned professional now found less prize money on offer and lack of TV exposure led to a reduced living from exhibition matches.

The historical governing body of the game in the UK was the British Darts Organisation (BDO). It had been formed in 1973 by Olly Croft in the front room of his house in Muswell Hill. The BDO was a founder member of the World Darts Federation. It comprised 64 member counties in Britain and organised tournaments for grass roots players all the way up to the professional level. This is how many of the leading players had developed 'up the pyramid'. The BDO set the rules which governed the game, such as the

They decided that, if the BDO was not going to recognise their organisation, the WDC players would not in future play in the Embassy Championships.

height of the board and size of the throwing oche. It organised the first World Professional Darts Championship in 1978 which, for many years under its sponsor, became known as the Embassy World Championships. All players were, until 1993, members of the BDO.

Many of the leading players now thought, however, that not enough was being done by the BDO to attract new sponsors. A group of players wanted the BDO to appoint a public relations consultant. They decided to form a new organisation to be known as the World Darts Council (WDC). The group included Phil Taylor, Eric Bristow, John Lowe, Dennis Priestley, Jocky Wilson and all the other world champions still active in the game. They became the 16 'rebels'.

The tension was felt by all at the 1993 Embassy Championships. As a mark of their campaign, the rebel players wore a distinctive insignia bearing the initials 'WDC' on their sleeves during practice sessions for the tournament. They were told by the BDO to remove the badges. The WDC players objected to an arrogance with which they were being treated. They decided that, if the BDO was not going to recognise their organisation, the WDC players would not in future play in the Embassy Championships.

The BDO, like any governing body, wanted to keep control of the game. It tried to quell the rebels. It wanted all players to stay within 'the family' of darts. The BDO sought to prevent players defecting to the WDC. It did so by passing resolutions which would have the effect of banning players who belonged to the WDC from playing in any events organised by the BDO, including all county darts and its super league competition. Indeed, also banned by the BDO would be any players who played in exhibition matches, even for charity, alongside WDC players. A civil war in darts had begun.

The WDC players retaliated by taking legal action against the BDO. It was reminiscent of the days of Tony Greig and the Packer revolution in cricket. They argued strongly that these bans by the BDO were in restraint of trade and illegal. They sought damages for loss of earnings over the years of the ban. A claim was brought in the names of Phil Taylor, Eric Bristow, Jocky Wilson and the other professional members of the WDC.

It was a bitter and protracted battle, lasting more than three years, and an expensive one for both sides. Eventually, a settlement was reached at the end of June 1997 after three days of negotiation before the start of the court hearing. The settlement was approved by the High Court. Basically, the WDC 'rebel' players had won:

- The bans imposed by the BDO were dropped. Each player was free to enter into such 'open' events as he wished. Eric Bristow said: 'For the first time in four years I am free to play in darts competitions all over the world.' In exchange, the WDC players dropped their claims for damages.
- The new WDC accepted that the World Darts Federation should continue to be the sport's regulatory body responsible for the rules.
- The WDC also agreed to drop 'World' from its name and was re-named the Professional Darts Council (PDC).
- A further term protected each party's lead championship event. Whilst both the BDO and the new PDC could hold its own 'world' championship, the top 16 players in each event in a particular year would not enter into the other organisation's event in the following year.

The court settlement did little to prevent the great darts divide. It effectively confirmed it. There would still be two world championships. Players would, in effect, have to choose to join one body or the other.

The first PDC World Championships were the 1994 Skol World Championships which commenced in late December 1993, a week before the BDO World Championships. They were held at the Circus Tavern in Purfleet. This started the unusual practice of the yearly championships of the PDC being commenced in December of the previous year. The first winner of the 'new' 1994 PDC World Championships was Dennis Priestley, who defeated Phil Taylor.

Darts followers still argue as to which tournament is the more prestigious. Generally, though, leading players have continued to join the PDC, attracted by the greater prize money. One of the most significant of these was Raymond van Barneveld, the Dutchman, who had won four BDO world titles including in 2006. Despite the agreed term in the 1997 court settlement, he played in the 2007 PDC World Championships. He won a dramatic sudden-death tie-break at five legs each in the final set to beat the previously invincible Phil Taylor 7-6 to win the PDC world title. It was a match to rank alongside that great 1992 final.

In October 2009, the PDC (through its chairman, Barry Hearn) made a takeover offer of £1m to buy the BDO and then invest a further £1m in the game. The bid was rejected. The divide continues.

70. STEPHEN HENDRY

World snooker in turmoil

A bitter divide in snooker was threatened as the prospect grew of a rival tour being established which would divide the players. Could the rival tour be stopped?

In December 2000 it was the turn of snooker to become embroiled in an ugly dispute destined for the courts.

Hendry was one of snooker's greatest-ever players. The 32 year-old Scot had been ranked the sport's number one on eight occasions. In 1999 he won the world championship at the Crucible Theatre in Sheffield for a record seventh time, defeating the rising Mark Williams in the final. In the spring of 2000 it was Williams who became world champion at the Crucible and ended the season as the game's top ranked player.

Behind both Hendry and Williams was their manager, Ian Doyle. Doyle was a tough, ambitious Scotsman ready to take on 'the establishment'. From his offices at a snooker club in Stirling, Doyle had for many years been fighting for a better deal for the players with the game's governing body, the World Professional Billiards & Snooker Association (WPBSA). In 2000, he saw his chance to apply further pressure. He agreed to merge his sports management agency with a new internet company, The Sportsmasters Network (TSN), which was keen to invest in snooker. Doyle became chairman of TSN.

Doyle, Williams and Hendry were dissatisfied, they said, with the 'amateurish' way in which the WPBSA was being run. Chaired by former player, Rex Williams, its board had no professional management with expertise in marketing or sponsorship affairs. Doyle was forthright: 'I don't believe that the sport can move forward with players or ex-players running the game. They've got a part to play but we need professional management. The problem is people on the board don't want to give up their own little fiefdoms.'

Doyle thought that the WPBSA was too dependent on tobacco companies for sponsorship; this source was destined to disappear and new sponsors should be found. Doyle complained generally that, as a regulatory body, the WPBSA should not also be the sole promoter of major televised tournaments.

With £10 million investment support from his City backers, Doyle approached the WPBSA with an offer to invest £3.3 million over three years in promoting four tournaments with new sponsors, in **Doyle was a tough, ambitious Scotsman ready to take on 'the establishment'.**

exchange for rights to transmit over the internet live streaming of WPBSA events. A deal seemed possible but negotiations became protracted. The WPSBA failed to give its backing. Doyle and TSN became frustrated and walked away.

On 6th December 2000, TSN issued a press release pledging a 'fresh vision for snooker' and announcing an intention to mount a rival 10-event global tour. New sponsors were planned with a significant increase in prize money. Events were planned in Dubai, Thailand, Malta and China. TSN subsequently announced that there would be a new world championship in 2002 to be staged at the National Indoor Arena in Birmingham with dates which would, deliberately, clash with WPBSA's World Championship at the Crucible. BBC snooker correspondent Clive Everton commented: 'This looks like a fight to a finish between competing tours, each with its own world championship.' It was civil war in snooker.

Many leading players committed to participate in the new tour. They included Stephen Hendry, Mark Williams and Jimmy White. Hendry was the first to back the breakaway tour. He signed a three-year contract to promote the organisation and its events. TSN proposed that, in the new world, the WPBSA should become solely a regulatory body. Was TSN making, in effect, an attempted takeover of the marketing of the professional game at the top level?

The WPBSA retaliated. Its main potential weapon was the BBC. The WPBSA's £20 million existing contract with the BBC for televising certain major events, including the world championship at the Crucible, still had several years to run. Pressure was applied to persuade the BBC to continue to honour its contract to televise WPBSA events despite the loss of the TSN players. The BBC confirmed that it would do so.

The WPBSA's second main weapon was Ronnie O'Sullivan. He was then ranked only number four in the world but was already one of snooker's major attractions. A substantial offer was made to Ronnie O'Sullivan to remain loyal to WPBSA tournaments and stay within the fold. After initial doubts, he eventually agreed to do so. Other leading players who stayed with the WPBSA included Steve Davis, John Parrott, John Higgins and Peter Ebdon. The professional ranks were being split. O'Sullivan won his first world championship at the Crucible in 2001.

The snooker war escalated. The WPBSA decided in March 2001 to make a number of rule changes for the 2001/02 season. A major new rule provided, in essence, that WPBSA members could not enter into or play in any snooker tournament, event or match without the prior consent of the board of the WPBSA.

The WPBSA indicated that this consent would not be given for a player to compete in an event being televised in any country at the same time as a WPBSA tour event being held in that country. The aim, clearly, was to prevent the rival tour being attractive for TV or commercial sponsors. If this rule were implemented, it would either kill off the rival tour or lead to the creation of two separate snooker circuits. This became the legal battleground.

Hendry, Williams and other leading players in the TSN camp fought back. They brought a legal action challenging the validity of the WPBSA's rule changes. The crux of their case was that the WPBSA was 'abusing its dominant position' as a governing body and imposing anti-competitive conditions on the players. It was very reminiscent of the fight by Tony Greig and Packer's 'World Series' tour against the established cricket governing bodies.

In March 2001, TSN relented. It announced that, at least for now, it was abandoning plans to form a new snooker tour. It did not wish, it said, to split the game. The TSN players would return to the WPBSA tour with 'considerable reluctance'. In practice, the BBC decision to stick with the WPBSA had been the key commercial blow. WPBSA also backed down by withdrawing its principal rule change for the 2001/2 season.

However, it was not peace. TSN would still proceed to challenge in the High Court the WPBSA's 'monopoly position' which it maintained was an 'unfair restraint of trade'. Hendry and Williams were encouraged to press ahead with their legal action. It was fought in the High Court.

Legal Question: Should the proposed WPBSA rule, which would have had the effect of preventing Stephen Hendry and others from competing in televised events run by the new tour, be declared invalid as being unlawful and in restraint of trade?

For: The rule affected the ability of a snooker event organiser to recruit players and therefore restricted the ability of any rival organisation to gain a foothold. Taken with the rule that only WPBSA-sanctioned events counted for ranking points, its effect was to limit significantly the events in which players could compete in order to earn their livelihood. It was contrary to UK and European competition laws. The WPBSA's interests should solely be as a regulator.

Against: The WPBSA was acting in good faith to protect and further the interests of all its members. Many of the rival tour events were likely to have restricted fields and so, in practice, would not be open to many WPBSA members. WPBSA events, on the other hand, were generally open to all members. Money made by the WPBSA from its tournaments was re-invested in the sport as a whole. The rule was necessary to support the broadcasting and sponsorship revenue of the WPBSA. It was therefore in the best interests of the sport.

Decision: The High Court hearing lasted six weeks. Judgment was given on October 2001.

On the major point, Hendry and Williams won. Justice Lloyd decided that the rule, requiring the WPBSA's consent for players to compete in other events, was too wide and was unreasonable under competition laws. It was declared invalid. Justice Lloyd explained: '*The WPBSA had market power and was in a dominant position.*' The effect of the new rule was to '*prevent competition – by limiting the sources to which the players can have recourse in order to earn their livelihood*'. He did not consider this restriction could be justified.

As to the challenge that certain other rule changes and actions of the WPBSA in the commercial field (e.g. as to the number of logos on a player's waistcoat) were an 'abuse of its dominant position' as a governing body, TSN failed. Both sides came away claiming victory. The WPBSA's chief executive welcomed the court's overall decision: 'This is a victory for the Association's right to protect the players and their assets against commercial predators.'

Hendry also claimed victory: 'All the big points we have won – and the other minor issues like logos and rankings were all peripheral anyway. Mark and I feel that we are very much vindicated in our decision to go to court.'

Each side had to bear its own substantial legal costs. It had been an exhausting battle and very little in fact had been achieved.

At the legal level, the case was important. It was the first judgment of the High Court to uphold a claim under English law that a sports governing body's exercise of its regulatory powers could amount to 'an abuse of a dominant position' in breach of competition law. It re-emphasised that decisions by a governing body must be 'proportionate'. If measures are introduced which restrict the ability of players and athletes to earn their living, those measures must be limited to the minimum reasonably necessary to protect the sport's interests.

At least snooker had avoided the position which emerged in darts of having, confusingly, two different circuits and two different world champions. There was for a period an uneasy aftermath. Some organisational changes were made in the WPBSA. A new chairman was appointed in 2003. Prize money was increased. Tobacco sponsorship was forced by law to end. Some new sponsors were found and, in 2010, responsibility for commercial promotion and exploitation of the professional sport was divested to a separate company, World Snooker Limited, in which the WPBSA holds a 26 per cent stake. The world championship is now being title-sponsored by Betfred.com.

71. THE DONS: WIMBLEDON OR MILTON KEYNES?

A passionate affair for supporters

Wimbledon FC proposed a controversial move 70 miles north to Milton Keynes. Should it be permitted by the football authorities?

By 2002, the great days of Wimbledon FC were in the past. The finest hour for Wimbledon's 'Crazy Gang' was the 1-0 defeat of Liverpool in the FA Cup Final in 1988 with a memorable winning goal from Lawrie Sanchez. It was now a fading memory.

It had been a rapid ascent for 'the Dons', founded in 1889 as Wimbledon Old Centrals, who had spent most of their history in non-league football. The club had only been elected to the Football League as recently as 1977. Fourth division champions in 1982/3, successive promotions saw the club reach the heady heights of the first division in 1986. Wimbledon FC became a founder member of the FA Premier League in 1992.

By 2002, however, the club was in disarray. Relegated from the Premier League on the last day of the 1999/2000 season, Wimbledon's finances and fortunes were collapsing. What could the club do? It was an unexpected and bold solution. Move 70 miles north to Milton Keynes!

Wimbledon were 'homeless'. Their home ground had for nearly 70 years until May 1991 been Plough Lane in Merton, south London. This was a spartan ground and did not meet the requirements of the Taylor Report enacted following the Hillsborough disaster. Plans to relocate to a new all-seater stadium in Merton failed. The FA had granted permission in 1992 for the club to play their 'home' matches at Selhurst Park in Croydon, sharing Crystal Palace's ground. Plough Lane was sold for redevelopment (originally for a supermarket). The club was losing, on one estimate, up to £4 million per annum in commercial income through not having their own ground.

It was an unexpected and bold solution. Move 70 miles north to Milton Keynes!

Wimbledon toyed with the idea of being bought by an Irish consortium and 'moving' to Dublin. This idea was stamped upon by the Irish FA who would not allow a team based in Ireland to play in the English league. It went no further.

Then, along came the Milton Keynes proposal in 2001. The man behind it was Pete Winkleman. A well-known music entrepreneur and football fan, he wanted top-class football for Milton Keynes. A number of possibilities were considered. There was an opportunity with other backers to build a modern new stadium as part of a large commercial development in the town. Starting a new club there would not, though, be enough to attract the necessary financial backing. Could an existing professional club be brought in from another town? Since 1998, Winkleman had been approaching without success other clubs in financial trouble, reputedly including Barnet, Luton and Queens Park Rangers. But Wimbledon FC, desperately looking for a new home, was a more promising proposition. A deal was agreed in principle.

Wimbledon applied, as required under the rules of the Football League, for permission to relocate to Milton Keynes. This was the first time permission had been sought in England for a league football club to make a significant geographical move of this nature. There was passionate opposition to the move from most Wimbledon supporters.

Such a geographical move of a club was unprecedented in English football – but not without some precedent in Scotland. In 1996, the Scottish Football League allowed Meadowbank Thistle FC to relocate permanently from central Edinburgh to a 'new town' more than 18 miles away, Livingstone, and to change its name. And in 2002 Airdrie United were, in effect, permitted to acquire Clydebank FC, taking its league position but playing at Airdrie's old ground.

The Football League rejected Wimbledon's application in August 2001. Wimbledon persisted. The matter was referred to an independent commission jointly appointed by the Football League and the Football Association. The commission met in May 2002.

Issue: Should the football authorities permit a league club to make such an unprecedented move of this nature away from its 'home' roots? If so, should 'Wimbledon' be regarded as the same club and keep their position in the first division of the Football League?

For: Football must be commercial. There was no land site in Merton or south London, claimed the club, where it was viable to construct a major football stadium. Wimbledon FC were a secondary tenant at Selhurst Park and there was no or little opportunity to promote their own colours, branding and marketing at the ground. Wimbledon were already playing a fair distance from their 'home'. A majority of the club's supporters came from outside Merton. There had been a steady decline in attendances. Milton Keynes offered a new stadium, excellent infrastructure and a potentially large fan base. A move was necessary to save the club.

Against:. The move broke the important bond between the club and the fabric of its local community. Wimbledon 'belonged' to south London. Long-standing Wimbledon supporters would not be able to associate with the new venue. Permitting a club to be bought and moved in this fashion would be to allow an American-style 'franchise' system to be introduced for owning professional football clubs, contrary to the English tradition. It would, in effect, become a 'new' club and should not be permitted to retain its league position as if it were the same club.

Decision: The commission opined. Wimbledon could move to Milton Keynes – and remain in the first division of the Football League. Exceptional circumstances existed. The commission noted that, in this case, the club's links with Merton were '*not so profound, or the roots go so deep, that they will not survive a necessary transplant to ensure the club's survival*'. The commission decided by a narrow 2-1 majority it was better that the club was saved. This, the commission stressed vainly, should not be regarded as a precedent.

The FA was not happy, declaring: '*The commission reached its conclusions despite evidence presented by the FA opposing such moves in principle. The commission has made it clear that their decision is based on exceptional circumstances. They see Wimbledon as a one-off. This is not the beginning of a franchise system.*'

2002/3 became Wimbledon FC's last full season at Selhurst Park. Fans deserted the club in protest and average attendances fell to fewer than 3,000. In October 2002 only 849 fans turned up for one league match against Rotherham, and 227 of them came from Rotherham! It was the lowest attendance ever recorded at a match in the Football League. Wimbledon FC subsequently went into financial administration.

Wimbledon played their first match in Milton Keynes in September 2003, against Burnley, and it ended in a 2-2 draw. Matches were played initially at the National Hockey Stadium in Milton Keynes. In Spring 2004, Pete Winkleman led the purchase of the club out of bankruptcy. A new 28,000 all-seater stadium was planned. On the pitch, results were poor. The club dropped to two divisions below where they were when they last played, as Wimbledon, at Selhurst Park. They were relegated to Coca-Cola League Two in 2006 but, in 2008, promoted as champions back to League One.

In June 2004, despite the FA commission's recommendations, Winkleman announced that the club would change its name to 'Milton Keynes Dons FC' and adopt a new badge and team colours.

Back in Wimbledon itself, the club's supporters formed a new club, AFC Wimbledon, which they saw as the direct descendant of Wimbledon FC and the 'true' club of

All that remains in Milton Keynes is the name 'Dons'. the people of Wimbledon. The new club started at the bottom of the football pyramid and enjoyed sizeable support from the start. The club (sharing a ground with Kingstonian FC) has been extremely successful, winning regular promotions and is now playing in the Football League (League Two).

In late 2006, agreement was reached whereby the replica of the FA Cup so proudly won in 1988, along with other club papers and memorabilia gathered under the name of Wimbledon FC, was returned to the London Borough of Merton.

AFC Wimbledon are now even engaged in plans to play again in Plough Lane with proposals, backed by Merton Council, for the site of the old greyhound stadium to be re-developed with a new 11,000 seater stadium – next door to Wimbledon's former Premier League ground. If it comes to pass, it would be a story-book return to the spiritual home.

72. THE BLADES ATTACK THE HAMMERS

Breach of rules and a rival's relegation

West Ham signed Carlos Tevez under transfer arrangements which breached the rules of the Premier League. Should they be 'docked' points? Could the decision affect which club was to be relegated?

The odds on it happening seemed very high. But that's football. It was the last day of the 2006/7 season in the Premier League. West Ham to win or draw away at champions Manchester United and Sheffield United to lose at home to relegation rivals Wigan – it was the only combination of results which would relegate Sheffield United and keep West Ham up. Sheffield United did lose. At Old Trafford, Manchester United pressed relentlessly against West Ham. Then, a counter-attack; the ball was played through and West Ham snatched a winning goal, and the scorer, inevitably, was Carlos Tevez. West Ham, astonishingly, were safe - or were they?

Should West Ham have been 'docked' points for a breach of the rules?

Should Tevez have been stopped from playing for West Ham? Should West Ham have been 'docked' points for a breach of the rules and Sheffield United be spared relegation? Did Sheffield United have a legal claim against West Ham for breach of the duties owed by one competitor in a league to another? These questions occupied the attention of commentators, fans and the media – and courts and tribunals – for months afterwards.

———————————

Tevez, an Argentinian international and once described by Diego Maradona as the 'Argentine prophet for the 21st century', was signed by West Ham from the Brazilian side Corinthians at the end of August 2006, along with fellow countryman Javier Mascherano. West Ham were cock-a-hoop. The players were duly registered with the Premier League.

Rumours spread early in the 2006/7 season that agent Kia Joorabchian's MSI Group still had 'economic rights' to the players, under arrangements not uncommon in South America, whereby Tevez could be transferred during a transfer window if and when the MSI Group said so and MSI would receive the fee – West Ham did not have full control. This 'third party agreement' had been hidden from the Premier League when West Ham obtained his registration. It was almost certainly in breach of Rule U18 of the Premier League Rules which prohibited a contract which 'enables any [third] party …to acquire the ability materially to influence' the policies or performance of a club.

The Premier League investigated but West Ham, through its managing director at the time, gave an emphatic assurance in September that there was no such agreement. The club lied to the Premier League. This was the real 'crime'. In late November 2006 West Ham came under new ownership and management, bought by an Icelandic consortium then led by Eggert Magnusson. The new management volunteered the true position regarding Tevez to the Premier League and in January 2007 handed over a copy of the agreement with the MSI Group.

Disciplinary charges were laid against West Ham by the Premier League for breach of the duty of 'utmost good faith' (Rule B13) and for the 'third party agreement' (Rule U18). A hearing of the Premier League's disciplinary commission took place at the end of April. West Ham pleaded guilty. They were fined a total of £5.5 million – £3 million in respect of the breach of Rule B13 and £2.5 million for Rule U18.

Crucially, the disciplinary commission did not deduct any points from West Ham, deciding that it would not be a *proportionate punishment* in the circumstances. The club was under new ownership and management. Moreover: '*A points deduction in, say, January … would have been somewhat easier to bear than today which would have consigned the club to certain relegation.*'

Actually, with West Ham lying 19th in the table and, with just a few games left, virtually certain of relegation in any event, many thought that the monetary fine was a severe punishment to go with the cost of inevitable relegation.

As far as the continued registration of Carlos Tevez was concerned, the disciplinary commission was weak. They did not require his de-registration but left it to the Premier League to be satisfied that the 'third party agreement' had been terminated. Given hurried and not very convincing assurances that it had been terminated by West Ham and that West Ham would resist any claim that it was still active, the Premier League allowed Tevez to continue playing.

And play he did! West Ham won their final three matches of the 2006/7 season – against Wigan, Bolton and Manchester United – with Tevez having a significant role in each match. He created two of the goals in the away win against Wigan, scored twice against Bolton and scored the only goal in the away victory against Manchester United. Remarkably, and totally against the odds, West Ham finished above Sheffield United who were relegated along with Charlton and Watford.

Did Sheffield United have any hope left? They launched a legal campaign to the effect that the disciplinary commission should have docked West Ham points – and that the Premier League should have been required to de-register Tevez for the final three games of the season.

The issue came before an independent three-man arbitration tribunal of the Premier League in June 2007. The tribunal had limited scope. It could not itself change the commission's decision – but it could order the disciplinary commission to re-consider. The arbitration tribunal said: 'No'. It would not order a fresh disciplinary hearing. The tribunal could only do so if it concluded that the original decision of the commission was *'irrational or perverse'. 'This is a very strict test and is very difficult to satisfy on a question very much of judgment and discretion.'* Tantalisingly, the arbitration tribunal had *'much sympathy'* for Sheffield United's grievances and *'…would in all probability have reached a different conclusion and deducted points from West Ham'*. The tribunal would have placed greater weight on the deception by the club's former management. But they could not say that the decision was irrational or perverse.

On the continued registration of Tevez, the arbitration tribunal recognised that, despite apparent termination, the MSI Group might still assert rights. That possibility was 'not entirely excluded'. However, there had been no attempt in practice so far by the MSI group actually to influence the club's policies or performance. The tribunal concluded: *'The arrangement may not have been legally watertight but it was a practical and workable solution to a difficult situation'* and, again, the decision not to de-register Tevez was not *'unreasonable in the sense of … being perverse or capricious'*. All a bit weak.

Time had virtually run out for Sheffield United to have any chance of staying in the Premier League for the following 2007/8 season. One last attempt was made to go to the High Court to appeal the arbitration decision. The High Court stamped on that last chance attempt. No leave was given to appeal to the court. It was the Championship next season for Sheffield United and an opening home match against Colchester United.

The row over Carlos Tevez's contract continued after the end of the 2006/7 season. Not surprisingly, the MSI Group claimed that they were entitled to any transfer fee – not West Ham – and that West Ham could not hold on to his registration. Further litigation was threatened. In the end, agreement was reached without further reference to the courts. West Ham did receive a small part of the transfer fee, the MSI Group received the lion's share and Carlos Tevez was transferred … to Manchester United.

Sheffield United were still angry. They faced a heavy loss of TV and other income as a result of relegation – a cost estimated isignificantly in excess of £30 million. Could they claim compensation by way of damages in a civil claim directly against West Ham? It was well worth a try. They would argue that West Ham broke the rules of the Premier League, including the duty of 'utmost good faith' which each club owed the others – and this had resulted in Sheffield United's relegation and financial loss. West Ham would counter that the Premier League's disciplinary regime should be the sole mechanism for punishing any breach of the rules. Surely, in any event, Sheffield United's own play on the pitch was a principal cause of their downfall?

The tribunal had 'no doubt that West Ham would have secured at least three fewer points over the 2006/7 season if Carlos Tevez had not been playing for the club'.

The lawyers found a route under the FA's rules, not previously used for claims directly between clubs, to an independent tribunal chaired by Lord Griffiths, former president of the MCC. Sheffield United's chances of success seemed small. Or would the story have one last sting?

Yes, it would. The tribunal announced its decision in September 2008. The Hammers were legally liable to pay compensation. Critically, the tribunal declared that, if subsequently discovered evidence of the club's assurances to Joorabchian's advisers had been known to the Premier League at the time of its original decision, it *would have suspended Mr Tevez's registration as a West Ham player*'. The tribunal had '*no doubt that West Ham would have secured at least three fewer points over the 2006/7 season if Carlos Tevez had not been playing for the club*'. The amount of compensation, likely to be multi-millions, would be assessed later.

Many were astonished at this unprecedented leap from the rule-book to compensation directly between clubs – and its implications for future disputes.

The Premier League must have squirmed uneasily. Sheffield United felt 'vindicated'. West Ham, facing forced sales of players, were stunned. It was now their turn to seek, despairingly, an appeal route. But the outcome was now for the accountants rather than the lawyers. An out-of-court settlement was eventually reached for payment of an undisclosed sum (believed to have been around £20 million).

Back to the football. At the end of the 2007/8 season, West Ham finished 10th in the Premier League and Carlos Tevez collected a winner's medal with Manchester United - although trouble and controversy would never be far from the Argentinian. For the Blades it would be another season in the Championship and not the Premier League.

73. GLASGOW RANGERS

The taxman blows the final whistle

Ten points were deducted in February 2012 and the league title was, in effect, forfeited to arch-rivals Celtic. Liquidation followed in June and a 'new' company had to settle for a place in the Third Division of the Scottish Football League. It was a terrible year for Glasgow Rangers. How did it happen?

No bigger club has fallen, or fallen further, than Glasgow Rangers. Hanging darkly over the saga was 'the Big Tax Case'. Never have so many football fans shown such interest in tax and insolvency law.

The proud Scottish club, with nine successive championship wins in the 1990s, sought to remain at the forefront of European football and to compete for foreign players alongside the major English Premier League clubs. Bank debt grew substantially under the ultimate ownership of Sir David Murray. How could costs be saved? Could the wage bill be managed more cheaply?

It was in 2001 that Rangers (or, more accurately, its parent company) established the Murray Group Management Remuneration Trust (MGMRT). This, as many Scottish football fans will now be able to explain, was a form of employee benefit trust (EBT), a structure used by several entrepreneurial companies. Money is deposited by an employer in the trust fund to be administered by independent trustees, usually offshore. Employees can apply for loans from the trust. Granting the loans is discretionary (i.e. not appropriate for pre-fixed wages or other contractual obligations). In most cases, the loans, once made, are not expected to be repaid. Such a scheme, it was thought, could be operated without deducting pay-as-you-earn (PAYE) and National Insurance from any such loans.

HM Revenue and Customs (HMRC) came on the attack. The tax affairs of the football industry were now under closer scrutiny. HMRC apparently discovered that, in relation to the operation of the Rangers EBT scheme, numerous emails or side-letters existed which in effect gave undertakings to particular players or other employees that payments would be made into sub-trusts of the MGRMT on their behalf. Their formal declared 'wages' were reduced. The EBT, if this was true, was arguably not being exercised with genuine discretion but as a way of paying contractual remuneration. Additionally, Rangers would not have properly disclosed its wage bill for players, as required, to the Scottish Premier League (SPL).

> **'It is a 10,000lb gorilla wandering around the room and we don't quite know what its appetite is.'**

Accounts revealed that more than £47 million was paid into the MGMRT by Rangers FC in the decade from 2001, with a further £10 million or so contributed by Murray International Holdings. 'Loans' had been made to more than 80 players, coaches and staff. If these had been wages subject to PAYE and National Insurance, a total of more than £49 million would have been required to meet the bill. Rangers had, arguably, an extra 'pot' with which to pay wages to sign and retain (potentially better) players during the decade in which the scheme operated. Was this a form of financial cheating?

On the pitch, Rangers continued to win cups and championships with league title victories in 2003, 2005, 2009, 2010 and 2011. Success, however, in Europe remained elusive.

The tax bill landed in 2010. HMRC considered that the MGRMT was a sham. PAYE and National Insurance should have been paid and, added to the bill, there would now be compound interest and penalties. Estimates varied but the total bill could be £50 million or even more. Alastair Johnston, then club chairman, acknowledged in March 2011 that the club could be in deep trouble if the tax claim succeeded: 'It is a 10,000lb gorilla wandering around the room and we don't quite know what its appetite is.' Could Rangers survive?

Sir David Murray's own financial empire was suffering and pressure grew to reduce the group's massive bank debt. Rangers could not be sustained financially under his ownership and the club was up for sale. In May 2011 he eventually sold his controlling interest (85.3 per cent) to Wavetower Limited (ultimately owned by businessman Craig

Whyte) for £1. Whyte pledged to pay off the bank debt and to invest money in the squad and stadium. He said he was willing and able to meet any liability on Rangers FC in the Big Tax Case with up to £15 million from his own personal wealth.

40 year-old Craig Whyte, a venture capitalist, was a controversial figure. (It was later revealed that he had previously been banned as a company director for seven years, a period that had expired, but this was not disclosed to the football authorities.) A subsequent Scottish Football Association (SFA) Judicial Panel found that the directors of Rangers had *very little disclosure of [Whyte's] personal financial circumstances or of the affairs or circumstances of any of his business interests, past or present .... or as to the source of his funding*. They had, however, *been made aware that Lloyds [the group's bank] were extremely enthusiastic about the potential purchase by Mr Craig Whyte of the MIHL majority holding*. Sir David Murray felt that 'he was left with almost no option' but to sell his shares to Whyte.

How quickly the walls came tumbling down! Whyte, seeking to save costs and repay the banks, appears to have adopted some extraordinary measures and systems. He compounded the conflict with the taxman by simply instructing that PAYE and National Insurance collected on wages since he took over should be withheld and not paid to HMRC. This 'policy' began, apparently, as a negotiating ploy to improve Rangers' position in any attempted negotiation with HMRC of a settlement in the Big Tax Case! A claim for unpaid tax built up of more than £13 million ('the Wee Tax Case'). HMRC commenced proceedings to recover it. Alongside other outstanding debts, it was now clear that Rangers could not meet its obligations as they became due. The club was insolvent. HMRC petitioned and on 14th February 2012 Rangers FC was placed in administration by order of the Court of Session. The club was now in the hands of two practitioners from the accounting firm of Duff & Phelps.

The administrators would attempt (with creditors temporarily at bay) to run the business of the same entity back into solvency by seeking a compromise arrangement with creditors. If this could not be achieved and liquidation ensued, the club as an entity would cease to exist.

Administration meant an automatic 10-point penalty under the rules of the Scottish Premier League (a measure, introduced in 2004, to deter financial mismanagement). The title challenge for 2011/12 was over. It had been forfeited to leaders, and arch-rivals, Celtic.

If the Wee Tax Case was the immediate cause of the administration, the dark cloud of the Big Tax Case still hung directly over the club. The case had been appealed by the club to the First Tier Tribunal (Tax). Several hearings had been held but judgment was still awaited. The delay in a final verdict remains a mystery in the saga. In a sense, however, the actual decision had become irrelevant. HMRC had made it clear that, even if it lost at the first hurdle, it would appeal. There was no foreseeable end to Rangers' financial difficulties. It was reported that total potential debt, including to the HMRC, could now exceed a staggering £134 million. The administrators sought to find another buyer.

While many were deep in insolvency proceedings and commercial negotiations, football's own judicial process continued. The SFA brought charges against Rangers FC and Craig Whyte for bringing the game into disrepute after the takeover by reason of the deliberate non-payment of tax, failure to disclose Whyte's previous disqualification, failure to provide accounts and failure to pay certain other clubs amounts due from matches. The SFA Judicial Panel Disciplinary Tribunal met in March and April under the chairmanship of Gary Allan QC. Their verdict, issued on 23rd April, was damning:

'On any view, the matters involved in this case are as serious offences against the ordinary standards of corporate governance as one could imagine.'

'On any view, the matters involved in this case are as serious offences against the ordinary standards of corporate governance as one could imagine.'

The tribunal imposed the maximum fine of £160,000 on Rangers FC. It also concluded that a 12-month ban on registering new players was appropriate. (It had considered whether it should expel or suspend Rangers FC from membership of the SFA but concluded that this punishment would be too severe.)

As for Craig Whyte, he had *'engaged in scandalous business activities which …. had a corrosive effect on the reputation of a proud football club'*. He was banned for life from participation in football in Scotland.

Rangers appealed but this was rejected. The club did succeed in persuading the Court of Session that the 12-month transfer ban should be removed as technically outside the sanctions available to the tribunal but the reprieve would be short-lived.

The SFA Judicial Panel had noted that *'there was scarcely a mention of any person lacing a boot or kicking a football'* in the course of the six-day proceedings before the tribunal.

Could liquidation be avoided?

There were potential buyers. The best offer was £8.5 million. Rangers could, however, only stave off liquidation if creditors would agree a compromise arrangement, formally known as a Company Voluntary Agreement (CVA). Creditors would have to accept a minimal amount in recovery of their debts.

HMRC made it clear that they would not approve the CVA for Rangers. Liquidation, in their view, would allow for greater investigatory powers into what went wrong at Ibrox and more effective legal weapons to bring claims against

'There was scarcely a mention of any person lacing a boot or kicking a football.'

wrongdoers, leading ultimately to greater recovery for the public purse. Others argued in vain that the taxpayer would be better served by a share of the proceeds available from a sale of the club and ongoing tax on higher earnings as a result of Rangers staying in the top flight with access to European football. Yet HMRC, the majority creditor, was resolved. Just two days earlier, the UK Government announced that it would be consulting on further measures to counter 'artificial and abusive' tax avoidance schemes.

Liquidation was now inevitable. Rangers Football Club PLC went into liquidation on 14th June 2012. The club's assets were sold off by the liquidators for £5.5 million to Sevco 5088 (and then transferred to Sevco Scotland Ltd) owned by a consortium led by former Sheffield United chief executive Charles Green. This transferee company was re-named The Rangers Football Club PLC, the 'newco'. (The 'old' Rangers, in liquidation, was less glamorously re-named RFC 2012 PLC.)

The 'newco', as a new entity, was obliged to apply to the SFA for membership in place of the 'old' Rangers and to the SPL to play in the top league. Was it still in the financial interests of the other SPL clubs to re-admit Rangers? The application was rejected by 10 votes (against), one (for) and one (abstention). The 'new' Rangers had no choice but to apply then to the lower Scottish Football League (SFL). The latter approved the club's admittance to the SFL third division. The SFA accepted the membership of the 'new' club but on condition that the new Rangers would accept the sanctions imposed by the SFA on the 'old' Rangers (including disciplinary decisions and a 12-month transfer embargo on buying new players).

The (new) Rangers, under manager Ally McCoist, played its first match in August 2012, a win in the Ramsdens Cup against Brechin City. The club's first home match in the SFL third division, against East Stirling, attracted a crowd of 49,118. It was a world record for a fourth tier football match.

Allegations and counter-allegations continued to abound. In August 2012, the SPL itself announced an independent commission (led by Lord Nimmo Smith) 'to inquire into alleged EBT payments and arrangements made by Rangers in relation to players during the period from 2000 until 2011' with a view to possible sanctions if breaches of its rules had taken place. Could a great club be stripped of titles won in a glorious past? For Sir David Murray, this was now 'not about sporting integrity' but a 'sense of tribalism' had taken over. In February 2013 the SPL commission decided that the scale and extent of the contravention of the disclosure rules required a substantial penalty – a fine of £250,000 – but that no unfair sporting advantage had been gained from these contraventions and Rangers would not be stripped of its past titles.

As regards the Big Tax Case, ironically, in December 2012 a majority judgment in the First Tier Tax Tribunal largely supported Rangers' arguments. HMRC promptly appealed to an Upper Tier Tax Tribunal.

Investigations, legal cases and recriminations will, one suspects, continue for years.

Chapter Nine

SEX, DISCRIMINATION AND PARTICIPATION

An athlete or player cannot win unless he or she can participate in the competition. Several of the most significant legal challenges in sport have concerned the right of a particular individual to play in a sport or to compete in an event.

It is fascinating how many of the cases recalled in this chapter have reflected changing attitudes or sensibilities in society at large as the courts have over the years encountered challenges for alleged discrimination on the basis of gender, youth, disability or race.

Groundbreaking cases include pioneering women seeking non-discriminatory rights to participate in training of racehorses, boxing and refereeing, a transsexual tennis player wishing to play in the women's singles at the US Open and an 11 year-old girl's desire to play football with similarly aged boys. We also follow a golfer's battle to be permitted to use a golf cart in professional competition, the challenge of a top-class disabled athlete and a cricket umpire's claim for racial discrimination when dropped from the elite umpiring panel.

74. FLORENCE NAGLE AND THE JOCKEY CLUB

A woman's fight for a trainer's licence

Florence Nagle wanted a licence to be a racehorse trainer. Was it unlawful for the Jockey Club to deny her a licence because of a 'men only' policy?

The cause of women in sport has, as far as the courts have been concerned, had no stronger champion than Florence Nagle.

Licences to train horses for racing in Great Britain were issued by the Jockey Club and no horse could race in meetings under their auspices unless trained by a licensed trainer. No trainer's licence had previously been issued to a woman. Florence Nagle owned and ran a racing stable at Westerlands, near Petworth in Sussex. She had extensive knowledge and experience of racehorses and, by 1966, she had trained them for more than 35 years. It was in her blood. How were her stables licensed for her horses to run? The Jockey Club had issued a licence to her 'head lad'.

A proud and determined woman, 70 year-old Florence Nagle now sought a trainer's licence in her own right. It was refused. The Jockey Club

70 year-old Florence Nagle now sought a trainer's licence in her own right.

said simply that it was a private institution and had complete discretion to decide to whom it issued a licence. Nagle was undaunted. She decided to take on the Jockey Club, alleging that the decision was based on sex discrimination and was an unlawful restraint of trade. She took the claim to the High Court. The Jockey Club tried to stop the claim.

Legal Question: Should the Jockey Club's decision be declared invalid as an unlawful restraint of trade contrary to public policy?

For: The Jockey Club's decisions affected people's livelihoods. It must act reasonably in the issue of licences. Its general practice, clearly based on sex discrimination, was to refuse to grant a trainer's licence to a woman in any circumstances. There was no objection on the grounds of Nagle's capacity and fitness as a trainer. The Jockey Club's practice was contrary to public policy and an unlawful restraint of trade.

Against: The Jockey Club was a private organisation. There was no contract or obligation to issue a licence. The sex discrimination legislation (as then existing) did not apply to the issue of licences by the Jockey Club. It was well established that a private club had complete discretion to decide whom to admit as a member. It was for the Jockey Club to decide its own policy. The courts were not entitled to interfere.

Decision: Florence Nagle won her battle despite losing in the first round. On appeal, the Court of Appeal allowed her claim to go ahead.

It was a landmark case. Although there were no applicable sex discrimination laws in force at that time, the court said that the general practice of the Jockey Club in refusing a trainer's licence to a woman was contrary to public policy and an unlawful restraint of trade. The Jockey Club had adopted, in effect, an unwritten rule. Lord Denning, one of the country's leading and most reforming judges, said:

'... *this unwritten rule may well be said to be arbitrary and capricious ... It is not as if the training of horses could be regarded as an unsuitable occupation for a woman ... We are considering an association which exercises a virtual monopoly in an important field of human activity.*'

Lord Justice Danckwerts added:

'*Her application is not considered [by the Jockey Club] simply because she is a woman. That is arbitrary and entirely out of touch with the present state of society in Great Britain.*'

The decision seems straightforward today but it was revolutionary at the time. Note that Florence Nagle even lost when the issue first came to the courts. It was only her perseverance and determination in pressing the case, and appealing, which won this famous victory. The decision was a clear warning that, even though sporting governing bodies may be private bodies, they affect peoples' livelihoods by making decisions such as whether or not to issue a licence to a particular individual. Decisions cannot be taken arbitrarily.

The gates had opened for the cause of equality of women in sport.

The Jockey Club capitulated and a trainer's licence was issued to Florence Nagle. In 1969, she became the first woman trainer in Britain to saddle a winner under the rules of racing.

The gates had opened for the cause of equality of women in sport – but not fully opened. The Jockey Club continued to resist calls for women to be allowed to ride as jockeys in races until 1972. The first woman to ride a winner in Britain was Meriel Tufnell on *Scorched Earth* at Kempton. It was 11 years after Florence Nagle's victory, in 1977, before women were admitted as members of the Jockey Club.

Subsequent female horse racing trainers of distinction have included Jenny Pitman (trainer of Grand National winners, *Corbiere* in 1983 and *Royal Athlete* in 1995), Jessica Harrington, Auriol Sinclair, Mercy Rimell and Henrietta Knight (trainer of *Best Mate*, which won three consecutive Cheltenham Gold Cups).

Florence Nagle is a name which should feature strongly in the history of women in sport.

75. RENÉE RICHARDS

Playing in the women's singles at the US Open

Renée Richards had undergone gender change surgery to become a woman. Should she be permitted to play in the women's singles at the US Open?

Renée Richards was a fine tennis player. She wanted to play in the women's singles event in the 1976 US Open at Forest Hills in New York. Her standard was good enough. The United States Tennis Association (USTA) denied her entry. The reason? She was born a male, Richard Raskind.

Richard Raskind went to Yale University and captained the men's tennis team there in 1954. After Yale, he went to medical school and then served in the US Navy. He pursued a career as an eye surgeon. He married and fathered one son. He continued to play amateur tennis and, in 1974, was ranked 13th in the US men's 35-and-over division. Nevertheless, for many years he had experienced a troubled sexual identity and was increasingly uncomfortable, psychologically, as a male. In the mid-1960s, he travelled Europe dressed as a woman, intending to have sex reassignment surgery. Finally, in early 1975 at the age of 40, he did go ahead and had successful surgery.

As Renée Richards, she re-established her ophthalmology practice in California and started playing tennis seriously again. She played in a few local amateur tournaments. Indeed, she played several before her gender change was discovered. It was after a prestigious amateur tournament at La Jolla, California which she entered under the name of Renée Clark, and won, that her past became public knowledge after a local media 'exposé'.

Inevitably, the question arose: what should the tennis authorities do? For the next year or so, Renée Richards played various US tennis tournaments. Some tournaments accepted her entry with knowledge of her transsexual background and indeed invited her. Some refused her entry. At one tournament, 25 women players withdrew in protest, claiming that she still maintained the muscular advantages of a male and genetically remained a male. The issue came to a crunch with her wish to play in the 1976 US Open.

The International Tennis Federation (ITF), when considering the issue of transexuality for events under its jurisdiction, decided to invoke sex chromatin tests which the International Olympic

'How hungry for tennis success must you be to have your penis chopped off in pursuit of it?'

Committee (IOC) had adopted in 1968 to test gender eligibility for the Olympic Games. The Barrbody test analysed membrane cells, taken by a smear test inside the mouth, for the presence of 'female' genes. The test was not without its critics. The USTA decided to require the same eligibility for entry into the women's events at the US Open.

Prior to 1975, no sex chromatin test had ever been asked of any competitor in the history of the US Open, nor had Richards been requested to undertake any such test for any event sanctioned in the USA. Although she had once passed the test, she had failed it (secretly) at two tournaments in Europe. She knew it was unlikely she would satisfy the test for the US Open. She considered that it was being introduced specifically in order to exclude her.

Richards questioned the validity of verifying gender through a genes test and insisted that 'bodily, psychologically and sexually' she was female. She had been issued official papers such as a passport and a certificate to practise medicine. She said: 'In the eyes of the law, I am female. It's a human rights issue. I want to show that someone who has a different lifestyle or medical condition has a right to stand up for what they are.'

She rejected the theory that 'the floodgates would be opened and through them would come tumbling an endless stream of made-over Neanderthals who would brutalise Chris Evert and Evonne Goolagong', adding: 'How hungry for tennis success must you be to have your penis chopped off in pursuit of it?' This was 'sheer nonsense'. She had the support of Billie Jean King and many other leading players.

Richards spent a year battling in the courts. She brought a legal claim to prevent the USTA from relying on a sex chromatin test for determining whether or not she was female and to require the USTA to permit her entry. It was a unique and challenging case. It came before the New York Supreme Court.

Legal Question: Renée Richards claimed that the sex chromatin test breached the anti-discriminatory code which was part of the equal opportunities legislation in the State of New York. Should she succeed?

For: Richards had undergone medically approved sex reassignment surgery. This was not a case of fraud. Her passport and other official documents legally recognised her as a woman. The sex chromatin test was introduced by the US tennis authorities solely in order to exclude Richards. It had never been required as a condition of entry previously or required of any other players. It was discriminatory.

Against: Although a difficult issue, in fairness to all female competitors, it was reasonable for the US Open to apply the same sex chromatin test as applied to events under the jurisdiction of the IOC.

Decision: After hearing conflicting medical and tennis evidence, the New York Supreme Court upheld Renée Richards' claim. The court decided that the requirement for her to pass the sex chromatin test in order to be eligible to participate in the tournament was '*grossly unfair, discriminatory and inequitable*' and violated Richards' rights under the human rights law of New York.

Renée Richards was free to play as a woman in the US Open.

When sex testing was first introduced by the IOC in 1968, several Eastern Bloc shot putters and discus throwers suddenly disappeared from women's sport. The only athlete known to have failed a femininity test at the Olympics is Ewa Kłobukowska, a Polish sprinter, in Tokyo in 1964.

The issue of transexualism has led to continued medical and legal attention. The Barrbody test was actually phased out by the IOC during the late 1970s in favour of different and technically preferable tests. (The most significant sporting 'gender' case since has involved South African Caster Semenya, 800 metres women's world champion in 2009. She was later required by the International Amateur Athletics Federation (IAAF) to take a gender test. Cleared for competition in 2010, Semenya won silver medals in the 800 metres at the 2011 World Championships and at the London 2012 Olympics.)

Renée Richards did play in the 1977 US Open. She lost 1-6, 4-6 in the first round to the third seed, Britain's Virginia Wade. Partnered by Betty Ann Stuart, however, the pair reached the final of the ladies' doubles that year when they lost to Pam Shriver and a youthful Martina Navratilova. She played in further US Opens until 1981 with moderate success, reaching the quarter-finals of the singles in 1978 and, in 1979, winning the US Open 35-and-over singles event. In 1981 Richards retired from professional tennis and returned to her other profession, ophthalmic surgery.

Perhaps fortunately for the British tennis authorities, when Renée Richards came to Wimbledon it was not as a player but during a successful two-year stint as coach and adviser to the future Wimbledon champion, Martina Navratilova – the highlight of which was Navratilova's dramatic three-set victory over Chris Evert-Lloyd in the 1982 Wimbledon final.

76. BELINDA PETTY

The fight to referee a men's competition

Belinda Petty wanted to be a full judo referee. Why couldn't she referee a men's competition at senior level?

A female referee of a men's competition? It was a case which could, if it succeeded, break through another barrier of male-dominated sporting practices. But would it?

By 1977, Belinda Petty had practised judo for nearly 20 years. A full member of the Budokwai, she held the qualification known as a Second Dan. In 1974 she gained the British Judo Association's club coach award and had been employed as a part-time judo instructor at various schools and clubs. She had also qualified as a judo referee, passing the national referee examination in 1976. The certificate did not differentiate between men's competitions and women's competitions. She had refereed competitions at club and area levels, including men's competitions.

She was proud of her qualifications. They assisted her job as an instructor. In October 1977 she was a referee in the national All England Men's Competition. Then, she suffered a blow to her aspirations. The president of the Judo Association intervened and stated that she should not have refereed in a men's national competition. It was not the association's policy. Since then, she had never again been selected to referee in men's competitions at national level. The association believed that 'it was not in the interests of the sport and not in the interests of women that they should referee male events'.

The president of the Judo Association intervened and stated that she should not have refereed in a men's national competition. It was not the association's policy.

Belinda Petty was very upset. She decided to fight the policy, alleging sex discrimination. Florence Nagle had won her case as a female trainer. Could Belinda Petty now achieve a similar result as a referee? The Sex Discrimination Act 1975 had by now been passed – but the Act exempted discrimination in sport 'where the physical strength, stamina or physique of the average woman puts her at a disadvantage to the average man' and the discrimination 'relates to the participation of a person as a competitor' in a sporting event. The scope of this so-called 'sporting exemption' was now in question.

Belinda Petty took her case against the Judo Association to an industrial tribunal in

London, where she won. The Judo Association appealed to the Employment Appeal Tribunal.

Legal Question: Should Belinda Petty be permitted to referee in men's national judo competitions? Did the Judo Association's policy amount to unlawful discrimination?

For: The policy of not selecting women to referee in national men's competitions was clearly discriminatory. Belinda Petty had plenty of experience and full qualifications. The sporting exemption in the 1975 Act only applied to discrimination relating to participation as a competitor, not as a referee. The national referee's qualification did not distinguish between men's and women's events. There were no physical reasons justifying the discrimination.

Against: The Judo Association should be free to decide, in its view, the best policy for selection of referees for national events. Refereeing fell within the sporting exemption since the role of referees related, in a general sense, to participation in competition. Discrimination was justified since women would not have the necessary physical or vocal strength, if necessary, to break apart two hefty male combatants in such an event. The policy was reasonable and consistent with the 1975 Act.

Decision: Belinda Petty won her case.

The Employment Appeal Tribunal decided that the sporting exemption in the 1975 Act only applied to the issue of who could, or could not, take part in the contest as a competitor. This did not extend to refereeing. A referee was not a competitor. '*We cannot see how provisions as to referees relate to the "participation" of the competitors in the contest,*' said the tribunal. Belinda Petty's qualifications for selection as a referee should be considered by the Judo Association on their merits. A general policy of excluding women from refereeing in senior men's competitions was unlawful.

The case was another significant step forward for women in sport. Any practice of excluding women from refereeing in sport, even in an all-male competition, was blown away.

Even the sight of a female assistant referee (no longer called a linesman) at football matches, and indeed as principal referee, has now become frequent – if not popular with all football managers. Wendy Toms became, on 27th August 1997, the first woman to officiate in the Premier League – as an assistant referee in a match between Arsenal and Newcastle. She

Any practice of excluding women from refereeing in sport, even in an all-male competition, was blown away.

was not daunted. Before refereeing earlier in a Championship match, she was reported as saying: 'If the players want to make it hard for me, I am happy to make it twice as hard for them.'

77. THERESA BENNETT

Why can't I play with the boys?

Theresa Bennett was an 11 year-old girl who loved playing football. She wanted to play with the boys in a local league but she was prevented from doing so by the rules. Was this sex discrimination?

Theresa Bennett was a good young footballer and played with the boys at school. She wanted to play more and join a boys' team which played in a local league run by the Nottinghamshire FA. They said: 'No'. It was 1978. Why could she not play in the same team as boys of her own age?

The rules of the regional Nottinghamshire FA and the national FA did not permit mixed teams. They stated in effect that, except for matches in a playing season in age groups up to the age of 10, 'players in a match must be of the same gender'. Theresa Bennett, or those acting on her behalf, challenged this rule. She was good enough to play in the 'boys' team. This was sex discrimination. Her case was supported by the Equal Opportunities Commission.

Why could she not play in the same team as boys of her own age?

The FA claimed that the rule was there for the safety of women and was justified under the Sex Discrimination Act which had a 'sporting exemption'. This permitted single sex competitions 'where the physical strength, stamina or physique of the average woman puts her at a disadvantage to the average man'. The FA wanted to encourage girls and women to play football, but age 11 was an appropriate cut-off point for mixed football.

Legal Question: Should Theresa Bennett succeed and be able to play in a mixed team at age 11 in the local league?

For: The physical differences, in terms of strength and stamina, between girls and boys at that age were not so great as differences between individuals of the same sex.

To prevent girls aged 11 playing with boys in a mixed team was discrimination and not the intention or policy of the Act.

Against: The rules were reasonable for the safety of girls and women. The 'sporting exemption' in the Act applied. The test was not based on individual attributes but whether the 'average woman' would be at a physical disadvantage compared with an 'average man' when playing football and the answer was 'yes'. The rules were permitted by the Act.

Decision: The case went first to the county court. Evidence was given of Theresa Bennett's skill and prowess as a young footballer. One witness said that 'she ran rings round the boys'. Another witness recalled that she 'was a vicious tackler and once tackled a 15 year-old so hard he had to be supported and taken from the field'. She won her case there but the FA appealed.

Theresa Bennett lost in the Court of Appeal. Despite the strong evidence about Bennett's individual position, the court decided that discrimination under the Act was permitted where 'the average woman' was at a disadvantage in the particular sport compared with 'the average man'. An average woman was, in the opinion of the court, at a disadvantage to the average man in football because she does not have the physique to stand up to 'the rigours of mixed football'. And, importantly, 'woman' for this purpose should be interpreted as a woman of any age – and not by reference alone to girls aged 11. One judge commented: '*We do not enquire about the ages of ladies.*'

The court (which included Lord Denning, one of the country's most reforming judges) had sympathy for Theresa Bennett – but allowing her to play would be '*stretching the bounds of judicial creativity beyond breaking point*'. No further appeal was allowed. So, Theresa Bennett lost her case.

Perhaps Theresa Bennett did have some partial success in that the cut-off point for mixed football was subsequently raised by the FA by one year. Nearly 30 years later, she also had a fine successor and campaigner in 10 year-old Minnie Cruttwell. Minnie was a key member of the Balham Blazers in south London and she wanted to continue to play for them when her age group included 12 year-olds. 'Girls are just as good as boys and if you've been with a team for a long time, you know them well and you don't want to have to make new friends.' She wrote to Tessa Jowell, then Secretary of State for Culture, Media and Sport, who went to see them play, saying: 'Women's football is England's fastest-growing sport and I'm concerned that we are the only country in Europe who have a blanket ban in place for mixed football at this age level.'

'We do not enquire about the ages of ladies.'

The result? In May 2007 the FA announced that it was reconsidering its age limit for mixed-sex teams. In the meantime, specified leagues would see how older mixed sides worked before the FA decided on a long-term policy. One of these allowed Minnie to continue to play for the Balham Blazers. Her father said: 'Minnie is the toughest tackler. I am glad the FA has decided to rethink'.

In May 2011 the FA announced that, after further studies, the age limit for mixed-sex teams would increase to permit under-13s to be included. The limit has since been increased further and in June 2014 the FA Council unanimously approved raising the limit to include under-16s. One suspects that Theresa Bennett approved.

78. JANE COUCH

The 'Fleetwood Assassin' fights for a UK boxing licence

Are there sports or events in which women should not participate? Is boxing one of them?

Jane Couch was born in Fleetwood, England in 1968. She later became known as 'the Fleetwood Assassin'. Expelled from her Blackpool school as a teenager, she lived what she later described as a 'life of booze, drugs and street fighting' until she was aged 26. Then she saw a TV documentary about women's boxing in the USA. She decided she could do that: 'It all looked so easy and feeble compared with some of the street fights I had been in.'

Her first official fight was against a female policewoman. Couch knocked her out in the second round. 'It was brilliant to flatten one and get paid for it,' she said. She burst on to the world professional boxing scene in May 1996 when she travelled to Copenhagen and outpointed French kick-boxing star Sandra Geiger over 10 rounds to win the Women's International Boxing Federation (WIBF) welterweight title. The fight attracted a peak TV audience across Europe of 3.5 million viewers. Geiger reportedly spent three days in hospital recovering after the fight with a broken nose and cracked ribs. Couch successfully defended her title in New Orleans in March 1997.

All her professional fights had been abroad. By 1998, Jane Couch, who trained at a gym near Bristol with her manager, Tex Woodward, wanted the opportunity to box professionally **Then she saw a TV documentary about women's boxing in the USA. She decided she could do that.**

in Britain. She sought the additional income which she could earn from fights held in her home country. It was her livelihood. The British Boxing Board of Control (BBBC) refused to give a licence to Couch, or any other female boxer, to box in Britain.

The BBBC justified its policy on the grounds that, if permitted to box professionally, women were more likely to suffer life-threatening blows to head and breasts and that pre-menstrual tension would make a female more liable to injury. One British promoter minced no words and put it another way: 'The only reason for women to be in the ring is as ring card girls.'

Couch decided to fight her cause with the BBBC. She alleged unlawful sex discrimination and had the strong backing of the Equal Opportunities Commission. She took the BBBC to an industrial tribunal.

Legal Question: Was the policy of the BBBC, in refusing to award boxing licences to women, unlawful sex discrimination? Should Jane Couch be entitled to box professionally in Britain?

For: The sex discrimination laws only justified discrimination in circumstances where men would be competing against women. The 'sporting exemption' was not relevant to single-sex competition. The BBBC's refusal to sanction female boxing in the UK was costing Couch money in lost earnings. Not to issue licences to women for boxing amounted simply to unlawful sex discrimination.

Against: The refusal by the BBBC to award a licence was based on objective and justifiable grounds. The risks of injury for women in boxing were greater than for men. There was medical evidence that women were potentially accident-prone and unstable emotionally when suffering from pre-menstrual tension. Professional boxing was inappropriate for women.

Decision: Jane Couch won by a knock-out. The industrial tribunal in Croydon, after a two day hearing, upheld her argument. The policy of the BBBC, in refusing to award any licences to women to box in Britain, amounted to unlawful sex discrimination. The 'sporting exemption' did not apply.

Jane Couch received her licence. British boxing history was made at Caesar's Palace Casino in Streatham, London on 25th November 1998 when she fought 18 year-old Simona Lukic from Germany in the first licensed professional women's fight in Britain. Couch won by a technical knock-out when the referee stopped the contest in the second round.

The policy of the British Boxing Board of Control, in refusing to award any licences to women to box in Britain, amounted to unlawful sex discrimination.

In February 1999, at the Thornaby Pavilion in Teeside, Couch took part in the first female title bout in Britain to be sanctioned by the BBBC. She successfully defended her WIBF welterweight title with a unanimous 10-round decision over European champion, Marischa Sjauw of Holland. Later in 1999, at the David Lloyd Tennis Centre in Raynes Park, London, Jane won the vacant WBF women's lightweight title with a 10-round decision over Sharon Anyos of Australia.

Jane Couch carried on her personal fight with the BBBC in 2001 when she sought a licence to fight an exhibition bout at Wembley with one of her male sparring partners. This was refused.

In 2007, Jane Couch was awarded the MBE in the Queen's Birthday Honours, declaring: 'I've been all over the world boxing in some of the biggest shows in front of millions of people and this is the biggest shock ever.'

In 2012, women's boxing was held as an official sport in the Olympics for the first time. The first Olympic women's boxing gold medal was won, in the flyweight division, by Britain's Nicola Adams.

79. CASEY MARTIN

A golf cart and the question: what is golf?

Casey Martin suffered from a blood disorder and he needed a golf cart to play. Could he be denied a place on the US PGA Tour?

Casey Martin holed his putt for a bogey on the 18th hole in the final round of the Nike Tour Championship. It was a disappointing 78 and he was slipping from his overnight position on the leaderboard. He waited nervously as other players finished. Would he remain in the top 15 of the money list on the Nike Tour and fulfil his dream of qualifying for the main 2000 US PGA Tour?

Yes. PGA Commissioner, Tim Finchem, presented Martin with his tour card, shook the golfer's hand and patted him on the back. But would he be allowed to play on the

US PGA Tour in the same way as he was now competing – using a motorised golf cart? That would depend, ultimately, on the verdict of the US Supreme Court.

Martin, born in Eugene, Oregon, was educated at Stanford University where he was briefly a team-mate of Tiger Woods. A promising golfer, he turned professional in 1995. His ambition was to play on the US PGA Tour. But he suffered from a birth defect in his left leg, a circulatory problem known as Klippel-Trenauny-Weber syndrome. This resulted in bleeding from blood vessels and difficulty in walking. He wore a special pressure stocking on his leg so that he could stand and walk. The constant tightness of the stocking had weakened his leg muscles. He could not walk the distances involved in PGA Tour events. He needed a golf cart between shots. He argued that he was entitled to a golf cart by reason of the disability legislation in the USA, the Americans with Disabilities Act: 'I just want to be given the chance to play.'

The US PGA said: 'No'. They maintained that use of a cart would give him an unfair advantage and take away a fundamental aspect of the athleticism and stamina involved in top-flight tournament golf. Many top golfers agreed. Jack Nicklaus was among those who took issue with the opinion that walking was not a fundamental part of the sport: 'I think we ought to take them all out and play golf. I think they'd change their minds. I promise you, it's fundamental.'

Martin filed a lawsuit in 1977 challenging the US PGA Tour's decision and obtained a ruling from a US magistrate that a golf course during a tournament was indeed a 'place of public accommodation' within the US disability legislation. The US PGA agreed that Martin could use his cart for the time being during the appeals process until the issue was finally decided. He continued to do so on the secondary Nike Tour.

In 1998, Martin achieved a career highlight that year by qualifying for and finishing 23rd at the US Open at the Olympic Club in San Francisco, briefly contending for the lead

> **But would he be allowed to play on the US PGA Tour in the same way as he was now competing – using a motorised golf cart?**

before falling back. He was the first player to use a cart in US Open history. Now, in 1999, he had qualified and was ready for the full US PGA Tour for the 2000 season.

In January 2000, at Indian Wells Country Club in the Bob Hope Chrysler Classic, 27 year-old Casey Martin teed off as a tour 'rookie' and, for the first time, a professional golfer on the US PGA Tour went to his golf cart – an EZGO. He finished with a four under par 68. The marshalls carefully guarded his golf cart during the round.

But could he continue? The appeals process finally reached the US Supreme Court in May 2001.

Legal Question: Could Casey Martin continue to compete, using a golf cart between shots, in US PGA Tour events? Were US PGA's objections contrary to the US disability legislation?

For: A golf course during a tournament was a place of public accommodation covered by the US disability legislation. Martin was disabled and entitled to a reasonable accommodation – which would include a cart. He didn't want a special advantage, just a chance to play. The cart did not give any advantage in golfing terms; if anything, it disturbed his rhythm.

Against: It gave Martin an unfair advantage. A golf cart was an 'outside agency'. It violated the spirit of competition. It took away a fundamental aspect of athleticism and stamina that walking brings to top-flight tournament golf. The area inside the ropes was no different from a playing field in any other professional sport. The disability legislation was not designed to apply to competitions in professional sporting events. In elite athletics, certain rules must apply equally to everyone.

Decision: One of the nine judges of the US Supreme Court (yes, nine judges to decide this issue), Justice Antonin Scalia, summed up the question before the court – perhaps with 'tongue in cheek' humour – in these polemic terms:

'It has been rendered the solemn duty of the Supreme Court of the United States … to decide What is Golf. I am sure that the Framers of the Constitution … fully expected that sooner or later … that judges of this august Court would some day have to wrestle with that age-old jurisprudential question, for which their years of study in the law have so well prepared them: Is someone riding around a golf course from shot to shot really a golfer?'

By a 7-2 majority, the US Supreme Court decided in Casey Martin's favour.

The Court, the highest court of the land, deemed that a golf course for a US PGA Tour event was indeed a 'public' place for the purposes of the US disability legislation. It was reasonable for Martin to use a golf cart in such a 'public' place. Justice Stevens commented: *'The purpose of the walking rule is … not compromised in the slightest by allowing Martin to use a cart.'* Accommodating Martin with a golf cart would not fundamentally change the game, said the court. *'What it can be said to do, on the other hand, is to allow Martin the chance to qualify for and compete in the … events [the PGA Tour] offers to those members of the public who have the skill and the desire to enter.'*

As for Casey Martin, he could only finish 179th on the Tour's money list in the 2000 season and failed to keep his elite level US PGA Tour card through his earnings. In the qualifying school for the following year, he narrowly failed to keep his spot (finishing tied for 37th when only the top 35 qualified), relegating him to the Nike Tour again. Playing only a limited number of events, he failed in subsequent years to regain his US PGA Tour card and, in 2006, he retired from professional tournament golf to become coach of the University of Oregon's men's golf team in his hometown of Eugene.

In 2012, with the US Open again at the Olympic Club in San Francisco, Martin decided to enter a local qualifying tournament and surprisingly clinched one of the remaining US Open spots. Despite his deteriorating condition but with the aid of his cart between shots, Casey Martin played well and narrowly missed the cut. His score over two rounds was better than those of Rory McIlroy and Luke Donald.

80. DARRELL HAIR

Racial discrimination and a cricket umpire

Darrell Hair was one of two umpires who decided that Pakistan had forfeited a Test match. He was later disciplined but his co-umpire was not. Was it racial discrimination against him?

Darrell Hair was a no-nonsense, straight-talking Australian. He was an international cricket umpire. He called it as he saw it, but did he call it once too often?

Born in New South Wales, Hair was a useful right-arm fast-medium club bowler in Sydney grade cricket until a knee injury cut short his playing career. He became a Test match umpire in 1991 and was appointed to the ICC elite umpire panel in 2002 when the International Cricket Council (ICC) introduced a policy that both umpires should come from nations not participating in the match.

Hair, a big man with a commanding presence, was not short of self-belief in his umpiring. This was evident at the Melbourne Cricket Ground in December 1995 when Australia were playing Sri Lanka. Hair (unusually, remarked *Wisden*, from the bowler's end) called Muttiah Muralitharan seven times in three overs for an improper bowling action - throwing. This, accompanied by other incidents and decisions involving Asian sub-continent nations, meant that he was always viewed with suspicion – and more – by India, Pakistan and Sri Lanka. No one was prepared, however, for the events of the fourth Test between England and Pakistan at the Oval in August 2006.

Pakistan, behind 0-2 in the series, were in a strong position with a first innings lead of 331 runs. Play began quietly on the fourth day with England on 78 for 1. After the dismissal of Alastair Cook by Umar Gul in the 52nd over of the England innings with a 'reverse swing' delivery, the umpires inspected the ball in customary fashion. Play continued.

At the end of the 56th over, just four overs later, Hair again inspected the ball and judged that, showing various scratches, it had been altered unfairly by human intervention – it had been tampered with. He reported this to his fellow umpire, West Indian Billy Doctrove. Hair wanted the ball changed. Doctrove agreed, although his initial preference had been to play on and try to identify the person responsible. A box of replacement balls was brought on. Hair signalled to the scorers that five penalty runs should be added to the England score.

Play continued in the afternoon until bad light intervened and tea was taken. The umpires decided to resume play at 4.45pm They returned to the field of play. But the Pakistan team did not. Indignation had turned to anger. The team, led by captain Inzamam-ul-Haq, decided to protest. The decision on ball-tampering was an allegation of cheating. It was, they considered, a direct and unfair challenge to their honour. The umpires left the field of play, leaving the bails intact. They went to see the Pakistan team in their dressing room. The exact verbal exchange is in dispute. The umpires stated that they were returning to the field of play – but it is not clear that any warning was given that the match could be forfeited.

At 4.56pm, the umpires symbolically removed the bails and awarded the match to England.

Hair and Doctrove walked out again on to the pitch at 4.53pm, along with the England batsmen and to the cheers of the bemused crowd. The Pakistan team did not follow. Wicketkeeper Kamran Akmal was seen on the balcony taking his gloves off and reading a paper. At 4.56pm, the umpires symbolically removed the bails and awarded the match to England. They were applying Law 21 which, in effect, stated that a match shall be lost by a side which in the opinion of the umpires refuses to play.

Chaos ensued. The 23,000 crowd jeered, with no idea of what was going on. Had the match really been forfeited? Crisis meetings took place involving senior cricket and match officials. In a surprising twist, the covers were seen coming off the pitch. The Pakistani team had apparently indicated, after their initial protest, that they would now take the field. They did indeed set out on to the pitch – but the umpires would not. It was a farce. It was not until 10.30pm that an announcement was made that the Test had been forfeited as an England win. It was the first time ever, in 129 years of Test cricket, that a Test match had been forfeited.

It was a public relations disaster for cricket. Recriminations abounded. The Pakistani team and management expressed outrage at the charge of ball-tampering. Others said it had only been a matter of time. The public perception was that the whole issue had been a shambles and handled badly. Hair's past record of controversy involving Asian sub-continent teams was raised by many

Holding aloft the infamous ball, Boycott declared: 'That's a good ball, not just a playable ball.'

commentators. Imran Khan called Hair an 'umpiring fundamentalist' and commented that 'such characters court controversy'. Wasim Akram called for Hair to be sacked. Michael Atherton said: 'The whole sorry mess was caused by the crassest and most insensitive piece of umpiring I have ever seen.'

The first official action, though, was a disciplinary action against Pakistan captain, Inzamam-ul-Haq, under the ICC Code of Conduct. The tribunal found that there was insufficient evidence to support the charge that his team had been guilty of ball-tampering. A turning point was dramatic evidence given by England's own Geoffrey Boycott. Holding aloft the infamous ball, he declared: 'That's a good ball, not just a playable ball.' Inzamam was, however, found guilty of bringing the game into disrepute by deliberately refusing to lead his team back on to the field of play when called to do so by the umpires.

The ICC then turned to 53 year-old Hair. The problem was that the decision to award the match to England, when the Pakistan team failed to return to the field of play, was in accordance with the laws of cricket. Hair knew his cricket laws. Many, however, considered that the umpires had acted insensitively and that much greater effort should have been made to continue the game in the interests of cricket. The growing swell of opinion was strongly anti-Hair. Hair recognised this and did his cause little good by secretly offering to resign in return for a payment of US$500,000.

In November 2006 the ICC formally met in Mumbai. After a short hearing by a three-man sub-committee who then reported to the full ICC, Hair, whose contract was due to run until March 2008, was banned from officiating in international matches. He was no longer a member of the ICC panel of umpires. Hair's umpiring career appeared to be at an end.

Hair did not take the decision meekly. In February 2007 he dramatically announced that he was suing the ICC on grounds of racial discrimination, saying: 'I believe that if I had been from the West Indies, India or Pakistan, I might have been treated differently.' It was an extraordinary and ironic claim given past accusations against Hair himself. Was Hair just trying to get his revenge? Yet, one could see his point. Why had he been disciplined and not his co-umpire, West Indian Billy Doctrove? Hair claimed that, as a result of the premature termination of his contract, his lost earnings would be in the region of US$4 million. The claim was heard in the Central London Employment Tribunal in October 2007.

Legal Question: Should Darrell Hair succeed in his claim for racial discrimination against the ICC?

For: No one questioned Hair's technical competence. He was accepted as being one of the ICC's best umpires before that incident. He acted in accordance with the laws of cricket in forfeiting the match. The decisions in the test at the Oval were taken jointly with his co-umpire, Billy Doctrove. No disciplinary action had been taken against Doctrove. The action against Hair was due to the pressure of the Asian cricket representatives. It was racial discrimination.

Against: Race was never mentioned in the deliberations of the ICC board or sub-committees. The decision was solely taken in the interests of cricket. Hair had clearly taken the lead in the decision to forfeit the match. Insufficient warning was given. The ICC had lost confidence in him. His actions and lack of judgment had damaged the reputation of cricket and could properly be taken into account in the decision to drop him from the international umpiring panel.

Outcome: Several days of mud-slinging and cross-accusation took place in the tribunal. Hair's counsel ripped into the ICC and their witnesses. Members of the three-man sub-committee, it was revealed, had summarily rejected the recommendation of ICC chief executive Malcolm Speed that Hair should be retained on the elite panel. This three-man panel was made up of representatives from Pakistan and Zimbabwe and Sir John Anderson from New Zealand who described Hair's actions at the Oval as 'appalling'. As Hair's counsel said: 'Hair didn't stand much of a chance did he?'

But no evidence of racial discrimination in making the decision really emerged. The ICC asserted that: ' … exactly the same decision would have been reached had Mr Hair been black or brown or even green.' Billy Doctrove himself found a reason not to attend.

Then, on the seventh day of the tribunal, the hearing was abandoned. Talks had taken place. Hair withdrew his claim for racial discrimination. He would be re-instated as an umpire with the ICC. He could umpire certain second tier matches, but not Test matches as a member of the elite panel. Hair agreed to work with ICC management during a six month 'period of rehabilitation'. The ICC would review his status as an umpire in March 2008 but would give him at least 12 months' notice of non-renewal. No financial settlement was made. The ICC would bear their own legal costs – which were, by then,

> **The ICC asserted that exactly the same decision would have been reached had Mr Hair been black or brown or even green.**

probably more than the $500,000 payment Hair had sought for his resignation in the previous November.

After the Oval incident, Hair was voted Umpire of the Season in the annual poll carried out by *The Wisden Cricketer* magazine, with more than one-third of the votes.

The possibility remained of Hair's return to top-class umpiring – and this was realised when, in March 2008, the ICC reinstated him to the full international panel of umpires. In July 2008, the ICC officially re-designated the Oval Test in 2006 as a draw. Later that same year, in August, Hair handed in his resignation to the ICC in order to take up a coaching role.

81. OSCAR PISTORIUS
Disability, tragedy and the Blade Runner

Oscar Pistorius, as a double ampuitee, could run with the use of prosthetic legs. Was he eligible to compete internationally against able-bodied athletes – even in the Olympics? Would responsibility for a tragic death lead to a fall from grace?

A more extraordinary question in sport can never have been before a court or tribunal. Could a man with no legs run against the fastest able-bodied athletes in the world and qualify for the Olympics?

Oscar Pistorius was born with a congenital defect. He had no fibula (calf) bones in either of his legs and his parents made the heart-rending decision, when Oscar was just 11 months old, that his legs should be amputated below the knee. Oscar himself did not grow up thinking he was disabled. He knew no different. 'I just didn't have any legs.'

From an early age, the South African turned to sport. He attended the boys' high school in Pretoria where, with the help of prosthetic limbs, he played rugby in the school's third XV team. He also played water polo and tennis. Then he suffered a bad knee injury playing rugby. He was introduced to sprinting in January 2004 as part of his rehabilitation. At age 17, using carbon-fibre 'legs' designed for disabled athletes and after just two months' training, he ran his first competitive race in his hometown of Pretoria. He broke the paralympic world record for 100 metres. In his own words, he 'never looked back'. He was a natural athlete.

Just eight months later, he represented South Africa in the 2004 Athens Paralympics. He was a sensation. He took the bronze medal in the 100 metres – and won gold in the 200 metres, breaking the world record with a time of 21.97 seconds. Watching him with his father was the surgeon, Dr Gerry Versveld, who undertook the original amputation operation. With tears in his eyes, Versveld exclaimed: 'Thank you! Thank you! This is the most amazing thing I will probably ever witness.'

Pistorius' thoughts turned seriously to competing against able-bodied athletes in open competition. In March 2005, he competed in the South African National Championships for able-bodied athletes. He proved he was fast enough by coming sixth in the 400 metres in a time of 47.34 seconds. With the aid of his high-tech carbon-fibre legs, he was almost as fast as the best able-bodied runners in the world over that distance. Was qualification for the Olympics within his reach?

Could a man with no legs run against the fastest able-bodied athletes in the world and qualify for the Olympics?

Attention turned to the rules. How should the authorities react? The International Association of Athletics Federations (IAAF) were uneasy. Were they to become the 'villains' in the piece? In March 2007, partly one suspects aimed at Pistorius but also at new forms of running shoes, the IAAF adopted a new rule to regulate the use of technical devices. It prohibited 'use of any technical device that incorporates springs, wheels or any other element that provides the user with an advantage over another athlete not using such a device'.

For running, Pistorius used a J-shaped prosthesis known as the Cheetah Flex-Foot supplied by an Icelandic company, Ossur. It is the 'Ferrari' of its kind. The model has been used by many single and double amputees, almost unchanged, since 1997. Despite admiration for his extraordinary achievements, many – including within the IAAF – thought that it should be regarded as a 'technical device' and that it did provide an 'advantage' compared with an able-bodied athlete. Fairness to all athletes required a strict approach to the rules.

How should the controversy be resolved? Pistorius agreed to participate in tests planned by the IAAF. He ran in a specially staged race in Rome in July 2007 which was videotaped by an Italian sports laboratory using several high-definition cameras from different angles. The video appeared to show that Pistorius was slower than other runners off the starting blocks and during the first 50 metres, the acceleration phase, and also around the first bend – but faster over the back straight where he appeared to have a longer stride than the able-bodied athletes.

The test was inconclusive. Further biomechanical studies were undertaken, on behalf of the IAAF, by Professor Brüggemann at the Institute of Biomechanics and Orthopaedics at the German Sport University in Cologne. The studies looked at his sprint movement, oxygen intake, blood lactate metabolism and various other measures agreed with the IAAF. On the basis of this study, Professor Brüggemann concluded that Pistorius' oxygen intake was 25 per cent lower than for the able-bodied athletes and that the 'energy return' to his artificial joints was higher than for human ankle joints. In total, he 'received significant biomechanical advantages by the prosthesis in comparison to sprinting with natural human legs'.

In January 2008, on the basis of this report, the IAAF Council concluded that the Cheetah Flex-Foot was a 'technical device' which gave the user an 'advantage over valid athletes'. Pistorius was declared ineligible to compete in IAAF-sanctioned events for able-bodied athletes. Were his Olympic dreams over?

Pistorius was not one to give up and he appealed to the Court of Arbitration for Sport (CAS).

Legal Question: Pistorius claimed that he should be permitted to participate alongside able-bodied athletes in competitions held under IAAF Rules, including the Olympics if he qualified, using his Cheetah prosthetic limbs. Should he succeed?

For: The Cologne tests concentrated solely on the 'advantages' for Pistorius. By excluding the start and acceleration phases, the results were distorted and did not consider the effect on his performance over the entire 400 metres race. Overall, there was no net advantage. The IAAF, by not searching for an appropriate accommodation for Pistorius' disability to permit him to compete on an equal basis with able-bodied athletes, had denied him his fundamental human rights and were guilty of unlawful discrimination.

Against: There was no discrimination by the IAAF. It was simply a question of applying a fair rule to prevent athletes, any athletes, having a technical advantage. If a technical device is used which provides an athlete with any advantage, in any part of a competition, the device must render that athlete ineligible to compete regardless of any compensating disadvantages. The tests showed that Pistorius did have, through the device, certain advantages which able-bodied athletes did not. The Cheetah device was therefore contrary to the IAAF rule.

Decision: Pistorius won. Or, more realistically, the IAAF lost. It was a carefully argued and sensitive judgment given in May 2008. It was a lawyers' judgment. The CAS panel accepted that the IAAF were not guilty of discrimination. Nevertheless, the question was: how should the rules be applied? . CAS judged that the rules, in the case of a passive device such as the Cheetah Flex-Foot, required the IAAF – and now CAS – to determine if it provided 'an overall net advantage'. In the context of sport, this should be the vital test:

'If the use of the device provides more disadvantages than advantages, then it cannot reasonably be said to provide an advantage over other athletes, because the user is actually at a competitive disadvantage.'

Crucially, the IAAF accepted that the burden of proof was on the IAAF. The evidence was therefore not sufficient. They had concentrated solely on particular advantages without assessing the effect of disadvantages. They did not demonstrate, on the balance of probabilities, that there was an overall net advantage for Pistorius. CAS noted that the IAAF appeared to accept that the rule would not prevent Pistorius from running in 100 metre or 200 metre races since such distances did not allow Pistorius to catch up from his slower start.

'I think this day is going to go down in history for the equality of disabled people.'

Moreover, the CAS panel was not persuaded in any event, on the evidence, that there were metabolic or biomechanical advantages in favour of a double amputee using the Cheetah Flex-Foot. The fact that Pistorius used less vertical force than an able-bodied athlete might actually be a disadvantage; many sprinters sought more 'spring' in their actions. The scientific evidence did not discharge the burden of proof.

CAS stressed the limitations of the panel's decision. This was not *carte blanche* for disabled athletes to race using other equipment. The decision was limited solely to the eligibility of Pistorius using the specific Cheetah prosthesis. Any other athlete or device would have to be assessed on a case-by-case basis. Moreover, it was possible that further and more definitive scientific evidence might be produced in due course to prove that Pistorius did have an advantage over other athletes. If all this imposed a new burden on the IAAF, *'it must be viewed as just one of the challenges of 21st Century life'*.

The 'fastest man on no legs' could compete in open competition. 'I think this day is going to go down in history for the equality of disabled people,' he said. The 21 year-old's quest for a place at the Olympics was no longer a dream.

For Pistorius, the challenge was now to reach the Olympic qualifying time. It was too tough a challenge for Beijing. But Pistorius did qualify for the London 2012 Olympics. There, he finished second in his 400 metres heat to reach the semi-final but did not progress further. He ran the anchor leg for South Africa in the final of the 4x400 metres relay.

On 14th February 2013 came the shock news. Pistorius had shot and killed his girlfriend, Reeva Steenkamp, at his home in Pretoria. He said that he had mistaken her for a possible intruder. His trial for murder began before Judge Thokozile Masipa in March 2014. On 12th September, he was found guilty not of murder but of culpable homicide. He received a prison sentence of a maximum of five years. In December 2014, Judge Masipa ruled that the prosecution could challenge her ruling of acquitting Pistorius of murder but that the State could not appeal the length of sentence. The case would now go in front of a five- person panel at South Africa's Supreme Court of Appeal later in 2015.

The extraordinary strory of the Blade Runner had moved tragically to a very different, and fundamentally more serious, legal setting.

Chapter Ten

SPORT AND EMPLOYMENT

Disputes between employers and employees have always been a frequent source of litigation. Disputes in the sporting workplace are no different.

Tensions arise if a player (or team manager) performs badly or is guilty of serious misconduct or if one party wishes to end the relationship for some other reason. Tension is exacerbated, in sports such as football, if a player wants to transfer his employment to another club.

Some disputes here are of lighter interest, including the rise of Mirabel Topham at Aintree. Groundbreaking claims include Newcastle's George Eastham, Belgian footballer Jean-Marc Bosman and Slovakian handball player Maros Kolpak. This area, more than any other, has been deeply affected by the all-pervasive scope of European law into which sport has, however unwillingly, been drawn.

82. MIRABEL TOPHAM

The Queen Bee takes over at Aintree

A boardroom struggle after the death of the long-serving clerk of the course, EAC Topham, would have a major effect on the future of Aintree. It led to the reign of Mirabel Topham.

The judge in the civil court would later sum up: '*[She was] a person of dominating and masterful character and personality and no doubt of considerable business acumen … Not only did she dominate everyone with whom she came into contact, but she completely dominated her husband.*'

Mirabel Hillier was an actress who had a number of smallish parts in West End and provincial shows. She was for a time a Gaiety Girl. In one showing of a musical comedy, *The Cinema Star*, at the Royal Court Theatre in Liverpool in 1914, she captured the eye and heart of Ronnie Topham. They married eight years later.

She had no racing background. Indeed, it was not until the death of EAC Topham in 1932 that Mirabel started to take a closer interest in Aintree, the racecourse leased to the family company from the Earl of Sefton.

The Tophams had been associated with Aintree since 1843 when Edward William Topham (the 'Wizard') became the official handicapper for the Grand National. He also became the lessee of the racecourse land. 'Wizard' Topham was succeeded by his sons and the family company was established in 1899. EAC Topham took over in 1905. 'EAC' was a formidable figure. The Grand National grew in popularity and became a national institution. A boardroom struggle after his sudden death in 1932 would determine his succession and the future of Aintree.

Captain Douglas Wood was EAC's natural successor as clerk of the course as he had known the Topham family for 31 years. He had been a director and secretary of the company since 1919 and had assisted EAC as clerk of the course for many years. He was very close to Bill Topham, EAC's younger brother, who played a much more active role in the business than Ronnie, the other brother. Bill Topham and Wood, together, ensured that Wood was appointed EAC's successor as clerk of the course at a short board meeting held just one day before the funeral. A little later, a written agreement

'Not only did she dominate everyone with whom she came into contact, but she completely dominated her husband.'

Behind the scenes, Mirabel was planning her move.

was signed appointing Wood deputy managing director of the company, and confirming his position as clerk of the course, for a seven-year period from 1st January 1934. All was relatively calm on the surface during 1933 and 1934.

Behind the scenes, Mirabel was planning her move. She did not like Douglas Wood and she decided to take over. She had plans, in effect, to oust Wood and to bring the company and Aintree under clear Topham family control again. Cleverly, she joined the board in 1935 and, by a surprise voting manoeuvre initiated by Mirabel and supported by Ronnie, a 'tame' cousin was appointed as chairman in place of Bill Topham. Life at Aintree was never the same again. Certainly not for Douglas Wood.

The first big row with Wood arose over the distribution of complimentary badges. Wood considered, as clerk of the course, that official and complimentary badges were his responsibility. He was not going to have any interference on race meeting matters from management of the company. They could let him know how many they wanted personally; he would deal with all others.

That was not the only issue. Even more emotionally, Mirabel wanted Wood's name removed from the race card and the name of Topham to have far greater prominence. Wood considered that, as clerk of the course, he was solely responsible to the stewards of the Jockey Club for the arrangements for the meetings and official race cards.

Senior figures of the racing world, including Lord Derby, expressed support for Wood. Lord Derby tried to broker peace with the board. He met them and expressed the opinion that 'the Tophams had no right to dictate to the clerk of the course in this way.' Asked later whether these views were accepted, he replied: 'There was only one director who spoke, and that was Mrs Topham. She didn't agree.'

Once Mirabel was on the board, there was only going to be one winner of this boardroom struggle. In 1937, within two years of joining the board, she pushed through a board resolution to dismiss Wood as an employee and deputy managing director of Tophams Ltd with immediate effect on the grounds of misconduct. Wood was sent a cheque for £220. He claimed, instead, damages for wrongful dismissal and breach of his seven-year employment contract.

Legal Question: Should Wood succeed in his claim for damages for wrongful dismissal? Should he be re-instated?

For: Wood had signed a seven-year contract of employment with the company. The complaints against him were trivial. He had not committed any act of misconduct. He was a highly respected clerk of the course. He was entitled to damages for wrongful dismissal and breach of contract.

Against: Wood had not carried out the instructions of the board. He had failed to advise the board properly about racecourse matters. He was acting beyond his authority. That was misconduct. It was perfectly in order to dismiss him.

Decision: The litigation came before the Civil Court at Liverpool Assizes in June 1936. Proceedings were widely reported in the Liverpool and national press. It was the 'Aintree Racecourse Lawsuit'. The racing fraternity was captivated. It became a daily show with Mirabel sweeping into court each morning in a variety of elegant outfits and hats, an actress in a star role.

The case was notable for the leading legal teams involved: Maxwell Fyfe KC leading for Tophams and Norman Birkett KC for Wood. The latter argued that the matters relied on by the defence were 'trivial and trumpery'. All along, Mirabel Topham had secretly plotted to get Wood out of the company:

'The real trouble is that Wood is not a Topham. All was harmony until Mrs Topham joined the board. Mrs Topham is the chief cause of all this trouble. She must be a very remarkable woman. Certainly it is plain from the evidence that she dominates her husband.'

Lord Derby, called as a witness, noted: 'There was a vast difference between the position when EAC Topham was clerk of the course and the present directorate. There was nothing EAC did not know about racing. Old Topham knew it all but the present directors know nothing about it.' Lord Sefton gave similar evidence to the court: 'Mr Topham, one of the directors, married a lady, an actress, who had no knowledge of racing.'

One lighter moment arose in the court proceedings when Ronald Topham was called to give evidence. Birkett KC asked: 'You have heard your wife say that she was the dominating mind in your marriage?' Topham replied: 'Well, most men are influenced by their wives. I use my own commonsense in some matters.'

Justice Lewis considered his judgment. It was no surprise when he decided in favour of Douglas Wood. The company was ordered to pay Wood £3,250 damages, plus the substantial costs of the case. And

> **'Well, most men are influenced by their wives. I use my own commonsense in some matters.'**

there were harsh words for Mirabel. It was clear to Justice Lewis that 'certain members of the Topham family' were determined to wrest management control out of the hands of Wood:

'The ringleader was Mrs AR Topham, a person of dominating and masterful character. Not only did she dominate everyone with whom she came into contact, but she completely dominated her husband.'

Wood was not, however, re-instated.

Despite the case, Mirabel Topham had made sure that control of Aintree would not pass out of the Topham family. She was now in control. She herself was appointed managing director in 1938 and she would be in sole control for the next 35 years.

Mirabel Topham would play a crucial role in determining the destiny of the course and its most famous race, the Grand National. She led the restoration of Aintree immediately after the war and the staging of the first post-war National in 1946. In 1949, she bought the freehold of the course from Lord Sefton and consolidated her power. She initiated the short-lived attempt to create a motor racing circuit at Aintree. She was determined to keep the Grand National alive, despite financial problems. But in 1964, to great uproar, she announced she was selling Aintree – returning to court and winning a battle in the House of Lords to overturn a restriction on the sale from Lord Sefton, namely that the land should only be used for horse racing or, in part, for agriculture. Mirabel wanted the Grand National to continue as a first-class event but run on another course. Eventually, in 1973, the course was sold for £3 million but on the basis that the Grand National would continue to be run there for at least five years.

It was, perhaps, fitting that Mirabel Topham's last Grand National was in 1973, the first victory for the great *Red Rum* – two figures forever associated with the famous race.

83. GEORGE EASTHAM
A landmark case for professional football

George Eastham wanted to leave Newcastle. The club refused to release him under the 'retain and transfer' rules of the Football League. Could Eastham challenge them as being invalid?

Newcastle's George Eastham was an elegant, skilful inside forward with superb ball control and a penetrating pass. In April 1960, he decided he wanted to leave Newcastle. He made the first of several unsuccessful requests to be released. They would lead to a fundamental challenge to football's transfer system.

Eastham simply wanted to earn more money. In 1960 the maximum wage in football was £20 per week during the season and £17 in the summer. He wanted a job outside football in the afternoons: 'We only trained in the mornings so I wanted something to occupy me rather than just wasting money on becoming a better snooker player. They

[Newcastle] said they'd get me a job but nothing was forthcoming, so I went down to London and started selling cork.'

Eastham had joined Newcastle in 1956 from Ards, a club in Northern Ireland managed by his father. In 1960, he was on the verge of the England team and he was a firm favourite at St James' Park. Newcastle refused to release him. 'If Eastham wants to play football, it will be at Newcastle,' said the combative chairman, William McKeag.

In 1960, the Football League still operated a so-called 'retain and transfer' system established at the turn of the century after professional pay for footballers had, somewhat reluctantly, been allowed by the football authorities. Players were engaged on yearly contracts with clubs. Under Football League

'If Eastham wants to play football, it will be at Newcastle.'

rules, a player was registered with a particular club and, while it held that registration, he could only play for that club. A club decided at the end of each season whether to 'retain' a player by offering a new contract (and, at that time, there was a maximum wage). If the player did not re-sign, he would not be paid. A club could decide to place a player on the 'transfer' list. If he was not on the transfer list, he could not be transferred and the club retained his registration. The club, in effect, decided whether a player would stay or go; it controlled the player's employment future.

Eastham was stubborn and he refused to re-sign for Newcastle. Crucially, he was supported by the Professional Players' Association (PFA). The PFA was becoming active under new chairman, former Fulham player Jimmy Hill, and secretary Cliff Lloyd. The fight for a better lot for professional footballers was underway. Eastham decided, with PFA support, to challenge the system. In October 1960, having been out of the game for three months, he issued a writ against Newcastle, the Football Association and the Football League claiming that the retain and transfer rules were 'an unlawful restraint of trade'. The Football League defended the existing system and declared that the law should leave football alone. It had no place interfering in rules which had served football well for over half a century.

Newcastle actually relented in the face of Eastham's persistence and, shortly after the start of legal proceedings, agreed that Eastham could transfer to Arsenal for a substantial transfer fee of £47,500. Eastham made his debut for Arsenal against Bolton Wanderers in December 1960 and scored twice. The PFA, however, had the scent of a breakthrough. They agreed to fund Eastham if he was prepared to continue his action as a test case against the Football League. He was and the challenge was on. The case went to the Chancery Division of the High Court.

Legal Question: Was the retain and transfer system operated by the Football League an unreasonable restraint of trade? Should Eastham, no longer in employment with Newcastle, have been free to move to another club?

For: The existing system treated players like chattels as if a relic of the Middle Ages. Eastham had been shut out from professional football for over three months. The retention system deprived him of his opportunity to earn his livelihood after his employment with a particular club had ended. It was an unreasonable and unlawful restraint of trade.

Against: The rules provided stability. If a player could do as he liked, the wealthier clubs would at once snap up all the best players (particularly when the maximum wage bar had been lifted). Smaller clubs would cease to survive or offer high-class football. Clubs would find it difficult to build up and maintain a consistent team. They would be discouraged from investing substantial sums in training and developing young players. It helped maintain competition and spectator interest. The system was not unreasonable.

Decision: Eastham won his case. The High Court decided that the retain and transfer system operated by the Football League was an unjustifiable restraint of trade. If a player wanted to leave at the end of his contract, he should be permitted to do so. Justice Wilberforce said starkly:

'Any system that interfere[s] with the player's freedom to seek other employment at a time when he was not actually being employed by another club would seem to me to operate substantially in restraint of trade.'

The Football League's justification of the existing system did not convince the court: *'The system is an employers' system, set up in an industry where the employers have succeeded in establishing a united monolithic front all over the world.'* The rules were more restrictive than necessary to protect the interests of the parties. The rules were invalid. Eastham had won a landmark case for the employment rights of professional footballers.

It was a breakthrough for the PFA. While the Eastham dispute was in progress, the PFA also challenged the maximum wage limit – and, with a threat of a players' strike, it was finally removed in 1961. The Eastham case, combined with the lifting of the maximum wage, broke the barriers. The best players were now free to negotiate longer and more lucrative contracts. Johnny Haynes of Fulham became the first £100 per week player. The transfer rules were changed. If a player did not want to re-sign on the offered terms, the dispute could be referred to a new independent transfer tribunal for arbitration. The balance of power was no longer held solely by the clubs.

Eastham also went on to claim another 'first' in English football history in 1963 when he made his international debut for England against Brazil. His father George 'Diddler' Eastham having represented his country in 1935, he became part of the first father and son combination to play for England. Since then, Brian and Nigel Clough and Frank Lampard senior and junior have also joined this 'two generations' club.

Eastham was awarded the OBE in 1976 for services to football. Rightly, he was given pride of place at the launch of the PFA's centenary in 2007.

84. JEAN-MARC BOSMAN

A decision that transformed football in Europe

Jean-Marc Bosman, a Belgian footballer, wanted to leave his club at the end of his contract and move to a French club. His club prevented his move taking place. Did this infringe the 'freedom of movement' rules of the European Union?

It all happened, perhaps, because his parents lived a few doors away from the girlfriend of an intelligent and adventurous young lawyer.

Jean-Marc Bosman was, in 1990, a 25 year-old midfield player with Belgian first division side, RC Liege. His early promise as a youth international footballer had not been fulfilled. As a litigant before the European Court of Justice, however, he succeeded in fundamentally changing the employment rights of footballers in Europe.

Bosman's contract with RC Liege, under which he received an average monthly salary of Bfr120,000, expired at the end of June 1990. The club offered him a new contract for one season but at a substantial, 75 per cent, drop in salary to Bfr30,000. Surely, RC Liege knew this was asking for trouble?

Bosman refused to re-sign for RC Liege and was placed on the transfer list. No Belgian club showed any interest at a fee fixed according to Belgian FA rules. However, Bosman made contact with USL Dunkerque, a club in the French second division. This led, fruitfully, to a proposed transfer. His monthly salary would be around Bfr1.2 million and he would receive a substantial signing-on bonus. A fee of Bfr1,200,000

Bosman succeeded in fundamentally changing the employment rights of footballers in Europe.

would be payable to RC Liege on receipt of the transfer certificate, which needed to be issued by the Belgian FA, with the approval of RC Liege, before the transfer could take place. It was initially a one-year transfer. USL Dunkerque would have an irrevocable option for full transfer of the player on payment of a further Bfr4.8 million by the beginning of August. All seemed well for Bosman.

But RC Liege scuppered the deal. They had doubts about the French club's ability to pay the full fee. They refused to support the issue of the transfer certificate before the start of the season, as USL Dunkerque wanted. The transfer could not go through. Since Bosman refused to re-sign, RC Liege then suspended Bosman but kept his registration, preventing him from playing for any other club without their approval. It was reminiscent of the 'slavery' ended in the UK 30 years earlier by the Eastham case.

Not surprisingly, Bosman was upset and commenced a claim. A Belgian court made a preliminary judgment in his favour, ordering RC Liege not to impede Bosman's transfer. In fact, Bosman did then sign yearly deals with successive lowly French and Belgian clubs, but each of these arrangements came to an end. Bosman was eventually signed by Olympic de Charleroi, a Belgian third division club. All these subsequent contracts were on personal terms less favourable to Bosman than the original proposed deal with USL Dunkerque. If he hadn't been such a mediocre player, Bosman's claim for compensation would not have arisen.

The saga was not over. Bosman was determined to pursue a claim for compensation to recover the income he had lost over the years as a result of the original refusal of RC Liege to allow him to join USL Dunkerque. It led to a protracted battle before the courts.

How should Bosman argue his case? His parents knew a young lawyer, Jean-Louis Dupont, whose girlfriend lived a few doors away. He wanted to have a go at the case. He was bright and seemed full of enthusiasm and ideas. He knew that the European Commission had started giving warnings to UEFA that football's rules needed attention in order to satisfy the EU's rules for a 'single European market'. UEFA had ignored these warnings.

Bosman, with his new young lawyer, brought an action against RC Liege, the Belgian FA and UEFA in the Belgian courts. Bosman's claim was not made on grounds of restraint of trade (or its Belgian law equivalent) but on the dramatic, groundbreaking basis that RC Liege's actions were in breach of the rules relating to 'free movement of workers' under European law.

The Belgian appeal court took the crucial step of referring the case to the European Court of Justice for certain preliminary rulings. Critical policy issues affecting the future of football in Europe were now in the hands of the European Court.. It was no longer a 'one-off' dispute. Did UEFA consider 'buying off' Bosman to prevent these issues finally going to court? Apparently not. The result could dramatically change football.

Legal Questions: First, was it unlawful for a club to require the payment of a transfer fee in respect of an 'out of contract' player like Bosman? Did the rules contravene European law on 'free movement of workers' by preventing him, a European national, from moving and being employed elsewhere in the EU?

Secondly, did the same European law principles render invalid 'quota' rules which in a number of national leagues restricted the ability of clubs to select more than a specified number of 'foreign' nationals for matches in certain competitions?

For: Each of these rules restricted Bosman's freedom, as a national of an EU member state, to join a club in another EU member state. A transfer fee was inappropriate and unlawful since Bosman was no longer employed 'under contract'. He should be free to negotiate his own employment as in any other industry. The nationality limit also restricted a club's ability or willingness to sign a 'foreign' player. The rules were an obstacle to freedom of movement of EU workers contrary to the Treaty of Rome and should be declared invalid.

Against: The courts should respect the autonomy of the football authorities in establishing rules for the best organisation of their sport. The rules aided stability within football. The transfer fee rules were needed to maintain a financial and competitive balance between clubs. Transfer fees supported clubs searching for talent and training young players (which would be discouraged if players could move freely at the end of the contract period without any compensation or transfer fee). The nationality clauses were also justifiable on sporting grounds. They helped to maintain the traditional link between each club and its country. They were necessary to create a sufficient pool of national players to provide teams in each national league with top players from the 'home' country. They also helped to maintain a competitive balance between clubs by preventing the richest clubs from simply acquiring the services of the best players.

Decision: Bosman won. The landmark decision was handed down by the European Court in December 1995. Efforts to argue that football should be exempt from European competition and employment law had failed. The football authorities had been putting their heads in the sand. Football was an 'economic activity' and the football industry was required to comply with EU law in a similar way to any other industry. As the Advocate General advised the Court:

'The right to freedom of movement and the prohibition of discrimination … are among the fundamental principles of the Community order. [The quota rules] represent an absolutely classic case of discrimination on the ground of nationality. [They] limit the number of players from other Member States whom a club can play in a match.'

The arguments in favour of the rules were not sufficiently strong. The court declared, if not convincingly, that the same aims could be achieved at least as efficiently by other, less restrictive means – such as the redistribution of broadcasting funds to clubs on a more equitable basis. The existing rules were invalid.

In December 1998, Bosman eventually accepted damages of Bfr16 million (around £312,000) from the Belgian FA.

The Bosman decision had a major impact on football in Europe. Transfer fees for 'out of contract' players now became illegal where an EU national was moving between one EU member state and another. Although the Bosman judgment was not strictly applicable to transfers between clubs within a single EU state, individual country football authorities – including the Premier League – quickly accepted that free movement for 'out of contract' players should apply to transfers between clubs within each EU country, with no fee being payable when players' contracts have expired. The principle of the Eastham case had moved an important and vital step further.

No single court decision has had a greater effect on the game of football.

The dynamics of the transfer market changed significantly. Clubs started signing players on longer contracts in order to avoid losing them on free transfers. Smaller clubs started to lose out on transfer fees unless they could commit younger players to sign long-term contracts. Other clubs saw the opportunity to acquire players who would shortly be 'out of contract'. Such players could negotiate substantially increased salaries since the new employer club would no longer be paying out a transfer fee. Leading players recognised their significant bargaining power as contract periods came to an end. Club loyalty could actually be financially disadvantageous. A large proportion of the new TV income in football has ended up in players' salaries rather than as club profits or money to be reinvested into the football business.

No single court decision has had a greater effect on the game of football.

The invalidity of the nationality limits also had major repercussions – and went far wider than the circumstances of the Bosman case itself. Clubs became free to sign and play as many EU players as they wished. Rules limiting the number of foreign players who could play in a particular match could not survive (for example, the previous rule in UEFA club competitions whereby only three foreign players plus two 'assimilated' foreign players could play for a team).

Top clubs now looked elsewhere for footballers, especially to continental Europe. Richer clubs were free to create multi-national superteams. History was made on Boxing Day 1999 when Chelsea became the first English side to field a starting team of 11 'all-foreign' players.

What does Bosman himself now think? He is a little sour:'I contributed to the enrichment of a whole host of players, but they did not, in turn, give me much recognition.'

85. MAROS KOLPAK

A Slovakian handball player and the game of cricket

Rules restricted the number of non-EU players who could be selected in a German handball league team. Should they apply to players from a country, such as Slovakia, which had a special 'association' relationship with the EU?

Seven-and-a-half years after Jean-Marc Bosman's court victory, another case before the European Court slipped quietly through the legal system. Who could have anticipated that a Slovakian handball player would lead a legal challenge that would transform the rights of players and athletes from Eastern Europe, South Africa and many Caribbean islands to compete in Europe – and substantially affect the organisation of cricket in England?

Maros Kolpak was a national of Slovakia but resident in Germany. Germany ran a strong professional handball league. Since March 1977 Kolpak had played as a goalkeeper for the German second division handball team, TSV Ostringen. His contract of employment was renewed, for a three-year fixed term, in February 2000. But he wanted a better chance to play in the team.

His problem was that the German national handball federation (DHB) placed certain restrictions on foreign players. Teams could not, in league or cup matches, field more than two 'foreign' players – classified by reference to a player's licence (issued by the federation) which regarded him as a national of a non-EU member country without, in effect, equal employment rights. Kolpak had been issued with a 'foreign' player's licence. This potentially restricted his ability to play in German league or cup matches.

Kolpak challenged his player categorisation. He considered that his selection should not be subject to any restrictions based on nationality. He wanted to be treated for this purpose not as 'foreign' but in the same category as

But he wanted a better chance to play in the team.

an EU national. His studious lawyers came up with a clever argument based on the 'association agreement' which Slovakia had with the EU by which the EU agreed a principle of non-discrimination on grounds of nationality in relation to employment and related matters. The issue came to the European Court in 2003.

Legal Question: Should Kolpak be free of any discriminatory rules based on nationality? Even though he was not an EU national, was he entitled to be classed for employment purposes in Germany in the same category as an EU national?

For: Kolpak was already lawfully employed in Germany. He should not be subject to any barriers of employment or selection based on nationality. By reason of the association agreement between Slovakia and the EU (which prohibited discrimination in employment matters based on nationality), he should have the same opportunity as EU nationals to participate in cup and league matches as part of his professional activity. Kolpak was entitled to a 'level playing field' and to be treated in the same way as EU nationals. The 'foreign' classification by the German association was invalid.

Against: It was going too far to equate a non-EU national with an EU national for all employment purposes. The EU rules should only apply to countries which enjoy complete equality of treatment vis-à-vis EU nations in respect of free movement. The association agreement with Slovakia did not create legally enforceable obligations in this way. It was proper for a sporting body to restrict the number of non-EU nationals who could play. This was reasonable on sporting grounds. It safeguarded the training of young players by German clubs and also helped to promote the German national team.

Decision: In another landmark judgment, the European Court decided in favour of Maros Kolpak.

The European Court agreed that, because of Slovakia's association agreement with the EU, he should indeed be treated in the same category as EU nationals for the purposes of eligibility to play in league and cup handball matches. The restriction in the rules of the German handball association was invalid. The court considered, but rejected, the association's attempt at a 'sporting' justification to exempt the application of this principle.

The principle of the Bosman case established that quotas or restrictions on selection of players from other EU countries were banned. The Kolpak ruling extended this principle so that it applied not only to EU nationals but also nationals of a wide range of countries merely having 'association' or similar relationships with the EU. Whilst the wording of many of these agreements may vary, similar 'rights' could now be claimed by nationals of countries such as South Africa and numerous countries in Eastern Europe, the Caribbean and the Pacific.

It is difficult to believe that the diplomats negotiating these 'association agreements' with non-EU countries could ever have contemplated their effect on sport!

What impact did the decision have in practice?

In Britain, the greatest consequence was for cricket. The decision enabled English county cricket clubs to sign up a multitude of cricketers from outside Britain. The earlier Bosman ruling had little effect on cricket, unlike football, since there were no other strong cricket nations within Europe. However, the Kolpak principle opened the way for cricketers to play in Britain from countries with strong cricket backgrounds such as South Africa, Zimbabwe and a number of West Indian islands – all of whom have association agreements with the EU containing anti-discriminatory employment provisions. So long as they possessed or obtained a relevant work permit and did not currently represent their 'home' country in Test cricket, cricketers from these countries could now be classed as domestic and not 'overseas' players. Restrictions limiting the number of 'overseas' players (then two per county team) would not apply to them.

English counties were not slow to take advantage. The first 'Kolpak player' in county cricket was South African Claude Henderson, who was signed by Leicestershire in 2004. A significant trend developd whereby counties bought 'Kolpak' players, not always of the highest quality, rather than spend money on coaching and developing young, home-grown British players. In 2008, there were

> **The Kolpak ruling extended this principle so that it also applied to nationals of a wide range of countries merely having 'association' or similar relationships with the EU.**

over 60 'Kolpak' players in county cricket and in one match, Northants v Leicestershire, they made up half the players taking the field. Many argued that the English national team suffered as a result of the smaller pool of talent available in county cricket. The other sport deeply affected by the Kolpak decision in the UK was rugby. The ruling enabled rugby teams (union and league) to sign players not only from South Africa but also Fiji, Tonga and Samoa.

Change did eventually come. The sporting consequences seemed far removed from the intent of the original diplomatic agreements. As a result of a campaign by the English Cricket Board (ECB) and supported by the French authorities, the European Commission altered its stance in 2008 in relation to the EU's Cotonou Agreement with many African, Caribbean and Pacific states, restricting its application only to free trade in goods and services and not free movement of labour. The UK's Home Office, in co-operation with the ECB, toughened up on work permit regulations. New rules now mean that only a player who holds a valid work permit for four years is able to continue to be employed by a county as though an EU citizen (but not if he has played one Test match in the past two years or five Test matches in the last five years). The ECB has also ensured that a significant percentage of its annual payments to counties is linked, on a per capita basis, to the number of England-qualified players in each squad.

The tidal wave of Kolpak players, caused by the European Court's decision, has now receded. However, its consequences have been considerable.

Ironically, if the situation of Maros Kolpak had arisen now, there would be no need to extend the principle of non-discrimination to non-EU countries. Slovakia became a full member of the EU in May 2004.

86. ADRIAN MUTU
Chelsea pursue a costly striker

The Romanian striker was one of the first buys under the ownership regime of Roman Abramovich. He was 'hot property'. He would also, a year or so later, test positive for cocaine. Chelsea wanted no more and sacked him. Could the club recoup any of its huge acquisition cost?

It all started well for Adrian Mutu. Six goals in his first five games, including two in a 4-2 win over London rivals Tottenham Hotspur. The 24 year-old Romanian-born striker, one of Europe's hottest prospects, had been bought in August 2003 for £15.8 million by Chelsea (under manager Claudio Ranieri) from Italian club Parma as Roman Abramovich's cash started to transform the London club.

Urbane and eloquent, with a law degree, Mutu was a footballer who read poetry and Dostoyevsky (he had just finished the latter's *The Idiot*). 'I guess I am the ultimate split personality,' he joked at an early press conference. Diamond studs in his ears, he was also a bit of a playboy.

In 2004 it all went wrong. His form declined and he went 13 games without scoring. Divorce proceedings with his wife, a well-known Romanian television presenter, were highly publicised – as were alleged liaisons including a 'sting' set-up with a porn star in Bucharest. Mood swings and missed training went with reports of clubbing and suspicions of drug abuse.

As the new season approached, Chelsea's new manager, José Mourinho, had his doubts about Mutu. They had several rows. The manager was particularly angry when Mutu insisted on playing in a match for Romania when the manager thought he was carrying an injury. A club fine ensued. After another poor performance in September 2004 and a missed training session, Chelsea ordered a drug test. The first sample tested positive for cocaine.

'I guess I am the ultimate split personality,' he joked at an early press conference.

Mutu faced an FA disciplinary charge. On advice, Mutu did not request that a B-sample be analysed. Better to confess and get the matter dealt with quickly. The FA disciplinary proceedings took place, leading to a £20,000 fine and a seven-month suspension until May 2005, including two weeks' rehabilitation at a clinic.

On 24th October 2004, Chelsea stunned Mutu, and the football world, by announcing that Mutu's employment had been terminated with immediate effect. Drug abuse was a serious breach of contract, stated the club. 'Chelsea has a zero tolerance policy towards drugs. This applies to both performance-enhancing drugs and so-called recreational drugs.' Chelsea had sacked goalkeeper Mark Bosnich for a similar offence two years earlier. Bosnich was, however, a player coming to the end of his career. Adrian Mutu, just 15 months into a five-year contract, was a major recent signing. Perhaps Abramovich and Mourinho were simply happy to get Mutu, a 'bad egg', off the club's books. The club would no longer have to pay his £2.3 million annual salary but would now not be able to get a transfer fee for Mutu. Were they just writing it all off?

In January 2005, Mutu signed for Juventus (although he could not play for them until May). It looked as if the Italian club had picked up the international striker for 'free'.

But the story was by no means over. It was only just beginning, at least for the lawyers. In February 2005, Chelsea dramatically announced that the club was seeking compensation from the player. Courts and tribunals have seen a constant flow of claims by players against clubs – employees against employers. Now the 'boot was on the other foot'. If it was a breach of contract, under legal principles the employer could bring a legal claim for damages for that breach. But what were the damages? This was a new one for football.

Estimates of damages varied from nothing (Chelsea would no longer have to pay Mutu's annual salary) to multi-millions for the club's loss of the striker's transfer value and write-off of the initial cost of buying him. It caused scratching of heads, much debate among the lawyers (amateur and professional) and eight years of dispute before numerous courts and tribunals.

First, a Premier League Appeals Committee confirmed that Mutu's drug abuse was a breach justifying the termination of the employment contract. Some clubs may, in such a situation, choose to help the player to rehabilitate and keep the player on their books, but it was the club's decision. As to the amount of compensation, the matter (after a lengthy dispute regarding jurisdiction) eventually fell in 2007 to be heard by FIFA's Dispute Resolution Chamber (DRC) in accordance with FIFA's Regulations on the Status and Transfer of Players.

What would be Chelsea's claim? Chelsea threw the book at Mutu, almost literally. The damages claimed included: the wasted costs of acquiring Mutu (i.e. the portion of the original transfer fee not yet depreciated over the remainder of the five-year employment contract), around £13.8 million; the cost of replacing the player, estimated at around £22.6 million; the unearned portion of the signing-on bonus, £44,000; other benefits received by Mutu, £3.1 million; legal costs, £391,000; and the unquantifiable cost to Chelsea in playing terms and damage to reputation. All in all, around £37 million (!) but 'at least equivalent to the replacement cost' of around £22.6 million.

FIFA's DRC usually assessed compensation for an early termination on the basis that it would be paid by a transferee club. How would the tribunal approach this one? The DRC decided that, in the '*exceptionally unique*' circumstances, the proper approach was to focus on the costs of buying the player (namely a substantial portion of the original transfer fee not yet depreciated over the five-year contract, associated costs and signing-on fee). Chelsea had made '*a massive financial investment*'. Players are an asset of a club in terms of their sporting role '*and also from an economic point of view*'. The final amount? The tribunal gave its decision in August 2008 and settled on compensation payable by Mutu to Chelsea of €17,173,990 (around £14 million) with interest if unpaid. It was a record sum payable by a player. A staggering sum. Chelsea called it 'a very significant decision for football', while Mutu considered it 'inhumane and unjust'. He appealed to the Court of Arbitration for Sport (CAS). The appeal was heard in 2009.

Legal Question: Should the damages claim against Adrian Mutu of nearly €17.2 million be upheld?

For: Chelsea had paid £15.8 million for the player. Mutu knew this. The costs were expended in reliance of Mutu performing his contract. They would be amortised over its five-year period. The transfer fee paid was a recognised item to be taken into account under Art. 22 of FIFA's Regulations. The breach justified termination. Mutu brought it upon himself. The club was entitled, on such a breach of contract, to recover these wasted costs of acquisition.

Against: Chelsea had a choice and elected to terminate, thereby foregoing any subsequent transfer fee. The club should bear co-responsibility for terminating the contract and its financial consequences. Mutu was not involved in the original transfer fee and had no input into it. It should not be taken into account. The club no longer had to pay Mutu's salary. The compensation should be nil or, at the least, the club should bear some of the risk and consequence of buying the player.

Decision: Mutu lost again. The CAS panel recognised that the solution must take into account *'not only the interest of players and clubs but, more broadly, those of the whole football community'*. Compensation based on the *'wasted acquisition costs'* was, it decided, a proper assessment under FIFA's Regulations and consistent with English law. The panel was unwilling to re-visit the circumstances of termination. It had already been decided that it was for *'just cause'*. The CAS panel confirmed the DRC's award of €17,173,900.

The exhausting legal battle was not, however, entirely at an end. CAS is, ultimately, subject to the constraints of Swiss law. Mutu claimed before the Swiss courts that the decision of CAS should be declared invalid. The Swiss Federal Court decided, in June 2010, that it was perfectly valid.

Could the money ever realistically be paid by Mutu? It would surely bankrupt him. Chelsea learned that Mutu owned three residential properties in Florida. Chelsea set off in pursuit, seeking remedies from local US courts. It would be a start. The arbitration award of CAS should be recognised, acknowledged a district court in Florida. Yet, enforcement is still a long way off. Chelsea tried a different tack. They obtained a ruling from FIFA in 2013 that Juventus had to contribute some of the money owed by Mutu to Chelsea since

The tribunal settled on compensation payable by Mutu to Chelsea of around £14 million with interest if unpaid. It was a record sum payable by a player.

they had benefited from Mutu's dismissal for breach of contract. It was shortlived. In early 2015, CAS over-turned FIFA's ruling and dismissed Chelsea's demands.

The decision is a landmark high for a legal claim against a player.

It remains doubtful whether Chelsea will ever get recovery. Interest on the payment is still accruing. It is probably only a club as rich as Chelsea who can afford to sack a player in this way and forego a substantial transfer fee. The decision is a landmark high for a legal claim against a player. Principal decisions of the courts, from Eastham to Bosman and Kolpak, have favoured the rights of players. Here is a significant one the other way. It is a warning by the courts, in these days of high fees and lucrative contracts, that clubs also have rights.

Mutu's football career, in the meantime, continued – with highs and lows. His spell at Juventus ended, after the Italian club's *calciopoli* scandal, with a successful transfer to Fiorentina. He made 112 appearances for the club and another 54 goals in Serie A brought much acclaim. He did, however, fail another doping test in January 2010 (for the banned appetite-suppressant drug sibutramine) resulting in a six-month ban. A night club brawl with a waiter also led to a public apology. In 2011 Mutu joined Cesena and subsequently moved to French club Ajaccio before returning to Romania and ending his football career in 2014. He remained a constant star of the Romanian national side, with 72 appearances and 35 goals, equalling the national all-time record.

It is not known whether he is still reading poetry.

87. AN INTERNATIONAL INJURY

A Belgian club, a Moroccan player, the G14 and FIFA

Abdelmajid Oulmers was injured playing for Morocco. He was a key player for his Belgian club. Could they claim compensation?

'It would be the end for international football. A World Cup would take place with only Spain, Germany, Italy, France and England and that would be the end.' A spokesman for UEFA, soccer's European governing body, expressed the fears of many if the case was decided against FIFA. It was a dispute which would change, perhaps fundamentally, the relationship between 'club' and 'country' in football in the 21st century. And it had all been triggered by a low-key match between Morocco and Burkina Faso.

It was a Belgian league club, Sporting Charleroi, who started it. Charleroi were going well in the 2004/5 season, heading the first division table until November 2004. Abdelmajid Oulmers, a left-side midfielder, was one of their best players. 26 year-old Oulmers was a Moroccan and he was called up for his first international cap for a friendly between Morocco and Burkina Faso. Charleroi wanted Oulmers to pull out on medical grounds claiming, not convincingly, that he was not fit. FIFA overruled and insisted that he should be made available for international duty under the FIFA rules for compulsory release of players for international matches.

Oulmers came on as a half-time substitute, scored and then was seriously injured – tearing ankle ligaments in an injury which kept him out of the game for eight months. Morocco, incidentally, defeated Burkina Faso 4-0.

Charleroi were angry since Oulmers was not insured against injury by Morocco and Charleroi, as his employer, had to bear the full cost of his continuing wages, the cost of surgery and of a replacement player. Moreover, the team's form dipped and Charleroi eventually finished fifth in the league – failing to win a place in the UEFA Champions League. They felt 'mugged'. The loss of Oulmers had severely damaged their league chances. Charleroi decided to bring a legal claim against FIFA for compensation for Oulmers' injury whilst on international duty.

It was a dispute which would change, perhaps fundamentally, the relationship between 'club' and 'country' in football in the 21st century.

Why does it always seem to be Belgium at the centre of these European legal disputes? Perhaps because Jean-Louis Dupont, the (then) young lawyer who led the Jean-Marc Bosman case, was behind it again. He was now advising Sporting Charleroi. He developed a claim that FIFA's regulations on the release of players breached European law. It was a Bosman-like attack on the well-established footballing rules of FIFA.

Crucially, Charleroi were backed by the powerful G14 group of clubs in Europe. (Only in football could this body keep the same name and comprise 18 clubs! Arsenal being one of the clubs added to the original 14 who included Manchester United and Liverpool but not Chelsea.) Oulmers was the case that the G14 had been looking for in their quest to challenge FIFA's rules. The G14 latched on to similar claims by French club Olympique Lyonnaise and Spanish club Atletico Madrid following injuries to their players during international fixtures. The G14 would cause FIFA's rules to be broken up.

It had been a long-running sore with the G14 who wanted more power for the clubs. They maintained that, since they paid the wages (and very high wages) of their employees, they should have a greater say in when they were released for international matches – and should be compensated if their employees were injured whilst on international duty. If the national associations would not bear responsibility, FIFA itself should do so and pay at least a proportion of the player's wages and/or give the clubs a greater share of the profits from competitions such as the World Cup and the European Cup in which 'their' players are performing.

Sporting Charleroi (or Jean-Louis Dupont) and G14 developed this frustration into a legal argument that, by demanding the obligatory release of players without some form of compensation, particularly in the event of injury, FIFA's rules amounted to an 'abuse of a dominant position' by FIFA under European law.

FIFA responded that this was a narrow and largely selfish view by the big G14 clubs. International football enhanced the experience and value of the players themselves. Clubs benefited from their players being internationals – both in terms of publicity and value. Importantly, the clubs were fully aware of the rules and the possibility of players being selected for internationals when they bought or developed players – including a 'foreign' player representing a country such as Morocco. England might be able to afford insurance (or at least partial insurance) for an injury to Michael Owen whilst on international duty – but a major fear of FIFA was that many national associations, particularly those in regions such as South America, Africa and Eastern Europe, simply could not afford to pay compensation for injury to star players. Could Ghana afford to pay compensation for injury to Michael Essien or the Ivory Coast for injury to Didier Drogba? Could they risk them playing international football?

The legal claim went first to a commercial court in Belgium, the Charleroi Tribunal of Commerce. The court decided in May 2006 that it would refer key issues to the European Court of Justice for guidance before it could judge on Charleroi's claim. They sought guidance on four rules which went to the heart of the 'club-versus-country' relationship in football. Were they valid – or did they infringe European laws on competition? The four were in effect:

- The obligation on clubs to release players for international duty
- The rule which meant clubs received no financial reward in return for releasing their players
- The provision that insurance cover was a matter for the clubs themselves (and could not be imposed on national associations as a condition for release by clubs of their players)
- The rule requiring clubs to be bound by FIFA's international calendar.

All were fundamental rules and all central to international football. The legal issue would turn on whether FIFA could successfully argue that the rules were reasonable, and proportionate, in the interests of maintaining a structure of international football – which was good for the game and all football followers. It would be necessary to justify each rule separately. It would be a long haul.

Once again, fundamental matters affecting football would be in the hands of the lawyers and judges of the European Court. Could a compromise be found 'within football'? Was there still time? Would FIFA and UEFA decide that it was preferable to work out a detailed 'football' solution, even if it involved some compromise, rather than face the stark possibility – as in the Bosman case – of the rules being swept aside entirely?

The answer was: 'Yes'. On 15th January 2008 in Zurich, before the European Court had given its judgment, FIFA, UEFA and the G14 announced the basis for a peace deal:

- FIFA/UEFA agreed in principle that they would make financial contributions for players' participation in the European Championships and World Cups.
- The G14 would in due course disband and a new independent European Club Association would be formed comprising over 100 clubs with membership across Europe determined 'solely on sporting achievements'.
- The G14 clubs would drop any court cases they had against FIFA and UEFA.

Initially there was simply a letter of intent and the parties agreed to work towards a 'memorandum of understanding'. A little more flesh to the deal was announced a few days later. UEFA and FIFA would pay clubs a daily rate for each player involved in the final stages of the European Championships or the World Cup. FIFA also agreed that clubs would only have to release players for one friendly a year played outside their own continent.

Could a compromise be found 'within football'? Was there still time?

Michel Platini, president of UEFA, told a news conference:

'*There is no winner here apart from football itself. It was utterly unthinkable for us that players might not have the right to play for their national team but of course we could see it was also logical the clubs who provide these players should also share in the profits from the competitions.*'

As far as the Charleroi case was concerned, strictly it remained in limbo. A G14 spokesman said that: 'As a sign of their commitment and goodwill, member clubs will take the formal decision to dissolve G14 and to withdraw its claims in court.' Karl-Heinz Rummenigge, chairman of the new European Club Association, added:

'*The lawsuits will be dropped … and the many misunderstandings and legal actions are now a part of the past.*'

Where would the funds come from for these compensation payments by FIFA and UEFA? The cynics pointed out that it would mean a reduction in the net profits from these tournaments available to FIFA/UEFA (for the benefit of the game as a whole) and more money diverted to the already successful clubs supplying most of the players. Was it, in reality, just another shift in favour of more power, influence and money for the major clubs?

The co-operation, or truce, continues - but at a price. In March 2012 UEFA and the European Club Association announced the signing of a renewed Memorandum of Understanding to run until 2018. The amount allocated to the clubs for the European Championships being held in Poland and Ukraine would be €100 million, rising to €150 million for the 2016 finals in France. Insurance (of an unspecified amount) for injured players would be part of the package - pending a worldwide FIFA package. Karl-Heinz Rummenigge said that the agreement '*reflects an improved balance between national teams and club football and is a great success for the European family*'. Talks were not always easy but '*we have reached a fair compromise,*' he said, perhaps hiding a smile. He urged FIFA to enter into a similar agreement.

Sepp Blatter, as FIFA president, duly responded. He announced that FIFA would, from September 2012, pay for a new worldwide player insurance project, covering all players involved in all international 'A' matches listed in the international match calendar. Payouts to a club for any injured player would vary according to salary up to a maximum of $27,000 per day (and a total maximum of $9.7 million). A provisional budget for the project amounted to $75 million. '*You have to take into account the best interests of the players … . The move will satisfy the clubs who have long campaigned for help to pay the salaries of their injured international players.*' Was there a sound of gnashing of teeth?

At least FIFA and UEFA appear to have learnt one of the lessons from the Bosman case – that it is preferable to reach a solution 'within football' rather for such fundamental matters to depend on the decision of the European Court. But it probably would not have happened without the trigger of a legal claim – and an injury to a 26 year-old Moroccan midfielder.

Chapter Eleven

LIBEL AND PRIVACY

Sporting stars are constantly in the news. Publicity is the fuel that drives sport's popularity and rewards for the participants. Newspaper articles, gossip magazines, internet sites, television and other broadcast media thrive on stories relating to sporting personalities. Some cause offence. Some contain allegations which, in the individual's opinion, cannot be allowed to rest.

The courts have seen a regular flow of actions where sportsmen and women have sought to protect or vindicate their reputations by bringing libel suits. In this chapter, we recall a few of them from different sports - including such well-known names as rugby's JPR Williams, cricket's Ian Botham and football's Bruce Grobbelaar. We include also the unfortunate story of the player labelled 'the world's worst tennis pro'.

Recent years have also seen a raft of legal cases seeking injunctions, super-injunctions and claims for damages as individuals fight the intrusion of the press. There has been no more determined litigant than motor racing's Max Mosley.

88. JPR WILLIAMS

'All the men ... merely players'?

JPR Williams, legendary rugby full-back, rarely shirked a challenge. He was Welsh captain in 1979 when a newspaper article accused him of 'shamateurism'. Was it libel?

JPR Williams, as Cliff Morgan remarked when commentating during that classic Barbarians match against the All Blacks at Cardiff Arms Park in 1973, 'never ever shirks not only a tackle but any situation at all'. In 1979, it was a serious off-field challenge he had to confront – an article in the *Daily Telegraph* that threatened his entire rugby future.

By 1979, John Peter Rhys Williams (one of the few world sportsmen instantly recognisable by the initials of his christian names – originally, and usefully, to distinguish him from his similarly named and very fine Welsh winger, JJ Williams) was at the zenith of his rugby career. Aged 29, captain of Wales, already holder of more than 50 caps and three Grand Slam titles, the finest full-back of his era, JPR was enjoying the final international season of his legendary rugby career – which he was planning to finish with the Triple Crown match against England at Cardiff Arms Park in March.

Then, in February 1979 and just weeks before the England match, the *Daily Telegraph* published a shattering article by journalist John Reason. JPR had been working on an autobiography which had been given some pre-publication publicity. The article in the *Daily Telegraph* was blunt. It alleged that JPR had infringed his amateur status by writing the book for money contrary to the rules of the International Rugby Football Board (IRFB). He was no longer an 'amateur' and he should no longer play for Wales. The article threatened his future in rugby.

Rugby union was still, proudly, an amateur sport. It was more than 80 years earlier, in 1895, when representatives of more than 20 prominent northern rugby clubs had met in Huddersfield to form the breakaway Northern Rugby Union which would permit payments to players – and lead to a changed rugby code, the 13-player per side Rugby Football League. The dispute about JPR's book may now seem from another age but, to use JPR's words, in the 1970s 'rugby union players walked on egg shells'. If found guilty of the charge, JPR would have been banned from any formal involvement in the

The article threatened his future in rugby.

game of rugby union – whether as an international or club player, a coach or on a committee.

The distinction between amateurs and professionals, between gentlemen and players, had already been removed in many leading spectator sports. The Football Association had permitted payments, initially up to a maximum wage, since 1885. The distinction in cricket was removed in 1963 – although high-performing amateurs (including, notoriously, WG Grace) had previously found ways of being compensated. Tennis, led by Wimbledon, had been open to all players since 1968. The Olympics were now largely 'open' in most sports. Yet, rugby union in the UK remained firmly and determinedly amateur, even if the walls were crumbling a little around the edges. Some players quietly received 'boot money'. (In fact, the term originated in the late 1880s in football, before professionalism was permitted, when it was not uncommon for players to find a half crown in their boots after a game.) But these payments were usually fairly small, often shared and a 'blind eye' was turned.

What about an autobiography – which could involve more substantial sums? Three of the Welsh greats, Gareth Edwards, Phil Bennett and Gerald Davies, had published autobiographies at the end of their careers. These had caused a stir but the players knew they had become 'professionalised' as they also accepted work in the media. But JPR was different. He wanted to keep his amateur status. He wanted, after retirement at international level, to continue playing at amateur club level while he pursued another career. He had trained to be a doctor and planned a career as an orthopaedic surgeon. It was a 'real' job. Indeed, two years earlier, JPR had even missed a British Lion's tour to New Zealand: 'My consultant told me to buckle down for my forthcoming surgeon's exams. Medicine had to come first.'

What were the rules? The IRFB rule said:

'No person shall … for remuneration … whether direct or indirect write a book or write an article … on the game or related matters. A person may be exempted … if he donates all such remuneration … through his Member Union … to a club or charity which should in no way benefit the person or his dependants.'

John Reason's article raised a storm. *The Sun* also joined the campaign. The Welsh Rugby Union (WRU) was forced to start an investigation. JPR's career was in serious danger, including his hopes of completing a final international season for Wales ending at the Arms Park. The rugby world held its breath.

JPR was summoned to a meeting with the WRU. He explained that he was not going to receive any of the money personally. He was going to give it all to a charity, a proposed new sports clinic in Bridgend. The legalities were complex and time-consuming. In the meantime, he had appointed an agency to receive any money from the book – and so he should remain an amateur provided he did not receive personally the money paid to them. The WRU accepted JPR's argument – and decided in his favour. He could finish his glorious career in style. He would play in yet another Welsh victory over England (27-3). JPR did not lose a single game in his 10 matches for his country against English opposition.

JPR had had 'a gutful of the innuendo in the newspapers'. He promptly served a writ alleging defamation.

But, off-field, John Reason was not satisfied. The *Daily Telegraph* published a further article in March bearing the heading 'BOARD SHOULD ACT NOW TO HALT SHAMATEURISM'. It claimed that the WRU had got it wrong. They had misinterpreted the regulations. The article alleged that JPR had infringed his amateur status under the rules by contracting in the first place to write his autobiography for money without getting prior exemption from the WRU or having established the charity or any binding arrangements to pass over the money. A simple intention (even if genuine) to give money away in the future was not sufficient. The article went further. It also seemed to suggest that JPR may already have indirectly benefited from some proceeds and implied that he may never have intended to give them to charity until the first of the newspaper articles appeared.

JPR had had 'a gutful of the innuendo in the newspapers'. He promptly served a writ alleging defamation. The defendants were the *Daily Telegraph*, journalist John Reason and editor Bill Deedes. A similar writ was brought against *The Sun*. The latter settled but not the *Daily Telegraph*. JPR was not prepared for a long drawn-out legal battle but, true to his nature, he refused to back down.

His claim eventually came before the High Court in February 1982. The hearing became a 'slanging match' between JPR and the journalist. The first leg of the libel match went well for JPR. After four days of the hearing, the judge directed the jury in a manner favourable to JPR's argument. The jury found that the articles in the *Daily Telegraph* had libelled him. He was awarded £20,000 in damages. JPR was satisfied.

But that was not the end of the saga. The *Daily Telegraph* appealed. The Court of Appeal, perhaps a little reluctantly, decided that the original judge went 'seriously wrong' in his direction to the jury. The judge should have given a different interpretation of the 'amateur' rule. The later court thought the more technical interpretation of John Reason and the *Daily Telegraph* had been correct. A new trial would be ordered before a new judge and jury.

Worse for JPR, new evidence could be asserted about the practice of 'boot money' which had now become available. Although not relevant to the specific question of an autobiography and amateur status, the Court of Appeal decided that it was relevant to the *Daily Telegraph*'s plea of justification when the 'sting' of the libel was based on a claim of 'shamateurism

Perhaps he really was 'one of the last of the Corinthians'.

and hypocrisy'. It should be left to a new jury to decide whether the newspaper was justified: '*Did [the evidence] compel the conclusion that this outstanding rugby football player, the idol of his native Wales, had stooped to make money while posing and playing as an amateur?*' There would have to be a new trial if JPR wished to pursue his libel claim.

JPR was 'furious at the outcome' but, by this time, just 'wanted an end to it all'. He wanted to complete his surgeon's qualifications in London and then go back to Wales to practise. He called an end to the litigation. He had not lost – but he had not won. It was 'very hard to walk away'. But it was over.

JPR became 'Mr Williams', consultant surgeon at the Princess of Wales Hospital in Bridgend. In 1994 the Sports Injury Clinic in Bridgend finally opened with financial help from the Mid Glamorgan Area Health Authority. Sideburns and hair a little shorter but socks still at half-mast, JPR continued to play club rugby – first for the St Mary's B team in London and then, for 16 'wonderful' seasons until the age of 54, for the second and third teams of Tondu in Wales. Perhaps he really was 'one of the last of the Corinthians'.

On 26 August 1995, the IRFB declared rugby union an 'open' game and removed all restrictions on payments or benefits to those connected to the game. The issue of shamateurism had become irrelevant. To adapt the words of Lord Justice Stephenson in the Court of Appeal in JPR's case:

' ... *the distinction between 'gentlemen' and 'players' [was now] dead and buried, not only on the cricket field, and, to give a new meaning to the words which Shakespeare's Jaques spoke in a theatrical context (As You Like It II. vii. 140), ' ... all the men and women merely players."*

JPR published a second autobiography in 2006. He offered some advice to sports people tempted to bring a libel action: 'Think carefully ... and think twice about what your lawyers say. Remember, they are the only ones who are certain to make money out of it.'

89. BALL-TAMPERING IN THE HIGH COURT

Botham, Khan and an infamous libel case

Ian Botham was deeply offended by newspaper articles by Imran Khan. Botham thought he was being accused of ball-tampering and lack of class. It would become one of sport's most infamous libel actions.

In July 1996 an England Test match at Lord's was about to begin. Two of the world's greatest cricket all-rounders were facing up to each other – not in a contest on the cricket pitch but in the High Court. It was a saga which lasted longer than any Test series. A judge would end up describing it, despairingly, as litigation 'which does no credit to anybody'.

Ian Botham was not popular in Pakistan. He did not like touring there. Once, during a radio commentary, he joked: 'Pakistan is a place to send one's mother-in-law, all expenses paid.' Matches between England and Pakistan in the early 1990s had been fraught, including Pakistan's victory in the World Cup final in 1992 at the Melbourne Cricket Ground. Botham was out for nought. One of the Pakistani players is reputed to have told him to send his mother-in-law in to bat next since she couldn't do any worse! More seriously, accusations or hints of 'ball-tampering' were constantly in the air as Pakistan's bowlers carved through the English side.

Imran Khan, Pakistan's captain, added to the friction. He was interviewed for an article in *India Today* in 1994 in which he discussed the issue of ball-tampering. He had previously admitted that he himself once tampered with a ball, using a bottle-top, in a Sussex county match in the early 1980s. The newspaper article reported Khan as saying that 'the English media and a certain section of cricketers' had been motivated by 'racism' when they kicked up such a storm over Pakistani bowlers. The article continued to quote Khan: 'Look at people who have taken a rational stand on this. Tony Lewis, Christopher Martin-Jenkins, Derek Pringle. They are educated Oxbridge types. Look at the others, Lamb, Botham and Trueman. Class and upbringing makes a difference.'

Shortly after, Khan followed up with an interview for *The Sun* in England when he appeared to assert that ball-tampering in certain forms was commonplace in world cricket: 'The greatest and most famous bowlers from England and around the world have been guilty of ball-tampering. The biggest names of English cricket have all done it. And when I say big names, I mean as big as you can get.'

No name in English cricket came bigger than Ian Botham. He claimed that the article in *The Sun* was calling him a 'cheat' and was a libel. He had never tampered with the ball contrary to the rules of cricket. He demanded a public apology. He also threatened to sue Imran Khan for libel for the other article, alleging that Khan was calling him a 'racist' and 'lacking in education, class and upbringing'. Allan Lamb joined him in this claim – but Fred Trueman did not bother.

Khan tried to quell the row. He said that he had been misquoted and was only trying to defend himself. He asserted again that he did not regard certain forms of ball-tampering as 'cheating'. He regarded Botham as a 'worthy opponent' and not a 'cheat'. But the apology was not sufficiently public or unequivocal for Botham. Perhaps Pakistani pride would not permit Khan to go that far.

The feud was taken to the courts. Khan first tried to get the claim based on *The Sun*

> **'The biggest names of English cricket have all done it. And when I say big names, I mean as big as you can get.'**

article struck out – on the grounds that, taking the article as a whole, it was clear that Khan was saying that the practice of lifting the seam and scratching the ball was commonplace and not, in his view, 'cheating'. 'To me, they are within acceptable limits,' he said. This issue went to the Court of Appeal. On this point, Botham won a partial victory. Whilst the jury should look at the article as a whole and it may not have been asserting that Botham was a 'cheat', the court considered that it could still be viewed as damaging Botham's reputation.

So, on 15th July 1996, the stubborn cricket rivals found themselves facing up to each other in a libel action before a jury in Court 13 of the High Court in the Strand. It would be an unpleasant battle – perhaps more fiercely fought than the Lord's Test beginning later that week. Khan even changed his defence to add a plea that the claim that Botham had been involved in ball-tampering was justified.

Witnesses from the world of cricket were called. Michael Atherton and England coach, David Lloyd, were forced to miss a day's training session for the Lord's Test to attend. David Gower and Robin Smith were called. Brian Close and Geoffrey Boycott, as usual, were on different sides – Boycott arousing Botham's wrath with a 'bravado' performance suggesting that ball-tampering had become as common as speeding. Charles Gray QC fought the case for Botham and Lamb. They were up against the legendary George Carman QC whose courtroom tactics managed suggestively to include stories of Botham's past off-field exploits. Khan, nine days into the proceedings, did at least drop his defence that the allegations of ball-tampering against Botham were justified. It was a 13-day hearing which came to a climax on 31st July.

The jury retired to consider its verdict. The courtroom was tense when they returned. By a margin of 10-2, the jury decided in Khan's favour. It was not libel. Botham and Lamb were left to pick up most of the costs of the case, estimated at around £400,000. Khan would bear a portion. The verdict came as a 'great shock' to Botham. He later said in his autobiography: 'And to the day I go to my grave I will never understand how they reached it.'

> **The verdict came as a 'great shock' to Botham.**

Botham and Lamb would not give up the feud. They appealed and were set to return to the courts in May 1999, but the case was suddenly dropped, with the statement: '*The parties believe that in the best interests of cricket their differences should not continue to be argued in the courts. Any remaining issues between the parties will be resolved between them.*'

The case was over – if not happily resolved.

In 2000, Botham did go to Pakistan to commentate on a series there. He took his mother-in-law, recalling his earlier comment as something silly said in his youth. He said that she had enjoyed a great time on the 'all-expenses paid' trip, especially shopping for carpets. Perhaps it represented some sort of closure.

90. BRUCE GROBBELAAR

Brilliant saves – inspired or unintentional?

The headlines in *The Sun* were astonishing. Were there really links between Bruce Grobbelaar, an Asian betting syndicate and a plot to fix matches? It would lead to an extraordinary criminal trial and libel suit.

The sell-out crowd enjoyed a dramatic match at Anfield in January 1994 between Liverpool and Manchester United in the Premier League. It was a match to be remembered – a match which would later be replayed, on videotape, in Winchester Crown Court.

Liverpool were losing 1-3 at one stage but pulled back to level the score. Bruce Grobbelaar was Liverpool's long-standing and sometimes eccentric goalkeeper.

(Who could forget his 'wobbly-legs' routine as Roma's Francesco Graziani missed his crucial kick in the penalty shoot-out when Liverpool won the European Cup Final in 1984?) Grobbelaar made two terrific second-half saves against Manchester United: first from a shot by Ryan Giggs and then a powerful half-volley by Roy Keane which struck his hand as United were thwarted. The result was a thrilling draw.

After the end of the 1993/4 season, though, Grobbelaar's fantastic career at Liverpool had come to an end. Thirteen seasons, more than 600 appearances, six league titles, a European Cup victory, three FA Cups and three League Cups had made him, in his words, 'the most decorated goalkeeper in the league'. Grobbelaar had been transferred to Southampton and was enjoying an extension to his playing career. In another lively match in early November that year, at Maine Road, Southampton drew 3–3 away with Manchester City.

Then, four days later, the world of football was astonished as *The Sun* published a series of articles concerning Grobbelaar. *The Sun* alleged that Grobbelaar, along with Wimbledon goalkeeper Hans Segers, had been accepting payments through middlemen – including former Wimbledon and Aston Villa striker John Fashanu and a Malaysian, Heng Suan Lim – on behalf of an Asian gambling syndicate. Tipped off by a former business partner of Grobbelaar with whom he had also served in the Rhodesian army, Chris Vincent, the paper contrived a 'sting' operation resulting in secret audio and videotape evidence of an extraordinary meeting between Grobbelaar and Vincent in a hotel room in Southampton.

The conversation seemed to be evidence of corruption. Was Grobbelaar building a 'nest egg' for his retirement? After initial talk about women, football and the old days of their failed safari business in Zimbabwe, the conversation turned to other matters. Grobbelaar appeared to be admitting that he had accepted a payment of £40,000 from a syndicate to make sure Liverpool lost to Newcastle in a league match the previous year. He also said that he blew the chance

It was the biggest media story of betting and alleged corruption in football since the scandal of the 1960s.

of making £125,000 when he 'accidentally' made two 'blinding saves' to defy Manchester United in that match at Anfield. When playing for Southampton, he said that he had deliberately let in an early goal against Coventry before Southampton stormed back.

Vincent was trying to interest Grobbelaar in 'working' for another Asian syndicate. Grobbelaar was seen apparently taking £2,000 in cash from Vincent as first of a series of advance payments for rigging future matches.

It was devastating. It appeared that Premier League matches were being fixed. It was the biggest media story of betting and alleged corruption in football since the scandal of the 1960s. An investigation, called 'Operation Navaho', was launched by the police. In March 1995 Grobbelaar was arrested and, along with Lim, Fashanu and Segers, charged with conspiracy to corrupt by giving or accepting money for improperly influencing or attempting to influence the outcome of certain football matches. Grobbelaar alone faced a separate charge of accepting a corrupt payment, on the basis of the 'sting' operation, on behalf of another (in fact fictitious) syndicate. The case went to jury trial before Justice Tuckey at Winchester Crown Court.

> **'I was returning to my days in the bush. As a tracker, you are out in front, doing your own thing, trying to find people.'**

The trial started in January 1997 amidst a continuing media frenzy in Court 3, the same courtroom used for the Rosemary West mass-murder trial a year or so earlier. Grobbelaar pleaded not guilty. He claimed, rather extraordinarily, that he was only stringing Vincent along in order to gather evidence on his former associate's affairs with the intent of taking it to the police. He was himself trying to entrap Vincent: 'I was returning to my days in the bush. As a tracker, you are out in front, doing your own thing, trying to find people.' As for his dealings with Lim, he said that he only gave 'advice' or 'forecasts' and he never 'fixed' or threw a match.

Curtains were drawn in the courtroom. The jury were entertained to excerpts of the goalmouth action in a number of matches, including the full 90 minutes of the 3-3 draw against Manchester United at Anfield. No evidence was produced that Grobbelaar had actually played in a way that amounted to match fixing. Witnesses included 1966 England goalkeeper Gordon Banks. (Grobbelaar's counsel raised laughter in the court when he asked Banks why he had not caught the ball when making his famous save from Pelé in the 1970 World Cup!) Banks, in his statement, said that he had studied the videotapes of the relevant matches and that, in his opinion, Grobbelaar had played in a 'thoroughly professional and competent manner'. Jimmy Armfield could see nothing untoward. Southampton manager and former World Cup player Alan Ball said that he had had no hesitation in continuing to pick Grobbelaar after his arrest. Other witnesses included Ron Atkinson, Alan Hansen, Nigel Clough and Bob Wilson. The Wykeham Arms in Winchester became a popular meeting point after the day's events.

After a trial lasting eight weeks, the jury were out for nearly 11 hours. They failed to reach a verdict on any of the charges. A re-trial was ordered. It began again in June 1997. After a 45-day retrial of evidence, followed by more than 26 hours of deliberation spread over five days, the second jury of six women and five men eventually reached a verdict on the main charges. The atmosphere was tense. 'Not guilty.'

The jury were still undecided on the separate charge against Grobbelaar based on the £2,000 received during the 'sting' operation. After a further three hours deliberation the following day, still no agreement. Judge McCulloch directed the jury to be dismissed and the prosecution withdrew the charge. That, after all the media frenzy, was the end of the criminal case.

Then to the civil courts. Grobbelaar decided, in the light of the criminal verdict, to take revenge and proceed with a libel action against *The Sun*. His reputation had been shattered. He should be compensated. The case opened in the High Court in July 1999. The jury found in Grobbelaar's favour with an award of damages of £85,000.

The Sun appealed. The tide turned firmly against Grobbelaar. The Court of Appeal overturned the lower court's decision on the grounds that the jury's verdict was '*perverse*'. Lord Justice Simon Brown said that it represented a '*miscarriage of justice which this court can and must correct*'. He found Grobbelaar's explanation '*quite simply incredible*'. It was the first time that a jury verdict in a libel case had been set aside as a perverse finding. But this was not the end. The case was eventually appealed by Grobbelaar to the House of Lords, the highest court in the land.

The House of Lords technically re-instated the verdict of libel – but gave Grobbelaar nothing. The Lords decided that, although the specific allegations of match fixing had not been proved, there was strong evidence of dishonesty on Grobbelaar's part. Grobbelaar had acted '*in a way in which no decent or honest footballer would act*'. It was a damning verdict.

It was the first time that a jury verdict in a libel case had been set aside as a perverse finding.

Grobbelaar no longer had any reputation which could be damaged. Lord Bingham remarked: '*It would be an affront to justice if a court of law were to award substantial damages to a man shown to have acted in such a flagrant breach of his legal and moral obligations.*'

The House of Lords slashed Grobbelaar's award of damages to just £1 and ordered him to pay *The Sun*'s legal costs, estimated at £500,000. It had been a terrible mistake by Grobbelaar to bring the libel action.

Grobbelaar was unable to pay the costs and was later declared bankrupt in England.

Grobbelaar would later remark: 'The Britons bankrupted me. I came to their country with £10 in my pocket and they gave me £1 back. But in between I had one hell of a ride.'

91. THE WORLD'S WORST TENNIS PRO?

Losing on and in court

The headline caught the attention of the tennis world. Had this been the worst run of defeats in professional tennis history? Was it libel?

'The world's worst tennis pro wins at last' ran the headline. Englishman Robert Dee had left school at age 16 to chase his life's dream of becoming a professional tennis player. He worked with the legendary Nick Bollettieri in Florida before joining a tennis academy in Spain and reaching a career-high world ranking of 1,466 in 2005. On 22nd April 2008 stories in the press, including the *Daily Telegraph* under that headline, changed his life. 'Having been previously unknown to almost everyone in the tennis world, I suddenly became famous overnight.' Even Roger Federer enquired to find out more.

The article in the *Daily Telegraph* was typical. The paper had printed a short front-page story beginning: 'A Briton ranked as the worst professional tennis player in the world after 54 defeats in a row has won his first match.' It went on: 'Robert Dee, 21, of Bexley, Kent, did not win a single match during his first three years on the circuit, touring at an estimated cost of £200,000.' Dee was upset. He sued for defamation, claiming that the piece exposed him to ridicule and could damage his ability to work in the tennis world. By suggesting he was absurdly bad at tennis, the piece made him 'look like the Inspector Clouseau' of the tennis world. He argued that the story was untrue since he had won many professional games on the Spanish domestic circuit during his 54-match losing streak on the international circuit – which came to an end in Reus near Barcelona when he beat an unranked 17 year-old, Arzhang Derakshani. Dee lost in the second round.

In fact, Dee was on a run bringing legal claims, a run more successful than any so far he had achieved on the professional tennis circuit. He had received apologies, and damages, from a series of well-known media organisations who ran the same story, including the BBC, Reuters, the *Guardian*, the *Daily Mirror*, the *Daily Mail* and others. These media organisations thought it convenient to settle with Dee rather than defend legal actions in court. The *Daily Telegraph* did not. The case came before Mrs Justice Sharp in the High Court in 2010.

Robert Dee lost. His claim was struck out.

Esoteric discussion took place in court as to whether allegations of 'want of skill' could themselves be defamatory. However, the primary defence of the *Daily Telegraph* was justification and fair comment. The articles in the paper should be read as a whole. Evidence

By suggesting he was absurdly bad at tennis, the piece made him 'look like the Inspector Clouseau' of the tennis world.

was submitted by such tennis players as Boris Becker and John Lloyd to the effect that 'the circuit' was understood in the tennis world to mean the international circuit run under the auspices of the International Tennis Federation (ITF) or the Association of Tennis Professionals (ATP). Domestic tournaments, not run by the ATP or ITF, did not qualify for world ranking points and were not part of the international circuit.

Mrs Justice Sharp in the High Court seemed to have little sympathy for Dee:

'*In every race, match or other sporting event, someone has to come last: that is the nature of competitive sport. Losing in sport is an occupational hazard.*' The *Daily Telegraph* was not saying that these matches were the whole of his playing record. '*The incontestably true facts are that [Robert Dee] did lose 54 matches in a row in straight sets in his first three years on the world ranking ITF/ATP tournaments on the international professional tennis circuit, and that was the worst ever run.*' His wins on the Spanish national circuit did not '*detract from the fact that he holds the longest record for consecutive defeats based on the official world ranking system….The characterisation of Dee as the world's worst is therefore simply a consequence of his unprecedented record of defeats.*'

The *Daily Telegraph* did not have to prove more in terms of playing skill or lack of it. The paper's case succeeded on the basis of justification – that the facts were true.

Dee's run of wins as a litigant had come to an end. His subsequent record as a tennis player showed little improvement. On the ATP website he is now classed as 'inactive'.

92. MAX MOSLEY

A chequered flag for privacy?

Max Mosley, a dominant figure in the administration of Formula One racing, was outraged by the sensational story. Was it an unjustified breach of his privacy? He decided to sue.

The story was blazened across the newspaper. Photographs which would have revealed a person's private parts were, however, discreetly blocked out in relevant places including, as the court later pointed out, 'in one instance by a chequered flag'. Another public figure had been exposed.

Max Mosley, in 2008, had been president of the Fédération Internationale de l'Automobile (FIA) for 15 years. A former barrister and amateur racing driver (and co-founder of March Engineering which became a fairly successful Formula One team), he was the youngest son of Oswald Mosley, former leader of the British Union of Fascists. His parents married at the home of Joseph Goebbels, with Adolf Hitler as a principal guest. He would later say: 'All my life I have had hanging over me my antecedents, my parents.'

Mosley first joined the Formula One Constructors' Association in the late 1970s as its legal adviser. He formed a close association with Bernie Ecclestone and, together, they forged a number of deals that established the commercial and operational framework for Formula One, which became one of the world's most commercially successful sports. First appointed FIA president in 1993, Mosley had been re-elected for subsequent four-year terms in 1997, 2001 and 2005. Mosley was a major figure in motor racing.

It was a Sunday in March 2008 when 68 year-old Max Mosley learned of the headline in that day's *News of the World*: 'FI BOSS HAS SICK NAZI ORGY WITH 5 HOOKERS'. It continued: 'Son of Hitler-loving fascist in sex shame.' The paper claimed that Mosley had been filmed 'romping in a torture dungeon'. 'Mosley - a friend to FI big names like Bernie Ecclestone and Lewis Hamilton - barks orders in German as he lashes girls wearing mock death camp uniforms and enjoys being whipped until he bleeds.' Short clips from the video material were made available on the newspaper's website. The source? One of the female participants (referred to as Woman E in court) had pre-agreed with the newspaper secretly to film the activity. She was paid £20,000 by the newspaper.

Mosley was outraged at the intrusion into his private life and particularly the allegation of Nazism. He decided to sue the *News of the World*. It became an important case for its ramifications - not only for the law of privacy but also for the sport. Mosley claimed damages, in effect, for wrongful infringement of privacy - a form of legal claim given stimulus in recent years by the European Convention on Human Rights and Fundamental Freedoms.

The case came before Justice Eady in the High Court. He accepted that such a claim could exist in law except that disclosure was not wrongful if justified by a countervailing public interest.

Counsel for the *News of the World* argued forcibly that disclosure was indeed in the public interest. Because of Mosley's position as FIA president, the activities 'call seriously into question his suitability for his FIA role'. Intrusion by clandestine filming was justified by the anticipation of a Nazi theme, 'mocking the humiliating way Jews were treated' or 'parodying Holocaust horrors', which was a matter relevant to Mosley's suitability

Mosley's counsel countered that 'what took place was simply a 'standard' S and M prison scenario' and nothing more.

for his post. (Other arguments, that the activity amounted to inciting or aiding the criminal offence of assault or keeping a brothel were quickly dismissed.)

Mosley's counsel countered that 'what took place was simply a 'standard' S and M prison scenario' and nothing more. (Justice Eady acknowledged, incidentally, that 'BDSM' was now the more common expression.) In the lead-up to what Mosley termed a 'party' (and the paper called 'an orgy'), one of the women arranging the event notified the others simply that: 'I'm doing a judicial on him at noon.' Enactment of domination, restraints, punishment and prison scenarios were 'neutral' and did not entail Nazism.

Justice Eady gave his judgment on 24th July 2008. Mosley won. The judge was persuaded that there was no evidence of Nazism. If there had been, that might justify disclosure. However, he said: '*I have concluded that there was no such mocking behaviour or, from material viewed, any evidence of Nazi behaviour.*' Could the disclosure and breach of privacy otherwise be justified? Justice Eady decided not. There was a pre-existing understanding of confidentiality between the participants. The secret filming of sexual activities (albeit unconventional) carried on between consenting adults on private property, knowingly induced by the *News of the World*, had breached that trust. Such sexual activity '*may be viewed with distaste and moral disapproval but in the light of modern rights-based jurisprudence does not provide any justification for the intrusion on the personal privacy of the claimant.... Titillation for its own sake could never be justified.*'

Mosley's right to privacy prevailed. The court awarded him an unprecedented £60,000 in damages. The *News of the World* also had to pay a large majority of Mosley's substantial legal costs.

Would the disclosures affect Mosley's position as FIA president? Criticised by many in the sport, his involvement in a number of high-level motor sports events was cancelled or limited and some clubs considered withdrawal from the FIA. Pressure built up and Mosley faced a formal vote of confidence as FIA president. Could he survive? Mosley, despite his embarrassment, pressed ahead. He was an astute politician. An extraordinary general meeting of the FIA was held on 3rd June. Mosley did survive, just: 103 votes in support and 55 against, with 7 abstentions and 4 invalid votes. Mosley declared that he would stand down at the end of his term in October 2009. (An internal dispute led Mosley at one stage to declare that he was prepared to run again but, to the relief of many, the dispute was settled and Mosley did stand down.) His preferred candidate, Jean Todt, was eventually elected as his successor.

Mosley was not, however, finished as a litigant. His case against the *News of the World* represented a high-water mark in the courts' support of an individual's right to privacy. Yet, whilst the risk of a damages claim might deter some newspapers from pressing ahead with a story, it is clearly far better (for the individual) to prevent any publication in the first place. For this, the individual needs to know that the story is pending.

Max Mosley himself took up the cause. He began a lengthy legal battle to try to force newspapers to warn people before making allegations about their private lives. The route he chose was to file an application to the European Court of Human Rights claiming that the European Convention on Human Rights was breached by the failure of the United Kingdom to impose a legal duty on journalists to give an individual at least two days' prior notice of stories about the misbehaviour of a public figure. He failed. In May 2011 the European Court ruled that the UK's domestic law was not in conflict with the Convention.

If a potential 'victim' does know that a damaging story is about to break, he or she may seek an injunction to stop its publication - either on the grounds that it would be libellous or that it would be a wrongful infringement of privacy. Yet, the fact of the injunction (and bare details involved) will be known and often lead to unwelcome speculation and exposure.

In order to prevent this, the practice grew of seeking so-called 'super-injunctions' whereby the judge would approve a gagging order prohibiting not only disclosure of the story but also of the fact that an injunction had been imposed at all! The practice of such super-injunctions began to arouse controversy, not least because they favoured rich and powerful celebrities with the resources (beyond most) to obtain the secret remedy. Two familiar sporting names in these pages (uncanny how their football and legal stories have been linked) were litigants in important privacy actions before the courts in early 2010 - John Terry and Rio Ferdinand.

John Terry (Chelsea and England star, but known initially to the court simply as 'LNS') sought a super-injunction in January 2010 to prevent publication of a story alleging an extra-marital affair with another person (now known to be Vanessa Perroncel, at the time a long-term partner of Wayne Bridge, a team-mate of John Terry with Chelsea and England). The judge leading such privacy cases in the High Court was now Justice Tugendhart. He was not impressed. Those who apply for super-injunctions must expect their applications to be examined in detail. The evidence gathered by John Terry was inadequate. Significantly, in the judge's view, his principal motive appeared to be to protect his reputation for sponsorship deals and other commercial interests. He turned down Terry's application. The courts should only act in secrecy where '*strictly necessary*'. It was important that the public should be able to debate moral questions and exercise '*freedom to criticise within the limits of the law the conduct of other members of society as being socially harmful or wrong.*' The days of super-injunctions being granted routinely in privacy cases were now over. John Terry had helped (unwillingly) to shape the law.

The ensuing publicity regarding Terry's alleged affair would, indirectly, lead – a year or so later – to the verbal fracas on the pitch at Loftus Road and to John Terry's trial for allegedly racially abusing Anton Ferdinand (and then to a disciplinary charge against the latter's brother, Rio). In the meantime, the publicity had other consequences. On the pitch, Terry was replaced as England's captain by Rio Ferdinand. Off the pitch, Rio Ferdinand would also find himself the victim of an 'exposure' by a newspaper. In April 2010 the *Sunday Mirror* ran a story under the headline 'My Affair with England Captain Rio'. Carly Storey gave an account of their alleged past relationship in return for £16,000. Ferdinand, following Max Mosley's precedent, sued the paper for damages for

The high-water mark in the law's protection of privacy, represented by Max Mosley's case, had long receded.

misuse of private information and breach of privacy. The owners of the *Sunday Mirror* countered that disclosure was in the public interest. Ferdinand had replaced Terry as England captain on the basis that Ferdinand was 'reformed and responsible'. This, it appeared, was not the case.

Justice Nichol in the High Court decided against Ferdinand. '*Overall, in my judgment, the balancing exercise favours the defendant's right of freedom of expression over the claimant's right of privacy… Stories may be in the public interest even if the reasons behind the informant providing the information are less than noble.*'

John Terry and Rio Ferdinand both failed. The attitude of the courts had changed. The high-water mark in the law's protection of privacy, represented by Max Mosley's case, had long receded.

Max Mosley himself was still not finished. He continued his crusade. He started a libel action against the *News of the World* and continued to apply for orders in various countries against Google, and other website operators, seeking to remove video clips featuring him and other content about his sex-life. The *News of the World* became embroiled in its own scandal of 'phone hacking' and other improper practices. The owners, News

International led by Rupert Murdoch, suddenly called an end to the paper; the last copy of the *News of the World* was published on 10th July 2011.

The press were again under attack. The Leveson Inquiry was set up by the government into the culture, practices and ethics of the press. There was no more determined witness before the Inquiry, advocating change and the establishment of a statutory tribunal to regulate the press, than Max Mosley.

Chapter Twelve

A CLOSING COCKTAIL

We end with a few diversions away from the main path and with a collection of sporting cases and incidents which have not changed the course of the law or the direction of sport – but which may provide some amusement or interest to the sports observer.

Perhaps there is a theme here. In many of the stories in this last 'cocktail' the claims have been somewhat unusual or optimistic in nature. They include a Scotland supporter's hopeful claim after a rather strange match against Estonia, a Leicester City fan seeking damages for shock after a referee's decision and two American fans fighting over a ball.

And we finish with a warning for the sports fan from the divorce courts.

93. DAVE WINFIELD

'He killed a seagull!'

An extraordinary incident in a night game in Toronto would lead to fans flapping their arms whenever Dave Winfield, lead hitter of the Yankees, appeared. What was it about?

It was a night game in Toronto in August 1983. The home team, the Blue Jays, were playing the New York Yankees. Dave Winfield, the Yankees' lead hitter and one of the game's greatest players, was getting ready to field before the Blue Jays started their fifth inning. There was a packed crowd at the Exhibition Stadium. Little did anyone know that one of baseball's strangest incidents was about to occur.

Winfield, at third base, was casually playing catch-ball with team-mate Don Taylor in the warm-up before play started. Winfield had spotted a large seagull sitting over on the pitch towards the dug-out. Many gulls perched in the stands, waiting no doubt for their post-match feed on half-eaten hot dogs and other scraps. This gull seemed keener on watching play. Winfield had seen him there earlier. Winfield threw the ball to the ball boy – but threw it in front of the seagull to scare him off. In Winfield's words: 'The ball takes a short hop off the artificial turf and *wop!* It flattens the bird. Right away I know he's a goner.'

Feathers scattered. The ball boy, rather dramatically, came on with a white towel, picked the bird up and put him on the towel and carried him off. The murmur in the crowd turned to a rumble, and then to widespread booing. Fences were rattled and objects thrown on to the pitch. The crowd booed Winfield for the rest of the match (won, incidentally, 3-1 by the Yankees).

After the match, Winfield was informed that the police wanted to see him. A complaint had been made and a warrant for his arrest issued. David Mark Winfield, the game's most expensive and renowned player, was taken by a squad car to the Ontario Provincial Police Station. He was charged with 'wilfully causing unnecessary injury to a bird, to wit a Gull, by using a ball' contrary to the criminal code. Maximum sentence: six months in jail. Exhibit 'A' laid sadly on the table, stiff, legs in the air. Questioning lasted an hour-and-a-half. When Winfield left the station, released on bail (posting a $500 bond), flashbulbs from dozens of reporters lit the sky. Winfield covered his face with a briefcase. He was required to return to court in August.

Exhibit 'A' laid sadly on the table, stiff, legs in the air.

Billy Martin, manager of the Yankees, could only say: 'They say he hit the gull on purpose? They wouldn't say that if they'd seen the throws he's been making all year. It's the first time he's hit the cut-off man.'

The following day, the charge was dropped. Dave Winfield was a free man.

At the Yankees' next match, when Winfield came out to bat, 40,000 fans flapped their arms like birds. 'He killed a seagull!' In an attempt to remedy his public image in Toronto, he assisted an off-season charity fund-raising event by contributing a painting to the auction. When he told his friends that he had been invited to Toronto, they said: 'Invited or extradited?' Speaking at the event, Winfield remarked that he had leather shoes, a lizard belt and an alligator briefcase. He jokingly remarked to the audience that he had feared he might get 'five to ten' if he visited Toronto!

For years, whenever Winfield returned to play in Toronto, his appearances would be greeted by fans standing and flapping their arms - until Winfield himself joined the Blue Jays late in 1991 and became a fans' favourite, leading the team to the World Series Championship.

94. A CARIBBEAN FARCE

Which way is the goal?

It was an extraordinary end to a football match in the Caribbean. Grenada were trying to score at both ends of the pitch – and failing! Why?

It did not reach a court or tribunal – we are allowed one exception in this book – but it was an example of a basic sporting doctrine, 'rules are rules', which should be retold. It was a match for the mathematicians and the lawyers. It ended in a farce.

Barbados were playing Grenada in a preliminary group match in February 1994 in the Shell Caribbean Cup, the soccer championship of the Caribbean. Grenada went into the match with a superior goal difference which meant that Barbados needed to win by two clear goals to progress to the final phase of the competition.

Under the rules of the tournament, if a match was level at the end of normal time, extra time would be played until a sudden-death winner. In order to encourage teams to attack for that winner rather than wait for penalties at the end of extra time, the rule-makers introduced a rule that a sudden-death winner would be worth two goals.

Suddenly, with around three minutes remaining, the Barbadians passed the ball – and deliberately kicked the ball into their own net.

It seemed like a good idea at the time – but what trouble it would cause!

Back to the match. Barbados were playing well and took a 2-0 lead. They had the necessary two-goal advantage. They held this lead until the 83rd minute. Then Grenada scored, making it 2-1. A frantic finish was in store as Barbados pressed forward trying to clinch the extra goal – but they could not get past Grenada's packed defence.

Suddenly, with around three minutes remaining, the Barbadians passed the ball – and deliberately kicked the ball into their own net. It was an own goal to tie the game 2-2. They had worked out that their best chance of getting a two-goal advantage was now to score in extra time!

Bewildered, Grenada did not know which way to turn. There followed the extraordinary sight of one group of Grenadian players trying to attack for a winner – and another group trying to score an own goal themselves to restore the one goal difference for Barbados which would be sufficient to see Grenada through. But, equally extraordinary, Grenada could not score at either end – Barbados were defending both ends of the pitch. The full-time whistle blew. Football being football, Barbados scored the sudden-death winner in the fourth minute of extra time and were awarded a 4-2 victory. Grenada were out.

Grenada complained, but there was no remedy. Barbados were playing within the rules of the tournament. Moreover, they could not be accused of trying to lose the match – they were trying to win. Rules are rules. So it was all the fault of the rule-makers, and no doubt the lawyers, who drew up the rules!

Barbados' success was short-lived, however, and they were eliminated in the next phase. Trinidad and Tobago, the hosts, went on to win the title.

95. A DISAPPOINTED SCOTTISH SUPPORTER

'There's only one team in Tallinn'

The floodlights at the stadium in Tallinn were poor. The time of Scotland's match with Estonia was changed – with unusual consequences.

John MacDonald was an enthusiastic Scottish supporter. It was October 1996 and Scotland were due to play Estonia in a group qualifying match for the 1998 World Cup. It was a 6.45pm evening kick-off in the Kadriorg Stadium in Tallinn, the Estonian capital. MacDonald was with a group of travelling Scottish fans and he was looking forward to the match.

Then, the arrangements changed. On the day before the match, temporary floodlights were erected at the Kadriorg Stadium. After testing, the Scottish FA claimed that the floodlights were unsuitable for such an international fixture. FIFA agreed and decided that the kick-off time should be brought forward to 3pm in the afternoon. Estonia were upset by the decision – perhaps because the revised time would interfere with the arrangements, and fee, agreed for live television transmission.

The kick-off time of 3pm arrived. Six hundred Scotland supporters, including John MacDonald, were allowed into the ground and took up position. A farce ensued. The tartan army sang 'There's only one team in Tallinn'. The fully-kitted Scotland 11 lined up for the national anthem and kicked off. Some noted that the Scottish team never put a foot wrong throughout the game! The match was abandoned after one pass. The Estonian team had failed to turn up. FIFA awarded the match to Scotland 3-0 by default.

Some noted that the Scottish team never put a foot wrong throughout the match!

John MacDonald was frustrated by his wasted journey and expense, despite the apparent Scotland victory. He wanted compensation. Whom could he sue? He brought a claim against FIFA alleging that the governing body was under a duty not to alter the kick-off time so close to a game that it would lead to the Estonian team not turning up. He also claimed that the Scottish FA should have taken reasonable care to ensure that the match could be played at the original time. His claim for compensation came before Judge McEwan in a Scottish court.

John MacDonald lost. The Scottish FA had only made representations to FIFA and had no control over the decision to re-arrange the match or the adequacy of the floodlights. As for the claim against FIFA, a spectator simply had no legal redress against the organisers for this kind of disappointment. A spectator could have no claim unless personal injury was caused. The court understandably declared: '*If the present kind of claim were allowed, it would open the way to many claims by an indeterminate class of people disappointed at the outcome or organisation of a sporting event.*'

Perhaps it was a sign of our litigious times that the claim could get as far as the courts in the first place.

To make matters worse for the Scottish supporters, FIFA changed its mind after a successful appeal by Estonia and, instead of awarding victory to Scotland, ordered the match to be replayed at a neutral ground. It was duly replayed, four months later, in Monaco – where it ended in a 0-0 draw. Scotland failed to qualify for the World Cup.

96. WHAT A REFEREE!

A Leicester fan's shock at a last-minute penalty decision

A Leicester fan tried to sue for damages as a result of a bad refereeing decision in a FA Cup match. Did he have any chance?

All football fans have suffered it - the refereeing decision which has cost 'our' team the match.

This one was at Stamford Bridge in February 1997 during the final few minutes of extra time in the fifth round of a FA Cup replay between Chelsea and Leicester City. The original match up at Filbert Street had ended in a 2-2 draw. The score in the replay was still 0-0 after 115 goalless minutes. A penalty 'shoot-out' was looming to settle the tie.

Chelsea's Erland Johnsen moved into the Leicester penalty area in a final attacking attempt. He appeared to clash with two Leicester defenders. Johnsen fell to the ground. Was it a dive? The referee, Mike Reed, awarded a highly dubious penalty. Chelsea scored. The final whistle blew and Leicester were out of the FA Cup. Leicester's manager, Martin O'Neill, was apoplectic. He attacked the decision as a 'disgrace'.

Leicester's supporters were in uproar. One, Tom Tyrrell, was so upset he later decided to take legal action. He issued a claim for damages against the Football Association (FA) as being responsible for the referee's alleged negligence.

The basis of his claim was novel. His loss, he claimed, was having to miss work for two days due to the trauma and shock he had suffered as the result of witnessing such a negligently given penalty decision. He claimed lost earnings of £100, travelling expenses and the cost of his ticket.

> He issued a claim for damages against the Football Association as being responsible for the referee's alleged negligence.

The FA applied to have the claim struck out. The case was duly heard in the Central London County Court in April 1997. It was a lost cause for Tyrrell. He was no more fortunate than his team. The court dismissed his claim. There was no reasonable cause of action. The referee, even if he was incompetent, owed no duty of care of this kind to a spectator. Tyrrell went away empty-handed – except for a bill for costs.

It is fundamental to sport that the decision of a referee, made in good faith in the course of the playing of the game, must be accepted – however reluctantly – both by players and also by spectators. The implications would be mind-boggling if a referee, or a sports governing body such as the FA, could be liable in law for financial consequences of a mistaken, but honest, decision in the course of play. Put legally, the risk of a referee making a mistaken decision is an inherent risk which a spectator takes when attending a match. Tom Tyrrell's claim was ill-founded in law. It had no prospect of success. But all football fans knew how he must have felt!

It was of little consolation to Leicester City fans that Chelsea went on to win the FA Cup in 1997. After beating Portsmouth in the semi-final, they defeated Middlesbrough 2-0 in the final.

97. UNSEATED AT NEWCASTLE

A supporter claims her seat at St James' Park

Jane Duffy paid £500 to guarantee 'her' seat at St James' Park. Could she be moved?

The promotional leaflet in 1994 featured Newcastle legend Kevin Keegan endorsing the offer: 'Your place at St James' Park is secure well into the next century … As a United bondholder your name … will be fixed to your personal seat.' Newcastle were offering season ticket-holders, on payment of £500, a 'bond' which would guarantee them a seat for the next 10 years at the applicable season ticket prices together with complimentary home cup tie tickets for three years.

Jane Duffy was a loyal supporter of Newcastle United. A 44 year-old City Council education adviser, she had been a season ticket holder for many years. These were exciting times at St James' Park and she wanted to continue to be part of it. Waiting lists for season tickets were building up. Jane Duffy took up the offer together with one for her father: 'I was, simply, scared of losing my seat.'

Jane Duffy enjoyed 'her' seat in the centre of the Milburn Stand. That is until, just six years later, Newcastle notified her that they were moving her. Around 4,000 season ticket-holders were being moved to a different place in the ground. The club needed the original seat positions as part of 'top-class' facilities to be offered to corporate clients in a new fund-raising scheme to

Jane Duffy said: 'I feel totally conned.'

support a £42 million redevelopment at St James' Park which would increase the ground capacity to 52,000. The club said that if Duffy and other season ticket-holders were not willing to pay the substantially increased prices for the 'corporate' seats, they would have to move to the newly-built upper tier. Jane Duffy insisted that the alternative seats 'up in The Gods' were inferior and destroyed the ambience built up among loyal season ticket-holders over the years.

She and many others were deeply upset. They set up a 'Save Our Seats' campaign. They claimed that the literature and advertising gave a clear impression that £500 would guarantee the same seat for a decade. 'Fans are incensed,' said a spokesman. 'The snub to ordinary season ticket-holders, shifted for corporate entertainment, is bad enough. But for those who bought bonds, this is an absolute disgrace.' Jane Duffy said: 'I feel totally conned.' She brought a legal claim against Newcastle to prevent 'her' seat being moved. Five other fans brought similar actions – together they became known as the 'Newcastle Six'.

Justice Blackburne praised the fans '*unswerving loyalty, even fanaticism*' but ruled in favour of the club. The Six appealed.

While the rest of the football world was absorbed with Euro 2000, the appeal was heard in London. Led by Lord Justice Woolf, the Court of Appeal confirmed that, in the end, this was a matter of interpretation of the contract terms of the bond. The club's lawyers had protected the position in the small print. Unfortunately for Jane Duffy, those terms did allow Newcastle to make this change. She would have to watch from another seat.

Newcastle, desperately trying to rebuild the club's public image, eventually agreed not to pursue Jane Duffy and the other members of the Newcastle Six for legal costs.

98. 'IT'S NOT A CATCH IF YOU DROP THE BALL!'

Two fans fight over a baseball

Barry Bonds hit a record-breaking home-run into the stands. Baseball fans fought for the ball. Who would own it?

It was the last day of the 2001 US baseball season in October at PacBell Park in San Francisco. It was a record-breaking season for Barry Bonds, lead hitter for the San Francisco Giants. He had already broken the major league record for home-runs in a single season. He was about to smash his 73rd, and final, home-run of the season into his favourite right-field stands.

The event was widely anticipated. Fans, in American tradition, were at the ready to catch and claim the historic ball. Many had come prepared with baseball gloves. The ball flew into the stands. Alex Popov, the owner of a healthfood restaurant in Berkeley, was the first to get to the ball, thrusting his gloved hand above the swarm of fans. Extraordinarily, the scene was caught on videotape by a cameraman. Popov held the ball very briefly, for less than a second, before disappearing under an unruly mob of excited and grasping fans. A minute later, Patrick Hayashi, a software engineer from Sacramento, emerged from the scrum with the ball in his hand. He smiled and showed it to the cameraman. Hayashi said he found the ball rolling free in the melée.

Was Hayashi entitled to retain the ball? Popov claimed that he had possession and that it had wrongly been taken from him. He was entitled to the ball. No, said Hayashi: 'It's not a catch if you drop the ball.' Popov started a lawsuit to reclaim the ball.

Did it matter financially? Well, a previous record-breaking home-run ball, Mark McGwire's home-run in 1998 which was the first to reach the magic 70th in a season, was purchased for $3.2 million by a major baseball memorabilia collector, Todd McFarlane. After months of wrangling between Popov and Hayashi, the dispute could not be resolved outside the courtroom – so to the Californian Superior Court.

'It's not a catch if you drop the ball.'

Judge McCarthy presided over an intense and often surreal three-week court battle. It raised deep theoretical questions. What constituted possession of a baseball landing in the stands? What was the nature of 'possession' in law? Did it require full 'dominion and control'?

Four distinguished law professors gave their views to the court. They all disagreed. Arcane arguments and precedents were drawn from pursuits such as whale hunting, fox hunting and the salvage of sunken vessels. Reference was even made to Herman Melville's 1851 novel *Moby Dick* and the customs and practices of whalers when a whale had been harpooned and subsequently captured – distinguishing between 'fast fish' and 'loose fish'. It was all very erudite and no doubt profitable for the lawyers, but frankly inconclusive.

After all the arguments, Judge McCarthy finally came to his decision, a 20-minute ruling in the mould of King Solomon. Both men, he said, had an equal claim under the law. He settled on a principle of *'equitable division'* discovered in the roots of ancient Roman law. He ordered the ball to be sold and the proceeds to be shared equally!

After all the arguments, Judge McCarthy finally came to his decision, a 20-minute ruling in the mould of King Solomon.

Popov did not, he judged, achieve full control of the ball but did attain something Judge McCarthy termed *'pre-possessory rights'* before he was attacked by the swarming crowd. It would never be known whether Popov would have been able to retain control of the ball if the crowd had not interfered. It was *'an out of control mob, engaged in violent, illegal behaviour'*. Judge McCarthy saw here, in the midst of America's national game, a need to assert a fundamental principle underlying American history and culture – the rule of law:

'Judicial rulings, particularly in cases that receive media attention, affect the way people conduct themselves. This case demands vindication of an important principle. We are a nation governed by law, not by brute force.'

As a result, Judge McCarthy decided that *'each man has a claim of equal dignity as to the other'*.

The consequence? With the aid of a sports memorabilia agent, the ball was auctioned. It fetched $450,000, bought by Todd McFarlane for his prestigious collection. The litigation could surely only have taken place in America. As one consequence, Alex Popov faced a legal bill for over $470,000 – twice his share of the proceeds from the auction of the ball in dispute.

99. KIM CHRISTENSEN

Moving the goalposts

The goalkeeper of one of Sweden's leading teams appeared to be moving the goalposts closer together! Was it really true?

Thirty year-old Kim Christensen, a Dane, was the regular first-team goalkeeper for IFK Gothenburg, one of Sweden's leading teams. (Christensen, in fact, had the unusual record of having played in every minute of every game for the club in the league in the previous 2008/9 season.) Gothenburg, level on points at the top of the Swedish league, were playing Orebro in September 2009. As common in Sweden, it was an artificial grass pitch and the goalposts rested on designated markings on the surface of the pitch – eight yards (7.32 metres) apart, or at least they were at the start.

After around 30 minutes of play, the referee was alerted by Orebro players that Christensen had been seen kicking the moveable goalposts several centimetres inwards. They were no longer eight yards apart at the base! (TV coverage later confirmed Christensen's actions.) The referee kicked them back into place and the match continued to its conclusion, a 0-0 draw.

Had Christensen done this before? The answer was 'yes'. 'I got the tip from a goalkeeping friend a few years ago, and since then I have done it from time to time', he admitted.

'I got the tip from a goalkeeping friend a few years ago, and since then I have done it from time to time.'

The incident was reported and considered by the disciplinary commission of the Swedish Football Federation. Sweden's disciplinary chief declared: 'I have never heard anything like this before. It's unique.' Surely Christensen faced punishment?

The commission deliberated but decided to take no action, saying in a statement: *'The referee did not note any fault and the incident would have merited a yellow card but not a red one. For that reason the disciplinary commission did not impose any subsequent sanction.'* A member of the commission added that, at the time, giving a penalty kick to Orebro would have been the correct response.

When the 2009/10 season came to a close, IFK Gothenburg had slipped to second place and could only claim the runners-up position in the Swedish league. Perhaps there was some kind of justice for moving the goalposts.

100. 'GOLF WAS HIS MISTRESS'

A warning from the divorce courts

Ken Lane was a keen golfer. Perhaps he spent a little too much time at the golf club?

Carol Lane was fed up with her husband's behaviour. The couple had been married for 14 years. Ken Lane's passion for golf was too much for her. The couple still shared the same home in Middlesex – a short drive from Moor Park Golf Club.

Carol complained that if her husband was not on the course, he could be found at the 19th hole, drink in hand: 'It was an obsession with him.' She declared: 'You have heard of the golf widow? I am it. I hate golf and because of it I just never saw my husband.'

They had three children, the oldest was 13 and the youngest was five. 'She obviously needed and deserved the support of an understanding husband. I do not think she got it,' Judge Goodman said when her claim for a divorce came before the Family Division of the High Court in June 1987.

Forty-six year-old Ken Lane saw things differently. A former county player, he enjoyed his golf. He was a film technician and mostly worked at nights. Sometimes he went straight to the course in the mornings. He denied his wife's allegations and believed their marriage had not irretrievably broken down: 'I have done nothing wrong. Okay, I played golf on Saturday afternoons followed by drinks at the clubhouse. Then I would be out at 6am on Sunday mornings and I occasionally played in the week. But I did not play or drink as much as they said.'

'Golf was his mistress. It was never another woman.'

Carol Lane told the court: 'Golf was his mistress. It was never another woman. I always knew where he was – out on the course. A woman I could handle, but not the sport.' She added: 'I did go to a golf "do" with him once and went up to him while he was chatting with his mates and said: "Do you know who I am?" His friends did not even know he was married.'

Judge Goodman granted Carol Lane a divorce.

Epilogue

FIFA AND AN UNFINISHED STORY

One final case. Sport and sporting personalities continue to encounter the law. We add here an unfinished story.

We may at the time of writing be barely into the first half of an extraordinary saga of alleged bribery and corruption, undercover informants, international police operations, early morning raids and arrests affecting a sport's world governing body. We have, however, already experienced a week of news-breaking events that the soccer world will not forget.

We revisit here key moments, background and characters relating to the drama in May and early June 2015 that engulfed FIFA.

101. FIFA UNDER ATTACK

America leads the charge

Seven leading FIFA officials were arrested, on behalf of America's FBI, in a dawn raid on a luxury hotel in Switzerland in May 2015. How did it begin? Why were the US authorities involved? Where would it lead?

Manhattan, New York: November 2011

Charles 'Chuck' Blazer cut an extraordinary figure. A heavy, corpulent 68 year-old man with a bushy white beard, he had been trailed by two federal agents, one from America's Federal Bureau of Investigation (FBI) and the other from the US Internal Revenue Service (IRS), as he rode his motorised scooter down the sidewalk of New York's Fifth Avenue on his way to a restaurant. One of the agents, according to the *New York Daily News*, offered him two options: 'We can take you away in handcuffs now - or you can co-operate.' It was a pivotal moment. He chose to co-operate.

Chuck Blazer had risen through regional football in the US to become one of the biggest names in world soccer. He was the head of the Confederation of North, Central American and Caribbean Association Football (CONCACAF) which comprises 35 member associations affiliated to the Fédération Internationale de Football Association (FIFA). CONCACAF is one of six regional confederations attached to FIFA and appoints three members to FIFA's key 24-man Executive Committee. Blazer had, since 1996, been one of them.

A colourful character, he enjoyed the high life – literally. He occupied two connected apartments on the 49th floor of Trump Tower above the New York offices of CONCACAF. An animal lover, one of Blazer's apartments (admittedly the smaller one) was apparently used mostly by his cats. Another pet was a blue-and-gold macaw named Max, often seen on Blazer's shoulder and indeed featured, perched on the basket of his mobility scooter in New York's Central Park, in a video uploaded by Blazer on his regular travel blog.

'We can take you away in handcuffs now - or you can co-operate.'

He was, though, an effective deal-maker. He had built his reputation, and wealth, as secretary-general of CONCACAF, second-in-command for many years to then long-time president Jack Warner from Trinidad. Blazer helped increase CONCACAF's commercial income to over $40 million a year during his tenure. He was 'Mr Ten Percent', apparently receiving 10% personally as commission on all TV and sponsorship deals he negotiated for CONCACAF.

The trouble (according to the IRS Criminal Investigation Division) was that Blazer didn't appear to pay enough tax or even, for a five-year period, file any tax returns at all. It's tax that gets them. Faced with demands for millions of dollars in unpaid taxes, Blazer agreed to 'co-operate' and blow the whistle on other FIFA officials and executives. An FBI investigation into FIFA had started, apparently triggered by a chance lead during an unrelated inquiry by the New York-based Eurasian Joint Organized Crime Task Force into aspects of Russian organised crime. Blazer worked as an FBI informant, collecting evidence while remaining (until late 2013) a member of the FIFA Executive Committee. During the 2012 London Olympics, he is even said to have secretly recorded meetings with several FIFA colleagues using a hidden microphone in the fob of a key-chain.

Brooklyn, New York: 25th November 2013

In November 2013, the scene moved to a courtroom in Brooklyn on the 10th floor of the courthouse of the Eastern District of New York. Judge Raymond Dearie ordered the doors to be locked for a secret hearing. Blazer, in his wheelchair and recovering from chemotherapy for rectal cancer, pleaded guilty to 10 counts including income tax evasion, money laundering, conspiracy to commit racketeering and wire fraud, and failure to report foreign bank accounts. One count that later stood out, when revealed 18 months later, was an admission that Blazer 'and others on the FIFA Executive Committee agreed to accept bribes in conjunction with the selection of South Africa as the host nation for the 2010 World Cup'. Blazer still faces the prospect of a prison sentence but his 'co-operation' may save him.

Chuck Blazer joined two others as FBI informants who, it was later revealed, had pleaded guilty in secret hearings to similar charges, namely Daryll and Daryan Warner, sons of the ubiquitous Jack Warner, former FIFA vice-president and former president of CONCACAF. Blazer was, though, 'the big catch'.

Zurich, Switzerland: 27th May 2015

In May 2015, the US authorities were ready. It would lead to a week that stunned even the world of football.

The drama started at dawn on Wednesday, 27th May. More than a dozen plain-clothes Swiss police, co-ordinating with America's FBI, arrived at 6am at the five-star

Baur au Lac hotel in Zurich. The hotel, according to its website, prides itself on 'the discerning tastes of its guests'. Awoken before they could enjoy the hotel's renowned breakfast, seven FIFA officials were arrested and led away, shielded from public sight by crisp linen bed-sheets. The raid was 'breaking news' worldwide.

One of those arrested was Jeffrey Webb, a FIFA vice-president and current head of CONCACAF. A successful banker from the Cayman Islands, 50 year-old Webb was regarded by many as a likely successor to Sepp Blatter for the FIFA presidency in due course.

Miami, Florida: 27th May 2015

That same day, as morning came in the USA, the FBI swooped on CONCACAF's offices in Miami. A further seven FIFA officials and senior sports marketing executives were arrested. They included former CONCACAF president and FIFA vice-president Jack Warner, once a close colleague of Sepp Blatter, and a number of other figures in North and South American soccer. Fourteen defendants were now in the FBI's net.

Brooklyn, New York: 27th May 2015

The spotlight, on that same dramatic day, switched to the US Department of Justice in Brooklyn. For many, the 'player of the week' was Loretta Lynch. A 56 year-old Harvard-educated lawyer, barely 5ft-tall, daughter of a Baptist minister from North Carolina, she was the first African-American woman to hold office as the US Attorney-General. Nominated by President Barack Obama with the comment: 'Loretta might be the only lawyer in America who battles mobsters and drug lords and terrorists, and still has the reputation for being a charming "people person"'. She had just completed her first month in office as Attorney-General. During her previous position as US Attorney for the Eastern District of New York, she had worked on the FBI investigation into FIFA. Now was the time for exposure.

'The indictment alleges corruption that is rampant, systematic and deep-rooted.'

The press conference began shortly after 11am. Lynch walked confidently to the podium, flanked by colleagues from the US Justice Department and representatives of the FBI and the IRS Criminal Investigation Division. She started calmly with a comment on a domestic political matter. Then, electrifyingly, she announced the background to the arrests:

'*The 47-count indictment against these individuals includes charges of racketeering, wire fraud and money laundering conspiracies spanning two decades… Beginning in 1991, two generations of soccer officials… used their positions of trust… to solicit bribes.… They did this over and over, year after year, tournament after tournament.'*

The alleged bribes and kickbacks, over a 24-year period, amounted to more than $150 million.

Allegations had abounded for some years about the bidding processes for the right to host the World Cups, culminating in the controversial decision to award the 2022 World Cup to Qatar. Loretta Lynch turned, however, to the award of the 2010 event to South Africa: *'Even for this historic event FIFA executives and others corrupted the process by using bribes to influence the hosting decision.'* She concluded devastatingly: *'In short, these individuals and organizations engaged in bribery to decide who would televise games, where the games would be held; and who would run the organisation overseeing organised soccer worldwide.'*

'The pantheon of world soccer has a new hero.'

The US law enforcement agencies had exploded a depth-charge that resounded around the football world. Criminal charges had been launched against key FIFA officials that – despite all the rumours, years of allegations of vote-buying, press investigations and threats of boycotts – no other country or authority had attempted or achieved. If proven, in the US Attorney-General's words, this was *'corruption that is rampant, systematic and deep-rooted'*. Many regard the bringing of these criminal charges as quite simply the finest contribution to soccer ever made by America. One commentator remarked of Loretta Lynch: 'The pantheon of world soccer has a new hero.'

Why the Americans? What did it really have to do with them? Lynch explained. Actions and meetings had taken place on American soil and, crucially, *'the defendants … used the banking and wire facilities of the United States to distribute bribe payments'*. America is strict on white-collar crime, its anti-corruption laws are amongst the toughest in the world and its jurisdictional reach is notorious and wide. (It has been observed that, apparently, Swiss-born Sepp Blatter has not set foot in America since 2011.) Zurich, the venue for the 2015 FIFA Congress, provided the perfect opportunity for the FBI to pounce, with many suspects all in one place. The US and Switzerland have a mutual extradition treaty and the Swiss authorities had co-operated fully.

Trinidad, West Indies: 28th May 2015

Jack Warner was released from jail on bail in Trinidad. He attended a political rally with many supporters, declaring: 'If I have been in FIFA for 30 years and I have been thieving all the money, who give me the money?' A crowd member called out: 'Blatter.' Warner responded to great applause: 'And why it is he ain't charged?'

Zurich, Switzerland: 29th May 2015

Two days after the FBI arrests, the scene of the drama moved to the 65th FIFA Congress held at the Hallenstadion in Zurich. Item 17 on the Agenda was the election of the FIFA president. FIFA's head of communications Walter De Gregorio (more on him later) had declared that Sepp Blatter was not 'dancing in his office' but firmly intended that the election would still go ahead. Blatter (once described in a Swiss newspaper as 'the dark prince of football, the godfather, Don Blatterone') was defiant; any problems were not those for which he should take responsibility.

FIFA's constitution entitled 209 member associations (more than the number of member states of the United Nations) to vote on a one member-one vote basis. Undaunted by the crisis, 79 year-old Sepp Blatter was elected to a fifth term in office as FIFA president, winning by 133 votes to 73 on the first ballot against challenger Prince Ali bin Al Hussein of Jordan. Not enough, by the rules, to secure outright victory on the first ballot but Prince Ali conceded an inevitable defeat. Blatter's long-standing support in Asia, Africa, the Caribbean and Central America

'You can't just ask people to behave ethically just like that' (influenced perhaps by FIFA's often generous grants for development projects, out of its $1 billion and more annual revenue, which made Blatter a hero in many of those countries) helped him to victory. Spain and France voted in support, as did Russia. England and the USA did not.

Re-elected as president, Blatter declared: 'For the next four years I will be in command of this boat called FIFA and we will bring it back ashore.' He added, to many with some bravado: 'We are at a turning point. We need to pull together and move forward. We can't constantly supervise everyone in football. You can't just ask people to behave ethically just like that.'

New York: 1st June 2015

'Follow the money' advised Deep Throat in the film *All The President's Men*. Here, the money trail quickly moved closer to the highest echelons of FIFA. Particular attention focused on the $10 million allegedly paid as a bribe to CONCACAF's Jack Warner in exchange for helping South Africa to secure the right to host the 2010 World Cup. Reports in the USA indicated that Jerome Valcke, FIFA's secretary-general and Sepp Blatter's right-hand man, was the previously unidentified 'high-ranking FIFA official' who aided the payment.

Was there a smoking gun? A letter emerged, from the South African Football Association addressed in 2008 directly to Valcke, requesting that FIFA in effect deduct

$10 million from the funds budgeted by FIFA for the 2010 World Cup organising committee in South Africa and 'thereafter advances the amount withheld to the Diaspora Legacy Programme... to be administered and implemented directly by the President of CONCACAF who shall act as fiduciary of the Fund.' Trailing the money, there seemed little evidence of any relevant development projects in Caribbean countries to support a 'legacy programme'. The US indictment alleged, instead, that the bulk of the money found its way to Jack Warner's personal accounts or to companies controlled by him – and that around $750,000 was paid by Warner to Mr Ten Percent, Chuck Blazer.

Valcke maintained that he did not 'authorise' the $10 million payment but that it had been properly approved by Julio Grondona, then chairman of FIFA's Finance Committee (who had since died), for legitimate development purposes. Whilst the original indictment did not say that the FIFA official knew that the money was being used as a bribe, the trail was getting uncomfortably close to the top of FIFA. Was the revelation that two of his closest colleagues had been linked directly to the alleged 2010 World Cup bribe the final straw for Sepp Blatter? Had the net closed in too far?

Zurich, Switzerland: 2nd June 2015

At 5.46pm on 2nd June, just four days after his re-election as FIFA's seemingly eternal president and six days after the FBI raids, Sepp Blatter stepped onto the podium before a hastily arranged and sparsely attended press conference at FIFA's offices in Zurich. He announced: 'I have been reflecting deeply about my presidency. While I have a mandate from the membership of FIFA, I do not feel that I have a mandate from the entire world of football - the fans, the players, the clubs, the people who live, breathe and love football as much as we all do at FIFA. Therefore, I have decided to lay down my mandate.'

Blatter urged FIFA's Congress to organise the election of his successor 'at the earliest opportunity' (probably in early 2016) when he would stand down: 'I shall not be a candidate.' His 17-year reign as president, and a 40-year career at FIFA, was coming to an end. A new era beckoned.

Berlin, Germany: 6th June 2015

A thrilling final of the UEFA Champions League reminded us of the 'beautiful game' on the pitch. Second-half goals from Luis Suarez and Neymar gave Barcelona a 3-1 win over Juventus.

Attempted humour was not popular at FIFA. Communications director Walter De Gregorio appeared on a Swiss TV show shortly after Sepp Blatter's resignation speech and was asked for his favourite FIFA joke. Gregorio responded: 'The FIFA president, secretary-general and communications director are all travelling in a car. Who's driving?' Answer: 'The police.' Three days later, FIFA announced that De Gregorio had 'relinquished his office with immediate effect'.

Where will all this lead? Writing in Summer 2015, many questions remain for the future. Criminal investigations by law enforcement agencies continue both in the US and separately in Switzerland, including into the awards of the 2018 and 2022 World Cups to Russia and Qatar respectively. Volumes of data and documents have been seized from FIFA offices. Numerous 'suspicious' bank transactions are being examined.

Will Sepp Blatter keep to his word and stand down? Will he and other high-ranking officials be charged? Will the venues for any of the forthcoming World Cups be changed? Will steps be taken to reform FIFA's constitution? Will the cases get to court? Will the allegations be proven? Will Chuck Blazer survive to give evidence and, importantly for the judicial process, be fit enough to be cross-examined by defendants?

It is likely to be many months before the defendants arrested overseas appear in a full US court trial. Extradition proceedings from Switzerland for many will be subject to complexity and appeal. The lawyers will continue to be fully involved. The words of the acting US Attorney for the Eastern District of New York at the dramatic press conference on 27th May resonate: '*This is the beginning of our effort, not the end.*'

This is a story which is not yet complete. But it has already produced a week that soccer will not forget. FIFA will surely not be the same. An encounter with the law has, again, had a material impact on the sporting landscape. The case continues.

ACKNOWLEDGEMENTS

This book is intended as an entertainment and certainly not an academic work. Nevertheless, many have elevated sports law to a respectable discipline. I am indebted to Jonathan Taylor and his team who ran the Post-Graduate Diploma in Sports Law at King's College, London which I was pleased to attend (and pass) as a 'veteran' student around 10 years ago. The seeds of this book were planted during that course.

I also acknowledge the leading texts in this field: *Sport: Law and Practice* by Adam Lewis QC & Jonathan Taylor (Bloomsbury, 2014) and *Sports Law* by Simon Gardiner, John O'Leary, Roger Welch, Simon Boyes and Urvasi Naidoo (Routledge, 2012).

Extracts quoted or cited from particular cases reflected in this book have principally been sourced, where cases have come before the courts, from the official *Law Reports* or, where decided by the Court of Arbitration for Sport, from the *Digest of CAS Awards*. Other background material and quotes derive from statements or interviews widely reported in the press, including the fine sport sections of *The Daily Telegraph* and *The Times* or the excellent website of *BBC Sport*.

Books which have provided particular background have included: *The Life of Senna* by Tom Rubython (Business F1 Books, 2004); *Soccer in the Dock* by Simon Inglis (Willow Books, 1985); *Setting the Record Straight* by Peter Swan with Nick Johnson (Tempus, 2006); *The Hansie Cronje Story* by Garth King (Monarch Books, 2005); ... *And Nothing but the Truth* by Deon Gouws (Zebra, 2000); *The Final Score* by Hans Segers with Mel Goldberg and Alan Thatcher (Robson Books, 1998); *Calcio: A History of Italian Football* by John Foot (Fourth Estate, 2006); *St Leger Goold: A Tale of Two Courts* by Alan Little (Wimbledon Lawn Tennis Museum, 1984); *Back Home: England and the 1970 World Cup* by Jeff Dawson (Orion, 2001); *Lester* by Lester Piggott (Partridge Press, 1995); *The Second Mark* by Joy Goodwin (Simon & Schuster, 2004); *The Tour de France 2006* by John Wilcockson (VeloPress, 2006); *Tony Greig: My Story* by Tony Greig (Stanley Paul, 1980); *The America's Cup* by Dennis Connor & Michael Levitt (St Martin's Press, 1998); *Bellies and Bullseyes* by Sid Wadell (Ebury Press, 2007); *Second Serve* by Renée Richards (Stein & Day, 1983); *Jane Couch: Fleetwood Assassin* by Jane Couch and Tex Woodward (Blake Publishing, 2000); *Aintree's Queen* by Joan Rimmer (SportsBooks, 2007); *An Aintree Dynasty* by John Pinfold (Trafford, 2006); *From Boot Money to Bosman: Football, Society and the Law* by David McArdle (Cavendish, 2000); *JPR: Given the Breaks* by JPR Williams (Hodder & Stoughton, 2006); and *Botham* by Ian Botham with Peter Hayter (Collins Willow, 1994).

These have been specific sources. More generally, the foundations for this book reflect the influence of my parents. My father introduced me to the addictive pleasures of sport. If it involved a ball, he played it. I also learned from him that the way to read a newspaper is from the back pages first. Equal gratitude is due to my mother who encouraged me to do something 'useful' and that included becoming a lawyer.

I sometimes declare to my wife, Jenifer, that this book is aimed at 'the thinking sports fan'. I remain firm in my belief that this category is more numerous than she suspects. I am nevertheless hugely grateful for her support during this project (including the preparation of this second edition) and especially for her encouragement when my pace slowed.

Ian Hewitt
1 August 2015

ABOUT THE AUTHOR

Ian Hewitt was a partner in a leading international law firm for over 25 years. Amidst a varied practice, he was involved professionally in the formation of the FA Premier League. After ceasing a full-time legal career, he took a Post-Graduate Diploma in Sports Law. He is a member of the British Association for Sport and Law.

A former Hampshire county tennis player, he sits on the management committee of the Wimbledon Championships. He is a lifelong, if now armchair, supporter of Southampton FC. He enjoys playing golf when time permits, ever seeking some glimpse of improvement. His sporting heroes include Seve Ballesteros, Roger Federer and Matt Le Tissier.

Ian has published five books, four being sport-related. He lives in London with his wife Jenifer.

Other books by Ian Hewitt:

- *Centre Court: The Jewel in Wimbledon's Crown*, with John Barrett (Vision Sports Publishing, 2010)
- *Wimbledon: Visions of The Championships*, with Bob Martin (Vision Sports Publishing, 2011)
- *Hewitt on Joint Ventures* (5th ed., Sweet & Maxwell, 2011)
- *Immortals of British Sport: A celebration of Britain's sporting history through sculpture*, with Sampson Lloyd (Vision Sports Publishing, 2013)